INDIANIZING FILM

NEW DIRECTIONS IN INTERNATIONAL STUDIES

PATRICE PETRO, SERIES EDITOR

The New Directions in International Studies series focuses on transculturalism, technology, media, and representation, and features the innovative work of scholars who explore various components and consequences of globalization, such as the increasing flow of peoples, ideas, images, information, and capital across borders. Under the direction of Patrice Petro, the series is sponsored by the Center for International Education at the University of Wisconsin–Milwaukee. The center seeks to foster interdisciplinary and collaborative research that probes the political, economic, artistic, and social processes and practices of our time.

INDIANIZING FILM

DECOLONIZATION, THE ANDES, AND THE QUESTION OF TECHNOLOGY

FREYA SCHIWY

RUTGERS UNIVERSITY PRESS

New Brunswick, New Jersey, and London

LIBRARY OF CONGRESS CATALOGING-IN-PUBLICATION DATA

Schiwy, Freya.
    Indianizing film : decolonization, the Andes, and the question of technology / Freya
Schiwy.
        p. cm. -- (New directions in international studies)
    Includes bibliographical references and index.
    ISBN 978-0-8135-4539-4 (hardcover : alk. paper) -- ISBN 978-0-8135-4540-0 (pbk. : alk.
paper)
    1. Indians of South America Bolivia--Government relations.   2. Video recording in
ethnology--Bolivia.   3. Mass media--Political aspects--Bolivia.   4. Indians in mass media.
5. Indian activists--Bolivia.   I. Title.
    F3320.1.G6S35 2009
    302.23'4308998084--dc22   2008036420

A British Cataloging-in-Publication record for this book is available from the British Library.

Visit our Web site: http://rutgerspress.rutgers.edu

Manufactured in the United States of America

CONTENTS

ACKNOWLEDGMENTS

The media activists, mentors, friends, and colleagues who have supported me in the years of research, writing, and rewriting are too many to mention, and I appreciate all of their help. I would like to thank first the media activists in La Paz, especially Iván Sanjinés, Reynaldo Yujra, Nila Ruíz, Franklin Gutiér- rez, and Marcelina Cárdenas for their generosity, sharing their thoughts, and making many of the materials I talk about here accessible to me. Without them this book would not have been possible.

Alessandro Fornazzari initially encouraged me to focus on indigenous media and read multiple versions of the dissertation and then the manu- script. His detailed critical comments and emotional support have been tremendously helpful. Thank you to Walter Mignolo for all his support and enthusiasm. Our conversations helped me to initially clarify the scope of this project. Jacqueline Loss read and commented on early drafts of the introduc- tion. David Wood did the same for chapter I. Long-distance from Bolivia, Keith John Richards carefully read several chapter drafts. His provocative questions proved instrumental in clarifying and rewriting entire sections. Michelle Raheja, Vorris Nunley, Jodi Kim, Mariam Lam Beevi, Susan Antebi, and Juliette Levy offered detailed comments on drafts of the introduction. Discussing my work with them was crucial in helping me to sharpen and focus my argument.

The National Museum of the American Indian granted me access to their video collection. Thanks to Carol Kalafatic for conversations and her assis- tance there. CEFREC's staff opened their video archive, even though I am not a filmmaker and have no technical knowledge to offer in return. When Iván Sanjinés, Jesús Tapia, and Marcelina Cárdenas were touring the United States as part of the Eye of the Condor/Ojo del Condor video tour, I invited them to screen and discuss their videos at Duke University. Sanjinés and Tapia's visit took place in Spring 2002 (Cárdenas was not able to attend) and spoke to the challenges of creating a dialogue between indigenous activists and U.S. academics. During my stays in Bolivia and at festivals in Guatemala, New York, and Rhode Island, I had long conversations with indigenous video makers, especially Reynaldo Yujra, Faustino Peña, Marcelino Pinto, Julia Mosúa, and Alfredo Copa, and with members of CLACPI, particularly Iván Sanjinés, Alexandra Halkin, and Marta Rodríguez. Members of CEFREC-CAIB and I collaborated on an academic panel during the Second International Conference of the Bolivian Studies Association (La Paz, 2003). In 2000 I interviewed employees of the CRIC consulate in Bogotá, Colombia. They graciously agreed to sell me copies of their videos and provided me with additional material about their bilingual education program, in which the videos play a vital role. (Because of a surge in paramilitary violence and kidnappings, I was not able to visit the Cauca at that time). Catherine Walsh organized an outstanding workshop and conference in Quito, Ecuador, in 2001, where scholars from various disciplines and countries, activists from the Afro-Ecuadorian coastal regions, as well members of CONAIE's communication department participated. As part of our exchange we visited CONAIE's offices, where the media activists Mario Bustos and Lucila Lema let me interview them and observe the editing process. Unfortunately, this book can only reciprocate in a limited fashion the time and patience of indigenous media activists and their collaborators from whom I have learned tremendously.

Between 1999 and 2006, I traveled repeatedly to Bolivia, Ecuador, Colombia, and Peru. During my visits other friends and colleagues provided support. I viewed films and videos in the National Cinema archive where Elizabeth Carrasco gave valuable assistance. Thanks to Delfina Yujra for companionship and to Silvia Rivera Cusicanqui for company, food, and several of her unpublished and out-of-print writings. Rosario Rodriguez and her family in La Paz offered housing and Guillermo Mariaca Iturri care when I was ill. Thanks also to the late Beatriz Palacios and to Derliz Barrero at the Centro Gregoria Apaza, Franco Gamboa, Blithz Losada, and Kathy Seibold for coffee and conversation in La Paz and for literature recommendations. In Colombia, members of the Instituto Pensar at the Pontificia Universidad Javeriana made my stay in Bogotá a truly enjoyable experience. Thanks to Santiago Castro-Gómez and María Luisa Eschenhagen, to Carmelita Millán de Benavides, Pilar Melgarejo, Erica, Carolina, Sandra, Alfredo, Ana Lucía, and Silvia.

Research travel was made financially possible though the Duke-UNC Program in Latin American Studies Tinker Mellon Travel Grants, an Ernestine

Friedl Research Award; a Duke University Graduate School International Research Award; and a Duke-UNC Program in Latin American Studies Ford Foundation Grant. Helpful were also two FLAS (Foreign Languages and Area Studies) fellowships that I received to learn Quechua and to improve my Spanish.

Many thanks to the anonymous readers of the manuscript for their detailed comments, to Patrice Petro for her enthusiasm, and to the production editors at Rutgers University Press for all their work. I especially appreciate Leslie Mitchner's unparalleled support and efficiency. Finally, thanks once more to CEFREC for permission to include production and video stills and for the cover image. The photo shows Teresa Muiba Moye of the Moxeño Trinitario People, member of the Puerto San Lorenzo community, Territorio Indígena Multiétnico (TIPNIS), Beni (Bolivia), and was taken during the production of a television program about indigenous women's rights and women organizing themselves in Muiba Moye's community in 2007.

INDIANIZING FILM

INTRODUCTION
THE QUESTION OF TECHNOLOGY

The film and video training center CEFREC (Centro de Formación y Real-ización Cinematográfica) in Bolivia recently published on its homepage an image of the Quechua media activist Marcelina Cárdenas in traditional fes-tive attire pointing a camcorder at the viewer (fig. 1).[1]

CEFREC's homepage brings together culturally diverse indigenous video makers from distinct geographical and climatic regions. A young boy from the lowlands rises from the Andean hills and trains his camcorder on Cárdenas, a middle-aged video maker from Potosí whose body dominates the river land in the foreground. Her camera points beyond the frame, at once interpellating us, the viewers, and invoking the widespread practice of video making among indigenous peoples in the high- and lowlands of the Andean countries. Indeed, since the video makers visually occupy spaces far from their origins, the composition refers to indigenous media's travels. No longer limited by the expense of cumbersome 16mm or 35mm cameras, film projectors, and production laboratories, analog and digital video enables the exchange of indigenous gazes interculturally among various ethnicities.

Exotic images of South American Indians in body paint holding cam-corders began to proliferate in magazines and on book covers in the United States in the late eighties (fig. 2). The appeal of such images for Western consumers still lies in the way they visualize a clash between the native body and new communication technology. As Robert Stam put it, "widely disseminated images of the Kayapo wielding video-cameras, appearing in *Time* and the *New York Times Magazine* [and on the cover of Stam's book itself] derive their power to shock from the premise that 'natives' must be quaint and allochronic, that 'real' Indians don't carry camcorders" (Stam 326). In other words, the photograph of the Kayapo cameraman joins two apparently incongruous time-spaces: the time of indigenous peoples inhabiting what the West has come to think of as the premodern, a timeless realm beyond history, and the time of digital technology, proper to the speed and time-space compression of postmodernity.

Like the images of Kayapo cameramen, CEFREC's homepage joins indigenous bodies with the global technological present. Both images play on a notion of temporal unevenness that is a construct of colonial discourse, reiterated in mainstream media. Audiovisual media have been deeply embedded in capitalist and colonial relations. As Beverley Singer argues, "Indians have been misrepresented in art, history, science, literature, popular films, and by the press in news, on radio, and on television. The earliest stereotypes associating Indians with being savage, naked and heathen were established

——— I. CEFREC's homepage, http://videoindigena.bolnet.bo (CEFREC). ———

with the foundation of America" (1). Michelle Raheja explains that "hundreds of actualities featuring Indians engaging in putatively quotidian practices were shown in nickelodeons from 1894 through 1908. These actualities and early documentary and ethnographic films simultaneously contributed to the myth of the vanishing Indian and helped to create a form of American spectatorship that coheres around the dichotomous relationship between Indian and white figures" (Raheja, "Reading" 1170). Though Singer and Raheja speak about North America, their words hold true for North and South American perceptions of indigenous peoples alike, not withstanding the ideological projects of racial assimilation or *mestizaje* dominant in Latin America. What Fatimah Rony calls "ethnographic cinema" (8)—educational and entertainment documentaries but also the polished, special effects–loaded fiction films produced and distributed by the global media corporations housing the North American film industry—has been key in fashioning colonial imaginaries across the hemispheres. These films represent travel

2. Kayapo video maker. http://www.amazon.de (Bernd Kulov).

and colonial others to Western selves. Ethnographic cinema offers viewers representations of indigenous archetypes: romanticized Indians or barbaric others who invariably inhabit modernity's past. "The exotic is always already known," as Rony puts it (6).

The Kayapo image in figure 2 conjures these conventions for an ingenious politics of the exotic. The Kayapo have successfully exploited the apparent temporal clash in images of native video makers to raise awareness about their struggle against the incursions of gold miners, ranchers, and state development projects. As Alcida Ramos argues, "in a phenomenon similar to what happened to the term Indian—which the Indians appropriated, purged it of much of its derogatory undertones, and turned it into a political tool—they have instrumentalized exoticism and turned it into a decoy to first attract national attention and then put across their own message" (99). In the late eighties the Kayapo's media politics secured the support of environmental organizations and the rock star Sting and thereby prevented the building of a hydroelectric dam on the Xingu River that would have flooded their territories. In addition, Kayapo leaders drew on audiovisual technology to coordinate the social protests among distant villages and different Kayapo, Xavante, Ashaninka, and Waiãpi communities.[2]

CEFREC's homepage may not command the same shock effect for Western (and indigenous) viewers as the photographs of Kayapo video makers, but it similarly resignifies colonial tropes that place especially indigenous women at a remove from audiovisual technology. CEFREC-CAIB's production is not primarily directed at Western viewers. Instead, the media collective documents rituals, celebrations, and other aspects of local culture for viewing in the communities. In that sense—like indigenous media made in Brazil, Colombia, Ecuador, and Mexico—CEFREC-CAIB changes not only who makes films about Indians but also who watches them. Featuring Marcelina Cárdenas on CEFREC-CAIB's homepage alludes to a tension in these cultural politics. Indigenous culture has become closely associated with the female body, but while the majority of aboriginal filmmakers in Canada are women (Nicholson 3), this is not the case in Latin America. Rather, particularly in the Andean countries, men have adopted Western clothing, mediate contact with Western agencies and authorities, or more readily migrate to urban centers. They are also more involved in indigenous media production. Confronting the gendered contradictions of anticolonial struggle, where women stand in as guardians of tradition but some also wield camcorders and demand social transformation, points to a critical reinvention of what at first sight might seem like a conservative politics of cultural rescue.

CEFREC is a center for cinematographic training that is dedicated to providing indigenous activists with video equipment and filmmaking skills. Since 1996 the independent filmmakers affiliated with CEFREC offer workshops in various rural locations and in its production centers in La Paz, Santa Cruz, Chuquisaca (Sucre), and Cochabamba. The center has been closely collaborating with CAIB (Coordinadora Audiovisual Indígena de Bolivia), a grassroots organization that was founded at one of the first workshops in the town of Yotala in the Department of Chuquisaca.[3] CAIB brings together indigenous media activists from the lowlands, valleys, and Andean highlands in Bolivia who reside primarily in rural communities. Jesus Tapia, an Aymara living in the tropical Yungas, directs the organization. CEFREC was founded in 1989 in La Paz by the *mestizo* Iván Sanjinés, the son of Jorge Sanjinés who had become famous in the sixties and seventies for his anti-imperialist and revolutionary films made with Quechuas and Aymaras. CEFREC and CAIB maintain a media network that connects over one hundred rural communities throughout Bolivia and in the transnational Amazon basin. In 2005 CEFREC and CAIB were actively involved in the preparations for Bolivia's Constituent Assembly. Their multimedia packages circulated information about the country's existing constitution and the proposals for reform that were put forth by indigenous and peasant organizations. Members of CAIB screened the materials and facilitated discussion in the communities and across ethnic boundaries about the goals and ideals the villagers wanted to see debated in the assembly. Reception of indigenous media is not limited to rural villages, however. Selections of CEFREC-CAIB's widely influential, award-winning fiction videos and docudramas have screened at regional and international indigenous film and video festivals in North and South America and in Europe.

CEFREC-CAIB's work is not a local, isolated effort, although it is the most comprehensive in Latin America. As a response to the needs of indigenous social movements, indigenous media has evolved simultaneously in different parts of the world. Aboriginal communities in Australia and New Zealand, native filmmakers in Canada and the United States, and indigenous organizations in Latin America began using video in the mid-eighties, when the technology first became available.[4] The most important centers for indigenous media in Latin America are in Bolivia, southern Mexico, northern Brazil, and

Ecuador. Smaller scale indigenous video production exists in many other regions in Latin America, and CLACPI (Coordinadora Latinoamericana del Cine y Video de los Pueblos Indígenas), as well as other technical advisors (some of whom identify as indigenous while others do not) have offered crucial support. CLACPI was founded in 1985 by independent filmmakers and visual anthropologists. The collaboration between CLACPI and indigenous media activists, however, has changed over time and is itself indicative of a decolonizing process lead by indigenous movements.

The boom in Latin American indigenous media opens up a series of concerns that I pursue in this study. How do video makers adapt a technology apparently "foreign" to their cultures for the goal of strengthening them? How significant is the representation and role of women? How do these videos compare to earlier efforts at creating an anticolonial gaze? How do they negotiate the openings and pitfalls of the global market for multicultural film? How might indigenous media contribute to a greater understanding of decolonization at the beginning of the twenty-first century? I explore these questions in light of indigenous media production in Bolivia, Ecuador, and Colombia.

Organizations like CEFREC-CAIB, CONAIE (The Confederation of Indigenous Nationalities of Ecuador) and the CRIC (Consejo Regional Indígena del Cauca) are producing analogue and digital video recordings: documentaries, docudramas, fictions, television news programs, educational videos, and films that do not fit easily into conventional genres. The screenings in rural communities and itinerant festivals allow different indigenous cultures—often for the first time, as the Quechua video maker Marcelino Pinto once pointed out—to learn about each other and to establish contact between different communities and language groups (Mosúa, Copa and Pinto, audiotape). Indigenous media help to overcome historical tensions and prejudice among these communities. Occasionally they serve as a means of coordinating social protests. In their more quotidian deployment they form part of a politics of cultural and epistemic revival that indigenous movements have been promoting with growing success since the late sixties across the continent.[5]

With strong indigenous movements in Bolivia and Ecuador, indigenous media in the two countries offer many parallels but also differences. The National Indigenous Plan for Audiovisual Communication (Plan Nacional Indígena Originario de Comunicación Audiovisual) has emerged as one of the world's most prolific and influential sites for indigenous media production. As I explain in more detail in chapter 1, the plan, despite the term "national" in its title, is both independent of the Bolivian state and transcends its boundaries. CEFREC-CAIB launched the plan in 1996 and secured the support of the country's major indigenous and peasant organizations.[6] It has received grants from governmental and nongovernmental institutions. The most important ones are AECI (International Development Agency of Spain) and Mugarik Gabe, a Basque nongovernmental organization. This indigenous media initiative is not centered in one community or language. There are thirty-nine indigenous ethnicities in Bolivia, and together they constitute a majority of the national population.[7] The National Indigenous Plan for Audiovisual Communication brings together ethnically diverse indigenous media activists, such as Jesús Tapia (Aymara), Regina Monasterios (Guarani), Julia Mósua (Trinitario-Moxeña), Alfredo Copa (Quechua), Marcelina Cárdenas (Quechua), Patricio Luna (Aymara), Humberto Paz (Quechua), Nicolás Ipamo (Chiquitano), urban migrants like Reynaldo Yujra (Aymara), and independent white and mestizo filmmakers, such as Iván Sanjinés, Franklin Gutiérrez, Max Silva, César Pérez, and Francisco Cajías. CAIB represents regional video production units and facilitators who are responsible for distributing the media to the communities included in their National Audiovisual Communication and Exchange Network (Red Nacional de Comunicación e Intercambio Audiovisual). The local facilitators are usually at least bilingual and in charge of organizing the screenings and guiding discussions of the videos. Parallel to the regular distribution through the Network, CEFREC-CAIB's annual Anaconda Film Festival communicates villages in the transnational Amazon region. In addition CEFREC-CAIB has stepped up community television production. The news shows include documentaries made by their video crews in Bolivia and Paraguay. While indigenous and peasant communities in Bolivia are the primary audience for CEFREC-CAIB videos, the National Indigenous Plan for Audiovisual Communication has garnered worldwide attention among indigenous and aboriginal film and video makers. In 2005, for instance, Maori television wanted to buy the rights to *Qati Qati/Whispers of Death*, as well as other fiction shorts.[8] *Qati qati* has won several international awards, among them the prize for the best mise-en-scène at the VI American Indigenous Film and Video Festival in Guatemala in 1999 and the Distinción RAL "Programa Latinoamericano" at the Latin American Television Encounter RAL in Uruguay in 2001.

Although of lesser continental influence and with a more modest reach, the communication department of Ecuador's national indigenous umbrella organization CONAIE similarly strives to connect diverse indigenous communities in Ecuador.[9] As Macdonald points out, "Andean Indians are about 95 percent (1.5 million) of the total Indian population, far more than the diverse linguistic nationalities of the Amazonian region, whose 75,000 members make up less than 5 percent of the total. However, Amazonian Indians have provided more than half of CONAIE's leaders. More important, it was the Amazonian Indians who provided the initial stimulus and structure for ethnically based organization in the 1960s, and these lowland groups consistently spoke to broad issues and concerns" (176). CONAIE'S video production has been more uneven than that of CEFREC-CAIB, beginning in 1994, and with different directors in charge. Yet its communication department has already released more than one thousand documentaries.[10] Quichua women of the regional organization ECUARUNARI have used video to open up additional spaces for representing indigenous women (Lema, n.p.).[11] CONAIE's Web page currently features a call to register for a workshop in communication. Organized by CLACPI (Latin American Council for Indigenous Film and Communication), the primary goal of the workshop is to create a permanent audiovisual production unit, which will make Ecuador's "indigenous peoples and nations visible at the local, regional and continental level."[12]

Colombia serves as a point of contrast. Its indigenous movement has been more fragmented, despite the ONIC's coordinating efforts.[13] The indigenous peoples of Colombia only constitute about 2 percent of the national population (Gros, "Indigenismo" 43; Jackson 107), a small number compared to Bolivia and Ecuador, where those who identify as indigenous constitute at least 50 percent of the population if not more.[14] ONIC has not employed audiovisual media in a consistent manner here, but the CRIC made a collection of videos in 1996 and 1997. The Nasa people (formerly known as Páez) are the strongest ethnic group represented in the CRIC (Jackson 110); they use the material primarily in their bilingual education program, which is a key element in the CRIC's efforts to recuperate and revitalize indigenous language and culture.

Despite the differences between indigenous peoples in Bolivia, Ecuador, and Colombia, the videos made by CEFREC-CAIB, CONAIE, and CRIC attest to similar preoccupations and goals. The activists employ audiovisual media in order to strengthen indigenous cultures, including modes of knowing and forms of transmitting social memory. By modes of knowing I am referring to myth, ritual, dreams, the interpretations of an animate life-world, and perspectives critical of colonization. Forms of transmitting social memory include storytelling, dance, song, weaving, basketry, clothing, cooking, etc. Both indigenous modes and forms of knowing have been suppressed, at times even destroyed or severely truncated since the conquest. Cast as superstition or folklore, they have become associated with what the West considers to be disappearing worlds. Yet as subalternized forms they have also survived and have become closely associated with the female body. When indigenous media opt for vindicating indigenous cultures and epistemologies, and for turning them into sustainable knowledge, they challenge this suppression along with the apparent temporal clash exploited in the Web images discussed earlier. In other words, indigenous media contest a process of colonial subalternization that has denied indigenous communities participation in the dominant discourses and practices that have shaped Latin American societies.

While Quechua and Aymara cultures have certainly informed national imaginaries in the Andean countries, indigenous movements seek to complete a process of decolonization. From the indigenous perspective, this process has remained inconclusive since Latin American nation-states became constituted and formally independent from colonial rule in the early nineteenth century.[15] No longer primarily concerned with ousting a foreign occupying power, I suggest that decolonization at the beginning of the twenty-first century focuses not only on the struggle over territory, legislation, and political representation but also, perhaps more important, on epistemes. In other words, indigenous movements recognize that representation—audiovisual, literary, and scholarly—entails the power to shape lived reality. There is an urgent need to decolonize knowledge. Gender becomes problematic here as women are cast as the guardians of traditional knowledge while also demanding cultural change. Using audiovisual technology itself similarly points toward a transformation of the cultural and epistemic traditions indigenous movements vindicate.

Using audiovisual media to create forms and spaces where sustainable knowledge is generated is a complex undertaking. The brochure *La otra mirada: Memoria del plan nacional indígena originario de comunicación audiovisual*, printed on the occasion of CEFREC-CAIB's participation at the international cultural convention EXPO 2000 in Hannover (Germany), for instance, affirms with great enthusiasm on the first page that "in Bolivia the indigenous peoples already have access to audiovisual technologies, which allows them to construct communication mechanisms and strategies that help them to better confront the issues of the new millennium" (CEFREC et al., *Otra* 1).[16] Scholars who see indigenous media as a means of articulating cultural activism and talking back to power (cf. Ginsburg, Abu-Lughod, and Larkin, "Introduction" 7–8) share this optimism: "The imperative to communicate places Indigenous peoples in a powerful position to take advantage of the many possibilities provided by globalisation. Through radio, film, video, recorded music and now the Internet, there is the potential for Indigenous peoples to tackle the problems posed by globalisation and to transform its technology in unique ways" (Smith, Burke, and Ward 9). Cautioning against such opinions, others argue that audiovisual media themselves risk reproducing the Western society of the spectacle.

As is well known, Heidegger proposed that modern technology implies a loss of technē or poiesis. Technology becomes separated from creative and intellectual activity when technology and the discourse that sustain it become subject to and constitutive of instrumental logic. Struggling with language and exploiting the effects of estrangement, Heidegger calls the integration of all elements of the world, including human activity, an enframing (*Gestell*) into a standing-reserve (*Bestand*). The process creates a functional difference between artisanal labor (*Handwerk*) and modern technology. The difference manifests itself as the separation of *techne* and *technē*. Heidegger asserts that precapitalist artisanal production, like that of the arts, involved a thinking and planning process: "*technē* is the name not only for the activities and skills of the craftsman, but also for the arts of the mind and the fine arts. *Technē* belongs to bringing-forth, to poiesis; it is something poietic. The other point that we should observe with regard to *technē* is even more important. From earliest times until Plato the word *technē* is linked with the word *epistēmē*. Both words are names for knowing in the widest sense. They mean to be entirely at home in something, to understand and be expert in it. Such knowing provides an opening up. As an opening up it is a revealing" (13). For Heidegger technology is now so integrated into the system of production and commodification that it has affected human activity (such as labor) and nature (the Rhine has become a commodity of the vacation industry) but also the very process of thinking about technology (16). Technology and knowledge have become thoroughly instrumentalized.

From this perspective media technology appears to present a step forward in a teleological continuum that stretches from oral culture, to literacy, to new media technologies. Some think it is therefore alien to cultures apparently inhabiting an oral, premodern time.[17] Following arguments by Jack Goody and Walter Ong, many similarly believe that technology determines cognitive processes and that "oral" cultures think differently and less complexly than those considered "literate." Others counter that, without doubt, "dominant Western cultural practices arise from an intersection between technology and subjectivity which marks a determinate break with premodern forms. . . . However, the brute fact is that, for virtually all indigenous and 'tribal' people within Western settler colonies and for many others as well, this break has already occurred. They are already 'viewers,' with all the disruption to indigenous subjectivity which this implies" (Hamilton 217). I argue that indigenous media challenge the teleological view of civilization and its inherent equation of intellect and technology. The activists use video to bring key issues of concern to indigenous communities to the screen, locating them squarely in the present. The documentaries privilege the indigenous subject as expert in his or her own right, and docudramas and fiction shorts counter the way race and gender have intermeshed in the patriarchal gaze of empire.

Indigenous video makers, however, are not the first to articulate an anticolonial gaze and audiovisual practice. In the early 1970s the Colombian Fundación Cine Documental—Marta Rodríguez and Jorge Silva—and the Bolivian Grupo Ukamau—filmmakers Jorge Sanjinés and Beatriz Palacios, Antonio Eguino, Oscar Soria, and others—insisted that anticolonial film must subvert the complacency of entertainment movies and find ways to incorporate the cultural values of colonized people (Sanjinés and the Ukamau Group 59–60; Wood 80). Although not a unified movement championing one aesthetic solution to U.S. cultural imperialism, third cinema filmmakers from across Latin America and Africa agreed that Hollywood film's hegemonic narrative form and visual style attested to the inseparable relation between capitalism and (neo)colonialism. Industrial cinema's mode of production and its aggressive imperialist forms of distribution seemed to demand a response grounded in revolutionary aesthetics. Some called it an "aesthetics of hunger" (Glauber Rocha), others an "imperfect cinema" (García Espinosa). Turning the dearth of resources into an advantage, they opted for stark documentary realism, sometimes black and white film stock, and handheld cameras. A key part of the revolutionary fervor of the sixties and early seventies, these films denounced class and race oppression along with economic dependency and often ended with calls to armed uprisings.[18]

In contrast with third cinema, CEFREC-CAIB fiction videos made since 1998—such as *Qati Qati/Whispers of Death*, *Vest Made of Money*, *The Forest Spirit*, *Loving Each Other in the Shadows*, or *Overcoming Fear*—incorporate not only humor but also suspenseful narratives and the stock codes of Hollywood film. Abundant close-ups, elements of the horror movie and the melodrama, as well as the focus on personalized stories rather than collective protagonists contrast especially with the images of Quechuas and Aymaras put forth in the Ukamau Group's famous 1971 docudrama *Courage of the People* that came to epitomize a Bolivian cinema with the people instead of for the people (Sanjinés and Grupo Ukamau 57–81; Jorge Sanjinés, "Problems"). For third cinema documentary realism was the style if not the form of choice. Indigenous media activists have also largely opted for the documentary form. Some of their videos are self-reflexive—such as *Lighting the Spirit* (*Kanchariy*) and *Rebellions and Hope* (*Rebeldías y esperanzas*)—but most of CONAIE's, CRIC's, and CEFREC-CAIB's productions include observational shorts or they privilege expository documentaries. This conventional format provides off-screen commentators or alternating talking heads who create a straightforward educational address. Like the fiction videos, indigenous documentaries break with the innovative aesthetics of anticolonial cinema. The question thus persists: How can the medium play a crucial role in decolonization if, at first sight, it no longer opposes the motion picture industry's dominant film language? How can it challenge traditional ethnographic film's claims to document what is real without questioning what and how the camera registers? And how are these films seen when they enter a global mediascape? Instead of changing a world economic system built on colonial and capitalist exploitation, isn't indigenous video doomed to merely become part of the multicultural global market for diversity? What does it mean to appropriate a technology commonly considered paradigmatic of late capitalism? I argue that indigenous media do not seek a bigger piece of the pie, rather, like the indigenous movements they are associated with, the activists seek to transform the system.

Indigenous media are embedded in a complex process of adapting media that works through video production and distribution practices and through film image. I call this process "indianizing," borrowing from Felipe Quispe

("El Mallku"), one of Bolivia's most outspoken and controversial Aymara revolutionaries turned politician. Quispe calls on Aymaras and Quechuas to stop buying into the discourse of *mestizaje* and instead "indianize the white man" (*indianizar al q'ara*) (Sanjinés, *Mestizaje* 165). My use of the term refers to the capacity of indigenous cultures to integrate European elements into their own symbolic and social orders (Rivera and THOA, *Pachakuti* 6).[19] Extending what Brooke Larson called the "adaptive vitality" of indigenous peoples, video makers build on a long Andean tradition of integrating what is foreign into traditional cultural and economic forms (Larson 12). The process is an example of how indigenous movements in the region are transforming dominant socioeconomic and political structures and largely hegemonic epistemologies.

Indigenous media's complex process of appropriation suggests theoretically reconsidering the question of technology. In contrast with Goody and Ong, we need to recognize that the conquest of the Americas entailed narrowly enforcing European medieval and Renaissance ideas about books, knowledge, and writing (Mignolo, *Darker*, "Signs"). Notions of orality and literacy (or the technology of the alphabet) separate what have always been much more diverse forms of semiosis. What Mignolo calls "alternative literacies" were subalternized, though not entirely destroyed, in the process ("Signs" 232). As Quijano and Mignolo have argued, the discourses and practices shaping technology are foundational to the coloniality of power.[20] Indeed, the constitution of power and knowledge implies an intricate relationship between geopolitical systems of economic exploitation, the construction of race, and epistemological hierarchies or Eurocentrism.

Film and video have reproduced the gaze of Empire, reinforcing ideas about indigenous peoples as inhabiting a primitive, pre-technological world first offered with the narratives of conquest. As my study shows, indigenous media challenge this view on screen. Yet audiovisual technology exceeds the parameters of representation. Although the final product may become part of what Diana Taylor calls "the archive" (20), the process of production and distribution enters audiovisual representation into the realm of performance. Communities discuss possible topics and ways of representing them on film; they act in front of the camera, and codetermine the process of distribution and collaboration between indigenous video makers and their nonindigenous technical advisors. In these instances, social relations are enacted and technology itself is redefined. It becomes a technology of

knowledge that entertains and educates but also allows for social practices
to be strengthened or brought back into existence. *Indianizing Film* hence
conceptualizes film/video/television as text and as a social practice.[21]

Film technology entails at once representation, enactment, and material-
ity. It comes into being as a response to social desire, and it shapes desire
and social relations. In other words, media technology begins as a discourse
before it becomes part of existing practices (Batchen 24). Likewise, once
technologies circulate, they become "objects [that] shift in meaning as they
move through regimes and circuits of exchange" (Ginsburg, Lughod, and Larkin, "Introduction" 5–6). It is not only the meaning of a given text—written or
audiovisual—that changes with every viewing experience; as an object, technology itself is far from ontological. Rather, "the meaning of texts or objects
is enacted through practices of reception" (6). Like Fernando Ortiz's notion
of transculturation, indigenous media refer not only to the transformation of
ideas (and not at all to the biological mixing of *mestizaje*) but also to culture
as matter and as practice.[22]

The cultural politics of indigenous video makers cast audiovisual technology as a technology of knowledge equivalent and to a degree preferable
to literacy, frequently considered a hegemonic epistemic form and means
of representation. As a social practice, video makers assimilate audiovisual
technology to a complex semiotic tradition of transmitting knowledge and
a pan-indigenous set of ethical guidelines that are themselves under construction. The process of indianizing creates continuities between complex
indigenous systems of signifying and audiovisual aesthetics. These systems
of signifying exceed the binary of literate versus oral culture. Indeed, these
lines of continuity call into question the idea that film technology is alien
to indigenous cultures. I maintain that, while video makers refrain from
explicitly opposing the dominant codes of commercial film, they integrate
the elements of Hollywood film with the formats of oral storytelling and the
arrangement of colors, borders, and iconography familiar from Andean textiles. Such forms and modes of transmitting knowledge are closely (though
not exclusively) associated with women. While anticolonial cinema and
much critical film scholarship have focused on experimental techniques
that undermine commercial cinema, indigenous video draws attention to the
way Hollywood conventions and aesthetics can be turned against themselves
in a process that is primarily about "intra-racial looking relations" (Kaplan
222) and creating what Raheja calls "visual sovereignty." As Raheja puts it,

"by appealing to a mass, intergenerational, and transnational indigenous audience, visual sovereignty permits the flow of indigenous knowledge about such key issues as land rights, language acquisition, and preservation by narrativizing local and international struggles. Visual sovereignty, as expressed by filmmakers, also involves employing editing technologies that permit filmmakers to stage performances of oral narrative and indigenous notions of time and space that are not possible through print alone" ("Reading" 1162–63). Yet adapting or indianizing film points to tensions between what the Bolivian video makers call a *rescate cultural* (cultural rescue), symbolized by the woman's body on one hand and the demands of indigenous women's movements on the other. I show that idealized notions of gender complementarity become symbolic of a vision of decolonization that relies on intercultural exchange. This vision subscribes to an Andean notion of duality that continues to be blind with respect to those who do not fit neatly into the binary of male and female.

What I call indianizing runs counter to the movement inscribed by transculturation in so far as it does not seek integration into hegemonic structures.[23] Indigenous audiovisual communication transforms existing structures of generating knowledge by situating itself on the border of dominant centers. Indigenous media circulate through autonomous communication networks sustained by indigenous facilitators who, in some cases, carry generators and equipment to isolated rural communities, or, in other cases, make use of existing facilities in order to screen and discuss documentaries and fiction shorts. The distribution of indigenous media corresponds to an ethos rehearsed by the Andean Oral History Workshop (THOA), whose Aymara researchers consciously answered to the ethical values and needs of their communities of origin. The THOA obliged its members to return the results of their findings to the communities and to submit them to their critical review. Indeed the THOA's innovative approach to indigenous historiography has fed on a process of refinement achieved through continuous interaction between research findings and community evaluations of these results (Rivera and THOA, "Potencial" 58; Stephenson, "Forging" 104–7). Although the THOA also produced some videos, it has mainly worked through oral Aymara history transposed into writing and through radio shows (Stephenson, "Forging"). Indigenous media activists also use manuals, and some are literate or, like Marcelina Cárdenas, even university educated. Many, however, have only marginally been exposed to the state education system, and their main venues of communication are audiovisual media. They have created and sustained a process of indigenous intercultural exchange of ideas where videos filmed in diverse rural communities are circulated back to them, thus placing different cultures in contact with each other. Only after more than a decade of inter-indigenous communication, where video has contributed to strengthening the value of indigenous culture and sought recognition and contact with indigenous and native viewers globally, are the media activists also focusing on the larger national society. CEFREC-CAIB and CONAIE strive to change power relations and dominant traditions of representing indigenous cultures largely bypassing the media industry and the sphere of literacy, long considered the hegemonic form of exerting and contesting power in Latin America.

In their study of different challenges to scientific racism in the nineteenth and early twentieth century, Nancy Leys Stephan and Sander Gilman once explained that the visions of ethnicity most profoundly critical and challenging of the objectivity claims in the scientific debate of the time did not directly impact scientific racism. Yet circulating in marginal presses and expressing views held in black communities, they constituted a radical reservoir for a different thinking (188). Indigenous media similarly have bypassed hegemonic discourses, even sites of knowledge production—be they the world of state-sponsored and private education, commercial film festivals, or mass media broadcasts. The activists in the Andean countries initially largely refrained from addressing intellectual elites or the broader civil society. The video makers and their collaborators instead have created an independent archive of videos treating social and economic relations, medicinal and agricultural knowledge, and myths and stories that are screened through autonomous networks. For the communities involved in audiovisual communication, the creation of audiovisual networks thus marginalizes the knowledge and perspectives dominant in urban centers. Indigenous media form a viewing context where indigenous peoples look at themselves. The problem of nation building that Latin American narrative fictions tried to solve—either advocating against or in favor of *mestizaje* (cultural and biological miscegenation) and transculturation as the merging of Western and indigenous languages and patterns of thinking—is here reversed. Rather, the goal has been to strengthen indigenous cultures and shape the conditions for creating sustainable knowledge within and among indigenous communities.

What video makers call "intercultural dialogue" is a goal, not a given. It implies a conversation among equals that has partially been realized but remains restricted. Intercultural dialogue is an ideal that first needs to rid civil society of the colonial subalternization at its heart. As Carlos Mamani Condori and Maria Eugenia Choque Quispe, the former directors of the THOA, put it, "the idea of interculturality is very different from the subordination of natives by whites. One of the objectives proposed by the *ayllus* is establishing a communication. Sitting down at the table and talking among equals with the goal of finding solutions to a common problem" (Mamani Condori and Choque Quispe 167). While emerging from the cultural border that colonialism has reified, the subaltern here bypasses the hegemonic center even as the video makers, like the sociopolitical movements they are associated with, ultimately seek dialogue.[24]

The question of technology—that is, whether a technology apparently alien to indigenous cultures can be used to "rescue" these cultures—implies a second problem of subsumption. If we consider that the use of technology necessarily transforms a culture and integrates it into an already existing one, such as the society of the spectacle or the multicultural market, our understanding of technology's characteristics inscribe a hegemonic logic. Like the idea of a subaltern voice perpetually out of reach and destined to lose itself once it comes into representation, indigenous media would seem to necessarily translate subalternized cultures into hegemonic frameworks, integrating them into the hegemonic domain along the way. The trope is familiar from the theorization of the relationship between orality and literacy. All change must necessarily pass through writing, wrote Angel Rama in *The Lettered City* (82). Although indigenous voices may be traced in literary representations (e.g., Lienhard), they ultimately become integrated into the established power structures of the institution of literature. *Testimonio*, some argue, has suffered a similar fate (e.g., Beverley, *Testimonio* 281).

Although indigenous media evolve from collaboration, they differ fundamentally from literary *testimonio*. *Testimonio* has been considered a prime entry point into the canon of literature for subalternized, often indigenous voices achieved through the mediation of a literate interlocutor and editor. Many on the academic left hoped that *testimonio* could thus contribute to destabilizing the idea of the canon and the literary institutions (and academic book market) that uphold it.[25] Indigenous media, in contrast, beg reconsidering the hegemony of literacy as technology of the intellect.

Instead of a juxtaposition between oral and literary means of expression, the process of indianization transfers subalternized ways of understanding into an audiovisual medium that is at once marginal to the powerful realm of letters and to mass media and central to it. Originating with the conquest, Latin America has been characterized by a correlation of power, knowledge, and literacy that the late Uruguayan literary critic Angel Rama called the "lettered city." The lettered city's power has rested in disciplining and integrating—particularly through literary fiction—vast oral cultures, thus figuratively remedying Latin America's foundational and violent cultural encounter, a clash that the nineteenth-century intellectual Domingo Faustino Sarmiento so influentially cast as the clash between civilization and barbarism. According to Rama, the social makeup of this lettered elite has continuously changed but not its logic of operation; yet, with the proliferation of mass media in the twentieth century, the concept of the lettered city has come into crisis. Jean Franco argues that the mass media contribute to the long-awaited decline and fall of the lettered city (*Decline and Fall* 11). As I elaborate in this book, however, the correlation of knowledge, power, and literacy that Latin Americanists have come to associate with the metaphor of the lettered city involves a "visual economy." Mass media can thus be more readily understood to extend the power of the lettered city's visual economy. The cultural politics of indigenous movements confront this configuration, particularly when contesting prevailing images in audiovisual form. By this I mean that indigenous media work through a key technology of mass media, including some of film's dominant aesthetic conventions, yet they circulate primarily outside of corporate-owned film and television industries.

In response to the great international interest in indigenous-made films, the media activists experiment with different ways of relating to the global market. Some organizations, such as the Brazilian Video in the Villages and the Chiapas Media Project in Mexico, choose to distribute and sell their films to international audiences. For the Chiapas Media Project, indigenous video has become one means of keeping attention in the United States focused on the Zapatista struggle. Others that are at the center of this study—such as the Bolivian media activists organized in CAIB and CEFREC, CONAIE's communication department in Ecuador, and the CRIC in Colombia—opt to bypass the multicultural film market in favor of autonomous distribution networks among indigenous communities. In other words, while some oral histories compiled by indigenous research institutions (such as the THOA) did

primarily circulate back to indigenous communities, the *testimonio* debate
was most invested in writing that addressed and traveled to the global north.
Indigenous media from the Andean countries, similar to the THOA, primarily addresses indigenous peoples and rarely seeks an academic solidarity
politics or commercial distribution.[26]

The question of whether indigenous communities ultimately seek to
integrate themselves better into existing market relations, or whether
decolonization actually seeks to transform existing structures is key. I claim
that indigenous media attest to both. On the one hand, video helps indigenous communities to articulate their demands for better healthcare, state
education, access to technology, and so forth. On the other hand, when the
Bolivian videos enter into marketing relations, the media activists tend to
demand that potential buyers adhere to the principles of an Andean reciprocal economy. In Bolivia, indigenous media activists extend a reciprocal
economy that has continued to exist parallel to capitalist market relations.
Often truncated in its reach and importance, video at once documents and
strengthens this tradition. Moreover, the process of indianization points to a
different logic. Instead of entering the dominant realm of cultural representation, indigenous movement organizations adapt audiovisual media to an
epistemic process of intercultural communication that bypasses established
centers. Indianizing film entails appropriating media not merely as a form
of entertainment but as an educational tool that allows for a decentralized
intercultural communication, a process whereby audiovisual media become
a technology of knowledge that is proper to the communities.

Parting ways with transculturation, this process of appropriating audiovisual technology more readily resembles the Zapatista's integration into
the Mayan indigenous movements in southern Mexico: "The EZLN [Ejército
Zapatista de Liberación Nacional/Zapatista National Liberation Army] gets in
contact and interacts with the indigenous communities and becomes part
of the indigenous resistance; it gets contaminated and subordinated to the
indigenous communities," says Subcomandante Marcos (Marcos et al. 149).
The Zapatista spokesman explains how the Marxist guerilla became incorporated into existing indigenous movements and organizations as a process of
dismantling and rebuilding: "We went through a process of re-education, of
re-modeling. It was like they unarmed us. As if they had dismantled all the
tools we had—Marxism, Leninism, socialism, urban culture, poetry, literature—everything that was a part of ourselves, and also that we did not know

we had. They dismantled us and put us together again, but in a different configuration" (151).[27] Marcos, too, has called this process "indianization": "the indianization of the EZLN tactically displaced itself, contaminated the urban part, and indianized it as well" (150).

Instead of ultimately integrating indigenous cosmovisions into Western civilization and concepts of modernity, indigenous media—similarly to the Mayan villages that the Marxist guerilla came in contact with—construct a pan-Indian ethos by assimilating Western thinking and technology. The process is not unique to the Andean and Amazonian peoples. Indigenous media are a means of political self-representation and communication that reflect internal discussions about the effects of mainstream media on indigenous societies. Aboriginal filmmakers in Australia have developed strategies to adapt the medium to cultural requirements in their own usage (Ginsburg, "Faustian" 96–98; "Embedded"; "Screen" 51). In North America, "under visual sovereignty, filmmakers can deploy individual and community assertions of what sovereignty and self-representation mean and, through new media technologies, frame more imaginative renderings of Native American intellectual and cultural paradigms, such as the presentation of the spiritual and dream world" (Raheja, "Reading" 1165). Singer writes that "as Native American filmmakers . . . what really matters to us is that we be able to tell our own stories in whatever form we choose" and argues that "the oral tradition is a continually evolving process [that] is apparent in Aboriginal and Native American films and videos, which are extensions of the past in our current lives" (2, 3). Isaac Pinhanta, an Ashaninka teacher and filmmaker affiliated with Video in the Villages in Brazil, writes that

> we are using the instrument of video in a different way, in our own way. We use it also to help society better understand us, in the way that we think, us here and you there. This is how we are, we have our own knowledge and it would be good if everyone were to begin to see this from now on. It is good for us to have this dialogue. There are people who say: "Ah! You're trying to be white." Today, everyone uses Japanese technology, but the Japanese is not Brazilian, nor is the Brazilian Japanese. This is the same. I'm not Xavante, I'm Ashaninka and he's Xavante. But we can organize ourselves using the same instrument that white people use, but with a different image and purpose. You use it according to your needs and your way of organizing yourself.[28]

This appropriation of media transforms the audiovisual technology's dominant inscription into the entertainment industry of Western capitalism and colonialism; it also impacts indigenous movements' cultural politics, as indigenous media activists are well aware. Pinhanta reflects that

> no matter how much we strengthen our culture and language, we are going to change; something will change inside our villages, just as changes have already occurred. . . . Today, to be very traditional, of an oral culture, is worthless in this global world. But for us, this is of great value. We are very proud of our knowledge, of our myths, of our beliefs. A small design of a hat of this size is significant because it tells a big story. How can we preserve this, so that it is not lost? That is our great challenge. Our clothing is very significant for our people. If we stop using this clothing, will we be the same Ashaninka or will we be different? We think about this, but nobody knows. A historian can imagine how it will be, but does not know. Will writing change us? It has already changed us, we have seen the change, and contact with another society has already changed us. If video is to help us to organize ourselves, if it in itself represents a change, it is us who are changing, not someone who comes from the outside. Someone from outside our village may teach us how to use video, but it is us who are making this change. (Pinhanta, n.p.)

Indigenous cultures, though on the one hand apparently fixed and immobile in the phrase *rescate cultural*, acquire a malleable, dynamic characteristic in the process of adapting media technology.

Subalternity, Literacy, and Academic Readers

Thinking about indigenous media in terms of a technology of knowledge places what Ginsburg has called the "Faustian Dilemma" of indigenous media—where Western technology seems to sit uneasily with indigenous traditions—into dialogue with ongoing reflections about representation and subalternity. Latin American subaltern studies has more readily engaged with the problematic of literary and historiographic representation. Drawing attention to indigenous media in this context opens these debates up to the role of media—an inherently collaborative form of representation and enactment—in producing and challenging relations of power and subalternity.

Writing a book about indigenous media that is sympathetic to the process of decolonization that indigenous movements promote, but that is not primarily addressed to the viewers and producers of indigenous media, enacts the move that indigenous media activists themselves, at least in the Andean countries, shy away from. This book thus risks being read as a translation of the subaltern into hegemonic space. The move is problematic because subaltern studies entails pitfalls that impinge on its very intent. As Gayatri Spivak put it, "there is always a counterpointing suggestion in the work of the [subaltern studies] group that subaltern consciousness is subject to the cathexis of the élite, that it is never fully recoverable, that is always askew from its received signifiers, indeed that it is effaced even as it is disclosed, that it is irreducibly discursive" ("Subaltern Studies" 11). In this sense, the subaltern remains a theoretical fiction that entitles the project of reading (12). To escape the predicament, John Beverley has suggested that "what subaltern studies can or should represent is not so much the subaltern as a concrete social-historical subject, but rather the difficulty of representing the subaltern as such in our disciplinary discourse and practice within the academy" (*Subalternity* 1). Mignolo has suggested thinking of subalternity in terms of epistemologies that colonialism often violently oppressed and sought to annihilate. His work engages with writers who have brought hegemonic and subalternized knowledge traditions to bear on each other, creating what Mignolo calls "border thinking" or "border gnosis" (*Local* 5–13). Mignolo asks, "how should we think from models and theories provided by Chicano/a thinkers such as Gloria Anzaldúa and Cherrie Moraga, among others? How should we operate in language from the edges of what disciplinary self-descriptions placed as the exterior of a disciplinary interior? How should we erase the disciplinary distinctions between external narrative forms, such as the myth, and internal narrative forms such as history? How should we rearticulate them in the sphere of human languaging, beyond discursive genres framed in imperial languages and epistemological structures of domination?" (262). Border thinking, for Mignolo, indicates "the emergence of new loci of enunciation, . . . subaltern reason striving to bring to the foreground the force and creativity of knowledges subalternized in a long process of colonization of the planet, which was at the same time the process in which modernity and the modern Reason were constructed" (13). My work strives to illuminate the way indigenous media functions as a technology of knowledge, an epistemic form that is in the process of becoming sustainable, at least for the communities engaged in audiovisual communication. Indigenous videos certainly offer complementary, even radically different representations of cultural, ethnic, and social heterogeneity than the literary and cinematic narratives that students and scholars of Andean culture are familiar with. Instead of comparing indigenous videos to literary and cinematic *indigenismo*, however, I focus on what the process of indianizing audiovisual technology contributes to thinking about decolonization in the age of multiculturalism. Taking such an approach to indigenous media conceives subalternity as a relative category that indicates the colonial subalternization of knowledge. This conceptualization specifies a process of subalternization, but it also widens the scope of what is considered subaltern and how subalternized discourse can be engaged.

For subaltern studies what remains inaccessible is not only a worldview and perspective that does not fit accredited parameters of historical understanding, but also a discourse transmitted through rumor and social practices (Spivak, "Subaltern Studies" 21–23). Scholars working in the Andes have long engaged this dilemma. Some have explored unfamiliar worldviews and, like John Murra, for instance, opened up an understanding of Quechua-Aymara economy and trade across different ecological zones. Brooke Larson and Olivia Harris, among others, have deepened our understanding of these economic relations and their changes over time. Their work allows us to conceive of indianization as a longstanding historical strategy where Quechua and Aymara communities have creatively appropriated and adapted capitalist forms of exchange while maintaining the characteristics of reciprocal economy.

Scholars such as Regina Harrison, Joanne Rappaport, and Denise Arnold and Juan de Dios Yapita have focused on the technologies and forms in which indigenous communities continue to transmit traditional worldviews and social relations in the Andean highlands. In the *Darker Side of the Renaissance*, Mignolo explored ways of reading worldviews expressed in the drawings of Mesoamerican maps. He discussed these worldviews in contrast with European understandings of geography, society, and technologies of knowledge. That is, indigenous epistemology here competes on equal ground with Western knowledge. Mignolo thus critically revised the parameters that allowed literacy and Eurocentrism to marginalize and partially destroy indigenous technologies and perspectives of knowing. The work of indigenous intellectuals like Maria Eugenia Choque Quispe, Carlos Mamani Condori, and those who have worked closely with them, such as Silvia Rivera Cusicanqui, articulates alternative epistemologies by bridging oral (e.g., radio) and literate forms of publication, an approach that again required reconceptualizing where and how knowledge transmission takes place. Raheja's notion of visual sovereignty discusses native appropriations of film but also indicates the search for a reading strategy. As she puts it, "visual sovereignty involves a revision of older films featuring native American plots in order to reframe a narrative that privileges indigenous participation and perhaps points to sites of indigenous knowledge production in a film otherwise understood as a purely Western product" ("Reading" 1162). These are not deconstructive approaches of reading against the grain, but rather sustained engagements with indigenous epistemologies. I seek to similarly engage with indigenous media—as text and as practice—in order to explore an understanding of decolonization articulated from subalternized perspectives in an audiovisual rather than an alphabetic or oral format.

My approach was originally inspired by a collective interdisciplinary research project under way for a number of years. Formulated once as a process of "thinking from the Andes" rather than "in the Andes" (Schiwy and Ennis 1), we have been exploring possibilities of entering into dialogue with the subalternized knowledges produced in indigenous, Afro-Colombian, and Afro-Ecuadorian social movements in order to promote the decolonization of academic thinking. The concept of the coloniality of power has constituted a key anchor for us as we have debated its continued theoretical significance under conditions of multicultural markets and neoliberal globalization.[29] While for many of us the coloniality of power indicates race as a key construct of colonialism, indigenous media activists have pushed my understanding of how the coloniality of power is anchored in constructions not only of race but also of gender. Indeed, I argue in this book that gender imaginaries and relations have become central to current processes of decolonization.

While the Andean Oral History Workshop and scholars like Xavier Albó or Pablo Mamani Ramírez maintain close working relationships with their communities, writing about indigenous media from the vantage point of the U.S. academy poses a different set of challenges. Although we may share the goal of decolonization, our dialogue is limited by the writing style required for academic publication. More important, indigenous communicators struggle for decolonization in a different place and under often quite dangerous conditions, which have little in common with the relative comfort of

working at a North American university. Can an engagement with indigenous
media lead not only to a solidarity politics to be effected outside the academy,
but also to further exploring the possibilities for pushing the decolonization of knowledge within the academy? My hope is that this book will offer
an engagement with indigenous media that goes beyond the study of an
object, however fascinating. While an important emerging cultural form,
indigenous media can also serve as an interlocutor, contributing to thinking
differently about indigenous cultures, decolonization and gender, and about
the question of technology.

By exploring indigenous media in the Andean countries in light of
questions about knowledge, gender, and decolonization, I depart from the
geographic focus of indigenous media studies, from its preoccupation with
documentary film, its thematic focus, and to a degree its ethnographic methodology. In stride with the native media boom in Australia, New Zealand,
Canada, the United States, Latin America, and elsewhere, critical research
on indigenous media has become a growing and multidisciplinary field of
inquiry. Several book-length studies have been published about Aboriginal
media in Australia (e.g., Michaels, Deger) and important monographs and
collected volumes have addressed the diversity of native and Aboriginal
media in North America (e.g., Singer; Nicholson; Raheja, *Redfacing*). There
are a few edited volumes that compare indigenous media activism globally
(e.g., Ginsburg, Abu-Lughod, and Larkin; Wilson and Stewart). Houston Wood
is currently preparing a monograph that maps and compares indigenous
feature films globally. Article-length studies on indigenous media have
appeared in a variety of publications (journals and collected volumes), and
there is a plethora of short statements and reviews circulated in house or
on Web sites by media activists involved in indigenous video making. For
Latin America the best-documented context is Brazil—Kayapo video making
and *Video nas aldeias* (*Video in the Villages*).[30] Due to Alexandra Halkin's presentation and distribution of indigenous videos from Chiapas and Guerrero
in U.S. universities, the Chiapas Media Project/Promedios is also garnering
increasing attention. Erica Wortham's book on indigenous media in Mexico,
Making Culture Visible, is forthcoming from Duke University Press. Despite
their importance, indigenous video and television in the Andean countries
are only beginning to receive scholarly attention. The Salvadorian filmmaker
Daniel Flores conducted an interview with the Bolivian video makers Marcelino Pinto, Alfredo Copa, and Julia Mosúa that I transcribed and that was

published in the journal *Bomb* in 2001. My article "Decolonizing" explores the process of indigenous media production in contrast with revolutionary third cinema. Jeff Himpele's article "Packaging" includes an interview with Iván Sanjinés and Jesús Tapia. Himpele's *Circuits of Power* includes a conclusion that treats indigenous media activism in Bolivia, and Ibazeta's and Wood's doctoral theses include some discussion of indigenous media in Bolivia.[31]

Most research on indigenous media has so far mainly treated the impact of video on indigenous societies and their constructions of identity. Publications often interrogate the role and importance of the (visual) anthropologist or independent filmmaker and collaborator in relation to the communities they work with. Ph.D. research attests, however, to indigenous media's growing interdisciplinary appeal.[32] *Indianizing Film* is not an ethnographic study. I am interested in the relation of indigenous media to the broader pan-indigenous and scholarly discourse on decolonization. I place indigenous media in relation to scholarly work on other collaborative texts with a revolutionary impetus, such as *testimonio* and third cinema. I argue that video bypasses literacy and thus overcomes the limitations of *testimonio*. My approach hence shares certain affinities with Michelle Raheja's forthcoming monograph, *Redfacing and Visual Sovereignty*, which includes analyses of videos, films, and written autobiographies. Raheja studies the different forms native critical interventions and forms of transmitting knowledge and cultural memory have taken over the last two centuries in North America, including native media. Her work takes a wider historical view than mine, and she concentrates on North America. Rarely have scholars interrogated the use of gender imaginaries in indigenous media, compared indigenous media production to the revolutionary third cinema of the sixties, or studied indigenous-made fiction videos. These are central concerns of my work. I contrast the revolutionary ethos and visual aesthetics of third cinema with indigenous fiction videos in order to understand how the concept of decolonization has changed since the 1960s. By analyzing how indigenous video negotiates the colonial gaze (racial and patriarchal) that mainstream and ethnographic film established, I hope to sharpen our understanding of decolonization.

As a study of audiovisual forms of discourse, I hope this book will shed light on a little known area of film/video production in Latin American media studies. Much of the critical focus has been dedicated to revolutionary films, particularly those from the 1960s and 1970s (e.g., King, *Magical*; Pick,

New; Chanan, *Cuban*) or to compiling histories of national cinemas (Stam, *Tropical*). The recent proliferation of independent internationally coproduced and commercially successful Latin American cinema has triggered a renewed critical interest in Latin American film that is being published in a variety of journals and collected volumes (e.g., Noriega, *Visible*; Shaw and Dennison, *Latin*; Shaw, *Contemporary*; and particularly the *Journal of Latin American Cultural Studies*). Some have begun revisiting the film and television industries, including commercial B-movies produced in Latin America throughout the twentieth century (Ruétalo). The field of Latin American media studies is becoming wider, encompassing research in literary and cultural studies, sociology, and communication studies. Perhaps because it is primarily distributed outside of commercial venues, indigenous media has remained marginal to these approaches. While linking up with the methodological and theoretical concerns articulated in the study of revolutionary films, I hope this book will contribute to creating a complex picture of the diverse media productions in contemporary Latin America.

Chapter 1, "Indigenous Media and the Politics of Knowledge" offers an overview of the different kinds of videos produced and circulated through indigenous audiovisual communication networks in the Andes and the transnational Amazon basin. I argue that these videos offer cultural entertainment but, more important, act as a technology of knowledge where the diverse genres of indigenous media, including the combination of documentaries and fictionalized mythological representations, acquire an epistemic power. The video makers and communities involved in the intercultural process of audiovisual communication question the perspectives, genealogies, subjectivities, and technologies of representation that, since the time of conquest, have been privileged in a global epistemic geopolitics. Video distribution turns rural areas in South America into a multicentered, rhizomatic epistemic network. In other words, decolonization no longer seeks the ousting of a foreign occupying power. Instead, indigenous media create the conditions of possibility for redefining where and how sustainable knowledge is produced. They contribute to the construction of a pan-indigenous positioning vis-à-vis colonial discourse that transcends the particularities of indigenous media processes in individual locations.

Chapter 2, "Casting New Protagonists," looks at who makes indigenous media. I contend that the collaboration between nonindigenous collaborators and indigenous video makers changes the notion of revolutionary consciousness. If third cinema was marked by urban vanguard intellectuals bringing consciousness to the people (rural and urban working class, peasants, and indigenous peoples), the slight unease some of these filmmakers may have felt with regard to applying the Marxist analysis of the origins of revolutionary consciousness to a context deeply shaped by colonialism has given way to a dialogic relation of a different kind. Indigenous communities and video makers focus on decolonizing the soul—that is, on strengthening indigenous cultures and their perceived value. This also means integrating independent filmmakers and consultants into a cultural politics designed by indigenous social movements. Unlike the collaboration between revolutionary filmmakers and indigenous communities in the testimonial third cinema of the sixties and seventies, indigenous video networks build on community demands for change by responding to a pan-indigenous ethos of accountability. The process is aimed at broadening the procedure of analyzing and generating proposals within the communities, rather than at raising consciousness from without.

Chapters 3 and 4 take issue with how indigenous media engage two central tropes of the cinematic gaze of Empire: temporal entrapment and the feminization of the colonized.

In chapter 3, "Cinematic Time and Visual Economy," I suggest that looking at indigenous video as part of a cultural politics of knowledge requires rethinking the teleology of orality, literacy, and audiovisual media as a shorthand for the way power and knowledge have played themselves out. It may seem reasonable to see indigenous media as part of a temporal accession that contributes to the waning importance of literature, or, in other words, to the decline and downfall of what Latin Americans have called the "lettered city" (cf. Rama, *Lettered City*; Franco, *Decline*). I make the case that, instead of mass media signaling an end to entrenched forms of power and knowledge, indigenous media activists confront a powerful visual economy that extends the lettered city. Graphic, painted, performative, photographic, and cinematic representations have accompanied the colonial and postcolonial inscription of knowledge and power. In contrast with cinema's colonial gaze, indigenous media inscribe their communities into the present rather than as occupying a premodern realm—be it monstrous or pastoral. The video makers resituate the cinematic management of time within the notion of *nayrapacha*, an Andean concept where the past guides the future, as I show in reference to a selection of fiction and documentary shorts.

Indigenous media's work with the cinematic time of *nayrapacha* at once invokes and challenges precolonial utopias of indigenous society that are part of indigenous discourse itself. This internal critique of indigenous culture feeds on changing gender roles within the communities (the participation of women in video production processes partially contributes to these changes) and on the confrontation with the patriarchal gaze of Empire. The lettered city's visual economy temporally displaces indigenous and colonized peoples and at once associates them with virgin territories, childlike irrationality, vengeful nature, and similar metaphors of femininity. On the other hand, indigenous communities themselves often negatively associate their traditional technologies of knowledge (such as weaving and storytelling) and the embodied performance of their ethnic identity (through clothing, language, cooking, etc.) with women.

Chapter 4, "Gender, Complementarity, and the Anticolonial Gaze," focuses on how indigenous video makers rework the tight relation between gender and colonialism. The representation of gender and knowledge in the video shorts *Our Word*, *Qati qati*, *Forest Spirit*, and *Loving Each Other in the Shadows* frame the critique of cultural self-deprecation in terms of a gender clash. Women are cast as the guardians of indigenous traditions, languages, and culture at large, while men appear as the victims of the self-denigrating effects of colonial discourse. Women become the tragic heroes of these films, redeeming their husbands and lovers through their violent deaths. These films reverse the patriarchal gaze of colonial discourse by framing female-identified indigenous culture as the object of indigenous desire. Yet revaluing traditions associated with the feminine also forces video makers and their audiences to review actually existing gender relations. Women's participation in audiovisual communication, just like their activism in political and community organizations, distances them from the parts they play on screen. The tensions mark an instance where a return to indigenous cultural traditions encounters its limits. Women's roles as filmmakers, as political leaders, and as privileged access points to indigenous traditions make clear that decolonization is as much about the rescue of indigenous culture as it is about transforming and reinventing the present. I suggest that the contradictions opened up by the gendered logic of anticolonial discourse hence indicate the drive toward a transformation within an otherwise conservative indigenous politics of cultural rescue. The revalorization of feminized culture, however, is not unproblematic. Women's presence on screen plays with their status as objects of the male gaze, a configuration of looks and narrative conventions that would reinscribe a patriarchal order. Gender relations further remain limited in view of "third gender" (Horswell, *Decolonizing* 23) and run the risk of reinscribing gender essentialism, and with it the binary thinking that structures colonial discourse.

Chapter 5, "Nature, Indians, and Epistemic Privilege," discusses the use of the documentary film form in a series of shorts: *Mother Earth* (*Tierra madre*), *The Nasa Garden*, (*Nasa tul*), *The Earth Is Bleeding* (*Sangra la tierra*), *Oil in Weenhayek Territory* (*Petroleo en Territorio Weenhayek*), *Creating Life* (*Creando vida*), and the independent U.S. production *Trinkets and Beads*. The films share a focus on the environmental problems affecting communities in the tropical lowlands and the subtropical Andean valleys. By comparing these films, I work through the ontological trace that persistently inscribes itself as film's apparent ability to capture reality. I argue that this trace remains active, even when using digital technology that, unlike analog film, no longer engraves light on the chemical composition of film. Indigenous video makers take advantage of this trace in order to construct a perspective on knowledge production that negates the possibility of objectivity in favor of a concept of episteme as always embodied and interested. Gender again comes to play a problematic role in this context. *The Nasa Garden* and *Mother Earth* represent nature as a maternal figure with whom the Nasa, Quechua, Aymara and Weenhayek, respectively, have traditionally had a symbiotic relationship. While *Mother Earth* invokes a problematic bond between woman and nature, *The Nasa Garden* essentializes the indigenous subject as a male caretaker of nature, thus leaving a problematic equation between femininity and nature intact. *The Earth Is Bleeding* and *Oil in Weenhayek Territory* use a compressed time line and a conventional format (alternating talking heads and contextual footage). Like *The Nasa Garden* and *Mother Earth*, these shorts shy away from self-reflexivity yet similarly challenge the notion of objectivity espoused in standard documentary and ethnographic film. The video makers abide by the idea of pedagogical clarity, even simplification. These indigenous documentaries employ the tools of documentary realism to make a case for indigenous epistemic privilege vis-à-vis the investment interests and development initiatives brought in from the outside. *Creating Life*, finally, follows the same expository format but complicates the idea of a homogenous indigenous identity that grows from an ontological symbiosis with the land. The film instead focuses on inter-indigenous relations and different approaches to agriculture by local and migrant indigenous peoples in the Andean valleys of Bolivia. Although these documentaries refrain from commenting on video making in the communities, they attest to a complex understanding of the relationship between image and identity.

Chapter 6, "Specters and Braided Stories," links the narrative structures and thematic conventions of Andean storytelling, the symbols, and the textile technologies of transmitting knowledge to the adaptation of Hollywood elements of style in *Vest Made of Money*, *Qati qati*, and *Cursed Gold*. I maintain that storytelling fuses with complex forms of transmitting social values through textiles, dance, song, rituals, and the reading of an animate lifeworld. Like the lettered city's visual economy discussed in chapter 3, these oral-visual and textile traditions of encoding knowledge and social memory exceed the dichotomy of literate versus oral culture. Indeed, these forms of transmitting knowledge subtly transform the conventional film genres. My analysis proposes that these videos rely on visuality and sound track more than on dialogue and subtitles. Video makers thus reinvent indigenous traditions of communicating aural-visually that again have more readily been associated with women than with men. Though taking a radically different approach than experimental anticolonial third cinema in the sixties and seventies, indigenous video thus indianizes the dominant language of fiction film.

Chapter 7, "Indigenous Media and the Market," concludes by exploring indigenous representations and enactments of labor and market exchange on screen in relation to film as a material practice. Film is a product of labor relations that enters the market. I contend that the strategies of transforming film from a capitalist/colonial art into a means of indigenous communication are rooted in what the Aymaras call *ayni* (reciprocity). Indigenous media production relies primarily on the tireless participation of indigenous communities and communicators bound by relations of reciprocity instead of monetary exchange. Indigenous video makers and their collaborators also take advantage of the currency of multiculturalism in the global web of foundations and nongovernmental organizations. As a product, indigenous film circulates through autonomous networks, free of charge, but also selectively through the global indigenous film market. When indigenous media take advantage of the global marketing of multiculturalism, the market continuously threatens to engulf indigenous cultural politics as a folkloric commodity, even as they may promote a solidarity politics, such as in the case of the

Chiapas Media Project. In other instances, such as the Andes, video makers indianize audiovisual technology by selectively distributing and pricing their films. Rather than seek inclusion of multicultural content into the existing global film market, dominated by the film industry's profit principle, this strategy subtly gives rise to alternative modes of film production and exchange networks. In the Andean countries, indigenous audiovisual communication thus strengthens what I call a "border economy" that has coexisted with Western capitalism since the time of conquest.

1

INDIGENOUS MEDIA AND
THE POLITICS OF KNOWLEDGE

Indigenous media centers have emerged in multiple settings throughout
Latin America. Although indigenous peoples in Brazil number less than 1
percent, the Brazilian nongovernmental organization Video in the Villages
(Video Nas Aldeias) and the Kayapo's use of video are perhaps most familiar
to readers elsewhere. The founder of Video in the Villages, Vincent Carelli,
started making video with Waiãpi Indians in 1990. Since then he has worked
with Nambiquara, Xavante, Waiãpi, and Ashaninka video makers and collaborated with anthropologists Virginia Valadão and Dominque Gallois, and
with filmmakers Tutu Nunes and Mari Correa (Carelli, n.p.). Video makers
like the Xavante Caimi Waiassé and Divino Tserewahú have traveled to
festivals, universities, and academic conferences in the United States, and
a selection of Video in the Villages videos are readily available for purchase
in North America.[1] Terence Turner has published widely on his collaboration with Kayapo video makers since the mid-1980s. The documentary _Tak-
ing Aim_, which circulates in North American universities, details how the
Kayapo have used video to record violations of their territorial rights and
as a way to connect communities that have traditionally had difficult and
tense relations. The Granada Television production _Kayapo: Out of the Forest_ is
also quite extensively disseminated and highlights the role video technology
played when Amazonian tribes organized across ethnic and linguistic differences in order to prevent the building of a major dam on the Xingu River
in the mid-eighties. The Mexican Promedios, known in the United States
as the Chiapas Media Project (CMP), has also become well known. CMP/
Promedios is an international solidarity organization founded in 1998 by
the independent filmmaker Alexandra Halkin from Chicago. This binational

nongovernmental organization promotes access to new video and computer equipment and training in the Zapatista-controlled areas of Chiapas and indigenous communities in the state of Guerrero, Mexico. The organization is extending its work with Tzotzil, Chol, Tzeltal, Tojolabal, and Mam Indians to other states like Guerrero, where paramilitary drug traffickers and the state are waging a low-intensity warfare, with the indigenous peoples caught in the middle. An important part of CMP video distribution is focused on universities in the United States, where screenings and film discussions foster awareness and international solidarity politics. CMP/Promedios's major effort, however, lies with the indigenous communities that it serves. As Halkin summarizes, "CMP/Promedios has trained over 200 indigenous men and women in basic video production, audio and satellite internet access; enabled the production of 22 videos for international distribution; and provided the means for hundreds of videos utilized internally by the indigenous communities in Chiapas" (Halkin, "Outside" 1).

Perhaps still of lesser notoriety, Zapotec communities in Oaxaca took advantage of audiovisual training and technology provided by the Mexican Instituto Indigenista (INI) beginning in 1989. Severing ties with the Mexican state in 1998, the INI became a nongovernmental organization called Ojo de Agua Comunicación, whose president is now the Zapotec media activist Juan José García (Wortham, "Between" 363–64). Dante Cerano, a P'urhépecha Indian, uses video to locally involve young people in the process of rethinking indigenous values in Michoacan. Ana Rosa Duarte and Byrt Wammack Weber direct the important video initiative Yoochel Kaaj that is expanding into community television in the Yucatan.[2] In Guatemala, international and national solidarity organizations support indigenous video makers who use the medium to remember the past decades of violence. They organized the VI International Indigenous Film and Video Festival in Xela (Quetzaltenango) in 1999, which brought together indigenous media activists from across the hemisphere.[3] According to Wortham, "many indigenous video makers in Mexico today . . . are activists in their communities, using video to refocus and revalorize community life" ("Between" 366).

Less well researched, but most influential and prolific, however, are the indigenous media centers in the Andean countries of Bolivia and Ecuador. Indigenous media activists in the Andean-Amazonian region share a focus on strengthening indigenous cultural traditions with their Brazilian and Mesoamerican counterparts. CEFREC-CAIB and CONAIE communicate large numbers of villages and diverse indigenous peoples through video. These are the countries where *indigenismo*—the complex literary and social science debate that addressed social and cultural heterogeneity, including the so-called Indian problem—had found fertile ground in the twentieth century. Documentaries such as *Let's Save the Forest and the Life of the People* (*Salvemos el bosque y la vida de los pueblos*), *The Earth Is Bleeding*, and *Woman, Wisdom and Power* (*Mujer, sabiduría y poder*), produced by CONAIE in Ecuador, convey cultural practices and key information about community problems across geographic and ethnic divides. The videos highlight traditional medicine, celebrations, rituals, and also offer histories of indigenous organizing. In short, they affirm cultural vitality and alternative epistemic regimes. In Colombia, a national context where indigenous peoples are a small minority (a total of 2 percent of the population), the CRIC has been using video for its bilingual education program in a similar fashion.[4]

The most prolific and creative site for indigenous media in Latin America is undoubtedly located in Bolivia. In 1996 the major indigenous peasant movement organizations in the country agreed on the need to create a broad communication strategy. Despite the term "national" in its title, the National Indigenous Plan for Audiovisual Communication is independent of the Bolivian state. The plan initially involved the collaboration of several different organizations: Confederación Sindical Única de Trabajadores Campesinos de Bolivia (CSUTCB; an Andean peasant union); Confederación de los Pueblos Indígenas de Bolivia (CIDOB; a national organization of thirty-four indigenous peoples of the Bolivian lowlands); Confederación Sindical de los Colonizadores de Bolivia (CSCB; an organization that represents the Quechua and Aymara speaking peasants of the Chapare, Bolivia's primary coca growing region and home of Evo Morales, Bolivia's first indigenous president who took office in 2006). These peasant unions and indigenous organizations underwrote the audiovisual communication plan developed by Centro de Formación y Realización Cinematográfica (CEFREC; a center for cinematic training) and Coordinadora Audiovisual Indígena y Originaria de Bolivia (CAIB; a nationwide organization of indigenous media activists).[5] CAIB was founded by "audiovisual communicators," who were appointed as representatives by their respective communities of origin, in the small village of Yotala following the V American Indigenous Video Festival that CLACPI and CEFREC organized in Bolivia in 1996. CAIB is a multiethnic and multilingual association that brings together mostly younger video makers who are critical of

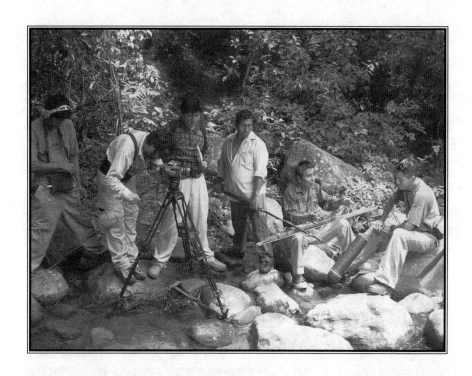

3–6 (above and facing). CEFREC-CAIB production images.
Courtesy of CEFREC.

some of their parents' and peers' desire to assimilate to Western culture. They connect with a generation of elders who want to preserve cultural practices as the basis for alternative knowledge and social ethics, and they are closely associated with indigenous movement organizations such as CSUTCB, CIDOB, CSCB, etc.

In the Andean countries of Bolivia, Ecuador, and Colombia, indigenous media has largely evolved independently of the state. While the CRIC has coproduced a few of their films with the Colombian Ministry of Culture, CONAIE's communication department produces most of the indigenous media in Ecuador. The most consistent financial supporters of the National Indigenous Plan for Audiovisual Communication have been Mugarik Gabe, a Basque nongovernmental organization, and Agencia Española de Cooperación Internacional (AECI), a development institution of the Spanish state. The South-South Exchange Programme for Research on the History of Development (SEPHIS), whose seat is in the Netherlands, have also provided support on a limited and project-specific basis.[6] More recently the videos are also crediting the Basque government (Eusko Jaurlaritza). CEFREC offers training workshops and technical advice, houses editing suites, television studios, and a Latin American indigenous video archive. The members of CAIB form regional production units and their facilitators maintain the National Network for Audiovisual Communication and Exchange through which videos regularly circulate in rural communities.[7]

Indigenous Media and the Decolonization of Knowledge

 CEFREC's fifteen-minute expository documentary *The Other Gaze* (*La otra mirada*) contextualizes indigenous video production in Bolivia for an international audience. It strings together footage shot during video training workshops, interviews with media activists, and clips from several indigenous-made fiction and documentary videos. This is a conventional short dominated by voiceover, yet the film makes far-reaching claims: Indigenous media "invite the exchange of gazes and perspectives on diverse realities, on issues that have to urgently be addressed, on stories gathered in distant communities. Most importantly, of gazes that change the order of things so they [the indigenous communities] may become protagonists, gazes that are born of the need to use communication in a world of changes and transformations that obligate the indigenous and aboriginal peoples to answer back, to not succumb to the pressure of big business interests" (transcript from *The*

Other Gaze). On the one hand, this documentary asserts that indigenous communities, having experienced a long history of colonialism, are now under constant pressure. Even those areas in the Amazonian lowlands that were initially peripheral to colonialism's impact are becoming more and more exposed to development projects, logging, oil drilling, etc. Quechuas and Aymaras have long struggled against the devastating effects of what—despite national independence in 1825—they see as ongoing colonialism. Like in the highlands, indigenous communities throughout Bolivia are now exposed to the profit-driven exploitation of natural resources in their territories, the effects of environmental contamination, and to neoliberal policies that privatize land and water.

On the other hand, the documentary proposes that indigenous media constitute a tool that allows these communities to challenge common perceptions about indigenous people. Since the conquest, and with more urgency yet since the formation of nation-states in the early nineteenth century, the dominant trend in Latin America for dealing with heterogeneity has been to envision bringing indigenous people into the national fold through biological and cultural mixing. Emitted in writing and in the mass media, this discourse today casts indigenous cultures as disappearing worlds or reduces them to folkloric icons of the tourist market. Indigenous media activists and their collaborators share an acute awareness that indigenous perspectives have been discounted in these national imaginaries, regardless of their high- or lowland provenance. As Lucila Lema puts it, in Ecuador, "Quichua women have had absolutely no access to the media and when they do enter into these spaces they become symbols of poverty, ignorance, domestication, etc. Election campaigns and commercial advertisements devalue, folklorize, and distort these images, submitting them to the supply and demand laws of the market" (Lema, n.p.). *The Other Gaze* highlights the importance of the audiovisual medium in strengthening indigenous cultures so they can "answer back." Indigenous video here is claimed as a technology of knowledge.

Directed by CEFREC's founder, Iván Sanjinés, *The Other Gaze* hence implicitly questions the epistemological anchors set in European histories of science and philosophy. The media activists see the West's tradition of knowledge production as steeped in colonial legacies and as an unreciprocated one-way export offering them little benefit. As is well known, colonialism established the basis for the economic exploitation of what was later to be called the "third world" by the "first" and justified this exploitation through an elaborate religious and philosophical framework. The coloniality of power articulates racial and gender constructs, the formation of a new global structure of labor and exploitation, and a Eurocentric epistemology.[8] Together they order space, time, and subjectivity in a way that privileges particular sites and subjects of knowledge production while disqualifying others. This tight intermingling of epistemic and economic regimes originates with the conquest of the Americas; it connects the experience of Spanish and Portuguese colonialism with the second wave of British, French, German, and Italian imperialism (Quijano, "Coloniality" 533–34). As Mignolo argues, "Western expansion since the sixteenth century has not only been a religious and economic one, but also the expansion of hegemonic forms of knowledge that shaped the very conception of economy and religion" (*Local* 22). In other words, the colonial experience not only led to the exploitation and annihilation of indigenous peoples, but also engendered an increasingly intensified global economic system and a powerful Eurocentric discourse that perceives, describes, and produces a global reality with profoundly unequal access to the regime of power and knowledge:

> [For the colonizing discourse] cultures of scholarship were precisely what people outside Europe either lacked (like the Aztecs or the Incas), or if they happened to possess them (like China, India, or the Islamic world), they became an object of study (e.g., the rise of "Orientalism"). Over the five hundred years of Western expansion and the creation of colleges and universities in colonized areas since the beginning of the sixteenth century, this belief became so strong as to make people doubt their own wisdom, when that wisdom was not articulated in Western educational institutions and languages. (Mignolo, *Local* 304)

The coloniality of power constructs the idea of modernity as a projection of European economy and epistemology. This geopolitics of knowledge hence affects Creole and Mestizo elites and also creates pressures on indigenous peoples to either abandon or conceal their traditional knowledge and religious beliefs. Colonial discourses and practices have thus hierarchically positioned complex constructions of knowledge and subjectivity. Alongside massive enslavement and death, indigenous peoples were marginalized and their systems of knowledge suppressed.

Cast as superstitions and devils' worship, many subalternized forms of knowing have nevertheless survived; they have been transformed and hidden along with the multiple material and embodied forms of signifying that transmit alternative ways of life and traditions of understanding. As *The Other Gaze* affirms, indigenous media activists seek to convert these subalternized viewpoints into "protagonists." The politics of knowledge promoted by indigenous media thus subscribe to the ambitious goals of indigenous movements in the continent to complete the process of decolonization. Culture is here understood as a resource for thinking alternative modernities and forms of development. The languages, perspectives, and genealogies of knowledge that the colonial discourse characterizes as barbarian, superstitious, or irrelevant are now cast as important resources for thinking otherwise. As I explain in more detail below, media activists across the Andean countries—such as Marcelina Cárdenas, Ofelia Condori, Alfredo Copa, Pedro Gutiérrez, Patricio Luna, Regina Monasterios, Julia Mosúa, Maria Morales, Faustino Peña, Marcelino Pinto, Reynaldo Yujra, Aidée Alvarez, and Jésus Tapia from Bolivia; Lucila Lema and Mario Bustos from Ecuador; and Inocencio Ramos and Carmen Vitonás from Colombia—foster the conditions of possibility for generating knowledge and consciousness through communication among their communities of origin.

Using video as a tool for decolonizing knowledge, however, raises questions about how it engages or resists mainstream cinematic codes that have inscribed colonial and patriarchal forms of seeing. Mainstream media are embedded in a powerful global industry, dominated by few multinational corporations. Both as discourse and labor product, film and video are tightly bound to the geopolitics of knowledge that comes into existence with the colonization of the Americas. Yet indigenous media activists are not the first to use film in order to challenge the coloniality of power in Latin America. In the face of U.S.-led neocolonialism, filmmakers in the sixties and seventies countered the hegemony of the Hollywood film industry, along with its promotion of an "American way of life." Against what was deemed cultural imperialism, third cinema elaborated an "aesthetics of hunger" (Glauber Rocha) and an "imperfect cinema" (Julio García Espinosa). Latin America's famous revolutionary filmmakers rejected Hollywood's narrative and visual codes in favor of an often stark, documentary realism captured with handheld cameras. They converted the dearth of resources into an asset. Their films included stunning denunciations of imperialism and internal colonialism and, particularly in Bolivia, its effects on native peoples. Indigenous media's articulation of an anticolonial gaze, however, could not be more distinct from anticolonial cinema's radical aesthetics.

Courage of the People, released in 1971, for example, is one of Jorge San-jinés and the Ukamau Group's masterpieces. It was produced in close collaboration with the mining community of Siglo XX in the Bolivian Andes and includes the participation of Domitila Barrios de Chungara, who later became rather famous for her provocative comments at the First International Feminist Conference in Mexico City in 1975. (She includes an account of the event in her well-known *testimonio*, *Let Me Speak*, which she authored with Moema Viezzer.) The Ukamau Group's dramatized documentary re-creates a history of Bolivia's largely Quechua and Aymara miners' resistance to capitalist exploitation in the twentieth century. Against the backdrop of the Andean high plains, the opening sequence shows the miner families marching in protest, the handheld camera moving inside the crowd and allowing the spectator to take the miners' perspective as they are massacred by young soldiers with machine guns. In a powerful montage of still photos, the film names those responsible, including members of the ruling military junta at the time. Unlike the Ukamau Group's earlier films, this docudrama is no longer shot in black and white, but it conserves the handheld camera technique, on-site sound recording, and natural light, which strengthen the documentary truth effect of the miner community's reenactment. Instead of highlighting the leadership of Barrios de Chungara—a typical choice for a more mainstream type of documentary—the filmmakers use long shots to capture a revolutionary collective and juxtapose it with close-ups of individualized soldiers, company representatives, and government officials. *Courage of the People* closes with a sequence where the miners return to march and protest yet again with revolutionary fervor. This time the military is absent, and the scene inspires hope, not despair.

Indigenous media activists today, in contrast, embrace the cinema industry's genres, such as the horror film and the melodrama, and they employ the emotional effects of close-ups and suspenseful soundtracks. Rather than focus on the links between external and internal colonialism expressed through racial and class oppression, indigenous fictions re-create myths and stories set in the present day-to-day life of rural communities. The narratives are full of suspense and laced with humor. Fiction shorts appeal to Hollywood genres and elements of style, and they feature individual protagonists.

The documentaries are often quite conventional. Alternating talking heads offer opinions and narrators pedagogically represent and simplify complex issues. Both aesthetically and in tone of argument, indigenous video could not be more distinct from the revolutionary films of third cinema. Yet it clearly exceeds the parameters of entertainment.

Angels of the Earth (*Angeles de la tierra*) like *In Search of the Warrior* (*En busca del guerrero*) for example, is set in a present-day urban environment and deals with the experience of migration. *Angels of the Earth* was first made as a pilot VHS recording in 1997. Remade in digital video in 2001, it tells the story of the young Quechua, Sinchi (Alfredo Copa), who goes to Cochabamba in search of his older brother, who had left the village as a child. Shot with stabilized camcorders and conventionally edited, the video offers no stylistic surprises. The older brother, Antonio (acted by the talented Aymara Reynaldo Yujra), has become successful in the city at the cost of denying his Quechua origin, language, and name. When faced with Sinchi, Antonio denies his family ties to the "*indio*" before him. He fears exposing himself to the racism of urban society that permeates deeply, even the relationship with his wife. The film ends tragically with Yujra's character falling ill and renouncing his cultural denial. On his deathbed he confesses to his brother, tearfully regretting his hardheartedness. Sinchi's ethnicity is marked by accent and attire. He speaks Quechua-inflected Spanish and wears a colorful poncho and white peasant pants that mark him aurally and visually as a newcomer to the city—and as an easy target for small-time crooks seeking to take advantage of him. Antonio similarly performs his *mestizo* identity through dress and through appropriating the racial invectives that urban society retains for rural Indians. The video individualizes the protagonists and tells a story of shifting ethnic identification. There is a tragic, if not violent tone to this film as it addresses the intimate effects of internal colonialism, but there is no military oppression, no reference to coca eradication taking place in the nearby Chapare, and no denunciation of the collusion between neoliberal corporations and government. The video instead counters the prevailing stereotypes about indigenous peoples that the cultural production of educated elites has helped to inscribe. In the face of increasing migrations and spreading state education, the pejorative vision of indigenous cultures issued in textbooks, novels, and mass media has become an ever-more urgent problem across ethnically diverse communities. Media activists seek to offer a new image of indigenous culture and its relevance for modern society. Against the

tropes of melancholic Indians struggling against a colonial order and incapable of rational thinking that is still taught through *indigenista* literature,
indigenous videos like *Angels of the Earth* revalue indigenous subjectivity and
family relations.

This dimension of decolonization bids on critically examining and revers-
ing the "colonization of the soul." The Bolivian scholar, filmmaker, and public
intellectual Silvia Rivera Cusicanqui spoke of the colonization of the soul as
one of colonialism's most nefarious effects. It denotes the pressure exerted by
colonial powers upon Quechua and Aymara populations to adapt to Christian
religion but more generally indicates the influences exerted through religious institutions and secular systems such as schools. The intimate effects
of colonialism thus refer to the power of the idea of "civilization" propagated
through diverse literary and visual representations, as well as in daily enactments of power. It has resulted in a general pressure on indigenous peoples to
deny their economic systems, native languages, religious beliefs, and ethnic
belonging (Rivera Cusicanqui and THOA, *Pachakuti* 5 n. 8). One of the lasting legacies of colonialism has been the conceptual reduction of ethnic and
cultural diversity to the racial category of the Indian, itself a complex notion
of ascribed identity and self-identification. The racial taxonomy that determines what or who counts as Indian in Latin America, and the Andes in particular, has never been stable. *Angels of the Earth* highlights that indigenous
identity is an unsteady category that has varied according to a person's ties
to agricultural labor and education, rather than strictly to biological "race."[9]
However, mobility in racial identification carries the threat of being revealed,
hence Antonio's refusal to recognize his brother. As Fanon had perceptively
analyzed in *Black Skin, White Masks*, the effects of colonialism are realized
in looking relations. Colonialism effects its work on the subject when, in
Fanon's example, the child cries out, "Look, a Black Man!" thus compelling
the colonial subject to see himself as object of the white gaze (111). The interpellation takes profound roots in the psyche of the colonized.

The African American political activist George Parker wrote in 1908 that
"if it be true that as a man thinketh, so he is, then the self-making power
becomes proportionately more powerful when applied to a whole race. For
years it has been constantly affirmed and reaffirmed that races of African
blood have contributed nothing to humanity's store of knowledge and civilization, and this incessant affirmation has produced a conviction of truth not
only in the minds of those who affirm it, but also in the minds of those whom

it wrongs" (quoted in Stephan and Gilman 179–80). In Latin America such affirmations have worked their effects over five hundred years. In the context of multiculturalism and neoliberal reforms that began to shape the Andean countries in the eighties, the pressure to assimilate, as Bolivians emphasize, continues to prevail and is supported by large parts of the national elites (cf. Rivera, *Birlochas* 2–8; Sanjinés, *Mestizaje* 10). "Indian" continues to be a contested term, at times assumed and at others rejected or reworded from *indio* (Indian) to *indígena* (indigenous) to *originario/a* (aboriginal). Indigenous movements in the continent have reappropriated the term *indio*, at least when spoken by those who self-identify as Indian, changing its meaning from a notion akin to the abject to a source of pride. Many nevertheless prefer to simply emphasize ethnicity: Quechua, Aymara, Guarani, Chiquitano, Moxeño, Huaorani, Shuar, Nasa, etc.

At first sight, *Angels of the Earth*'s focus on the colonization of the soul appears to resemble a different film made by the Ukamau Group. *Blood of the Condor* (*Yawar mallku*) was produced in 1969, two years before *Courage of the People*. The film is spoken mostly in Quechua (a scripted dialogue, rather than the improvised style favored in *Courage of the People*) and subtitled originally in Spanish. The film denounces sterilizations that the Peace Corps allegedly performed on indigenous women without their knowledge during the sixties.[10] The filmmakers mixed neorealist style with surreal elements in order to create a revolutionary message that projects indigenous political agency and choice, rather than entrapment by overwhelming circumstances. In a key scene, the urban migrant Sixto (Vincente Salinas) cries out, "*yo no soy indio, carajo!* (I am not an *indio*, damn it!"). Like Antonio in *Angels of the Earth*, Sixto serves as the paradigmatic migrant who denies his ethnic origin. As John Hess explains, "Sanjinés goes beyond the naturalist determinism of neo-realism to analyze the situation of his characters and show the possibility and source of change. He juxtaposes time to compare life in the city with life in the *altiplano*, the life of the Quechua with the life of the Spanish in the city" (Hess 113). The film thus achieves temporal equivalency by placing the Quechuas in the city, but even more forcefully by crosscutting village and urban scenes dominated by two narratives of quest: Ignacio's efforts to find out who is doing harm to the women in the village and Sixto's stymied struggles to obtain blood to save his brother's life.[11]

The solution to cultural and ethnic self-denial in *Angels of the Earth* and *Blood of the Condor*, however, are as distinct as the aesthetic strategies that the filmmakers deploy. In his failing, Sixto can no longer ignore the racism and self-centered lack of compassion of the urban society and of the medical elites eager to please their U.S. visitors. After his brother's death, Sixto returns to his community wearing traditional clothes. His fiery look (captured in a compelling close-up of his face) embodies the two perspectives on colonialism that have informed anticolonial struggle by indigenous movements, where one eye sees economic oppression and the other sees racism.[12] The film ends in a freeze frame of guns raised victoriously. The solution to ongoing colonialism that *Blood of the Condor* proposes is armed resistance. *Angels of the Earth*, in contrast, parts with neorealist aesthetics, surreal soundtracks, and rejects the violent uprising that both *Blood of the Condor* and *Courage of the People* promote. The indigenous video indicates that the problem is no longer (only) a clash between indigenous communities and outsiders, although racism still prevails. Instead, the gaze is turned inward as both brothers look at each other. Yujra's character dies but bequeaths a final question for Sinchi and the spectators, how to resist the effects of colonialism on the soul?

Indigenous media are primarily directed at indigenous and peasant viewers in rural communities. In Bolivia, members of CAIB's network facilitate technology and biweekly screenings of video and multimedia packages that include fiction shorts such as *Angels of the Earth*. After the screenings the videos are put up for debate, raising awareness about self-denigration and implying that change has to start with the decolonization of the soul at the very heart of the communities. Most indigenous videos are even more explicit than *Angels of the Earth* in this sense, since they are set in the context of daily village life. The fiction short *Cursed Gold*, for instance, is characterized like *Angels of the Earth* by stable frames and extreme close-ups. Its tragic love story takes place in Chipiri, a rural community in the subtropical coca growing Chapare, near Cochabamba. The video opens with a shot of a truck arriving, carrying a young man, fluent in Quechua, who comes to town in search of gold. Although in a less explicit manner than the more recent *In the Name of Our Coca*, this video is set within the contemporary context of coca leaf trade and coca eradication programs and, allegorically, criticizes both the militarization of the region and the search for easy riches that motivates cocaine production. The video makers enact scenes from the town market, record in a *chichería* were patrons drink and sing, show market women complaining about the scarcity of coca leaf, and focus on the evolving romantic relationship between the two young protagonists, Tito (José Escalera) and

Juanita (Aidée Alvarez). The camera follows Tito on his foray into the jungle and to a waterfall, where he hopes to gain access to gold by ultimately offering a human sacrifice. He does not heed the warnings of the young Juanita advising him that the waterfall and pond are enchanted, and Tito ultimately pays for this disregard with his own life. *Cursed Gold* ends with the devil, an elderly fellow, rising from the waters with a roar that sends Juanita running back to town in panic. Juanita's flight is shot with a much-celebrated improvised traveling technique where the camera is attached to the cable tire-slide on a children's playground, "to give it a little more life," as Marcelino Pinto explained (Flores 35). Again, this is not an experimental or self-reflective film, so the spectators do not see how the shot was realized. Instead the effect of the last scene enhances the drama and suspense. Like much of the rest of the film, the images here are underlined with a computer-generated sound track that brings the drama to its completion. Again, there are no overt calls for resistance but instead a subtle examination of the effects of colonization on the soul as the protagonist disregards local knowledge and his own dreams of premonition.

As the offscreen spectators and the devil's eyes within the frame look on, *Cursed Gold* like *Angels of the Earth* constructs interracial-looking relations: on screen, Quechua speakers look at each other, while the primary audience off screen—Quechua, Moxeño, Guarani, Chiquitano, Aymara, and other indigenous communities—see each other. The topics of indigenous videos, as much as their mise-en-scène, create contemporary relevance. Most important, however, both *Angels of the Earth* and *Cursed Gold* criticize those who have lost connection with their villages and no longer believe in the traditional knowledge and social ethos that survives in cultural memory and the daily practice of parts of the communities. The issue is urgent, and not only in the highlands and the Chapare. *The Forest Spirit*, filmed in the Moxos lowland jungle, equally violently punishes its protagonist for failing to believe. In this film, two brothers lose their lives to the forest spirit, manifested alternately as a seductive woman dressed in red and as a jaguar only audible through her growl. *Vest Made of Money*, an Aymara short set in a village in the highlands, shifts perspective by showing how avarice and greed constitute deviations from the traditional community ethos of reciprocity, again sanctioned by death and insanity. Yet the final reference is again to regimes of knowledge as the protagonists invariably disregard key premonitions, such as dreams or the flight of a blackbird.

Unlike the Ukamau Productions from the sixties and seventies, none of these videos call for armed revolution; rather they provoke introspection. Stylistically the video makers do not reject the codes of mainstream cinema outright; rather they recontextualize familiar Hollywood shots and techniques and make them work in a new way. Teresa de Lauretis once suggested that, if the gaze is a combination of narratives (and their cumulative effect through history), of affective identification with diegetic elements in the film (the production of desire) and of the camera eye, the power of preexisting discourses can be negotiated but not in terms of a binary resistance: "The terms of semiotic space [are] constructed in language, its power based on social validation and well-established modes of enunciation and address. So well-established that, paradoxically the only way to position oneself outside of that discourse is to displace oneself within it—to refuse the question as formulated, or to answer deviously (though in its words), even to quote (but against the grain)" (*Alice* 7). CEFREC-CAIB's fiction videos do not offer narratives of violent clashes between colonizers and colonized. The media activists certainly do not film from the perspective of the explorer, but neither do they reverse the gaze and "place the camera on shore with the natives," as did Nelson Pereira dos Santos's parody *How Tasty Was My Little Frenchman* (*Como era gostoso o meu Francês*).[13] Although the stories usually end violently, with death as a harsh punishment for disbelief, this violence symbolizes the consequences of abandoning indigenous cultural practices—and more specifically systems of knowledge—as contributing to cultural extinction. The perspectives on the process of decolonization, on the other hand, are open-ended. They concur only that decolonization in the age of multiculturalism requires the revision and reevaluation of indigenous traditions by members of the community themselves.[14]

The concept of decolonization has changed and with it the notion that the anticolonial gaze must necessarily reject commercial cinema's visual codes. Indigenous documentary and fiction shorts largely follow the industry's aesthetic conventions: close-ups, melodramatic love stories, horror film, suspense, and in the documentaries alternating talking heads, expository and observational formats. These conventions are employed, however, as indigenous media turn the gaze toward the inside. The communicators explore the problems experienced and discussed within indigenous communities and the intercultural relations among different indigenous ethnicities. The stories told and enacted in indigenous fiction videos become an indicator of a surviving knowledge. This knowledge is not merely a repository of ancient tales, but a dynamic resource of stories that are continuously adapted to changing ways of life. Their moral lessons, nevertheless, unceasingly inform ethical, social, and economic regimes. The media activists begin by critically evaluating traditions that have already entered into crisis within the communities. While there are idealizations—the grandmother in the video fiction *Qati qati* states that "before there were no thieves"—the videos at once question these idealizations. In accordance with traditional Aymara law, the robber in *Qati qati* is found and punished by whipping and expulsion from the community. The law exists precisely because crime has also existed in the past.[15] Framing myths, stories, and cultural practices vindicates them as reservoirs for another way of thinking.

In other words, indigenous media do not prescribe a single form of anti-colonial struggle but provide spaces for debate about multiple ways that ongoing colonization may be reshaped. If racist discrimination has found increasing echoes within the younger generations in the communities and expresses itself in disregard for elders, storytelling, and the social ethos of reciprocity, the video makers reevaluate cultural practices and transmissions of knowledge by reinterpreting these traditions as a resource.

This focus on epistemology is not unique to CEFREC-CAIB's media activism.[16] In the Colombian Cauca, the CRIC's documentaries and docudramas form part of education packages that include *cartillas* (textbooks), compact music discs, and videos. They are part of the organization's longstanding politics that include the struggle to recuperate ancestral territory, language, and culture (Rappaport, *Cumbe* 10–11). The use of these media in the CRIC's bilingual education program reflects an effort to reform pedagogy, to take it out of the classroom, and to make it "more like a lived experience," as Graciela Bolaños of the CRIC Consulate in Bogotá explained. She commented that the CRIC realized during the late seventies that visual images are a more adequate method of transmitting information than literature: "they stimulate profound reflection." The use of video in adult and children's education is an outcome of this insight.[17] Some of the CRIC's video documentaries are meant to reinvigorate the use of indigenous language (e.g., *The Nasa Language* [*Nasa yuwe' walasa'*] made in 1994); others, like *The Nasa Garden* (*Nasa tul*), advocate sustainable agriculture. The CRIC also uses video to represent a history of the organization's struggle for land rights and autonomy, for self-regulated government, and for bilingual education. The CRIC's 1996 video *Opening a Way*

(*Yi pyandena*) establishes links between present-day indigenous struggles and a long history of anticolonial resistance, highlighting particularly the success of Quintin Lame's efforts to regain Nasa territory in the 1920s.[18] In the Cauca, video makers like Inocencio Ramos, Daniel Cuetocué, Daniel Piñacué, and Carmen Vitonás interlace their own contemporary documentary footage with nonindigenous archival material shot for television. The videos cast communities and elders as successful protagonists of anticolonial resistance rather than as victims of colonial oppression. Though in a locally restricted area, Nasa video makers and their audiences thus construct a history of cultural survival that again focuses on regimes of knowledge and ways of telling their own history.

In Ecuador, Quichua women have created alternative media productions that, according to Lucila Lema, have had profound internal effects. Their use of video, radio, and publications has strengthened "identity, women's self-esteem, and women's organizations" (Lema, n.p.). The power to shape external perceptions, on the other hand, requires elaborating clearer and more sustainable media politics on the part of indigenous organizations (Lema, n.p.). Again, the emphasis on vindicating indigenous epistemologies is explicit. As Lema writes, "global knowledge has not led to dignifying humanity and neither to creating respect and the peaceful coexistence of peoples. In Latin America the 'network society,' the 'society of flows,' and the 'global village' have not achieved 'progress.' On the contrary, they have led to more poverty and marginalization, more 'cybernetic illiteracy.' Its time to value local, quotidian knowledge, the non-academic knowledge of our ancestral cultures. Perhaps only in this way global knowledge can be valid and it will only be valid if it contributes in favor of life" (Lema, n.p.).

Knowledge Flows and Audiovisual Networks

While the CRIC's educational use of video is locally focused on Nasa language and communities, and CONAIE is still seeking ways to effectively and sustainably ensure interethnic video networks, the National Indigenous Plan for Audiovisual Communication has a wide range and communicates different indigenous ethnicities and cultures. The plan is a carefully thought-out and continuously reevaluated and adjusted strategy, which (at the time of writing) has been growing in reach and influence, uninterrupted, for twelve years. Its goal is to provide indigenous communicators with access to audiovisual technology and to place diverse indigenous and peasant communities in contact with each other so they can discuss and envision alternatives to the effects of neoliberal globalization (cf. CEFREC, "Plan," n.p.). In CEFREC's words, the National Indigenous Plan for Audiovisual Communication enables "the formulation of methods and instruments of communication that are appropriate (and can be appropriated) for participation, information, learning, and training. The goal is to place indigenous peoples in a better position, so they can participate in active ways in the processes of development, in generating proposals and joint reflections, and can influence the processes of change that they are facing" ("Plan nacional"; my translation). The distribution of videos made in culturally distinct communities is a key component of the plan.

CAIB facilitators regularly distribute CEFREC-CAIB's video programs through the National Communication and Exchange Network that they maintain. The packages include diverse selections of films: documentaries, docudramas, and fiction shorts like *Cursed Gold*, *Angels of the Earth*, and *Vest Made of Money*. Most of the shorts are from Bolivia, but occasionally the packages include indigenous productions from other regions, including Mexico and Canada. The video packages are approximately sixty minutes in length and typically follow a structured arrangement of video shorts. Video Program Number Three is typical. It contains first, a seven-minute video letter (*video carta*), in this case from the lowland community Bermeo, in the northern Department of the Beni; then a seven-minute "video memory" (*video memoria*) about a festival in honor of a patron saint in Cotoca in the eastern lowlands near Santa Cruz; third, two video reports or news briefs, one Quechua and the other from the Mosetén. Video memories and letters are usually documentaries about rituals and ceremonies, filmed with stabilized cameras. They serve as a kind of video snapshot, but without the voiceover commentary that is familiar to Western viewers from ethnographic film. Video memories can also be slightly longer testimonial denunciations or docu-fictional re-creations of oral history of approximately fifteen to twenty minutes. Sometimes they follow a conventional realist documentary format, juxtaposing different viewpoints and interviews tied together by a voiceover narrator. They may also include reenacted parts and references to myths. Characteristic of the programs' arrangement is the compilation of contributions from diverse regions and ethnicities. The documentaries in Program Number Three are followed by a "video debate" (*video debate*), an educational short of about fifteen minutes that makes extensive use of voiceover narration and didactic summaries. Again, it refers to yet another geographic and ethnic context. The video debate *Traditional Medicine: Health in Our Communities* (*Medicina tradicional: La salud en nuestras comunidades*) juxtaposes the advantages and disadvantages of both Western medicinal practice and so-called traditional medicine in the highlands. This short sets the theme for the discussion in villages that may share similar problems but not the same language or geographic location. *Traditional Medicine* argues that both medical traditions are valuable but that traditional medicine is less costly, thus vindicating indigenous medicinal practices. These realist videos are distinguished as documents from "video stories" (*video cuentos*) like the Mosetén fiction *Forest Spirit* that concludes this package.

The video fictions complement CEFREC-CAIB's vast documentary production on video and increasingly on community television. In anticipation of Bolivia's Constituent Assembly, which began deliberations in August 2006 after the election of Evo Morales as the first indigenous president in South America, CEFREC-CAIB responded to the demands of the indigenous and peasant organizations in Bolivia by initiating the "National Communication Strategy—Indigenous Rights—Towards the Constituent Assembly." This strategy expands on the production and circulation of the video compilations, now making use of multimedia packages containing CDs and DVDs (fig. 7).

Like the earlier VHS video compilations, these multimedia packages are viewed in structured settings where local facilitators affiliated with CAIB guide the discussion of the material. "Multimedia Package no.1," for instance, includes Spanish language radio programs featuring interviews with leaders and representatives of indigenous organizations. They explain what the Constituent Assembly is and urge the communities to participate in the assembly. The leaders also discuss issues such as human and cultural rights, questions of land and territory, autonomy, and systems of justice. The DVD mixes indigenous-made television news shows on the same topics with docufictional representations. *A New Country, A New Path* (*Un nuevo país, un nuevo camino*) frames the efforts of a lowland indigenous community in eastern Bolivia as it prepares to generate proposals for restructuring the Bolivian state. The docudrama *Whose Truth Is It Now?* (*¿Ahora de quien es la verdad?*) re-creates the history of indigenous resistance to the Spanish conquest, to the exploitation and extermination of indigenous peoples during the colonial regime and under the national republic until the present. While much of the film focuses on highland Quechuas and Aymaras, it ends by insisting

7. Cover of CEFREC's multimedia package no. I.

that the Constituent Assembly has been convened thanks to the protests and demands of both high- and lowland indigenous movements. Mixing documentary, dramatization, educational film, and fiction within the video packages, indigenous media activists offer a variety of genres that integrate the different modes of educational address associated with Western pedagogical formats, with the stories, legends, and myths that have long transmitted moral lessons and social ethos within the communities.

The arrangement of the video packages and their genre distinctions in the VHS compilations and in the more recent multimedia packages differ from the criteria used in ethnographic and literary compilations for distinguishing different kinds of Quechua and Aymara narratives. Jesús Lara's famous anthologies, like many others, arrange tales chronologically from narratives of genesis to stories about precolonial power struggles, stories set in the colonial period, and those that show strong influence of Western and Christian thinking. One might say that such compilations correspond to the Western reader's need for clarity and chronological order. CEFREC-CAIB's video packaging also differs from endogenous arrangements of storytelling—for example, the structure of Denise Arnold and Juan de Dios Yapita's recent collection and analysis of Aymara tales about the potato. Arnold and de Dios Yapita combine a chronological order with a taxonomy derived from prevailing concepts in Andean thinking: the distinction between the superior world/the spirit, which is also the faraway time and symbolized by birds of prey and the condor; the world on this earth, whose connection to the spirit world is mediated by the fox and the spider; and the underworld that is symbolized by transitional animals like the toad who bridge land and water. Water is also a reference to the path that leads to the land of the dead and the Garden of Eden, the latter a result of Christianity's influence (Arnold and De Dios Yapita, *Madre Melliza* 135). In *Hacia un orden andino de las cosas*, Denise Arnold, Domingo Jiménez, and Juan de dios Yapita suggest that the Aymara in Qaqachaka distinguish the Spanish term for story (*cuento*, rendered *kuñtu* in Aymara) as gossip from other kinds of stories about wild animals, a literary genre that is called *parlanaka. Layra parla* (stories about the past) and *awil achach parla* (stories transmitted from the ancestors) are again different genres. CEFREC-CAIB does not follow this latter taxonomy, although the fiction videos in particular include elements of different genres of storytelling and forms of transmitting knowledge.

While literary and ethnographic compilations distinguish the tales of origin from contemporary variations on those tales, indigenous video in the Andean-Amazonian countries most often forgoes the reenactment of historical epics. Unlike their famous counterparts, such as the Inuit film *Atanarjuat the Fast Runner*, most of the Bolivian films do not re-create stories of origin set in the far past.[19] There are exceptions, *Jichi Woman* (*La mujer jichi*), for instance, is a legend of origin. More commonly, however, indigenous video makers opt for dramatic re-creations that tie the past to the present. Like the constant transformation that narrators perform in order to keep stories relevant to the present, the video makers set legends, tales of the walking dead, and other stories of fortune and misfortune in the present.[20]

According to Regina Harrison, Quechua speakers distinguish different degrees of complexity for seeing and understanding. Taken from a reading of a ritual poem in Santacruz Pachakuti Yamqui's 1613 text, Harrison lists four verbs that refer to increasingly complex ways of gaining knowledge: *rikuy* (to see), *yachay* (to know), *unanchay* (to understand) which can be used indexically or acquire iconic properties), and *hamuttay* (to understand allusion and metaphor). *Yachay, unanchay* and *hamuttay* "all refer to cognitive processes, modes of understanding which indicate a particular type of knowledge not readily evident at first glance in the translations" of Santacruz Pachakuti Yamqui's writings (79). *Yachay* commonly indicates practical knowledge and refers to teachers. While *unanchay* can indicate a standard, an insignia, a coat of arms, it is also used "in a more figurative sense as when referring to the images of the deity in the drawings of the Coricancha" (80). *Hamuttay*, in turn "would seem to indicate a more complex level of understanding in that there are allusions to perception, observation and ordering of thoughts and actions on the basis of this comprehension. Also included is an element of predictive knowledge (*conjecturar*) and the intimation that this information is conveyed through spoken discourse" (80). Video builds on this close relationship between seeing and signifying meaning at different levels of complexity. While documentary shorts like the video memory *Traditional Medicine* might be classified as a *yachay* video that indicates how much teaching has become associated with state education and pedagogical documentaries, CEFREC-CAIB's fiction videos lend themselves to the literal and metaphorical readings of *unanchay* and *hamuttay*, as I explain in more detail in the following chapters. On screen these videos similarly represent the act of storytelling or dreams as pointing toward levels of meaning not immediately apparent.[21]

Categorizing the videos according to Quechua concepts, however, would privilege highland perspectives. Given the strong intercultural emphasis of CEFREC-CAIB's media productions, it comes as no surprise that these terms are not used. Instead CEFREC-CAIB video makers have found a need to invent film genres while, at the same time, being aware that the mere need to categorize their films is part of the dialogue with film conventions. As Ivan Sanjinés, Reynaldo Yujra, and Franklin Gutiérrez commented, CEFREC-CAIB has struggled to differentiate genres in order to denote the diversity of their films without however reifying these genres. From their perspective, genres and the distinction between fiction and documentary are always ultimately insufficient.[22]

To question the limits between fiction and documentary film seems, at first sight, to resonate with the Ukamau Group's revolutionary filmmaking. Yet indigenous media's emphasis on mythical events—such as the search for the Loma Santa in *Our Word*—and the reenactment of legends of origin in the Colombian indigenous videos *Seed and Memory* (*Semilla y memoria: Chumbe nasa*) and *We Spin and Weave Giving Life to the Universe* (*Hilamos y tejemos para darle vida al universo*) point to a different rational. If the blurring of documentary and fiction for third cinema created political realism and revolutionary relevance, indigenous docudramas highlight the recuperation of indigenous epistemologies that are anchored in these stories. The video and multimedia packages combine documentaries that subscribe to the form's "discourse of sobriety" (Nichols, *Representing Reality* 9) with video stories and docudramas referencing mythical events and spiritual forces. Indigenous media thus construct an equivalency between mythical-spiritual and rational epistemologies. Fiction shorts such as *Our Word* and *Vest Made of Money* complement the vast body of indigenous documentary production that addresses diverse topics, including traditional dances, environmental pollution, and human and indigenous rights.[23]

While blending genres and mixing different modes of address in the video packages form two ways of strengthening indigenous epistemologies in the face of a dominant Eurocentric scientific tradition, language is another key means through which culturally specific ways of understanding is transmitted.[24] It comes as no surprise that many indigenous videos are spoken in the native languages. Most of these are fictions subtitled in Spanish for circulation in Latin America and in English when shown at international festivals elsewhere.[25] Documentaries, on the other hand, are frequently spoken in Spanish. Both documentaries and the subtitles in fiction films attest to the importance of Spanish as a lingua franca among indigenous peoples in the continent. Facilitators, however, may opt to simultaneously translate films spoken in a different indigenous language and subtitled in Spanish or those spoken in Spanish into the language spoken locally. Unlike literature, film allows for the simultaneous use of spoken and written work, of native languages and subtitles, and ad hoc interpreting. The use of subtitles and the combination of fictional and documentary formats establishes an equivalency between indigenous languages and those of the colonizers (in this case, Spanish, Portuguese, and English). In addition, at community screenings indigenous facilitators may speak the subtitles for those who do not read. In other words, indigenous media flexibly engage with opportunities that the technology offers in strengthening indigenous languages. The activists appropriate colonial languages such as Spanish and create a multilingual and intercultural politics of knowledge that transcends idiomatic boundaries and the limitations of print media.

Indigenous video thus largely bypasses literacy requirements. They challenge what Angel Rama called the "lettered city"—that is, the configuration of power, knowledge, and literacy that colonialism lastingly inscribed and that forms part of the coloniality of power. The lettered city serves as a metaphor for the process of colonial subalternization inaugurated with the conquest. It builds on a geospatial imaginary. Following Rama's argument, urban planning created an inner circle from where literate elites exercise their power (Rama, *Lettered* 16–28). This inner circle produces the discourse that defines modernization, technology, and civilization while setting itself off against widening concentric rings where rural areas are considered farthest from the proper sphere of knowledge production (32). One might add that both literacy and spatial order furthermore carry profound gendered connotations where the urban sphere is associated with masculinity and opposed to a countryside peopled by colonized subjects that literature frequently has cast as emasculated in unison with a femininized, though not necessarily docile nature.[26]

Rama argued that the colonial layout of Latin American cities spatially mirrors the lettered city's social order on a regional geopolitical scale. Smaller urban centers were connected with the metropoles, but communication among them was limited. A decentralized communication infrastructure in the countryside remained virtually unthinkable. CEFREC-CAIB's *The Other Gaze* claims that indigenous media generate a process that allows indigenous communities to "answer back," not primarily by entering the spatial design of the city, but rather by placing diverse cultures and ethnicities in contact with each other. The documentary indicates that there is a double process at work. On the one hand, indigenous audiovisual communication incites discussions in rural communities where ideas and proposals are generated. On the other hand, against the subalternization of rural space that the lettered city inscribed, indigenous media create networks through which indigenous communities exchange information and thus create the possibility of developing alternative forms of political and economical organization. Audiovisual media form a key component of the cultural politics of indigenous movements because they open up a communication process (CEFREC, *Comunicar* 35–62). In other words, rather than foster isolated protests or individualized artistic expressions, media technology allow for the exchange of perspectives among diverse indigenous communities.

Indigenous audiovisual communication thrives on the fervor and time invested by the activists, their communities, and their technological advisers. The indigenous facilitators associated with CAIB in Bolivia take advantage of lightweight VHS screening equipment and circulate video and DVD packages containing a selection of indigenous videos, television news shows, and radio programs among villages in the Andean highlands, in the subtropical valleys, and the river plains. They carry generators, television sets, videos, and DVDs by small aircraft or on foot, even to villages where there is no electricity. Within Bolivia and the transnational Amazon basin, this distribution network links over one hundred rural communities on a regular, biweekly basis, traversing extreme geographical and cultural differences. As the map on CEFREC's homepage illustrates, the Indigenous People's audiovisual network has achieved a representative regional coverage that includes thirteen of the approximately thirty-nine indigenous ethnicities in Bolivia.[27] The map initially visualized indigenous media as emerging from one center and spreading out to the diverse geographic and cultural regions within Bolivia. CEFREC-CAIB now edit their films in several production facilities, one in La Paz in the Andean highlands, another in the lowland capital of Eastern Bolivia, Santa Cruz, and additional emerging postproduction sites in Sucre and Cochabamba. These centers offer editing islands and other postproduction equipment as well as television studios. The videos themselves are filmed in diverse geographic and climactic settings, with the participation of the communities and a film crew that is composed of indigenous communicators from different ethnicities as well as technological assistants who may or may not be indigenous or Bolivian. Since 2004 the rural distribution network has been complemented by broadcasts on community television. After at first being granted half an hour of airtime on national television (Canal 7), Evo Morales's government expanded CEFREC-CAIB's broadcast time to an hour and a half at prime time. The television news shows include interviews and footage from within Bolivia and from neighboring countries, such as Guarani communities in Paraguay. (CEFREC-CAIB still refuses to allow for the usual flow that characterizes mainstream television in Bolivia. Like elsewhere in the Americas, Bolivia's television is commercially oriented, interspersing television shows with advertisements, product placement, and integration; its main purpose is selling audiences to advertisers.)

CEFREC has advised indigenous video makers in Chile and Colombia and collaborated in screenings and training workshops in Brazil and elsewhere. Although the image of the audiovisual communication map now attests to the multicentered production of indigenous media, the plan is progressively transforming into a distribution network that may better be characterized as becoming ever more densely connected, rhizomatic, and increasingly transnational. Indigenous media activism, to be sure, is continuously evolving. CEFREC-CAIB is expanding communication networks and building more cross-national and cross-cultural indigenous contacts, including video collaborations with indigenous film and video makers in Mexico, Ecuador, Brazil, Colombia, and Chile.[28] Indigenous audiovisual communication thus subverts the traditional flows of knowledge that, like the railroad systems built in the nineteenth century, discouraged contact among rural areas and populations.

If indigenous media largely bypass the lettered city's configuration of literacy and power constituting instead autonomous networks of knowledge production, it does not mean that indigenous media entirely forgo the city—postproduction, after all, takes place in urban production offices. CEFREC's members as well as those of CONAIE's communication department are urban residents, although they may maintain ties and property in their villages of origin. The city as dominant site for generating knowledge is, however, decentered because indigenous media is filmed and enacted primarily in rural locations and then distributed back to villages. It relies on the key participation of rural media activists and their communities. Unlike those literary *testimonios* that bring subalternized voices into the hegemonic realm of first-world readers through the literary form, indigenous media in the Andean countries largely bypass these audiences as well. This tendency holds true across all contexts of indigenous media production in Latin America. Even the Chiapas Media Project/Promedios, who most actively distributes indigenous videos to university audiences in North America and who partially relies on the income generated from these sales, still primarily targets and involves indigenous communities.[29] Most important, the stories enacted in front of the camera and projected into diverse indigenous and nonindigenous communities elsewhere challenge established sets of expectations regarding the modes of knowledge production, at least for those communities that indigenous media connect. Yet as the activists move toward engaging national society, they reencounter entrenched beliefs about their cultures formulated in a nationally venerated tradition of both literary and audiovisual representations that spans decades if not centuries.

It is important to reiterate that although the Bolivian process of audiovisual communication is coded in national terms, its distribution networks and production transcend the boundaries of nation-states. *The Other Gaze* includes footage from the training workshops where, alongside the Bolivian communicators whose dress and accent mark them as coming from diverse regions and indigenous cultures in Bolivia, there are also images of Juan José García, the Zapotec director of Ojo de Agua Comunicación in Oaxaca,

Mexico, who currently also directs CLACPI; Alberto Muenala, a Quichua independent filmmaker from Otavalo, Ecuador; and Iván Sanjinés, the Bolivian nonindigenous director of CEFREC. Premio Anaconda, an itinerant video festival organized by CEFREC-CAIB yearly since 2003, encompasses lowland indigenous communities in the Amazonian river lands, including parts of Peru, Ecuador, Brazil, and Bolivia. The prominent role that CEFREC-CAIB's videos play in Latin America is due, in part, to the scale of their production and collection. CEFREC's La Paz office houses the most extensive Latin American indigenous video archive in Latin America.[30] The archive contains a vast compilation of videos, films, and unedited footage filmed in digital and super-VHS format. Most of the material is from the Andean-Amazonian region, but the archive also collects indigenous film material from elsewhere in Latin America as well as some native productions from the United States and Canada. It provides an intercultural audiovisual resource center that distributes films to the growing number of rural communities linked through the National Indigenous Plan for Audiovisual Communication and beyond. CEFREC-CAIB's films are seen widely, both within Bolivia and at international indigenous film and video festivals. Indigenous audiovisual communication thus establishes contacts between communicators and communities in the entire region.

Throughout Latin America indigenous video makers and their collaborators are well aware of each other as they exchange films and ideas at the regional and international indigenous film festivals. The festivals and training workshops bring together native filmmakers from northern Canada to southern Chile, and occasionally even from New Zealand. In addition, indigenous media activists throughout Latin America—including, from Bolivia, Julia Mosúa, Reynaldo Yujra, Marcelino Pinto, Alfredo Copa, Jesús Tapia, and Marcelina Cárdenas—travel to international indigenous film and video festivals, such as the biannual Native Film and Video Festival, organized by the audiovisual department of the National Museum of the American Indian, located in New York City. Although the media activists, just as the indigenous movement organizations in the region, may at times promote national goals or seek to reshape the national imaginary (in Benedict Anderson's sense), the connections between culturally diverse indigenous communities are creating a process of pan-indigenous identification beyond the boundaries of the nation.[31] The indigenous media centers in Latin America are heterogeneous in their creation and growth, but they do not operate in isolation from each other. Shot in diverse cultural contexts, Latin American indigenous media form part of a booming global indigenous media production.

If indigenous videos incite debate over what is valuable and worth beholding in indigenous culture, they also provide a space for negotiating relations among different ethnicities and regions that have traditionally been isolated from one another. As the Quechua video maker Marcelino Pinto emphasizes, audiovisual technology brings together indigenous people that have been mutually unaware of each other's existence (Flores 35). On the one hand, indigenous media act against the discrimination of indigenous peoples and their ways of life; on the other, they begin to remedy not merely isolation, as Pinto has highlighted, but also a tradition of inter-indigenous conflict and distrust. CEFREC's Web page spells out that, "the Plan has brought about contact among indigenous peoples of the lowlands, the Amazon, the peoples living in the highlands and valleys in the western part of the country. What has geographically and historically been difficult to connect is now already an emerging reality, thanks to the space opened up by interethnic communication."[32] When the Bolivian state offered concessions to the demands of protesting low and highland populations by passing the INRA land reform law in 1993, the lowland indigenous organization CIDOB accepted, while the highland Aymaras accused CIDOB of being gullible. The split occurred at the same time that the highland movement itself fragmented (Rivera, "Presentación" 1). These tense relationships were already indicated in the colonial writings of Garcilaso Inca de la Vega, who displaced accusations of savagery onto the lowland Indians in his effort to portray the Inca Empire and civilization as equivalent to that of Spain. Such attitudes continue to prevail in Aymara claims to leadership and their having resisted Spanish colonialism more effectively than lowland peoples. When indigenous media put isolated and distant communities in contact with each other they counter entrenched interindigenous prejudice. The videos attest to similar problems in high- and lowlands, and they highlight successful strategies of resistance in the lowlands.

In this process, indigenous media redraw a line of "colonial difference."[33] On one side of this line, they position Western modernity; on the other side are diverse and discriminated indigenous peoples who are, however, not merely multiethnic victims. Lema formulates this line as a difference between "internal" and "external" communication (Lema, n.p.). From this vantage point, indigenous peoples share in a common struggle to preserve their cultural practices. At least as important as their positioning vis-à-vis the effects of racism are what indigenous communities see as a shared social ethos. Indigenous videos portray cultural practices as diverse yet guided by a similar respect for an animate life-world and a socioeconomic system that commands redistribution rather than individual profiteering. This is a moral imperative, to be sure, uttered with renewed urgency by indigenous movements who see parts of their communities (especially the younger generation most exposed to state education) despising indigenous traditions and seeking entry into the capitalist market. Intercultural communication through video injects indigenous alternatives to capitalism with relevance and reach. Fictional and documentary videos contribute to a continentwide movement to create awareness of such a pan-indigenous ethos. The process is characterized as strengthening indigenous culture and identity (CEFREC, *Comunicar* 32). These are problematic terms for some of us in the academy, for they invoke a tradition of celebrating authenticity and essence in the face of dynamic changes, hybridity, and the complex enactment of identities within the constraints of dominant discourses. Despite the use of these loaded terms, however, indigenous media include controversial representations that defy the notion of identity or culture as immutable entities.

2

CASTING NEW PROTAGONISTS

The question "Who is actually making these films?" comes up frequently when indigenous media are screened outside the communities and the indigenous film festival circuits. The question points to a doubt generated in part by the apparent temporal clash between indigenous bodies and digital video technology that the images in figures 1 and 2 bring to the forefront. The doubt over whether these are really indigenous peoples making the films also indicates the desire to determine authorship and creative origin, and perhaps meaning as well. This interest in the authorship of joint projects is not new. The critical debates over Latin American *testimonio* unpacked the process of collaboration between editors and those telling their stories in the literary testimonial. Opinions varied as to how much control either the editor or the person giving testimony maintains over the narrative product. There has been a certain consensus that the ambiguous nature of authorship itself leads *testimonio* to interrupt the bourgeois autobiography and bildungsroman, along with a profound Western sense of individualism, where intellectual work seems based on individual reflection. The *testimonio*, in contrast, is the product of a collaborative process where those telling their stories represent or embody a larger group, a collective voice that is enunciated individually and translated into book form by an editor.[1]

Unlike the essay, novel, and autobiography, film is linked to industrial labor and the fragmentation of the creative process. Or, to put it in different terms, film has long been a collective enterprise that sits uneasily with the idea of authorship.[2] In the film industry the producer frequently influences the final cinematic product as much if not more than the scriptwriter, director, actors, or other members of the crew. Yet despite the cult of the director figure—whether as an effort to reconstitute cinema as an art form (e.g., Truffaut, Bazin, Sarris) or as a marketing tool—the Hollywood industry, socialist and testimonial third cinema, as well as indigenous video share from the outset a certain disenfranchisement of the author as creator. Indigenous media, like literary and the cinematic *testimonio*, however, emerges from a process of collaboration that entails relations of subalternity.

In the widely read nineteenth-century text *Facundo, or Civilization and Barbarism*, the Argentine writer Domingo Sarmiento proposed an important task for the emerging national literature of his time: the assimilation of oral culture to modern civilization, the domain of letters. Literature was to purge the oral of its disruptive and arbitrary barbarism and create the cultural grounds for a Latin American national identity different from that of Europe (59–71). Making the link between literacy and intellect explicitly, he wrote that "if the glimmer of a national literature momentarily shines in new American societies, it will come from descriptions of grand scenes of nature, and above all, from the struggle between European civilization and indigenous barbarism, between intelligence and matter" (59). The late cultural critique Angel Rama argued that with the conquest literacy became an auratic practice in Latin America, sustaining a class of *letrados* (lettered men) who, at the service of the colonial Empire and later of the independent nation-state, controlled the symbolic and discursive production of reality (Rama, *Ciudad* 62–63). This group of writers, bureaucrats, church officials, and intellectuals formed a sphere of power that has proven tremendously resilient through time. Although the makeup of this group has changed and broadened, the lettered city has continuously re-created an intellectual elite whose practice disciplines a mostly illiterate population. In other words, literacy is a power that at once represents and produces reality. The collaboration between indigenous communities, their "audiovisual communicators" (*comunicadores audiovisuales*) as the media activists call themselves, and independent, nonindigenous collaborators entails unequal positions with respect to technological know-how and motivates preconceptions regarding intellectual expertise that are associated with literacy. The tendency is to either attribute intellectual agency and initiative to the nonindigenous filmmakers involved in indigenous media or to conceptualize the indigenous video makers as organic intellectuals. So who is actually making indigenous media?

[handwritten: Who is actually making indigenous media?]

Indigenous Activists, Independent Filmmakers, and the Question of Initiative

In creating a narrative of indigenous video, one could easily focus on the verbs that CLACPI deploys to describe its role: CLACPI "has *promoted* and *[handwritten: CLACPI]* *stimulated* training opportunities and developed opportunities for exchange [among indigenous communicators] in the same way in different countries" (CLACPI, "Festival," n.p.; my emphasis). Independent filmmakers and visual anthropologists founded CLACPI in Mexico in 1985. Among them were Marta Rodríguez (Columbia), Claudio Menezes (Brazil), Jeannette Paillán (Chile), Ana Piño S. and Juan Francisco Urrusti (Mexico), Gustavo Guayasamín (Ecuador), Alejandro Camino (Peru), and Iris Sanchez D. (Venezuela).[3] Together with those who, like Alberto Muenala, Guillermo Monteforte, and Alexandra Halkin, joined the organization later on, CLACPI members have trained indigenous media activists in video production and helped them to acquire technological equipment. In collaboration with local indigenous organizations CLACPI has organized nine international indigenous film and video festivals over the last two decades—in Mexico (1985), Brazil (1987), Venezuela (1990), Peru (1992), Bolivia (1996), Guatemala (1999), Chile (2004), Mexico (2006), and most recently again in Bolivia (2008)—and has published film and video catalogs.[4] Again in CLACPI's own words, the organization has served "as a motivating and coordinating force with regard to a series of different initiatives in training, production, and distribution of indigenous video and cinema in Latin America. In order to achieve this objective it [CLACPI] makes use of agreements and contacts with different organizations in the countries of the continent" (CLACPI, "Festival," n.p.). Since CLACPI states that it "has promoted" (*ha promovido*) and "stimulated" (*ha impulsado*) indigenous video, that it has served as a "motivating force," one might argue that audiovisual technology was handed to indigenous communities so that they may represent themselves. Focusing on the independent filmmakers who do not identify as indigenous might thus create a genealogy of indigenous video making that goes back to ethnographic filmmakers' experiments with photography and film among the Navajo (Worth and Adair). It would constitute a narrative that tends toward a vision of indigenous peoples as victims or constituents of Western agency, be that colonial or emancipatory. Most significantly, such a misrepresentation clouds a crucial change in the relation between indigenous communicators and their collaborators that has taken place since filmmakers like Jorge Sanjinés, Beatriz Palacios, Oscar

Soria, Antonio Eguino, Marta Rodríguez, Jorge Silva and others in the sixties and seventies collaborated with *campesinos* and miners in order to denounce neocolonial exploitation and racism. Indigenous video is not testimonial cinema.

Contrary to constructing indigenous communities as reluctant recipients of audiovisual technology, individual members of CLACPI and other independent collaborators characterize the origins of indigenous media as a response to indigenous communities' desire to access the technology. Anthropologist Terence Turner, for instance, has argued that he brought video equipment from the outside into the Brazilian Kayapo villages. The communities received this equipment as compensation for their participation in Granada TV documentaries (Turner, "Social," "Visual"). Turner has described his efforts at facilitating the technology for the Kayapo, but he has also stressed that "the initiative for the acquisition of technical competence in using video cameras, and the foundation of archives for the accumulation and storage of videos originated with Kayapo leaders like Megaron of the Mentuktire ("Visual" 69). The film *Taking Aim*—directed by the independent filmmaker Monica Frota but largely based on Kayapo footage—similarly emphasizes that the Kayapo specifically demanded video equipment as compensation for their participation in the Granada TV documentary *Kayapo, Out of the Forest*. The Kayapo later contacted independent filmmakers in order to produce films such as *Taking Aim* that show why and how Kayapo communities use audiovisual technology. In his recent discussion of Amazonian video, Turner emphasizes that the Kayapo, like the Inuit and Australian Aborigines, appropriated audiovisual media for their own ends, again placing the agency squarely with the indigenous video makers ("Representation, Politics" 75).[5] Halkin, founder of the Chiapas Media Project/Promedios, offers a similar account. Her article details how she raised the initial funds and how her own role changed in the process, which eventually led to the creation of various indigenous media production centers in the Zapatista-controlled territory of southern Mexico. Initially, while producing a documentary for a U.S.-based nongovernmental organization in 1995, "we ended up in a community that was swarming with press (both national and international), with photographers and TV news cameras all 'capturing the story' of the Zapatista representatives and community members who were present. It is important to note that this media presence was not a by-product of the Zapatista struggle; rather it was extremely intentional on their part, yet it was forged out of a dependence on outside (both mass and independent) media." Halkin adds that, "several people in the community came up to ask about my Hi8 camera (where I bought it, how much it cost, etc.), clearly demonstrating an interest in and awareness of this technology. I was impressed with the Zapatista organization and their obvious interest in communicating their message to the outside world" ("Outside" 4). The initiative and interest in acquiring audiovisual technology in her account also arise from the Zapatista communities themselves.

In the Andean countries indigenous audiovisual communication grows from a process of collaboration where CLACPI has played an important role. The Colombian filmmaker and former member of CLACPI Marta Rodríguez explains that the Fourth Latin American International Indigenous Film and Video Festival, held in Cuzco, Peru (1992), constituted a turning point for CLACPI, as it became increasingly focused on workshops and training opportunities. CLACPI itself began to see the need for greater involvement of indigenous video makers within its organization (cf. Dominguez, note lxvii). Once dominated by non-Indians, CLACPI's leadership changed hands from Iván Sanjinés to the Zapotec Juan José García in 2004.[6] The turning point mentioned by Marta Rodríguez, who together with Jorge Silva was herself part of the sixties and seventies revolutionary film movement, points to a regional if not global tendency that reflects growing indigenous movements. The new generation of nonindigenous collaborators does not assume the role of vanguard intellectuals.[7] Independent film and video makers—such as Iván Sanjinés in Bolivia, Alexandra Halkin and Guillermo Monteforte in Mexico, and Vincent Carelli in Brazil—see themselves as technological facilitators, acting according to the needs of indigenous media activists and their communities of origin. They train indigenous directors, camera people, scriptwriters and editors, and participate in the communities and activists' regular evaluations of indigenous media strategies without, however, prescribing aesthetic solutions to Hollywood's formulas or avenues for achieving social change.

Iván Sanjinés, the director of CEFREC and former director of CLACPI, is without a doubt an exceptionally dedicated and energetic figure in the indigenous communication process, and not only in Bolivia. He has directed CEFREC since its foundation. Yet Sanjinés does not see himself as leading indigenous media activism. In a 1996 bulletin CEFREC writes that the goal of indigenous audiovisual communication is to move from an " 'external vertical' communication to forms of communication that are internal to the culture and defined directly by the indigenous people in accordance with the processes that they are living and their needs" (CEFREC, "Presencia"). CEFREC's crew has conducted ongoing training workshops since 1996 in its offices in La Paz (located in the highlands), in Santa Cruz (in Bolivia's eastern tropical region), and in various rural locations. These workshops provide indigenous communicators, such as Patricio Luna (Aymara), Marcelino Pinto (Quechua from the Chapare), Marcelina Cárdenas (Quechua from Potosí), Jesús Tapia (Aymara migrant living in the Alto Beni valley), Julia Mosúa (Moxeña), Regina Monasterios (Guarani), and others who form part of CAIB with the fundamental skills in each area of video making, from sound and lights to camera and editing. Recently, these workshops have begun training the participants in the particular production aspects they feel most drawn to. CEFREC has thus promoted the use of video by members of indigenous communities. Some of the video makers have only had limited exposure to literacy and formal education, others, like Pinto, were already involved in teaching and communication, or even hold university degrees, such as Marcelina Cárdenas. In the Andean countries indigenous video extends the use of radio for social organizing in the high and low lands. The Guarani Peoples Assembly, for example, had already established a functioning network of radio communication that also included video distribution before they became involved with CEFREC. Similarly, though less interconnected, other lowland ethnicities also made use of radio and new information technologies (CEFREC, *Comunicar* 35–67). For the Andean valleys and highlands, Pinto and the Quechua Alfredo Copa expressed in an interview with Daniel Flores (an independent filmmaker from El Salvador) that when video presented itself as a technological opportunity, indigenous communicators readily took up the offer to extend a project already shaped by the use of community radio (Mosúa, Copa, and Pinto, audio recording).[8] In other words, the indigenous media activists insist that they took advantage of the technology when it presented itself. They cast themselves as agents of audiovisual communication rather than as passive recipients of the technology (CEFREC, *Comunicar* 16). Instead of becoming integrated into a cultural politics designed in the urban centers by lettered elites, indigenous communicators emphasize that they make use of technological advisors, who are incorporated into a cultural politics designed and promoted by indigenous movements.

Intellectual Agency and the Bolivian Integral Process

The changing relationship between urban intellectuals and their subaltern constituents in the countryside informs the process of adapting audiovisual media to indigenous cultural politics. Some video makers hone their particular skills and talents as actors, scriptwriters,[9] and directors, yet the culturally diverse indigenous communicators organized in CAIB frequently avoid the term "director" (*director, realizador*) and with it the idea of the individual creator and intellectual author. Instead, CEFREC-CAIB's films credit either a *responsable* (a person responsible) or simply the producer. Omitting the word director in the credits places emphasis on the collaboration between indigenous communities, CEFREC, and CAIB. Instead of self-proclaimed intellectual privilege over an uneducated rural mass steeped in oral traditions, these filmmakers and communicators insist on partnership. The Aymara Jesús Tapia (director of CAIB), Marcelina Cárdenas (the Quechua video maker responsible for *Loving Each Other in the Shadows*) and Iván Sanjinés (director of CEFREC) maintain that the process of audiovisual communication grows from a *proceso integral*, or integral process. As Jeff Himpele summarizes, "rather than claiming the image of authenticity, framed by [Western?] audience desires for purity, originality, and individual subjectivity, however, Tapia and Cárdenas frequently described the value of their work in terms of collectivity with the word *integral*. As Cárdenas explained to me, *integral* indicates that the work involves the collective input of the community in which the communicator is working . . . *integral* is also a value that can be extended to the coordinated work of media makers and organizations that are involved in the process of making video" (Himpele "Packaging" 358). The *proceso integral* strives to tie communities, video makers, and independent filmmakers into relations of reciprocity and a research ethos of accountability. Whatever idealization of actual power differentials such a representation on the part of Tapia and Cárdenas may involve, it is important to acknowledge that the *proceso integral* points to a new conceptualization of collaborative epistemic processes that has its historical roots in indigenous scholarship.

The THOA's important work in Bolivia started from the dual realization that on the one hand, Eurocentric scholarship did not adequately account for the history of Aymara resistance to colonialism, and on the other, that research traditions had primarily been exploitative of indigenous communities, extracting knowledge and distributing its findings elsewhere (Rivera Cusicanqui and THOA, "Potencial"; Stephenson, "Forging" 103, 105–6). Carlos

Mamani Condori argued that "one of the THOA's fundamental beliefs was that this knowledge must be returned to the indigenous communities so that a fortified sense of collective identity and unity might enable indigenous peoples to face their common problems and empower them to move together into the future" (paraphrased by Marcia Stephenson, "Forging" 106). Mamani Condori calls attention to Roberto Choque Canqui's work on education and to research centers and journals such as *Mink'a*, *Qhatati*, and *Chitakolla* and the Centro Pusisuyu as important precursors invested in undertaking "the difficult task of reexamining prevailing historiographic and intellectual paradigms from the point of view of indigenous peoples" (Stephenson, "Forging" 103). The critique of Eurocentrism and the search for more accountable forms of scholarship among Aymaras parallel discussions among other indigenous peoples and have led to the creation of intercultural universities where the university structure, curriculum, and research ethos are modeled on indigenous ideals.[10] These indigenous-led approaches to decolonizing knowledge do not presume research to be independent, objective, and disinterested; instead, they question the objectivity of any kind of historical or anthropological narrative.

Linda Tuhiwai Smith, a Maori scholar, starts her book *Decolonizing Methodologies* by arguing that "from the vantage point of the colonized, a position from which I write, and choose to privilege, the term 'research' is inextricably linked to European imperialism and colonialism. The word itself, 'research,' is probably one of the dirtiest words in the indigenous world's vocabulary" (1). Smith elaborates on the possibilities for doing indigenous research, which would acknowledge the social political context in which it is produced and which it serves. Smith suggests that communities ask critical questions that need to be answered without cynicism: "Whose research is it? Who owns it? Whose interests does it serve? Who will benefit from it? Who has designed its questions and framed its scope? Who will carry it out? Who will write it up?" (10). The work of the THOA evolved from the same preoccupation. It consciously became a form of knowledge production that answered to the ethical values and needs of the Aymara communities, a research that obliged itself to return the results of their findings to their communities and to submit to their critical review (Rivera and THOA, "Potencial" 58, 61; Stephenson "Forging").

Indigenous media operate according to the same ethos. The production group—consisting of indigenous activists from diverse cultures and language groups and members of CEFREC, some of whom identify as indigenous while others do not—and the communities where the filming takes place—collectively discuss scripts, editing, soundtrack, cinematic style, etc.[11] In some cases, more decision-making responsibility is delegated to the film crew made up of members of CAIB and their outside advisors, who are often but not always members of CEFREC or CLACPI.[12] In other cases, as, for example, in the making of *Dusting Off Our History* (*Desempolvando nuestra historia*), members of Copa's community codetermine the topic and the content of the video (Flores 32). Indeed, the term "audiences" is misleading, since the process of video making involves active participation of the communities, not only in terms of acting or reception but also in the creation of the films.[13]

The indigenous media activists are bound into relations of reciprocity and accountability, an integral and intellectually collaborative relationship with community elders and peers. As Alfredo Copa, Marcelino Pinto, and Julia Mosúa struggled to explain in their interview with Daniel Flores, although not all members of the indigenous communities are trained in video making, consciousness is not conferred or raised by the video makers. Copa claims that "I help the community on a continual basis, not only when I am making a video. I guide them. I work with them. And together we express the needs of the people" (Flores 31). He simultaneously insists and clarifies that the initiative for making video arises from the community: "I ended up doing the film because it represents the most urgent need of my community, to see this, their story told. I had already *escrito a pulso* (written out freehand) part of our history, but the community said, 'If our history becomes images, like memory it will help in remembering what our past was like'" (Flores 32). Copa then describes the process in detail: "I ask questions—although the story of a town is large and I do not know all of it. At first, they gave me a general idea. Then, I met with [the] elders and asked them, 'which part should we expand upon? Which part do you want to save? What is being lost? Then we recorded those replies" (Flores 33). In this last quotation it becomes clear that although Copa may "guide" his community, he is not the most knowledgeable person, "the story of a town is large and I do not know all of it," he emphasizes. Indeed, the selection of information and the length of its representation are decided together, by this Quechua video maker and the elders in his community. Julia Mosúa from the lowland Moxos explained with clear resonance the issues that the THOA and Smith raise, that "we work very closely with the communities we film. When we wrote the script for *Nuestra palabra* [*Our Word*], we told the community, 'This video, these images are not going to be sold; these images will return here where we made them.' So people participated enthusiastically" (Flores 31). Sometimes, but again not always, the community is presented with the video material before the final cut, as in the case of Copa's documentary (Mosúa et al., audio recording). Video makers acquire special skills as well as status; their abilities, however, are seen as being put to use by the communities rather than enlightening them from without.

CEFREC argues that the process of audiovisual communication strengthens the tradition of collective decision making in the communities (cf. "Communication Strategies," n. p.). Indianizing video production indeed invokes traditions of shared labor, called *mit'a* or *minga* in the highlands, where the community works together in harvests or hunting, but also in the construction of schoolhouses, churches, or roads. Such collaborations require the community's collective endorsement and participation. Like political and administrative decisions, film proposals pass through community assemblies that are nominally democratic and seek to generate consensus. (The fiction videos *Overcoming Fear* and *In the Name of Our Coca* both include condensed and idealized representations of such community assemblies in the Yungas and the Chapare respectively. These are tropical Andean valleys where Quechua and Aymara migrants from the highlands have settled.) Power relations within the communities constrain the participation of women and unmarried young people in political decision making. In the Andes governmental structures in the communities favor a heterosexual regime and a complex process of occupying political office on the basis of rotation and experience that favors the most wealthy elders (Ticona Alejo 127–35). Women video makers such as Julia Mosúa, Regina Monasterios, Maria Morales, Marcelina Cárdenas, and Aidée Alvarez have been key participants in the National Indigenous Plan for Audiovisual Communication. The Quichua Lucila Lema has been credited in the filming and editing of CONAIE's productions in Ecuador. Yet unlike in Canada where First Nation women constitute the majority of indigenous media makers (Nicholson 3), in Colombia, Bolivia, and Brazil indigenous audiovisual communication has so far mostly been in the hands of young men. The Bolivian CAIB's intercultural collective of indigenous communicators comprises both men and women, but men are in the majority. Although internal power differences, political goals, and tensions in the communities certainly impact on who determines video content, these are precisely part of the "forms of communication that are internal to the culture" (CEFREC, "Communication Strategies," n. p.).

Despite hierarchical social structures within the communities, the *proceso integral* marks one of the sites where indigenous media activists and their collaborators begin to transform an epistemic hierarchy linked to alphabetic literacy and shaped by the coloniality of power. The media activists utilize their nonindigenous collaborators while also taking their advice into account. This is not the same as submitting to the guidance of an educated elite. Similarly, the communities make use of the video makers' ability to filmically address issues of concern. Again, this shift in epistemic agency did not occur spontaneously but correlates with the growing importance of indigenous scholarship and social movements.[14]

Testimonial Cinema and the Vanguard Filmmaker

The *proceso integral* that drives CEFREC-CAIB's indigenous media reshapes a traditional, key relationship between leftist intellectuals and subaltern constituents. Iván Sanjinés suggests that indigenous video in Bolivia arises not only as an extension of community radio but also of the socially committed filmmaking of the sixties and seventies. Particularly important were also the experiences of those youths who, in the early eighties, began to train as video makers with the Cine Minero (the Bolivian miners' cinema). The Cine Minero, financed by the French government and lead by Ateliers Varan, a cinema institution that Jean Rouch founded, remained a short-lived effort (Sanjinés, "Panorama" 37–40). The revolutionary filmmakers of Latin America's third cinema—such as the Bolivian Ukamau Group, who began working with the miners in their film *Courage of the People*; Octavio Getino, Fernando Solanas, and Fernando Birri in Argentina; and the filmmakers in Cuba's film institute ICAIC, among others—in contrast have had lasting, provocative aesthetic and political influence. This radical part of *cine social* (cinema of social relevance) turned the fragmented industrial process of filmmaking into a socialist production practice that countered the capitalist logic inscribed in the globally dominant film industry.[15] Solanas and Getino advocated nonspecialized training for their production crew. Their vision was grounded in revolutionary needs and urgency:

Each member of the group should be familiar, at least in a general way, with the equipment being used: he must be prepared to replace

the Camera feeds the REVOLUTION

another in any of the phases of production. The myth of irreplaceable technicians must be exploded. The whole group must grant great importance to the minor details of the production and the security measures needed to protect it. A lack of foresight, which in conventional filmmaking would go unnoticed, can render virtually useless weeks or months of work. A failure in guerrilla cinema, just as in the guerrilla struggle itself, can mean the loss of a work or a complete change of plans." ("Towards" 50)

guerrilla Cinema

Solanas and Getino were not alone in likening revolutionary cinema to the ongoing guerilla struggle but spoke for a generation inspired by the successful armed struggle in Cuba. Like CEFREC today, the revolutionary filmmakers in the sixties and seventies made a commitment toward training every member of the production crew in all of the functions necessary. However, unlike Cine Minero and the CEFREC production group, they did not permanently include members of the impoverished or indigenous communities they worked with. Third cinema filmmakers and film critics continued to ascribe creative and critical force to the director, or at least to the production crew. The filmmaker was seen as an intellectual imbued with a critical consciousness and the will to serve as a leader in ending the economic and social injustices that result from capitalist and neocolonial conditions. They were adamant that their films should incite action beyond the viewing and propel the people to transform the existing order (Gutiérrez Alea, "Viewers Dialectic 123). After the Cuban revolution in the sixties and early seventies, "action" was understood quite unequivocally as armed revolution. Echoing the militant language of the time, for Solanas and Getino the camera was "the inexhaustible expropriator of image-weapons; the projector a gun that can shoot 24 frames a second" ("Towards" 50).[16] This subversive cinema sought a populist revolutionary appeal but shunned the easily consumed image. The filmmakers tried to reach and enlighten the audience and to create a continuity that would extend representation on screen into active audience participation in revolutionary action, "stimulating and channeling spectators to act in the direction of historical movement," as the Cuban filmmaker Tomás Gutiérrez Alea phrased it (128). The filmmaker collective became the cadre that led the people to clarity and action.[17]

the camera as a weapon

camera = gun

The Bolivian Ukamau Group's notion of *el pueblo* (the people) was perhaps most sensitive to the internal racism that shapes social relations in Latin

internal racism

American countries, particularly in places like the Andes, where a majority of the population continues to self-identify as indigenous. Films like *Blood of the Condor, Courage of the People,* and *Out of Here (Fuera de aquí)* that Jorge Sanjinés directed were, like the indigenous videos today, primarily intended for consumption by indigenous and *campesino* viewers. The films were also shown in urban settings and were received with critical acclaim at international film festivals. They continue to be screened in Ukamau's theater in the city of La Paz. The Ukamau Group's film practice was itself deeply transformed by their contact with Quechua and Aymara communities. Jorge Sanjinés and his production group moved from the idea of making a cinema for the people to a cinematic practice with the people. As I mentioned earlier, in *Courage of the People* the stories and ideas of the mining community determine the narrative, along with their improvised dialogues and acting. In this sense, the Ukamau Group's filmmaking changed profoundly from two years earlier, when they negotiated the rights to make *Blood of the Condor* with local authorities and gave nonprofessional actors the scripted scenes.[18]

The Ukamau Group elaborated what one might call, in analogy to the idea of border thinking (Mignolo, *Local* 49–88; *Idea* 9–10), a "border cinema." They fused Quechua-Aymara social organization with Marxist class-analysis and a critique of neo-imperialism. The filmmakers were inspired by massive protests and a general euphoria over "history being made by the people themselves," the anticolonial struggles in Asia and Africa that were dominating world news at the time, and by the writings of the Peruvian Marxist intellectual José Carlos Mariátegui.[19] At the beginning of the twentieth century, Mariátegui had placed Marxism in dialogue with what he saw as a proto-communist indigenous society.[20] The Ukamau Group sought collaboration between the Western, intellectual filmmaker and the Quechua and Aymara people in a project that could fuse socialism and those elements of indigenous practices compatible with communism.[21] Director Jorge Sanjinés, scriptwriter Oscar Soria, cameraman Antonio Eguino, and others who formed part of the Ukamau Group progressively incorporated the perspectives, narrative frameworks, and acting of Quechuas and Aymaras (Sanjinés, "Problems" 64), but they did not hand over the camera to members of the mining communities already involved in communication, like those operating the community radios of Siglo XX.

To some degree, sharing access to the technology was constrained by the cost of making film in 16mm and 35mm format. Cinematic *testimonio* was embedded in expensive technological structures that, unlike relatively cheap digital video camera and editing equipment, severely limited access to production.[22] Despite their sensitivity to the racism internal to Latin American society, the Ukamau Group, like the revolutionary filmmakers elsewhere at the time, never fully relinquished directorial control. While continuously evolving their narrative strategies, framing techniques, and choices of soundtrack, they envisioned the Marxist-indigenous fusion on screen and in the production process as a means of propelling revolutionary struggle (cf. Sanjinés and Grupo Ukamau 66). The Ukamau Group sought to give voice to the people, but it maintained the role of the modern intellectual that enlightens and guides the people: "Anti-imperialist revolutionary cinema needs to provide the labor of clarification, recovery and adoration. It needs to contribute toward raising consciousness about the validity of national cultures and participate in contributing to their development" (54). The means of intellectual production—technology and intellect—pertained to the immediate film production group. In this sense, perhaps not so much had changed from when Mariátegui viewed indigenous resistance to colonialism as disarticulated, victimized, and in need of guidance. The revolution, for Mariátegui in the early twentieth century and for the revolutionary filmmakers in the sixties and seventies, was to be led by the indigenous masses but brought together into an organic force from the outside (Mariátegui 49).

In the political analysis of the time, the integration of the peripheries into the global capitalist world-system called for a class rebellion against the forces of U.S. neocolonialism. The actions of national elites (landlords and capitalists who themselves were most often descendents of the colonial Creole ruling classes) could thus be understood as determined by colonial, and later neo-imperial, global economic relations. The solution for some was a national-populism (Argentine Peronism for Solanas and Getino) that pointed toward socialism; for others it was a socialist revolution with ultimately a global reach. Indebted to José Carlos Mariátegui's vision of Andean society, the Ukamau Group understood indigenous peasants as a social class that could be united with the struggle of the working class, particularly the miners, for global socialism and an end to neo-imperialism (Sanjinés, "Problems" 65–66). The Ukamau Group concentrated on the plight of indigenous peoples in their testimonial cinema, learned from the communities, and accommodated themselves to the requirements of local authorities, yet the acceptance of indigenous and subalternized thinking was limited by

[handwritten: thinking limited by Marxist frame works]

preconceived Marxist frameworks. In Saldaña Portillo's estimation, there was a fundamental disconnect between "the people" and the Latin American left. Latin American revolutionaries constructed a masculinist narrative, casting themselves as leaders of a feminized population within a modern teleology of development toward socialist ends, with the promise of thus acquiring "full masculinity" (Saldaña-Portillo 42). This revolutionary vision structurally resembles the liberal discourse of development now being run by international agencies, particularly in the way it rearticulates colonial imaginaries and civilizing discourses (22). Leftist revolutionaries, such as Che Guevara and Payera, as well as the Sandinista agrarian policy, correspondingly "represent political consciousness among indigenous peasants or urban blacks as dangerously contaminated by premodern prodigal tendencies and in need of reformation" (33). In other words, Marxist revolutionaries and testimonial filmmakers shared a predicament: a fundamental incompatibility between Marxist understanding of anticolonial struggle and what has been called indigenous messianic thinking.

[handwritten margin: Masculinity]

[handwritten margin: Marxism incompatible w/ indigenous thinking]

Framing Collective Consciousness

The difference between testimonial cinema and indigenous media's understanding of where and how thought occurs correlates with the representation of cultural practices on screen. Ukamau, it is important to emphasize, did not represent coca readings and similar practices as superstition. Yet the representation of ritual drinking, for example, differs markedly from indigenous videos. Consider the representation of alcohol consumption in the Ukamau Group's films *Blood of the Condor* and *Courage of the People* in contrast with CEFREC-CAIB's fiction shorts *Loving Each Other in the Shadows* and *Cursed Gold*. The Ukamau Group frames drinking as an intoxication that obstructs clear revolutionary consciousness and serves to maintain the oppression of the people. In *Blood of the Condor* drinking leads to wife beating and a general loss of orientation. The scene depicting a village celebration is filmed with a hand-held camera that emphasizes the dizzying effect that leaves little dignity for the community. In *Courage of the People*, drinking is in part to be blamed for the miners' inability to escape the massacre of the night of San Juan. The nightly drinking scenes and subsequent military attack are recorded with natural lighting and without the filters and complex arrangement of key and fill lighting familiar from Hollywood cinema, thus emphasizing the darkness and loss of orientation in the community. Whether

[handwritten margin: drinking maintaining oppression ↓ loss of orientation of community]

intentional or merely a result of limited technical equipment, the confusion that marks the massacre thus appears as an extension of an obscured consciousness induced by alcohol.

In contrast, in the Quechua fiction short *Loving Each Other in the Shadows* video makers portray drinking in the context of a *fiesta* that generates community. A camera fixed to a tripod stabilizes the frame while high contrast lighting emphasizes colorful dress and clear features (fig. 8). Takes that would portray extremely drunk or unconscious individuals are not recorded or are eliminated in favor of ritual toasts and dances. In the prenuptial negotiations for the arranged marriage, the parents' abstinence from alcohol marks their protestant religious affiliation, not a greater critical awareness. Even in *Cursed Gold* drinking is festive, and, though in the case of the protagonist it is excessive, it gives way to clairvoyance in terms of a dream that forewarns him of violence and death. That he does not heed the premonitions is not the result of drunken stupor but rather of his general alienation and disbelief in the value of dreams and storytelling.

CEFREC-CAIB's fictions and docufictions also break with the resistance the Ukamau Group developed toward personalized narratives and corresponding camera angles and shots. The Ukamau Group recognized the community as an important Quechua/Aymara sociopolitical institution; its role was to be privileged not only in the cooperation between filmmakers and actors but also in terms of narrative and framing (Sanjinés, "Problems" 62–66; Sanjinés and Grupo Ukamau 61–66). The Ukamau Group's interpretation of the social structures of Quechua community invokes traces of literary *indigenismo*'s representation of indigenous collectivities and Mariátegui's search for a nonindividualist subjectivity: "The *Indios*, because of their social traditions, tend to conceive of themselves as a group rather than as isolated individuals. Their manner of existence is not individualist. The individualist is opposed to the other; the *Indio*, however, exists only when he is integrated with the rest of the community" (Sanjinés y Grupo Ukamau 65). In *Courage of the People*, as well as in *The Principal Enemy* (*El enemigo principal*), Jorge Sanjinés and the Ukamau Group moved to a preference for long shots that could capture the people as a group or, more precisely, as a revolutionary collective agent. Antonio Eguino (the group's cinematographer at the time) made use of the handheld camera in *Courage of the People* in order to bring the spectator into the center of protesting crowds. Close-ups were avoided in favor of the medium shot so as not to offer an unnaturally close view of

8. Community celebration. *Llanthupi Munakuy/*
Loving Each Other in the Shadows production still.
http://videoindigena.bolnet.bo (CEFREC).

protagonists. Long shots contextualized individual action instead of isolating it. The Ukamau Group discouraged emotional identification with any individual character; instead, viewers were held to reflect critically. The Ukamau Group believed that the length of the shots provided the intellectual distance necessary for critical thinking, both for the spectator and for the collective protagonist at the center of the screen, now free to act and invent (Sanjinés and Grupo Ukamau 64–65).

Indigenous videos, in contrast, break with the resistance the Ukamau Group developed toward personalized narratives and corresponding camera angles and shots. The actors in indigenous fictions are mostly framed as individuals or in small groups. In *Vest Made of Money*, long shots pan across the landscape, introducing the scene, as the camera slowly moves in on the main characters, who are finally rendered in extreme close-ups (figs. 9 and 10). Individuals and conversing couples are set against the backdrop of the Andean landscape. If the Ukamau Group's films included the emotional and revolutionary movement of Quechua communities resisting oppression and marching toward a socialist future, the only time the community advances in *Vest Made of Money* is to place the protagonist Satuco (Reynaldo Yujra) to

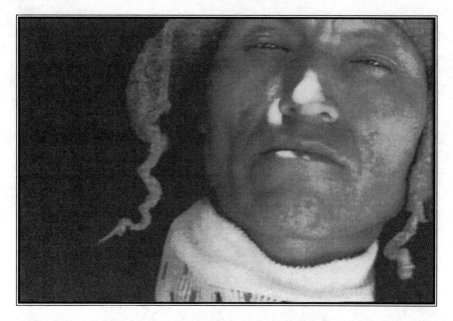

9. Close-up of Satuco (Reynaldo Yujra)
in *Vest Made of Money*. Video still.

rest in the cemetery. The scene is filmed from a low angle as a long shot in which human figures walk in small groups or alone on the film horizon, thus giving an entirely different sense of community than the revolutionary mass in *Courage of the People* that traverses a wide Andean valley, coming progressively closer to the camera and finally engulfing us as viewers.

In *Vest Made of Money* the community gathers on two further occasions, but without inscribing dynamic movement: first to deplore the protagonist's death and to console his wife and then again in the final scene to listen to the *jilacata* (the community authority) as he spells out the meaning of the story represented and enacted on screen. *Vest Made of Money* is a parable of the perils of greed and avarice that requires introspection, not revolutionary action. The deployment of long and medium shots and the use of close-ups in *Vest Made of Money* combine with the framing of individuals in small groups, providing a visual quality that holds individualism and collective responsibilities in tension, rendering neither into the other. Rather than constructing a collective, *Vest Made of Money* frames exemplary individuals, personalizing them like storytelling would, by elaborating their idiosyncrasies. The framing of the characters thereby enhances the intimate affective relationship between protagonists and spectators. The narrative construction of identification combines not only with camera distance but also with camera positioning. As is common for CEFREC-CAIB's fiction shorts, a steady camera alternates between point-of-view shots of the protagonists and a third-person spectator position. As if listening to a story told, the spectators watch the drama unfold; they are not immersed in revolutionary crowds. Yet since the audience is primarily made up of indigenous communities, they become the object of the legend's moral. Their identification is emotional, rendered through the close-ups and drama experienced by the protagonists.

Other CEFREC-CAIB fiction videos—such as *Cursed Gold*, *Angels of the Earth*, *Qati qati*, and *The Forest Spirit*—dispense all together with framing the collective. The inhabitants of Chipiriri in *Cursed Gold* are seen in daily activities such as the marketing of coca or relaxing in the local *chichería*. *Qati qati* also relies on individual protagonists and small groups, and *Angels of the Earth* contains no representation of Sinchi's community of origin. The Moxos production *The Forest Spirit* is set entirely in the jungle and works with only

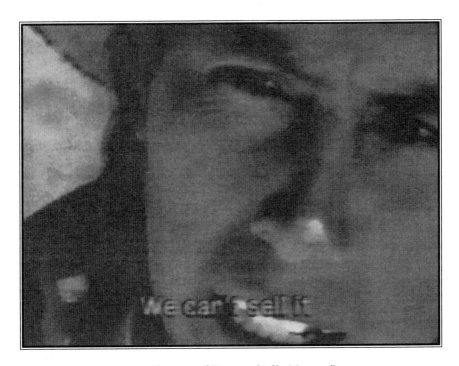

10. Close-up of Tomasa (Celia Mamani) in *Vest Made of Money*. Video still.

three actors. The construction of community in these films entails a slight but significantly different conception of collectivity and of where thinking takes place. It is a collectivity that works as an interpellation to its members, a community that is imbued with an ethos of solidarity yet is fractured by class, gender, migration, individual desires, or by the division between Evangelists and Catholics, as in *Loving Each Other in the Shadows*. On the one hand, these videos highlight individuals; on the other hand, indigenous media insist that the community is the place where social memory is transmitted and where traditional epistemologies are kept alive.

Indigenous community and organizational leaders have integrated independent film and video makers into the process of decolonization devised by indigenous movements. Although these filmmakers and visual anthropologists are not guerrilla fighters, their integration into the indigenous process of decolonization resembles the practice of "double translation" that has marked the relation between indigenous organizations and Marxist revolutionaries in Chiapas (cf. Mignolo and Schiwy, "Translation"). A growing self-confidence among the members of indigenous movement organizations and communities and the crisis of the political Left have changed the terms of their interaction. Instead of the Marxist revolutionary artist-intellectual translating indigenous social relations into the framework of anti-imperialism and socialist revolution, indigenous movement organizations are integrating independent filmmakers, like their revolutionary counterparts in southern Mexico, into the framework of decolonization that they envision. The political horizon for decolonization thus remains quite open. Decolonization constitutes a process where communities and individuals experiment with and evaluate different strategies for relating to the state and the global market. CONAIE's shifting relations with state power and recent trends in Bolivia attest to these multipronged strategies and processes of evaluation.

Organic Intellectuals?

Indigenous media activists hence do not fit neatly into Gramsci's notion of the organic intellectual. Gramsci's influential division between traditional and organic intellectuals refined the humanist conception of the intellectual as a thinker and professional commentator on culture and society. Gramsci's intellectuals are products of the state education system, and his distinction arises from relating the activity of the intellectual to the emancipation of the proletariat. The organic intellectual shares with the traditional intellectual not a political vision and social provenance but rather an inscription into notions of literacy, vanguard leadership, and a relation to the proletariat (not indigenous peoples). As Beverley puts it, "for Gramsci every relationship of hegemony was necessarily an educational relationship, expressing both a position of moral and intellectual leadership and the possibility of a bloc of different social agents around a common program articulated by that leadership" (*Subalternity* 12). For Gramsci, the organic as well as the traditional intellectual are leaders of groups or classes whose class interests they may (organic) or may not (traditional) share (cf. Gramsci 3–23; 56 n. 5). Instead of confronting a divide between different regimes of knowledge created by colonialism, the subaltern here are seen as lacking class-consciousness. Organic intellectuals emerge because they put subaltern sensibilities in contact with historical materialism. The communication between different regimes of knowledge takes place in the mind of the intellectual before he transmits his ideas to the masses, thus becoming their leader. To a certain extent the Marxist understanding of class conflict, however, predetermines the outcome of this communication between different regimes of knowledge. One might consider the work of the revolutionary filmmakers in the sixties and seventies as an effort to forge these organic ties between (educated and relatively well-to-do white or *mestizo*) filmmakers and "the people" (at best marginally literate, poor, and often indigenous). Both find themselves in sub-alternized positions vis-à-vis the state and global neocolonialism.

Indigenous communicators, however, are not organic intellectuals in Gramsci's sense. The notion of the intellectual as individual is replaced by a collaborative research ethic that extends from the communities to the video makers, encompassing the relationship between these and independent filmmakers. The new collaboration forms an integral part of indianization that in Latin America constitutes a new understanding of decolonization itself. No longer a project of armed resistance and aiming to construct a socialist society, it now appears only nominally socialist (and not necessarily liberal democratic either). Decolonization more readily constitutes itself as an effort to reconstruct an indigenous sociopolitical order, for example, in the movement to reconstruct the *ayllu* (Choque and Mamani Condori, "Reconstitución" 147). In other cases, the process refers to an idealized vision of the Inca Empire (cf. Asamblea Nacional; Choque Huanca). Transcending specific ethnic and geopolitical locations, indigenous organizations collaborate or work in loosely connected ways to further alternative proposals and a pan-indigenous social ethos. "Interculturality" creates a common denominator for indigenous movements working to strengthen different yet similar political projects (cf. Schiwy, "We Are All Presidents"; "Entre").

Yet there is another aspect to consider. For Gramsci, the process of state education and literacy are crucial in shaping intellectual capacity. Organic intellectuals are formed as individuals who reinterpret state discourse (transmitted through state education) while maintaining a link with the subaltern classes from which they emerge. Organic intellectuals then instruct and guide the subaltern, who provide what one might call the raw material of experiences and interests that the organic intellectual translates. Certainly, some video makers, such as Marcelino Pinto and Marcelina Cárdenas, have passed through the state education system. This description, however, does not fit others, like Julia Mosúa. Indeed, not all of the indigenous communicators are literate. Indigenous media at once bring into crisis the common assumption that an intellectual, whether traditional or organic in Gramsci's sense, is an individual with a standard education (usually steeped in the genealogies of Western thought) and certainly a person who is alphabetically literate, expressing him or herself more or less eloquently in alphabetic writing.

Indigenous media instead privilege the ideas generated within the communities and through the intercultural process of audiovisual communication itself. Consciousness is generated from within the communities and on the grounds of their traditions. Yet this is not a local process; rather it feeds on the information flows and exchanges enabled by video. The collaboration between indigenous communicators and their nonindigenous technical advisers constitutes a new practice and points toward the key importance of decolonizing knowledge. The dynamics of collaboration that come into effect in indigenous media are part of the process of indianizing the film medium—that is, of adapting it to a pan-indigenous social and epistemic order itself under construction.

3

CINEMATIC TIME
AND VISUAL ECONOMY

Does the proliferation of audiovisual media among indigenous communities respond to a change in the way literacy, literary representation, and power have congealed in Latin America? Urban elites in Latin America have enacted power relations by constructing an opposition between the realm of literacy and civilization, on the one hand, and the rural expanses inhabited by oral cultures, on the other. The opposition is at once spatial and temporal, where oral culture has become associated with stasis and literacy with progress and development. The Argentine Domingo Faustino Sarmiento famously called this the clash between civilization and barbarism. Already in the mid-nineteenth century he called for a literature that could fuse the two by integrating oral traditions into the lettered culture of the newly independent nation-states (59–78). The realm of civilization and literature formed the lettered city; its history is a narrative of coercion and colonial power, "where writing eventually looms over all human liberty, because new emerging groups can effectively assail positions of social power only on a two-dimensional battlefield of line and space" (Rama, *Lettered* 37).

Since the conquest, native speakers of indigenous languages have opted for the book and the essay as one important means of bringing subalternized indigenous perspectives to the forefront.[1] The alphabet, whether used by individual authors or through the collaborative form of *testimonio*, has been a privileged though certainly not the only venue for speaking back to power. The Aymara Fausto Reinaga wrote (and struggled to find publishers for his) books and essays in the sixties, severely criticizing Bolivia's National Revolution for framing indigenous people as a social class of peasants or *campesinos*. As Reinaga vindicated the racial identity of Indians, he also bid for inclusion in the lettered city. Change is to be affected from within. Domitila Barrios de Chungara and Rigoberta Menchú in the seventies and eighties sought out editors who adapted their stories and thoughts to the book form. Others have preferred to communicate their positions and research findings back to the communities they have worked with, often opting for community radio or inexpensive publications directed at indigenous readers.[2] Indigenous media in Bolivia largely bypass the realm of literacy, while the CRIC uses video parallel to alphabetic and other visual and aural media in their bilingual education program. Indigenous authors in Ecuador are prolific publishers, but the CONAIE is also seeking to expand its use of video. Opting or emphasizing audiovisual media may not seem surprising. Some argue that the lettered city as a configuration of power and analytic concept has recently come into crisis. At the end of the twentieth century, Jean Franco suggests, "radical change for most people came about not through armed struggle but from unanticipated changes as media and the new information economy were consolidated . . . the printed book, once the instrument for acquiring cultural capital, now encountered powerful rivals in radio and television" (*Decline* 11).

While some highlight the democratic openings mass media has offered, others maintain that media are not automatically democratic or emancipatory.[3] Octavio Getino, like indigenous media producers, insists that for audiovisual media to become true expressions of the people the current logic of access, production, and distribution must be profoundly reshaped (*Cine y televisión* 251–63). Cinema and photography, moreover, prolong a colonial gaze inaugurated with the conquest of the so-called new world (cf. Shohat "Imaging"; Shohat and Stam, *Unthinking*). Alexandra Halkin, founding director of the Chiapas Media Project, and Amalia Córdova, from the National Museum of the American Indian, argue that

indigenous communities are often on the frontline of corporate globalization and government efforts to privatize natural resources. Rarely does mainstream media address scenes of inequality so prevalent in these communities. When they do, they present the people as stuck in poverty and unable to draw on their own communities and cultures. Alternatively, media representations often include romantic portrayals and superficial analyses of culture. Through silence and misrepresentation, mainstream media contributes to economic injustice and lack of respect toward indigenous communities. (1)

One might more adequately understand the lettered city as invested with a visual economy that has enacted a teleological effect, where humanity is seen to develop from what Dipesh Chakrabarty called the "imaginary waiting room of history," characterized by oral culture toward literate and technological civilization (8). Such a teleology builds, however, on the fundamentally flawed assumption that literacy and orality are binary opposites.

The Lettered City's Visual Economy

Angel Rama's notion of the lettered city correlates the opposition of orality and literacy with subaltern and hegemonic forms of representation. Certainly, as a product and form of representation literature has inscribed ethnic and epistemic power relations. Literature has not only represented but also reproduced a fundamental heterogeneity. Cultural, ethnic, and economic differences pattern social identities and limit access to alphabetic literacy and the publishing apparatus. The disjuncture is particularly glaring in those texts that construct an indigenous referent but are read by the well-to-do middle classes (Cornejo Polar 79–80), even or especially when the novels and short stories denounce the abuse of Quechua and Aymara peasants.[4] As a concept, the lettered city indicates the complicity of intellectuals, poets, essayists, novelists, and bureaucrats with the state, despite its changing social makeup since the conquest. Yet the paradigm of literacy has also interpellated those critical of the existing order (Adorno 9).[5] Not just literature but also the alphabet becomes a hegemonic technology through which all change must pass: "Any attempt to ward off, defy or defeat the imposition of writing passes necessarily through writing," as Rama stated (*Ciudad* 82; my translation). On the level of technology then, Rama's analysis conceptualizes alphabetic writing as an encompassing technology of power that comes to substitute for oral tradition. In this sense the lettered city is not irrevocably tied to the state or the nation but to the struggle for power itself.[6]

Visual forms of signifying (maps, engravings, paintings, illustrations, graphs, photographs, film, etc.), however, have accompanied the performance and discourse of literacy. It may be useful to recall that in many contexts alphabetic literacy communicates less efficiently than pictographs, hieroglyphs, musical notes, or mathematics. Public service symbols, for example, proliferate in spaces such as airports, where communication is required across languages (Boone 16–17). Despite its focus on literacy, even Rama's account emphasizes that already in the sixteenth century the

lettered managed not only written documents and the law; they also created symbols and graphic diagrams. According to Rama, the educated elites
thus constructed a sense of inalterable signs in opposition to an apparently
ephemeral orality, signs that comprised both visual semiosis and alphabetic
writing. He argues that the urban design of the newly founded cities in what
later became Latin America visually re-created concentric circles of power,
where those located farthest from the center had the least possibilities of
partaking in the production of reality. The design of the city thus produced
a lived experience in physical space that corresponded to a Eurocentric
geopolitics of knowledge (Rama, *Lettered* 3–15). Sustainable knowledge was
tied to the city of letters, and rural, frequently indigenous modes of knowing
were marginalized or suppressed. Far from a dichotomy of letters and speech,
the colonial enactment of power relied not only on the alphabet but also on
architectural design and urban planning, visual and performative transmissions and contestations of authority (such as the creation and display of
religious paintings and iconography), the enactment of the *requerimiento* (the
Spanish ritualized taking possession of the land during the Conquest), the
use of clothing, etc. (Gruzinsky; Taylor 53–63).

photog   Gruzinsky argues that the colonial period was marked by a war of
images where Amerindian representations became replaced by Christian
iconography and where the understanding of representation itself was under
negotiation.[7] The process was not smooth but inaugurated complex forms of
indigenous adaptations and syncretism: "It is undeniable that the choice of
the visual compensated for gaps in a rather unsatisfactory linguistic communication. . . . The emphasis placed on the western image, on nonverbal
communication and ritual, and resorting to a liturgical staging in order
to win over the Indians are all in the same vein" (Gruzinsky 47). Gruzinsky
suggests that visual representation was at once more powerful than alphabetic writing in imposing itself on indigenous peoples and more permeable
to subaltern appropriation than the sphere of literacy (176–207). Similarly,
often elaborately adorned and illustrated maps visualized colonial contact
and rendered a dominant Europe-centered cosmovision, competing with the
visual representations of space and power produced by Mayans and Aztecs
(Rabasa; Mignolo, *Darker* 219–313).

     Photography came into existence at the height of the second wave of colo-
nialism and extended the power of the visual. Based on multiple reports of
photographic experiments in the eighteenth and early nineteenth century,

Batchen asserts that the desire for a photographic method of fixing "nature's writing" permanently began to be expressed at the beginning of the nineteenth century. The discourse on photography was part of an epistemological crisis regarding the understanding of nature, culture, and subjectivity. Photography was the expression of a scientific desire to subject nature, to fix it on the photographic plate, while acknowledging its autonomy from human action: "It would seem that the desire to photograph is here being projected—as its own nomenclature will later confirm (*photography*: light writing, light writing itself)—in terms of a will to power that is able to write itself even as it is written. Situated within a general epistemological crisis that has made the relationship between nature and her representations a momentarily uncertain one, photography is conceived in these first imaginings as something that is neither one nor the other, but is at the same time a parasitical spacing that encompasses and inhabits both" (Batchen 24). The body is intimately inscribed into this process where the camera extends the phallic powers of pen and gun. Batchen adds, "if photography is a mapping of bodies in time and space, then it is also a material production of those bodies, just as it is a reproduction of modernity's particular conception of the time/space continuum" (25).

The desire for photography grows, at least in part, from the experience of colonization and the wish to visually manifest and control what the colonial gaze sees: nature, natives, and the enactment of colonial superiority. Visual technology forms part of colonial history; it seeks proof for a colonial vision long rendered in visual representations. Since its inception, photography was harnessed not only to policing European populations but also to the perpetuation of a way of looking established in colonial travel narratives and paintings (Pratt 111–43). Photography was the means desired and then implemented for producing visual proof of the existence of race (Poole 118–41). The technology's indexical claim, the "ontology of the photographic image" (Bazin 13–14), imbued the paintings and drawings of nineteenth-century travelers with a new, seemingly objective value, as it promised unmediated access to what was once in front of the lens. Disavowing the effects of lenses, lights, angles, posing, and mise-en-scène, visual technology helped scientific racism construct the idea of race and produced what we might call a "reality effect." As a means of defining and producing what is real photography became a contested medium for representing Quechua and *mestizo* subjectivity in the Andes. On one hand, photography here constructed the Quechua as racially abject through posing and manipulations of light and shadow, despite the camera's apparent objectivity (Poole 118–41). On the other hand, photography entered into the rivalry between highlands and coast. Against coastal claims to Spanish heritage and privilege (that supported Lima's role as leading the Peruvian nation), *mestizos* in the highlands carefully staged photographs visualizing the romantic image of the Inca past as a blending of Andean and Greek imagery that shaped civilization in the Cuzco region (Poole 168–97). At the same time, middle class Quechua families appropriated photography, contesting the homogenizing racial discourse of the times by fashioning themselves as bourgeois subjects (198–216). Although access was constrained, photography constituted an important site where colonial and anticolonial perspectives were fought out. Indigenous media confront this tradition—one that became only more entrenched with the creation of moving images.

Time and the Colonial Gaze

Visual productions, alongside other discourses, re-create the conceptual parameters through which virtual and actual travel is made sense of. Film heightens the indexical sense of the relationship between film and reality. Cinema's transformative effect on society is attributed to its ability to represent time (an indexical effect) and to manipulate time—especially through montage, flashbacks, and the contrast between real time (the actual duration of an action or event) and cinematic time (condensing or extending an event's duration through cutting or slow motion, for instance). This dialectic relationship—representation and manipulation of time—has inscribed the apparent temporal disjuncture between Western civilization and its colonial others. The representation of the colonized other has been crucial to creating what Johannes Fabian called the denial of coevalness. In other words, the temporal disjuncture projected in film negates simultaneous, albeit unequal, economic and technological experiences in the cohabitation of global time. Film technology seems to allow for the preservation of time while positioning itself as an indicator of historicity, progress, and modernity. As Catherine Russel puts it, "in the cinema, the pastoral allegory becomes exaggerated by the role of technology in the act of representation, further splitting 'the modern' from 'the premodern'" (Russel 5). For its Western viewers, cinematic representations have supplied an apparent proof of the difference between modern technology (and supposed Western superiority) and people cast as occupying a prior stage of development.

The effects of this temporal ordering have profound implications regarding power and knowledge. Ethnographic film extended "the scientific dilemmas created by the positivist/empiricist frameworks in anthropology" (Ruby, "Exposing" 169), but more important, as Ella Shohat argues, "cinema has . . . operated as an epistemological mediator between two spaces—that of the Western spectator and that of the culture represented on the screen—linking two distinct loci and figurally separate temporalities in one moment of exposure" ("Imaging" 42–43). Film became an important tool for visualizing the tropes and metaphors of conquest and colonization put forth by popular fictions and exhibitions. It thus continued the spread of enthusiasm for the imperial projects beyond the elites and into the popular strata (Shohat and Stam 100). Film is the product of a modern desire that is at once a colonial one: "Cinema was invented at the height of colonialism at the end of the nineteenth century. The camera was crucial as a machine used by western travelers . . . —scientists, anthropologists, entrepreneurs, missionaries, and the entire array of colonial agents—to document and control the 'primitive' cultures they had seen and found" (Kaplan 61). Film, like literature, is an integral part of the coloniality of power.

With modest appeal to scientific objectivity, but with an even more powerful reach than ethnographic documentaries, the colonial gaze of Hollywood movies perpetuates the notion of "primitivism" as a perceived lag in development. The temporal disjuncture—on screen and off—contrasts apparently premodern indigenous peoples with the film technology in the hands of modern man—sitting comfortably in the audience or wielding the camera on screen. Camera eye and narrative construct a colonial gaze that boosts the foundational ambiguity of colonialism: an ever-present pastoral desire that coexists with a nightmarish fear of otherness. The *King Kong* movie (originally released in 1933 and remade twice, most recently in 2005), for example, draws our attention to cinema's role in framing the modern as opposed to the premodern. The film is at once about the power of representation and the power of representing. *King Kong* distinguishes clearly between those who wield the camera and inhabit the present and those who do not. In a self-ironic fashion, the film confirms that the camera focuses on the natives in the service of lucrative spectacle, a spectacle that produces itself as a clash of temporalities. In the 2005 remake of *King Kong*, Jack Black's character points the camera yet again at the inhabitants of Skull Island. Just as in 1933 when the white cinematographer on screen called upon his companions—and the spectators in the theater—to "take a look at that" spectacle of sacrifice unfolding before their eyes, in 2005 we are still located on the explorer's side. Indeed, Jackson's remake further accentuates the temporal difference created in the 1933 version. Black's camera sees indigenous peoples as the walking dead, zombies inhabiting an ancient realm, a time of dinosaurs, incompatible with modern civilization and yet, it seems, a part of its most ancient history. The giant ape is at once the embodiment of tenderness, chivalry, and innocence, a potential commercial spectacle, and the West's greatest fear and threat.

By situating the colonized other in a different spatial and temporal realm, cinema participates alternately in the creation of the ethnographic pastoral and its nightmare (Rony 194). On the one hand, film exhibits a desire for an Edenic past, a utopian nature-space devoid of the corruption of Western society. On the other, it incites spectators to experience the ever-present threat of colonial retaliation, ultimately banning this threat into the time of humanity's infancy. For its Western viewers cinema and ethnographic film thus create a kind of false film memory of a premodern past. But this film memory is deeply problematic; it refers to a past that never was and maps a stone-age imaginary onto the indigenous subjects captured in the frame.[8] The colonial discourse lingers in conventional ethnographic films broadcast on television and in classrooms where "the conventions of explanatory voice-over narratives and rural, impoverished people of color with exotic customs have become reified as a generic commodity in Western culture" (Russel 14.) Hollywood cinema, in this sense, forms part of a larger body of ethnographic film, including works of " 'art,' scientific research films, educational films used in schools, colonial propaganda films, and commercial entertainment films" (Rony 8). These audiovisual texts are deeply embedded in educational institutions and in the realm of public and commercial communication. They constitute a crucial part of the lettered city's visual economy.

This visual economy has rendered a colonial gaze that continues to coexist with postcolonial cinematographic "unthinking Eurocentrism" (Shohat and Stam). Film's indexical quality has endowed film with a powerful reality effect, since, whether fiction or documentary, it usually avoids showing the way even the most objective camera constructs what it and we see.[9] This sense of reality appears most powerful in documentary film and live television coverage but lingers even in fiction films, contributing thus to the sway of screen fantasies. Like standard ethnographic documentaries, motion picture cinema has assisted the global construction of racial otherness. Its colonial gaze, "which situates indigenous peoples in a displaced temporal realm," has "proved staunchly resilient" (Rony 8).[10] Indigenous video makers confront familiar representations of indigenous peoples in ethnographic documentaries, in Hollywood's globalized audiovisual discourse, as well as in the cinematic imaginary put forth in national productions. Movies made in the United States shape thinking about indigenous peoples in the Andes because U.S. films still dominate the Bolivian, Ecuadorian, Peruvian, and Colombian markets. Hollywood films circulate not only at local cinemas but also at urban markets—such as those in Latin America's largest indigenous city, El Alto—as affordable pirated DVD and VCD copies. Particularly in Bolivia, where filmmaking has been at least as important as literature, cinematographers have, however, created their own vision of the country's indigenous peoples.[11] Although films made in Latin American are much harder to come by than the ubiquitous Hollywood blockbusters—even at the pirate market stalls—Bolivian films have influenced the way indigenous subjects, cultures, and knowledge are commonly perceived in the country.[12] Similarly, one can argue that Ecuadorian and Colombian audiences may be less familiar with their national cinemas than with Hollywood blockbusters, yet local television production and national film contribute to shaping the national imaginary of indigenous peoples there.[13]

When I write that indigenous media confront these cinematic traditions, I mean that they do so in a double way. On the one hand, when indigenous media enter the national mediascape they compete with ethnographic film. On the other hand, even when the films circulate among the rural communities, they counter what viewers there are familiar with seeing on screen. The staples of Hollywood film, the ubiquitous soap operas, U.S.-produced television dramas, news shows, and advertising are today all within reach of indigenous audiences, even if they cannot afford to go to the movies. Television itself is spreading beyond the urban centers, reaching audiences that have only intermittent access to electricity and may share one television set with an entire community. The spread of audiovisual media is precisely part the urgency indigenous communicators and community leaders feel to "answer back."[14]

Indigenista Film

Until the advent of indigenous media, Bolivians' ideas about Aymara, Quechua, Guarani, and other indigenous peoples were informed, in part, by two

cinematic tendencies: (1) *indigenista* cinema and the newsreel production of
the Bolivian Cinematic Institute (Instituto Cinematográfico Boliviano, ICB)
in the sixties; (2) revolutionary, experimental third cinema, in Bolivia associated primarily with Jorge Sanjinés and the Ukamau Production Group, who
also filmed and distributed their cinema in Ecuador. In Colombia, Jorge Silva
and Marta Rodríguez shaped the sense of a national, revolutionary filmmaking sensitive to indigenous peoples' perspectives.[15]

In the sixties Bolivia's most prolific filmmaker, Jorge Ruiz, directed a
vast amount of documentary and news shorts for the ICB as well as several
motion pictures.[16] These films provided a convincing imaginary of Bolivia as
a modernizing country, in no small degree due to the quality and creativity
of Ruiz's work. *Come Back, Sebastiana* (*Vuelve Sebastiana*), considered Ruiz's
masterpiece, continues to present the indigenous legacy to Bolivian and
foreign audiences. The docudrama accompanies museum exhibitions and is
still occasionally screened at events in honor of the filmmaker, such as when
he won the National Culture Prize in 2001. A 35mm copy of the film was
restored and subtitled on the initiative of José Sánchez-H. at California State
University, Long Beach, and shown at the 8th Latino International Film Festival in Los Angeles in 2004. The Smithsonian National Museum of Natural
History in Washington considers the twenty-eight-minute black-and-white
documentary on the Chipaya "one of the most memorable ethnographic films
produced in the last century. Although not as well known, it merits a place in
the same illustrious category with classics such as Robert Flaherty's *Nanook
of the North* (1922), Jean Rouch's *Les maîtres fous* (1954), and Robert Gardner's
Dead Birds (1963)" (Smithsonian n.p.). The Smithsonian awarded Ruiz the
James Smithson Bicentennial Medal in 2005 and exhibited the film in Washington, D.C. Ruiz's international fame has only strengthened his relevance as
a filmmaker within Bolivia.

Come Back, Sebastiana, is a tender representation of a Chipaya community
that situates the Chipaya people of the Andean highlands as a disappearing culture. As the Bolivian film historian Alfonso Gumucio Dagrón put it,
"the film gives us a very clear idea of the slow destruction that victimizes
the Chipaya as western civilization penetrates their culture" (*Historia* 176).
Through a voiceover in direct address, the film narrates the dire situation
of the Chipaya and appeals to the young protagonist, Sebastiana (Sebastiana Kespi), not to run away from her community but to return and keep
it alive. Poetical and beautifully filmed, the docudrama avoids references to

contemporary political events (such as the National Revolution of 1952). It constructs Chipaya authenticity by contrasting Sebastiana's community with an Aymara town that has had closer contact with the West. The film fails to mention that the Aymara have also had a long history of resisting colonial rule. Urging Sebastiana to return, in this context, resonates with arguments inspired by Alcides Arguedas, who, at the beginning of the twentieth century, advocated against *mestizaje*.

Ruiz's treatment of indigenous sensibility does not correspond to Arguedas's racist judgment regarding the cause of Bolivia's poverty and lagging development. For Arguedas the demise of Bolivia's potential to modernize laid in the indigenous character, determined by the influence of highland geography and climate: "Note, in the man of the Altiplano, the harshness of his character, the aridity of his feelings, his absolute lack of aesthetic emotions" (180), wrote Arguedas. In the writer's estimation, racial mixing had combined the worst aspects of Spanish and indigenous character and resulted in a *Pueblo Enfermo* (a Sick People). As Javier Sanjinés emphasizes, for Arguedas, the "Indian was all but irredeemable, but deserving of protection" (*Mestizaje* 47). Though more forgiving of Chipaya culture than Arguedas of the Aymaras, it is difficult not to perceive *Come Back, Sebastiana*, as coming to a similar, custodial, conclusion. Rather than active participants in shaping the new postrevolutionary Bolivia, the Chipaya are ultimately cast as in need of Western protection.[17] As Himpele puts it somewhat more generously, "*Vuelve Sebastiana* [*Come Back, Sebastiana*] is formulated with urban nostalgia, in which people from the capital sympathize with the destruction of a rural past they claim as their own, and then turns to the fantasy of heroically rescuing the cultural ruins" (*Circuits* 120–21).

Nine years later Ruiz directed what he considers the last film he "gave to the Revolution [of 1952]" (Valdivia 82). *The Mountains Don't Change* (*Las montañas no cambian*), like *Come Back, Sebastiana*, is a docudrama. It ends pointedly with the argument that indigenous peoples cannot remain outside national society. The protagonist (Gabino Apaza) discovers that "he can no longer be a man who merely follows his routines: with dramatic dynamism, social reality has changed. He discovers that his is a new country: it has asphalted roads, factories, and agricultural machinery that alleviates the burden of physical labor" (Valdivia 83). According to Ruiz's own account, he discovered that the film was received with unanimous applause by state officials at the time since "it was not ideologically offensive" (83). Yet the sixties was precisely the time when indigenous movements resurfaced, and when the Aymara writer Fausto Reinaga claimed that the National Revolution had failed and that racism could not be reduced to class conflict. Ruiz's gaze is benevolent, but it mirrors the urban perspective on rural indigenous peoples, relegating them to a site beyond agency that either excludes them from the national project as in *Come Back, Sebastiana*, or subsumes them to the West, as in *The Mountains Don't Change*. Ruiz's influential imaginary thus rearticulates ethnographic film's temporal displacement in terms of the *indigenista* project. The two documentaries are closely aligned with the predominant options articulated in the Andean debates over the so-called Indian problem in the twentieth century: integrate and assimilate or be excluded and marginalized.[18] What does this mean for indigenous media?

Film and video are not neutral or even exclusively Western technologies; they are a key part of capitalism and colonialism. As objects of representation—at times returning the gaze, as when the "indigenous" (African American actors) in the first *King Kong* movie look straight into the camera— indigenous peoples have long taken part in cinema history. Even more, the dichotomy of literacy and orality was never quite what it seemed to be; rather, the lettered city has been bound up with visual semiotics and performance. In this sense, indigenous video does not operate entirely outside the lettered city's realm. Rather, indigenous media squarely confront not only the lettered city's national and regional visual economy but also a global configuration of media power. From this perspective, the spread of mass media is not necessarily an indicator of the waning power of educated elites or of an increasing popular access to the means of representation. Instead, the proliferation of images forms part of an expanding activity of the lettered city, not a radically novel and necessarily more democratic form of knowledge and representation. As Ana López writes, since the advent of film in Latin America, "the cinema was welcomed first and foremost as a sign of and tool for expressing the rationalist impetus of the modern. It was thoroughly aligned with the civilizing desires of the urban modernizing elites and disassociated from the 'barbarism' of national 'others'" ("Early" 57).

While the breach between those writing and reading and those who are being written about is closing, social heterogeneity still marks the production and consumption of fictional and nonfictional texts. Mass media, similarly, grant very limited access. Since the beginning of the twentieth century forceful cultural industries have established monopolistic distribution methods.

They intensify a visual regime that has long been at work, now largely subject to corporate control and profit interests. The global production and distribution of film remains dominated by a few media corporations (Miller et al. 50–110). At the beginning of the twenty-first century, newspapers, studies led by academicians and nongovernmental organizations, along with corporate media and cinema, often continue to disqualify indigenous subjectivity for being oral, backward, and irrational. In light of the continuity of colonial ideas and the limited access to mass media, it may be more appropriate to speak of a rearticulation of the lettered city, rather than its decline and fall. At minimum, if the power of literacy has declined, the principle of elite power joined with elite control of representation seems alive and well. The transformations of the lettered city, in this sense, attest to a lively dynamism, rather than decay and stagnation.

If the colonial gaze entails temporal displacement and exoticization—alternately the construction of savagery by casting monstrous others and the projection of timeless Indians as victims or romanticized placeholders of a past that never was—the solution is not just replacing "negative" images with "positive" ones.[19] It does not help much to merely exchange the one-dimensional characteristic of colonial others with another one-dimensional representation. In an early groundbreaking article Robert Stam and Louise Spence insisted that when analyzing film "a comprehensive methodology must pay attention to the *mediations* which intervene between 'reality' and representation. Its emphasis should be on narrative structure, genre conventions and cinematic style rather than on perfect correctness or fidelity to an original 'real'" (11). According to Stam and Spence, anticolonial film does not merely create "positive images" (9); it reclaims a past that has been left out of the frame and it speaks in the indigenous language. Anticolonial film reverses the spectator positioning of Hollywood movies. It places the camera (and thus the spectators) behind the lines of the colonized, or with the Indians circling the encampment. It creates viewer identification with those struggling against colonial rule instead of with the white male explorers (11–12). Reshaping the colonial gaze requires casting complex characters situated in the contemporary world.

Nayrapacha

Against the lettered city's visual economy and its temporal displacement of indigenous and colonial selves into a premodern time, indigenous media

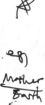

vindicate the notion of *nayrapacha*, not a circuitous concept of time, but one where "the past can also be future" (Carlos Mamani, quoted in Rivera and THOA, *Pachakuti* 1). Quechuas and Aymaras manage at least three key temporal concepts: *pachakuti* (the radical turnaround of time and space); the Inkarrí myth, that is the Inca's return and reestablishment of the Tawan-tinsuyu (Inca Empire); and *nayrapacha*, where the past is seen as a guide for the future. Two of these, *pachakuti* and *nayrapacha*, structure indigenous videos. The Inkarrí myth has so far not been visualized in indigenous media, perhaps because its reference is somewhat ethnocentric as it looks back upon Quechua dominance and a highland empire. Indigenous media in Ecuador and in Bolivia integrate very diverse indigenous peoples from the highlands, the Andean valleys, and the lowlands, and the CRIC in Colombia serves primarily the Nasa. Lowland indigenous organizations have, in fact, been paramount in shaping indigenous social movements in Ecuador. They have provided most of the leaders of CONAIE (Macdonald 176), and in Bolivia lowland peoples have played a significant role in CAIB and in the Indigenous National Plan for Audiovisual Communication.

Placing indigenous peoples into the present time has been a key strategy of both anticolonial cinema and indigenous media, as we already saw in the discussion of *Angels of the Earth* and *Courage of the People*. CEFREC-CAIB's doc-umentary *Mother Earth* more explicitly addresses the longstanding anticolo-nial struggle of indigenous peoples working toward another *pachakuti* that would reverse the order established with the conquest. The video highlights the 1829 Guarani resistance to the invasion of their lands, the Quechua and Aymara struggle for land reform during the National Revolution, and details the current Weenhayek fight for territorial rights in the eastern lowlands of Tarija (Chaco). *Mother Earth* depicts the Bolivian lowland indigenous move-ments' protest marches organized during the early nineties that demanded "*tierra y territorio*" (land and territory) and links the struggle over territorial rights in the tropical eastern parts of Bolivia and the transnational Amazon basin with the environmental discourse of indigenous communities who denounce the contamination and environmental destruction brought on by ranchers, petrol companies, and the logging industry. The documentary includes footage of the indigenous march for land rights that took thousands of lowland Indians to the frigid heights of La Paz in a grueling 4,000 km hike in 1990. The documentary thus portrays both lowland and highland move-ments as equal historical agents resisting the occupation and exploitation of their lands. By including still images of colonial paintings and sketches, *Mother Earth* proposes a historical account but at once joins different temporal moments into a narrative of an inconclusive process, thus marking what Rivera Cusicanqui called the long memory of anticolonial struggle (*Oprimidos*) with a new geographical depth. The film in fact brackets the lowland struggle; its perspective shifts from the historical highland efforts to obtain land to the diverse indigenous ethnicities of the lowlands and finally back to the highlands. An interview with Eduardo Yañez A., secretary of the CSCB (the organization of Quechua and Aymara migrants to the Andean valleys) is interspersed and provides contextual information. In other words, *Mother Earth* not only refuses the colonial gaze's temporal entrapment but also establishes the coevalness of diverse indigenous peoples. The leveling of historical agency in this documentary is key since it counters colonial stereotyping that has also informed indigenous intercultural relations.

This film furthermore challenges official historiography. It invokes a history of oppression but subordinates it to the narrative of a successful struggle. *Mother Earth* claims, similar to the THOA's comprehension of Bolivian history (Rivera Cusicanqui and THOA, "Potencial"), that the revolution was not the result of co-optation or even collaboration of the peasantry with the *mestizo* elite, facilitated in great part through the disastrous experiences of the Chaco war, but instead the outcome of indigenous struggles only later to be betrayed by the new *mestizo* powers. *Mother Earth* frames the Revolution of 1952, despite its problems, as the successful redistribution of land and the end to *latifundismo* in the highlands that results not from benevolent state legislation but from organized indigenous efforts. Similarly, the INRA law, the new land reform signed under the presidency of Gonzalo Sánchez de Losada and the Aymara vice president Victor Hugo Cárdenas in the mid-nineties, is represented as an outcome of the solidarity between the indigenous struggle in the lowlands and the highlands but in need of further reform.[20] Cárdenas, a controversial figure whom many Aymaras have accused of selling out to a politics of superficial multiculturalism instead of insisting on real change, is never mentioned in the video.

Mother Earth thus constructs a pan-indigenous and intercultural constituency beyond party politics. In the process of representing solidarity the video asserts indigenous cultural diversity. At the same time, it depicts indigenous peoples in Bolivia (and implicitly beyond) as sharing a similar, ongoing experience of colonialism now most urgently expressed as the resistance to national and transnational development projects. Indigenous communities inhabit a common time shaped by historical processes where indigenous peoples have confronted similar aggressions (Rivera Cusicanqui, "Prólogo" 67). The road, one of Bolivia's key metaphors of modernity and progress, featured in Jorge Ruíz's *The Mountains Don't Change*, is here reduced to a brief reference on the precariousness of roads that regularly turn into impassible mud allies—a state-sponsored modernization that has still not succeeded. CEFREC-CAIB's video calls state-supported and initiated development into question. At the same time, it resituates the road as a metaphor for the coming together of indigenous organizations in political struggle. A new modernity determined not by state-driven development initiatives but a pan-indigenous modernity to be defined through intercultural communication. The documentary thus contrasts profoundly both in style and message with the Ukamau Group's *Blood of the Condor* and *Courage of the People*, which also positioned Quechuas and Aymaras as critical social agents in the present but concluded with an appeal to join the armed revolution.

Perhaps surprisingly, during the first eight years of the Indigenous National Plan's existence CEFREC-CAIB has otherwise largely shied away from documenting road blockades and indigenous, peasant, or urban migrant protestors clashing with police or military forces that have marked Bolivian life since 1999. The decision was preemptive and part of a strategy that placed emphasis elsewhere: To denounce military or governmental actions risks serious repercussions (cf. Flores 35). Instead, CEFREC-CAIB opted for documentaries that, like *Mother Earth*, promote intercultural understanding and overcoming the historical tensions between highland and lowland indigenous peoples.[21] Recently, however, in the context of the low-intensity warfare in the coca-growing Chapare region and even before Evo Morales became president, CEFREC-CAIB has become more outspoken. *In the Name of Our Coca* is an urgent fiction short, shot under precarious conditions in the Chapare's militarized zone in 2005. It denounces the violent abuses and infractions of human rights committed by the military, the government's collusion with the military's murder and abduction of union and community leaders, and the inscription of young Quechuas and Aymaras into the military machine. The video also highlights the importance of local radio stations in denouncing these crimes, warning the population about military presence, and articulating resistance to the eradication campaigns targeting coca leaf plantations. The video's release precedes the moment when Evo

Morales's election to the presidency seems to guarantee some protection to the filmmakers and promises a change in policy. The film is an exception— even if a more outspoken denunciation than most other CEFREC-CAIB productions, it ends with a call to join the protest marches, not a revolutionary war. While it again locates Quechuas and Aymaras squarely into the present, this is a time of patient sociocultural transformation, which includes protests and road blockades, reconstituting traditional forms of governance and law, agriculture and language use, etc., but not rifles and machine guns.

Indigenous protests have been prevalent in Bolivia and Ecuador but also in Colombia. The Colombian CRIC's documentary *Opening a Way* (*Yi pyandena*) proudly depicts how the CRIC is born out of social protests and the struggle for land, but, similarly to the Bolivian *Mother Earth*, it does not prescribe militant anticolonial guerilla war. Rather, these documentaries become historical narratives that take their place among other documentaries of cultural and political practices, like *This Is How We Organized* (*Nawëthaw püt'*) or *Our Language Is Important* (*Nasa yuwe' walasa'*). The videos are integrated into the CRIC's bilingual education program that serves both children and adults.[22] In Ecuador, where the percentage of indigenous people is closer to Bolivia, CONAIE has perhaps most readily documented indigenous movement protests, although much of their more openly political films focus on resistance to environmental destruction (e.g., *The Earth Is Bleeding* and *Let's Save the Forest*). Even in Ecuador, however, most indigenous films center on cultural practices and none advocate armed revolution. Instead, as Macdonald has emphasized, the CONAIE prides itself on a nonviolent tradition (175).

Indigenous resistance to colonization has been pervasive and longstanding. It has included armed struggle, the defense of symbolic orders and cultural cosmovisions, as well as the defiant or secret exercise of rituals and cultural practices. Indigenous media build on varying strategies of cultural survival, from which Quechua, Aymara, Guarani, Moxeño, and other indigenous ethnicities have "drawn moral force and legitimacy in order to question the colonial order" (Rivera Cusicanqui and THOA, *Pachakuti* 5). Like testimonial cinema, the videos compel viewers to identify with the indigenous protagonists, rather than with the exploratory eye of Empire. Yet indigenous media and testimonial cinema do so with different consequences. The videos create a balance that does not replicate the Ukamau Group's militant conclusions. While indigenous peoples inhabit the present tense, these videos part ways with Ukamau's reformulation of *pachakuti* as the time of socialist revolution.

Indigenous media work primarily through the notion of *nayrapacha*, a concept that resonates across different indigenous cultures. The *nayrapacha* of indigenous media politics involves both a celebration of cultural traditions alive in the present and a critical revision of tradition. *Nayrapacha* entails a look toward the past, but it does not cinematically embalm indigenous communities in distant time. Key to cultural survival, the concept has been mobilized in other contexts, such as the writings of the Aymara intellectual Fausto Reinaga. Indigenous media invoke this tradition but also part ways with Reinaga's influential discourse articulated in the late sixties. For Reinaga the task was to maintain the difference—forged by the colonial experience—between Quechua and Aymara worldviews on one side and European cosmovision on the other in order to achieve social betterment without becoming Western (Rivera Cusicanqui and THOA, *Pachakuti* 2–3). In other words, he cast Quechua and Aymara identity as opposed to that of the West in order to exalt cultural and economic orders, social relations, and philosophical views perceived as opposite to and better than those of the West. With clear resonance of the sixties' and seventies' revolutionary prose, Reinaga wrote, "the West is an individualist system based on private property; the Tawantinsuyu, the Inka society, is a collective social system based on socialist property. The West, since it is based on private property is a system of war, the Inka society, in contrast, is social property and therefore a system of peace. The West has made of man man's worst enemy while the Inka order has made of man man's brother in a society of labor and love" (Reinaga, "Mi palabra" 61).[23] Reinaga constructed a utopian precolonial past that reiterates aspects of the Inkarrí myth in so far as the dominant alternative to the present is cast as an idealized Inca order.

Indigenous media similarly propose recovering indigenous knowledge, ethics, and social memory. Like Carlos Mamani Condori, former director of the Andean Oral History Workshop (THOA), indigenous communicators see *nayrapacha* as "the ancient times. But they are not ancient in the sense of a dead past, gone and without importance for renewal. Rather they imply that this world is reversible, that the past can also be future" (quoted in Rivera Cusicanqui and THOA, *Pachakuti* 1). The video makers, however, purge *nayrapacha* of its highland-centric implications. The shift is a result of the intercultural process of indigenous audiovisual communication. For Reinaga precolonial culture was Andean in nature, a fusion of Aymara and Quechua social and economic practices, values, and technologies, synthesized as the Inca society (*Inkanato*). Although Reinaga also constructed similarities with the precolonial indigenous societies of Mesoamerica, tensions among indigenous peoples across the hemisphere and within Bolivia—manifested in the Aymara resistance to the Inca Empire, the Uru struggle against Aymara dominance, and the displacement of the notion of the savage by Quechuas and Aymaras to lowland indigenous peoples—were not brought into debate.[24]

Indigenous media continue the cultural politics of knowledge that Reinaga helped to map out. They do not endorse a superficial multiculturalism that exhausts itself in folkloric posturing but instead mobilize the potential of cultural memory to radically alter power relations and forms of understanding that have been hegemonic since the conquest. However, while the writers and political figures associated with the Bolivian highland indigenous movements—such as Reinaga in the sixties and seventies and Germán Choque Huanca or Felipe Quispe (El Mallku) today—continue to subscribe to the view of Aymara leadership, indigenous audiovisual communication in Bolivia and Ecuador has a strong base in lowland ethnicities. In Bolivia the influence of lowland organizations such as CIDOB on indigenous media is equal if not greater to those of the highlands. Multiple video productions address the issues confronted by lowland peoples in Bolivia and Ecuador (such as environmental destruction). While the Inkarrí myth remains important for highland peoples, indigenous media's intercultural approach de-centers its relevance. Nevertheless, video provides a common tool for all involved and strengthens a pan-indigenous process that seeks to strengthen cultural resources and knowledge traditions. In other words, as the communities linked through the audiovisual communication process become increasingly aware of each other, they understand themselves to be similarly situated within a long colonial history that has homogenized native communities into the racial category of the "Indian." No longer marked by the cold war or the utopian horizon of a socialist society, they articulate positions from the perspective of indigenous movements in a context of global multiculturalism. Social struggle is not absent from indigenous video. The solutions, however, are not grounded in the violent ousting of foreign occupying powers but in painstaking social organization and the building of inter-indigenous alliances. *Nayrapacha*—invoking the past as guide for the present—lends itself as a common denominator that transcends cultural particularities and avoids invoking the contested memory of Tawantinsuyo.

When indigenous video reconfigures the colonial entrapment of cinematic time it unmistakably places indigenous social memory into the future tense.[25] Myth and storytelling become key themes for rendering *nayrapacha* on screen. Indeed, almost all of CEFREC-CAIB's first generation of fiction films re-create traditional stories in contemporary settings: *Cursed Gold* places the story of an enchanted lagoon that beckons those in search of easy riches into the time of trucks, coca markets, and Andean pop music; in *The Forest Spirit*, a mythical jaguar woman haunts two young Moxeños whose Western clothing and Spanish dialogue emphasize the contemporary feel of the video. *Vest Made of Money*'s mise-en-scène includes a bicycle and wads of colorful Bolivianos (the national currency); *Loving Each Other in the Shadows*' protagonists communicate in writing and escape an arranged marriage on a bicycle. At the same time, these films highlight the potential of myth and storytelling for thinking in terms of cultural survival.

Qati qati, for instance, tells a traditional story about a flying head and is set in the context of contemporary daily life in an Aymara village in the Andean highlands near Lake Titicaca. The story evolves around the central conflict between a husband and his wife, who tries to convince him of the credibility of such stories. At the end of this film, when his wife dies and turns into a flying head, the husband comes to reconsider what he deems superstition and the greater social ethos attached to it. Myth here becomes indicative of an epistemic order that has been subalternized. It now grounds a social ethos and social memory that is productive for thinking about alternative modernities.[26] *Vest Made of Money*, a twenty-five-minute fiction short shot in digital video format in 1998, brings this link to the forefront. The video can be read as a critique of capitalist accumulation. The film opens with striking colors of the sunrise; then, through a series of shots, slowly approaches an Aymara village; and finally renders extreme close-ups as one of the protagonists fights with his wife over whether or not to sell a cow. Saturated yellows and blues dominate this quotidian tale of greed and insanity. Individuals and small groups are set against breathtaking mountain ranges and ample pastures. The short ends with the villagers gathered and the authorities reminding everyone that avarice does not pay off: one protagonist has become a ghost that haunts the entire community, and the other has lost his wits. More than cultural survival, the story of the rolling head that structures *Qati qati* invokes a social ethos of reciprocity and an animate lifeworld that is explicated in *Vest Made of Money* as the protagonists stray from community ideals and find their supernatural punishment. The myth, the story, and the power of an animate life world are upheld, like in *Qati qati*, as equivalent if not privileged epistemic systems vis-à-vis the enlightened rationalism that guides modern thinking in the West.

Some might read the videos' emphasis on myth as part of an indigenous movement's cultural turn in the eighties. Jorge Sanjinés engages with this debate in *The Secret Nation* (*La nación clandestina*). The film reacts to the emergence of a folkloric politics exploited by figures such as the media savvy Aymara politician Carlos Palenque.[27] The harsh criticism of the Aymara Victor Hugo Cárdenas's vice presidency in the mid-nineties drew further attention to the way indianism could be emptied of its critical content and demands for social transformation.[28] *The Secret Nation*, to my mind, insists on the primacy of social struggle over cultural revival.[29] In this film the lost prodigal son returns to his indigenous roots and community at a time of social protest and road blockades, in which his community is actively participating. Like Sixto in *Blood of the Condor*, Sebastián Maisman (Reynaldo Yujra) in *The Secret Nation* is a victim of the colonization of the soul. After having betrayed his community, Sebastián eventually struggles to return and recover his Aymara last name (Mamani). In the central scene he performs the ancestral dance to his death, the only means left to redeem himself. The dance reintegrates him with his estranged community, whose members are just returning from their participation in the blockades, but his sacrifice appears utterly meaningless in this context. Rather, the victim of urban racism remains divided from his politically engaged community. His sacrifice returns him to the community, but he no longer actively contributes to the present struggle. *The Secret Nation* thus seems to flatten the powerful Andean concept of *nayrapacha*. Instead, the film integrates indigenous culture at large into the Marxist-*indigenista* view that prioritizes class struggle against capitalism. The film does not open up a broader debate over the meaning and potentials of indigenous social and cultural memory, techniques, and epistemic forms for current, indianist social and political projects.

Directed by Reynaldo Yujra (*The Secret Nation*'s protagonist), *Qati qati* proposes a different view. Although Valentina (Ofelia Condori) dies at the end, her death redeems her husband as he tells his children that it might be best to regard the traditions. In the video the past becomes an ethical guide, but,

maybe time to believe in ancestors

more than that, it points to particular forms of understanding and relating with the lifeworld and society. In this video, myth and storytelling acquire a key relevance for ending the nefarious effects of colonialism.[30] The media activists' use of *nayrapacha* thus defines anticolonial struggle as a cultural recovery from which alternative knowledge can be teased out and used to inform the construction of alternative modernities.

The stories re-created in indigenous fiction videos thus serve a similar function to those recovered in oral history docudramas and documentaries (e.g., *Our Word* and *Dusting Off Our History*). They also resemble the role oral history played for the Aymara research institute THOA. In the 1980s and early 1990s the THOA laid the groundwork for a broad sociopolitical movement that reconstructs traditional forms of community and government in the Bolivian highlands (Mamani and Choque Quispe 163–68; Stephenson, "Forging"). Critically engaging with the oral history of Aymara communities, the THOA worked with the epistemic potential of myth in order to theorize anticolonial struggle. The problem that this poses is familiar from yet a different context. As is well known, for the East Indian Subaltern Studies Group the problem consisted in recovering a subaltern consciousness from history. In this sense, subaltern studies implied questioning the very process of producing knowledge about the subaltern in an epistemological context marked by the Eurocentrism of historiography and its analytical categories, particularly those provided by Marxist readings of revolutionary struggle.

In the essay "The Prose of Counter-Insurgency," Guha explores the possibilities for accessing subaltern thinking, or what he calls "consciousness," from the perspective of postcolonial historiography. This subaltern thinking expressed itself in India in violent and messianic rebellions—a perception, one might add, that resonates with the way the mainstream press perceives anticolonial indigenous social movements in Latin America. (The unease grows into a profound anxiety if these social movements take political power in the name of indigenous constituents, such as in Bolivia in 2006.) The problem for the historians of the subaltern studies collective, writes Guha, was that history as a scientific discipline of universal reach and European origin did not provide the methods and concepts that would allow access to subaltern consciousness. On the one hand, existing documents do not justify subaltern perspectives. Guha suggested approximating subaltern consciousness, therefore, through a methodology that parallels literary deconstruction and consists in reading against the grain and in the gaps of narratives and historical records. On the other hand, however, by showing that East Indian rebel thinking was profoundly contradictory, at least in relation to the Marxist trajectory mapped out for acquiring proletarian consciousness, Guha indicated the limitations of a leftist national historiography. History cannot escape its own teleological vision: "There is nothing that historiography can do to eliminate such distortion altogether, for the latter is built into its optics. What it can do, however, is to acknowledge such distortion as parametric—as a datum which determines the form of the exercise itself, and to stop pretending that it can fully grasp a past consciousness and reconstitute it" (Guha, "Prose" 77). Guha thus marks a limit of academic understanding. He concludes that the historiographic narrative of anticolonial rebellion should point out the contradictions to the teleological perspectives of Western liberation opened up by these rebellions and by the myths that guided them.[31]

The labor of negativity—that is, the analysis and deconstruction of how power reconstitutes itself—is necessary and important. Yet if we are interested in the way power is contested and reshaped, there is also a need to further develop forms of engaging with the epistemic potential of subalternized knowledge without thereby falling into uncritical celebration or becoming bound by political pragmatics.[32] The THOA in Bolivia indeed approached the issue in a slightly different way than the Subaltern Studies Group. Like the video makers, the THOA's researchers work in close contact with their indigenous communities of origin. For both THOA and indigenous media activists, myth acquires a hermeneutic value. The stories collected by the THOA and narrated in oral testimony indicate cycles of Aymara resistance against colonialism and racism. Aymara history becomes one of coherence and survival, rather than of a disappearing culture's doomed and dispersed struggle:

> the rebellions that were always seen as a periodic reaction to abuses by the Creole and Spanish society could thus be read in a different manner. They became key moments in an underground ideological accumulation that cyclically came to the surface. They expressed the continuity and autonomy of Indian society. We have thus overcome the instrumental notion of myth, either understood as a space of eternal and universal "savage thought" or, at the other end of the spectrum, as a mere fabrication of the imagination that is completely

disconnected from "objective" reality. (Rivera Cusicanqui and THOA, "Potencial" 59)

No longer caught by the dilemma of having to choose between mythical orders, the demands of rational enlightenment, or a Marxist history of liberation, myth itself has become a genre for thinking otherwise.

Indigenous fiction films indicate a complex process of reinventing and reevaluating social memory "but . . . thinking about the future" (CEFREC, *Comunicar* 22). This dynamic conceptualization of *rescate cultural* (cultural recovery) resonates with Rigoberta Menchú's well-known dictum: "I think that we as indigenous people should take advantage of all the great values and discoveries of science and technology. Science and technology have achieved great things and we can't say: 'the indigenous peoples we are not going to be a part of that' because, well, we are a part of that. We have not been isolated creatures, immune to everything during the past 500 years. No, we have been the protagonists of history" (Menchú, "Hemos sido" 212). Indigenous media break the temporal configuration of the colonial gaze. Rarely have the Latin American video makers made films that are set in a past and mythical time, however. Of CEFREC-CAIB's productions, only *The Jichi Woman* allocates legend to a timeless realm. More frequently the stories are accommodated to present village life or even set in contemporary urban environments, like in *Angels of the Earth* and the Guarani video *In Search of the Warrior.* Time here is not mummified; instead, traditional stories and myths are resituated into contemporary contexts. The strategy responds to the logic of storytelling as a constant reinvention, where myths of old are continuously reshaped and re-accommodated to the needs and context of the present. If myth becomes a resource for recovering the past as a guide for the future, it joins the use of audiovisual technology as a form of transmitting knowledge. In other words, indigenous media both on screen and off indicates that indigenous cultures can change without necessarily being lost.

4

GENDER, COMPLEMENTARITY, AND THE ANTICOLONIAL GAZE

When viewing indigenous fiction and documentary films, it is striking how often they frame women as cultural guardians and men as the victims of the self-denigrating effects of colonial discourse. Documentaries and fiction shorts highlight the way cultural practices, religious beliefs, and knowledge are transmitted in embodied ways. Women become the symbolic bearers of indigenous identification; they are the ones with privileged access to indigenous languages, stories, and ethos; they are the ones transmitting social memory. Even ethnically marked clothing is frequently (but not exclusively) associated with women rather than men. In the fiction shorts men often appear as those who no longer believe in the stories and myths told by their wives. The male protagonists, who favor more secular and rational perspectives, are criticized for their loss of faith in the animate lifeworld and the social ethos that storytelling transmits. Their views mirror the lettered city's long-standing discourse that disqualifies indigenous belief systems as superstitions. In fiction shorts like *Qati qati* and *Loving Each Other in the Shadows*, women, in contrast, become the tragic heroes who die violent deaths, thus redeeming their husbands and lovers along with indigenous cultural tradition at large.

At first sight, the salience of gender in indigenous video seems to contradict the way some Latin Americans have understood power to be constituted in the context of colonialism. The principle of race, says Aníbal Quijano, "has proven to be the most effective and long-lasting instrument of universal social domination, since the much older principle—gender or intersexual domination—was encroached upon by the inferior/superior racial classifications. So the conquered and dominated peoples were situated in a natural position of inferiority, and, as a result, their phenotypic traits as well as their cultural features were considered inferior. In this way, race became the fundamental criterion for the distribution of the world population into ranks, places, and roles in the new society's structure of power ("Coloniality" 535). Quijano identifies race as the crucial lynchpin of power relations in the global world system.[1] According to this understanding, we would expect indigenous video, like the anticolonial cinema of the sixties and seventies, to focus on racial discrimination and exploitation. Why do indigenous media insist on gender instead of race?

On the one hand, highlighting women as the bearers of indigenous knowledge and culture and juxtaposing them with men who no longer believe in the relevance of traditions, corresponds to lived experiences. The imposed (and self-imposed) deculturation of the aboriginal peoples (*pueblos originarios*) in Bolivia has a gendered dimension that has affected differently "how one is indigenous," whether in rural communities, in the cities, or in indigenous movement organizations (Rivera Cusicanqui, "Desafíos" 17). On the other hand, when the videos construct masculinity and femininity as two distinct forms of subjectivity that relate differently to the pressures of colonialism, they also respond to the way the cinematic gaze—as part of a lingering colonial discourse—has intertwined constructs of race and gender. Does the indigenous enactment of femininity as closer to home and traditions hence mirror the dilemma of Asian and African anticolonial movements, where prescriptive dual gender relations rendered women the safeguards of tradition, inhibiting their struggle against patriarchal oppression? Or does women's participation in the indigenous movements and in the social practice of video making (on and off screen) constitute a kind of revolutionary action? Paraphrasing Frantz Fanon, one might ask if indigenous media create women that are no longer silent, whose sacrifices and fight for liberation develop new values governing sexual relations? Has woman "ceased to be a complement for man?" Has she "literally forged a new place for herself?" (Fanon, "Dying" 109). Finally, what are the pitfalls of juxtaposing femininity and masculinity? What becomes of those who do not fit neatly into either category? Must not decolonization itself overcome dichotomous thinking?

The Patriarchal Gaze of Empire

Certainly, racial thinking has become paramount since the conquest. Racial difference has been inscribed and enacted through discourse, social practices, and visual representations. The idea of race, before it was even called such, evolved from the debates over the humanity of the people that Spanish and Portuguese conquerors and clerics encountered. The debate has been transformed since the sixteenth century, moving from a focus on purity of blood and religious difference to biological racism. Literary, photographic, and audiovisual texts have added to the representations found in the chronicles and engravings from colonial times. The construction of racial subjectivity has served as a bodily metaphor for ordering economic, political, as well as epistemic relations. It has created lived exclusions and abuses but also forms of organized resistance and quotidian subversion. Today, the multicultural acknowledgment of different ethnicities structured in relation to the market seems to go hand in hand with the renewed mobilization of religious and ethnic differences in the imaginaries of war and terrorism (Mignolo, *Local* 27–33). Yet constructs of masculinity and femininity have been crucial to all of these dimensions. They influence relations between women and men as well as the treatment of those who do not fit smoothly into these binary categories.

Colonial discourse has employed gender as a metaphor and means of subalternization, a metaphor that casts territories as female virgin lands, penetrated by conquerors with the sword in hand. Latin American cities were built as male-dominated bastions in the middle—or perhaps better, on the borders—of "natural" spaces associated with femininity—whether virgin or indomitable. Caucasian men have thought of themselves not only in opposition to women but also to colonized (or postcolonial) men, represented as effeminate or as part of an irrational nature. Nature itself is bound up with tropes of femininity and opposed to civilization (Shohat, "Gender" 53–55; Williams, *Keywords* 219–24). As Anne McClintock put it in her analysis of British colonialism, "race, gender, and class are not distinct realms of experience, existing in splendid isolation from each other; nor can they be simply yoked together retrospectively like armatures of Lego. Rather, they come into existence *in and through* relation to each other" (5). Ojibwe scholar Andrea Smith argues that "patriarchal gender violence is the process by which colonizers inscribe hierarchy and domination on the bodies of the colonized" (23). The continuous reinvention of gender as a social category does not lose power with the emergence of ethnic Otherness; the invention of race cannot be seen to supplant the gender imaginary with the onset of Spanish and Portuguese colonialism. Rather, both constructs interact. They coalesce into gender specific forms of oppression and mesh long-standing imaginaries in order to justify economic, political, ethnic, and epistemic hierarchies.

In Andean indigenous and peasant communities gender relations are usually hierarchical and intimately tied to ethnic identifications. *Mestizo* ethnicity can be adopted or ascribed; it is derived from the kind of labor a person engages in and from appearance (dress, hairstyle, etc.), but it affects men to a greater degree.[2] Within many communities women who are considered *misti* or *mestiza*, for instance, are socially positioned above men who are considered *indio*, and indigenous women are at the lowest rung (De la Cadena, "Mujeres" 186). While indigenous communities thus create dynamic concepts of identity, women are more readily and—in de la Cadena's case study of a Peruvian village—negatively associated with indianness: "If the colonizing project supposed the feminization of the peoples they called "indigenous," the entrapment of the patriarchal project is the indianization of women ("Matrimonio" 149). In Bolivian society, "the peculiar articulation of ethnicity, class, and gender has lead to a complex chain of postcolonial stratification . . . that privileges westernized masculine sectors with greater economic income and formal education, while relegating women and indigenous migrants to the less demanding and worst paid occupations that hold the least amount of prestige and social acknowledgement" (Rivera Cusicanqui, "Desafío" 51–52). Indigenous movements cannot but bring to the forefront gender's crucial importance in the coloniality of power: "the point is that because gender and sexuality are so integral to the construction of racial and ethnic identities, the movements that form around these identities are inevitably affected by this" (Wade 103).

When video makers reframe the way audiences perceive not just indigenous subjects but also indigenous women, they and their audiences face the viewing conventions created by cinema's colonial gaze. Like the narratives of conquest, the colonial gaze has bolstered the intertwined constructs of race and gender; it is both masculine and imperial. As is well known, the male gaze has been theorized as a compelling force that combines narrative with the visual. The plot and camera eye together construct subjectivity and spectator identification by controlling dimensions of space (through camera distance and editing) and time (through editing and narrative). Following the argument in Laura Mulvey's classic article on the male gaze, mainstream (Hollywood) narrative film thereby creates a world based on "scopophilia," the pleasure of looking and being looked at that corresponds to male desire

(Mulvey, "Visual" 59). Women are cast as erotic spectacles whose lack of power causes the spectators to unconsciously transform the image of woman into an object of voyeurism and fetishism. Even women protagonists remain the objects of a desire constructed as male.[3] When the male gaze coalesces with colonial desire, film constructs a patriarchal imperial-looking convention. As a tool of colonial and patriarchal imagining, the cinematic gaze posits woman as the object of desire and man as fearless agent: "Heroic status is attributed to the voyager (often a scientist) come to master a new land and its treasures, the value of which the 'primitive' residents have been unaware. It is this construction of consciousness of value as a pretext for (capitalist) ownership that legitimizes the colonizer's act of appropriation. The 'discovery,' furthermore, has gender overtones" (Shohat, "Imaging" 50–51). As Shohat continues, "the camera relays the hero's dynamic movement across a passive, static space, gradually stripping the land of its enigma. . . . The unveiling of the mysteries of an unknown space becomes a rite of passage allegorizing the Western achievement of virile heroic stature" (51). Colonial rape is thus converted into one of ethnographic film's aestheticized tropes. In plain disavowal of colonial power relations, film shows us the white male hero who defends his wife and family against the attacks of savage Indians, apparently proving his masculinity along with the civilized superiority of the West. The camera meanwhile does not fail in locating us as spectators behind the settler's line, where we see ourselves attacked along with them (Stam and Spence 11–12).

Indigenous video makers confront the gendered dimension of the colonial gaze, "an imbrication reflective of the symbiotic relations between patriarchal and colonial articulations of difference" (Shohat, "Gender" 45). We have already seen, however, that indigenous media do not explicitly return the gaze of Empire. That is, they largely refrain from reenacting violent colonial encounters. As in the response to cinema's denial of coevalness, indigenous video reconfigures the patriarchal gaze of Empire by quoting deviously, rather than by making colonial rape explicit, as in Jorge Sanjinés's first feature film, *The Way Things Are* (*Ukamau*). The videos, instead, reveal three strategies for engaging the problem: casting complementarity, veiled critique through melodrama, and directly vindicating changes in gender politics.

The representation and enactment of gender and knowledge on screen constitutes a productive but problematic pan-indigenous strategy for countering the colonial cinematic gaze. It is a site where the *nayrapacha* utopia of the past is critically examined and reshaped to fit the needs of the present. Yet by insisting on a gender binary, indigenous media reinforce a set of taboos that are themselves products of colonial discourse.

Casting Complementarity

Qati qati is an adaptation of the Aymara story of the rolling head (*q'ati q'ati*), set in the Andean highlands of Carabuco.[4] This award-winning thirty-five-minute short weaves together a complex plot centered around two main threads, the story of a robbery and the tragic death of the protagonist's wife, herself turned into a *qati qati*. The video contrasts two modes of knowledge, a Western rational mode and an Aymara one based on premonitions, dream interpretations, and stories transmitted over generations. These competing epistemic modes are embodied by *Qati qati*'s protagonists, Fulo (Pedro Gutiérrez) and Valentina (Ofelia Condori) (fig. 11).

Qati qati opens with a scene showing a nightly potato thief and then cuts to a couple performing their early morning chores. Valentina goes to fetch water and Fulo watches the village authorities inspecting a potato field in the distance. We follow the couple's preparations for building a shelter in their own field so that Fulo may guard against potential robbers and finally witness Valentina's mysterious death. In this fiction short, Valentina worries about a snake hiding in the straw and representing peoples' intestines, and she tells a story about a flying head, warning her children to drink water before they go to bed so that their head does not fly off at night in search of something to quench its thirst. Valentina also enacts rituals to appease the forces behind the flying head, much to the amusement of her husband and children, who do not take her seriously. As she insists, her knowledge is ancestral, transmitted orally from her grandmother to her and now from her to both of her children.

Fulo, meanwhile, experiences dreams of premonition that he, however, fails to read accordingly. These dreams add validity to Valentina's perspective. Ultimately Valentina's death anchors her stories of the *qati qati* in a diegetic reality that Fulo can no longer deny. The short maintains a tension between male and female identified orders that is reinforced by its braided plot. *Qati qati*'s narrative structure mirrors the structure of Andean legends where two stories are connected, one shedding light upon the other. Besides the story of the *qati qati* told by Valentina, there is the story of the *qati qati*

———————— II. Fulo (Pedro Gutiérrez) and Valentina (Ofelia Condori) ————————
in *Qati Qati/Whispers of Death*. Production still.
http://videoindigena.bolnet.bo (CEFREC).

experienced by Valentina, the version of it rendered in Fulo's dreams, as well
as the story of the robbery that seems, at first glance, unrelated. While the
characters in both story lines (rolling head and robbery) interact, editing
conventions in the opening sequence imply that Fulo is likely the culprit of
the robbery. The community authority's inspection of the potato field where
the robbery occurred is cut to a close-up of Fulo's face. However, Fulo's
implication is never made explicit, and it turns out he is innocent. The robber is eventually found and turns out to be an unnamed character, a man
dressed in a poncho and *ch'ullu* (a traditional knitted hat). This figure interrupts the equation between dress and identity, perhaps even undermines the
grandmother's assertion on screen that there existed no robbery in former
times. *Qati qati* thus questions a possible link between crime and cultural
alienation.[5] The story of the robbery, at first sight, then simply provides a
context for the representation of Valentina and Fulo's labor in constructing an overnight shelter, which Fulo uses when guarding their fields against
potential thieves.

When I saw this video for the first time I did not understand, from my Western frame of mind, what was being illuminated, how these two tales were linked. It was not that the loss in belief and tradition had led to both crime and death. Where then is the key dramatic moment where a decision is taken that inevitably leads to the tragic end? The solution lies indeed with agency, male agency, but is based on the beliefs of the woman. The narrative gap that the viewers need to fill lies in the knowledge about rituals that the viewer brings to the reception process. If Fulo had reacted to his premonitory dream by performing a ritual, as the tale of the robbery suggested, he could have saved his wife from dying.[6] The scenes of the crime, investigation, and punishment of the robber provide a background, or secondary strain, that complements Valentina's enactment of feminized indigenous knowledge with an intact order of law embodied by men. The narrative itself centers on Fulo's emotional journey and spiritual redemption as he ultimately promises to venerate his communities' stories, knowledge, and ethos. *Qati qati*, like many of the other fiction films by CEFREC-CAIB, thus ultimately creates viewer identification with the male protagonist.

The video vindicates female-associated knowledge, but *Qati qati* does not simply discard masculinity or the importance of men in the community. The video's narrative argument together with the look of the camera strives to create a gaze that is both male and female. On the one hand, the film subverts the colonial gaze by excluding the colonizer from the frame and by creating a looking relation where indigenous communities see themselves (on screen and when the film is shown to its primary audiences). On the other hand, instead of casting Valentina as the erotic object of male (indigenous) agency, *Qati qati* seeks a dual gaze (through camera eye and narrative) that reflects gender duality. The camera eye complements the narrative's dual approach. Unlike other shorts, such as *The Forest Spirit*, *Loving Each Other in the Shadows*, and *Overcoming Fear*, *Qati qati* avoids the eroticization of its female characters. The video makers, furthermore, privilege a neutral camera eye instead of point-of-view shots from the male characters. Close-ups are distributed equally between both protagonists while looks between Fulo and Valentina are mostly averted. Fulo gazes at Valentina actively only twice, once in his dream where she waves good-bye, and once at her deathbed when her look can no longer return his. The crucial scenes in *Qati qati*—Fulo's dreams and the encounter of his dead wife–are filmed from Fulo's perspective but they are not eroticized.

The spouses' bickering over the relevance of traditional beliefs and ritual takes place in front of their two children, a boy and a girl. Like the children, the viewers identify with Fulo through the use of humor. As he laughs at his wife's superstitions and at the flying head he sees in his dreams, so do we. Some of the viewers' laughter is perhaps elicited without intention, rather a result of the scarcity of technological means that could create a more realistic rendering of the flying head. Nevertheless, this improvised representation successfully echoes the doubts of those spectators who already, like Fulo, question the mythical and spiritual dimensions of indigenous orders of knowledge. Affective identification with Fulo is reinforced with regard to overcoming these doubts in the final scenes. After his utter desolation when his wife dies, Fulo and his children walk away from the grave and the camera into a long shot of the Andean highlands, and Fulo pronounces: "perhaps it would have been better to believe." *Qati qati* posits its viewers as extensions of the couple's children—that is, as both male and female. Both are equally important participants in the process of decolonization. In the end, the children on screen will have to decide together with the viewers about what is worth preserving of indigenous traditions. As the last images fade out, the video seeks to integrate the duality at its base.

The figure of the village elder and owner of the targeted potato field, Tata Anselmo (who is not explicitly identified in the credits) is interesting, since he invokes a certain ambiguity. Tata Anselmo corroborates the epistemic system that Valentina invokes, a system that is also visually inscribed into the landscape. For instance, Tata Anselmo lifts the thief's footprints and takes them to the grave of the *chullpa* (the ancestral mummy), rendered on screen as the badlands of an eroded hillside. In the film, the *chullpa* correctly identifies the culprit. Set against the backdrop of the wide Andean highplains with glimpses of Lake Titicaca, the elder later reprimands Fulo for no longer believing in the mountains towering above the high plains, for no longer respecting the lake and *Pachamama* (Mother Earth). The figure of Tata Anselmo signals the support for Valentina (and an indigenous epistemology) by the older men in the community, but he does not fully break with the notion that "women are more Indian" (De la Cadena, "Mujeres"). Rather, the character draws attention to the social construction of gender, which is not identical in Aymara and Western traditions.

The gendered division of labor and space among Quechuas and Aymaras jars with the Western notion of private (associated with the feminine) and public spheres (associated with masculinity). Yet even where traditional gendered divisions of labor dominate, the roles of men and women are not interchangeable.[7] Among Quechuas and Aymaras, ideal femininity differs from the Victorian housewife, whose desired attributes are those of passivity, emotionality, and purity. Allison Spedding suggests that Aymaras have distinct expectations of women depending on their lifecycle. Even for the childbearing ages of fifteen to forty-five, the feminine ideal includes the ability to work, to have children, active sexual desire (although, as in the case of men, ideally to be addressed solely to the legitimate partner), and a penchant for economic calculus. Women are encouraged to travel (to markets), but their prestige does not depend on their talent as public speakers, one of the measuring sticks for male status ("Esa Mujer" 337–38). The gendered division of labor is very strict, although generally women are seen as more able to assume male tasks (working the land) than men to assume female tasks (preparing food, washing clothes) because of the difference in value attributed to each. In addition, women are able to find paid male labor, while men cannot find paid female labor (334–35).

Qati qati includes extensive footage dedicated to the representation of the gendered division of labor, social relations, and different forms of economic exchange. Its setting creates a community that has largely maintained social traditions. Aymara justice (the finding of the robber with the help of the *chullpa* and the whipping of the culprit once he is identified) is in the hands of men and is depicted as fully intact. *Qati qati*'s labor relations are based on self-sufficiency, reciprocity, and barter. Valentina, like other women in the village, fetches water from a natural source and not a mechanical well. She prepares the food and helps to build the shelter, while Fulo is responsible for guarding their potato fields, chopping wood for building materials, braiding ropes, etc. Valentina cares for the children when at home, while Fulo takes charge of them in her absence. Valentina cares for the smaller animals, and she trades potatoes (a high-plains crop) for apricots (from more temperate regions) in the marketplace. *Qati qati* highlights the market as a place traditionally dominated by women. Most important, in this video Valentina and Fulo are profoundly dependent on each other. Their equal value, constructed on screen through the representation of labor relations, underlies the ultimate tragedy of Valentina's death. Hence Fulo's lament, "Valentina, why have you left us, who will now take care of the children?" is more indicative of this mutual dependency than of relegating her exclusively to the role of child care provider.

In Andean cultures, older men traditionally lose their power and authority once they are no longer able to fully participate in agricultural and other
forms of physical labor (de la Cadena, "Mujeres"). The victim of the robbery,
Tata Anselmo, still works his fields. From an Aymara perspective he would
thus command the respect of a male elder. From a Western perspective,
however, he might not be ascribed complete masculinity given his advanced
age. Placing him alongside Valentina, therefore, also attests to a generational
power struggle, where many younger men in the community have been challenging the authority of the elders along with their critique of indigenous
cultural traditions. The colonial difference here runs through the community and divides epistemic orders along gender and age lines. *Qati qati* thus
reframes a logic of colonial power that has hitched gender and racial subjectivity together.

Qati qati draws attention not only to the value of tradition (in terms of
a cultural gendered practice), but also to the link between cultural traditions and knowledge, both embodied and transmitted primarily by women.
Valentina's representation as a guardian of tradition—that is, as having
privileged access to indigenous knowledge and ethics—conflicts with the
metaphor of femininity in the colonizing project. The metaphor had created
femininity as a marker of unsustainable knowledge, contrasting with male-
dominated science and technology. *Qati qati*, in contrast, invokes feminized
knowledge as sustainable. Although the privileged perspective is male, *Qati
qati* hence can hardly be reduced to an oedipal narrative, characteristic of
the male cinematographic gaze.[8] The object of desire in *Qati qati* is both an
idealized woman (capable of fulfilling her traditional gender roles and of
bearing children—male and female) and a feminine-identified knowledge.
The film renders an order that is embodied by women and the elderly, not a
straightforward patriarchal regime. Yet this is no feminist retooling of cinema aesthetics. Woman is the object through which man finds his redemption as Valentina's death compels Fulo, the children, and the viewers toward
accepting the power and relevance of indigenous knowledge and traditions.
Valentina may be the prize of male action that Fulo forsakes, but there is no
contention between male actors nor is there ultimately a patriarchal order of
knowledge to be perpetuated. *Qati qati* does not advocate the abandonment
of rational forms of knowledge embodied by the male protagonist, however.
After all, it is the woman who dies and the man who survives. Rather, Fulo's
rationality is complemented by the position of Valentina and by the explicit

moral in the final scene. Indeed, this film constructs complementarity as a paradigm in the service of decolonization.

In the Andean highlands, gender complementarity and the philosophy of duality mutually inform each other. Duality pervades not only human individuals but also the entire lifeworld, including features of the landscape, the spatial location of fields, and agricultural produce.[9] As Tata Anselmo's intervention in *Qati qati* makes clear, Valentina's mode of knowing and Andean philosophy are both intimately linked to the presence of otherworldly forces embodied in mountains, lakes, mummies, etc. Landscape features are also gendered—rounded hills and lakes are considered female and mountain peaks and rivers are male. Similarly, depending on the shape and number of eyes, potatoes may be male or female. Corresponding to the complex ordering of space in terms of female and male attributes, Aymara and Quechua subjectivity itself is understood as the result of interacting male and female elements, as well as other factors. Community members will define gender differences primarily according to the different but complementary responsibilities that men and women assume (Canessa 236).

Gender complementarity acquires paradigmatic value as it comes to stand for the possible coexistence of different orders of knowledge in indigenous media activism. *Qati qati*'s dual cinematic gaze affirms the value of such coexistence. It claims that Aymara gender relations are based on complementarity, and this gender complementarity sustains the possibility of having a Western worldview and an Aymara order of understanding coexist on equal terms. This approach is not unique to indigenous video. Complementarity has been the paradigm for other forms of decolonizing knowledge as well, such as in the structural layout of the Indigenous Universidad Intercultural in Quito. Instead of one order subalternizing or displacing the other, its programs strive to create the conditions for the coexistence of indigenous forms and modes of knowing and Western science (Lozano, "Síntesis" 51; Walsh, "(Re)articulation" 85–87). Moreover, the appeal to gender complementarity has historical precursors.

When Aymara intellectuals such as Fausto Reinaga and his son Ramiro Reynaga (the different spellings of the last name are intentional) began challenging racial politics in the Andes in the 1960s, they invoked gender complementarity as a defining element that distinguishes indigenous from Western societies. Without reflecting on their own misogynist discourse (cf. Stevenson, "Uso" 158–59), these thinkers reversed the feminization of the colonized subject in an effort to render the West morally abject.[10] For Reinaga and his son, Western culture is dominated by patriarchy, while Aymara gender relations are more just (Reinaga, *América* 129; Reynaga 89–90). Ramiro Reynaga explains that colonization is alive in its construction of unequal gender roles and images (89–90). Male/female complementarity, in contrast, emerges as the defining trait of indigenous highland culture. These indianists underscore that couples led the Quechua/Aymara rebellion of 1781, before Bolivia and Peru became separate and independent nations: Tupac Katari and Bartolina Sisa in the highlands around La Paz; Tupac Amaru and Micaela Bastida in Cuzco. The Peruvian indianist Guillermo Carnero Hoke similarly invokes an idealized precolonial past where "men and women were morally obligated to intervene and participate in debates from the same hierarchical positions and without any kind of discrimination or *machismo*" (116). At the same time, he affirms that being the father of the family entailed fulfilling a representative role. Carnero Hoke casts political representation as a male responsibility while affirming that women have full participation in the decision-making process. If there is a contradiction here, this past utopia is not questioned any further. Carnero Hoke furthermore asserts that the equality of the sexes is guaranteed by language structure, since Quechua has no gendered pronouns, articles, or suffixes: "The same endings and pronouns were used for both genders thus indicating that men and women were considered equal" (117). Another indianist, Virgilio Roel Pineda, suggests that due to the poverty of the Spanish language, in contrast, it lacks a term that would at once express the nucleus of Quechua wisdom as an outcome of paternal and maternal functions, instead obliging speakers to specify or use the male term as an inclusive (133).

More recently, in the late 1980s, the populist Bolivian politician Carlos Palenque enacted gender duality for a constituency of migrants in the urban center of La Paz (Archondo 139). The Aymara leader Felipe Quispe is sure to invoke his wife as enabling his political struggle (Quispe 15), just as Luciano Tapia does on several occasions in his autobiography.[11] The concept of complementarity continues to be productive for pan-indigenous cultural politics because it transcends the highlands context. For the Shuar in the Ecuadorian Amazon, gender complementarity is grounded in social and symbolic divisions (Mader 40); for the Nasa (Paéz) Indians in Colombia the gendered division of labor renders male and female contributions to sustaining life equally dependent on each other (Nachtigall 205–6).[12] Today, gender complementarity sets the ground for indigenous intercultural relations but also for envisioning epistemic and social relations with the West that are based on equal value and status.[13]

Yet gender relations in indigenous communities are a controversial topic. The representation of complementary gender relations in *Qati qati* contrasts with the criticism that some indigenous women have leveled against their communities. For the Aymara historian and former director of the THOA, María Eugenia Choque Quispe, gender complementarity is an ideal that the colonial experience itself has compromised (12). Choque Quispe invokes the image of the colonizers as those who, "obsessed with gold and silver, raped, kidnapped, and defiled, bringing dishonor to Indian women" (12). She asserts that "the imposition of colonial order meant the institutionalization not only of the irrational exploitation of the people and resources of this continent but also of gender relations between indigenous women, indigenous men, and the Spanish, marking them with conflict and violence" (12). Gender complementarity since then has therefore not necessarily meant equality or equal value. Basing herself on Palma Milagro's work, Choque Quispe adds that "the declining indigenous population and the appearance of castes (in colonial times) transformed the indigenous woman into a commodity whose value hinged on her reproductive abilities as the primary resource for a new identity; for Indian males the possession and control of the Indian woman acquired dramatic significance. The creation of a new prevailing order prompted indigenous thought to make women responsible for their suffering and problems" (12). Choque Quispe's critique may idealize precolonial gender complementarity, but her emphasis lies on a dual transformation: Woman's body becomes a means of anticolonial resistance where her value lies in biological reproduction. Yet, as the bearer of an identity despised by the colonial order, she is also negatively made responsible for indigenous suffering. Rivera Cusicanqui insists that ethnic organizations cover up issues related to women's social presence ("Desafíos" 18) and agrees with Choque Quispe that the pressure of internal colonialism has created gender inequality. For Rivera the increasing separation between gendered private and public spheres, where women are identified with the preservation of indigenous culture and tradition and excluded from political representation, results from internal colonialism in rural areas (51). Among the urban lower classes, "indigenous migrant women are applauded for working in a great variety of self-employed jobs where they maintain their autonomy" (52). In the dominant *misti-criollo*

society, in contrast, women favor occupational roles that go hand in hand with the modern construction of femininity as a kind of social maternity such as schoolteachers, nurses, and domestic servants.[14]

The participation of women as communicators in the National Indigenous Plan for Audiovisual Communication in Bolivia, in the CONAIE's communication department, or as independent video makers in Colombia conflicts with the idealized vision of women as community-bound caretakers of culture and social memory that is projected on screen. Women's participation in indigenous political movements and in the process of audiovisual communication contradicts precisely the "traditionalness" of indigenous gender roles that would have them remain closer to home, fields, and children. According to the transculturated indigenous social order that has evolved from the contact between a colonial history and indigenous communities and their gender philosophy, as well as from the still-dominant nineteenth-century Western ideal in *mestizo* society, opting to be active in political organizations or in video making contradicts traditional notions of women's roles and responsibilities unless this activity is explicitly framed as "helping" men and of a temporary nature.[15] Julia Mosúa (Trinitario-Moxeña), Marcelina Cárdenas (Quechua from Potosí), Regina Monasterios (Guarani), Ofelia Condori (Aymara), Aideé Alvarez (Quechua from the Chapare), Carmen Vintonás (Nasa), and Lucila Lema (Quichua) are taking advantage of this tension. When indigenous media vindicate an indigenous tradition deeply associated with femininity, they open up a crack from which to argue for change. Joined by many in the production crew and in the communities, these activists see a need to redress inequality within their communities. In addition, international concern for women's rights enables indigenous video makers and their collaborators to garner support for women's participation and for treating the issue of gender in the videos.

When the THOA (Aymara Oral History Workshop) began recovering the subalternized memory of Aymara political struggles, their interviews highlighted the protagonism of men's resistance to the colonial regime. Women themselves defined their roles as supportive of male struggle and as acting mostly in the background (Rivera Cusicanqui et al., *La mujer andina*). The same can be said about women's current self-perception in the indigenous organizations of the lowlands (cf. Rivera Cusicanqui, "Desafíos" 56–64; Lehm and CIDDEBENI, "Saber"). Even in those indigenous videos directed by women, complementarity remains the overarching paradigm. CONAIE's documentaries on medical practices, *Woman, Wisdom, and Power* and *Between Spirits and Humans* (*Entre los espíritus y los hombres*), claim a high status for women shamans, whose knowledge is cast as complementary to that of men. The Bolivian short *Mother Earth*, and most explicitly, perhaps, Julia Mosúa's *Ethnicity and Gender in the Moxos Plains* (*Etnicidad y género en los llanos de Moxos*), revalue the importance of women's labor and participation in anticolonial struggle on the base of it being just as important as that of men. Carmen Vitonás's interview of her grandmother highlights the value of transmitting knowledge along female lines in the two-part docudrama *Seed and Memory: Nasa Weaving* (I), *We Spin and Weave, Giving Life to the Universe* (II). The documentary complements the representation of a male genealogy of knowledge transmission in films produced by the CRIC, such as *The Nasa Garden*. In CEFREC-CAIB's videos, viewers glimpse the problem of violence, such as in *Vest Made of Money*, where the avaricious husband physically threatens his wife. More recently, *Overcoming Fear* overtly addresses this problem, reflecting an ongoing discussion among the production crew and in the communities where the urgency to interrogate gender power relations has become ever-more pressing in recent years (cf. CEFREC, "Communication" n.p.). Issues such as rape, violence against women, or spatial confinement, however, have not been at the center of indigenous videos, and the fate of lesbian, gay, or bisexual people continues to remain entirely outside the frame.

Much has been written about political representation and contact with the outside lying in the hands of indigenous men. Women have been seen as, at best, indirectly exerting influence on political processes (Ticona Alejo 132). Both low- and highland cultures have been characterized as patriarchal and even misogynist.[16] Just like reciprocity, complementarity does not necessarily exclude hierarchy and usually places men above women (Canessa 239–41). Complementarity can be used to justify a hierarchical order, but it can also be used to claim equal social and political power and influence, including the power to produce intellectual and cultural representations. Enacting indigenous tradition in gendered ways addresses the coloniality of power's collusion of racial and gender constructs in a creative though not unproblematic way. On the one hand, as Madhu Dubey suggested for the postcolonial resolution of nation building, "decolonizing nationalist discourses summon the metaphorical figure of 'woman' to resolve the inescapable contradiction of their project, which is to lay claim to post-Enlightenment European categories of progress and modernity, while reviving pre-colonial traditions to safeguard the nation's cultural difference from the West" (Dubey 2). The media activists organized in CAIB, CONAIE, and the CRIC are reshaping the devaluation of indigenous culture and identity that is bound by the constructs of gender and race. Their claims to European categories of liberal democracy are limited, but they do engage with the global currency of multiculturalism, human rights, environment, and women's rights. Yet casting women as the guardians of indigenous traditions and as a resource for thinking an alternative modernity runs the risk of leaving the gender imaginary underlying the coloniality of power unchallenged. Male indigenous leaders could be seen as reaffirming male dominance and as placing themselves in charge of elaborating from the raw material of feminized culture.

The award-winning docufiction *Our Word* (*Nuestra palabra: La historia de San Francisco de Moxos*) from the Moxos region in Bolivia's eastern tropical lowlands, for instance, highlights the value of oral history transmitted by women elders, yet their stories cannot stand on their own.[17] In this video, directed by Julia Mosúa, three female elders tell the story of the town San Francisco de Moxos in their native language. Their narrative is crosscut with the communities' dramatized reenactments in front of the camera. Oral history structures the seven different episodes, including the mythical migration in search of the *Loma Santa* (sacred hillside), the founding of the village, the arrival of colonizing forces (ranchers), their abuses, and the resistance of the Moxeño community. The women storytellers conclude on a positive note, stressing that the indigenous people have continued to organize themselves despite their oppression by white ranchers. As one of the women closes the door to the church—and to history—the image cuts to a symbol of the future: a shot of children playing. If the narrative appears to establish a female genealogy of knowledge transmission, its final sequence gives way to a relatively young man who confirms the historical antecedents of the indigenous *cabildo*. In a rational mode that contrasts with the women's mythical narrative, he outlines dates and the ongoing effort to recover the land. Political representation in this video is in the hands of men, exemplified by this switch in narrator and narrative mode. The dramatic reenactment gives way to the talking head. The young man explains that women are fundamental and necessary in helping the *cabildo* and its suborganizations. Shots of women as caretakers of children, harvesting food, and other activities illustrate this "helping." Similar to the images in *Qati qati* and in *Ethnicity and Gender in the Moxos Plains*, *Our Word*'s final shots are meant to counter the devaluation of women's labor as insignificant "helping" or "doing things" instead of "real work."[18] Women perform social memory and its oral transmission but also a gendered division of labor where women are defined by their responsibility for preparing food, raising children, and maintaining the indigenous language. Complementarity here runs the risk of ultimately privileging the male-embodied rational mode, since the film ends with male talking heads affirming the validity of women's social memory.

Melodrama's Subversive Potential

In the videos made by CEFREC-CAIB, CONAIE, and the CRIC, the prevailing approach has been to claim the equal value of female labor. Since 2001 CEFREC-CAIB has also begun producing fiction shorts with a more overt critique. According to Marcelina Cárdenas, who is responsible for the fifty-minute Loving Each Other in the Shadows, this video is meant to address the rift in her community caused by the tensions between Catholics and a rising number of families who have converted to Protestantism.[19] Yet this video more obviously scrutinizes a Quechua patriarchal order and its tradition of arranged marriages. The video makers of CEFREC-CAIB here take an approach that is almost opposed to that of Qati qati and Our Word, both in argument and genre. Loving Each Other in the Shadows is a melodramatic love story with an eroticized protagonist. It could be seen as classic example of the male cinematic gaze. Like other melodramas it nevertheless exploits the openings created by melodrama's emotional excess. The video's take on gender and the order of knowledge points more radically than Qati qati to the way that the nayrapacha of indigenous cultural politics involves a critical debate and process of renewal rather than a mere return to an idealized past.

Loving Each Other in the Shadows deploys its melodramatic elements in order to give weight to a female protagonist. In what begins like a version of Romeo and Juliette, a young woman from an economically privileged protestant family resists the marriage arranged by her parents with a member of another wealthy family of the community.[20] Together with her lover, who is from a poorer background, Rosita (Aidée Alvarez) flees on a bicycle and both end up hiding in a cave. When Rosita returns to her parents' house to collect a few belongings, her father unwittingly kills her, thinking she is a robber. She rejoins her lover and continues to haunt him, even when he realizes, with the help of the local yatiri (a healer and wise man who reads coca leaves) that she is indeed a ghost. In the last scene, Juancito (Samuel Vedia Callamullo), disregarding the *yatiri*'s advice, takes the hand of Rosita's ghost and releases her in the form a bird. She soars toward the sunlit sky from the waters that separate the living from the dead. He survives and is free to return to the community. Rosita pays for her transgression with her life, but the video shares the love story's optimism, since her death and love for Juancito set both of them free. This moment of release is the allegorical key to overcoming the divisions that haunt the community where the video is filmed. It is at once the moment where male agency is restored.

Melodrama has certainly been one of Hollywood's most powerful cinematic forms and it is at the center of feminist film criticism. The genre, however, is not simply an ideological tool of existing power. Rather, it "always addresses questions of individual (gendered) identity within patriarchal culture," as Ana López described melodrama's subversive potential ("Tears" 150). In addition, melodrama reflects on moments of crisis that are opportunities for change. It is indeed "a fictional system for making sense of experience as a semantic field of force" that "comes into being in a world where the traditional imperatives of truth and ethics have been violently thrown into question."[21] It appears an appropriate genre for the process of decolonization. If *Loving Each Other in the Shadows* represents the generational conflict where young couples are resisting the marital plotting of their mothers and fathers, Rosita's death does not merely mark her as a victim of tragic circumstances. Rather, she embodies female agency and a desire to interrogate the confines of patriarchal rule.

The last scene resonates deeply with several scenes of breaking free that structure the video. In a moment of foreshadowing, for instance, Rosita is allowed to engage in the traditional highland pasturing, despite her mother's well-founded anxieties about the sexual liberties that pasturing enables. The camera frames the narrow doorway where the families' sheep are pushing and shoving through, coming toward the camera, and sweeping the viewer along. The shots of the sheep intensify the viewer's affective identification with Rosita, thus amplifying melodrama's subversive potential, where even when melodrama's "narrative work suggests utter complicity with the work of the law, the emotional excesses set loose and the multiple desires detonated are not easily recuperated" ("Tears" 153). The interior shots of the house and courtyard, of Rosita's bedroom, and Juancito's family dwelling contrast powerfully with this scene of liberation. The sheep's eager need to break free of their confinement speaks to the young protagonist's less visible yet ardent desire to free herself of parental constraints and instead connect with the land (*Pachamama*), which is rendered through dramatic wide-angle takes of the Andean highlands and whose impact is only restricted by the visual shortcomings of digital video.

Although Rosita diegetically embodies the erotic object of male desire, this film opens up space to address gender relations as well as the links between tradition and the female body. In de la Cadena's research on gender and ethnicity in Chitapampa, Peru, fleeing the community and becoming part of the urban society becomes the younger generation's privileged solution to constricting marital traditions ("Mujeres"; "Matrimonio"). *Loving Each Other in the Shadows*, in contrast, takes a more critical stance toward Western modernity. Rosita's protestant parents are criticized when Rosita refuses to marry the indigenous *mestizo*. (César León sports a shoulder-length haircut, a sign of having spent time in the city.) If César has become more like a "*mestizo*," according to de la Cadena's intricate analysis of the interrelations of gender and ethnicity in the power structures of Chitapampa ("Mujeres"; "Matrimonio"), his Roman imperial name invokes patriarchal power and social status and so does his Spanish surname (that renders the common Quechua surname Poma into Spanish). Rosita's choice to marry Juancito instead of César León implies not only a desire to follow her emotions but also a more equitable relationship. As de la Cadena explained, in a society where power relations are structured by ethnicity and gender, if a more "*mestiza*" (more wealthy, more educated) woman marries "down" (a more "indigenous" man) she is in a better position to negotiate power and freedom of movement in the relationship with her husband and his family than if she marries "up" or "horizontally" ("Matrimonio" 128–33). Within both orders— "western-Christian-colonial" or "indigenous"—Rosita is better off living with Juancito, the "Indian," than with César, the "*mestizo*."

Rosita's choice is both pragmatic and supportive of those indianists who (like Choque Quispe and Silvia Rivera Cusicanqui) claim the urgent need to rid indigenous order of patriarchy. Yet Rosita does not immigrate to the city; instead, her flight takes her and Juancito to a cave where the couple is symbolically reborn and their relationship set on female grounds.[22] The indigenous order of knowledge in this film is again, like in *Qati qati*, referenced through spectral figures and dreams. In *Loving Each Other in the Shadows*, Rosita is the protagonist of the narrative and at the center of the camera's look. This time the dreams are those of the female protagonist. In the first one Rosita and Juancito share visions of walking together on water as the camera cuts back and forth between their sleeping faces. The dream's symbolism announces to both that a death is pending.[23] This black-and-white scene is repeated similarly in a second dream that shifts the narrative perspective fully to Rosita; from now on the dream scenes are only crosscut to her. Her last dream already casts the young woman as a ghost, jealously witnessing how Juancito and Rosita's best friend dance together after her death. The point-of-view shots here emphasize the narrative construction of Rosita as protagonist. The jealousy that the dream awakens propels the dramatic action, where Rosita commits to her feelings and decides to flee her parents' home and authority. Yet like the male protagonists in *Qati qati*, *Cursed Gold*, and *Vest Made of Money*, Rosita does not heed the dream's warning. When *Loving Each Other in the Shadows* frames female agency it thus unties epistemic regimes from their gendered embodiment. Rosita is no more knowledgeable in the meaning of dreams than Fulo in *Qati qati*. Like Satuco and Cihualcollo in *Vest Made of Money*, she defies the existing social order and ethos. Symbols of modernity (pen, paper, and the bicycle) become her tools of liberation.

The emotions set free through the melodramatic love story place us as spectators closely by her side. We wish the lovers to unite and are struck by her death. If Rosita fails to abide by the rules of the village, there is no moral reinforcement of these rules. Unlike in *Qati qati*, where we feel compelled to support the traditions of community life and ethos, here these arguably more recent traditions appear deeply unjust for her and the audience. On the other hand, the ancient order of knowledge embodied by the yatiri's reading of coca leaves is also lacking.

Rosita's wake provides the key sequence symbolically representing this doubt toward both tradition and modernity. The mirror images cut back and forth between two dimly lit scenes. In one, Rosita's body appears surrounded by candles in her father's home; in the other, she lies, in almost identical position, as if pinned down by candles, in the yatiri's courtyard. The sequence constructs a patriarchal complicity between the Christian wake and the *yatiri's*, as both seem to trap not only her corps but also the young woman's spirit in identical ways. The *yatiri*, who comes close to understanding the danger of the ghost, ultimately fails. His predictions all come true, except for one. Instead of drawing Juancito into death, Rosita achieves her freedom without killing Juancito. Since Rosita ultimately escapes the *yatiri's* comprehension, his power is questioned, not by Western rationality but by the couple's strong trust of each other. In other words, the video does not prove the *yatiri* entirely wrong and neither does it disavow the existence of ghosts and the relevance of dreams. Rather, the critique of social order goes both ways. Both modern patriarchy and Quechua tradition call for reform. *Loving Each Other in the Shadows* thus does not confront the subjects of colonial relations (the colonizers) but their religious and epistemic regimes, themselves devoid of any purity. Evangelists, Catholics, and the Quechua *yatiri* are all proven at least partially mistaken.

All traditions need to be analyzed as to whether they "promote love," says Marcelina Cárdenas, the video maker responsible for this film.[24] Community cohesion and nonviolent conflict resolution rather than oppression, division, and death are the ethical goals that *Loving Each Other in the Shadows* promotes. Indigenous communities are not the abysmal sites of female oppression that needs to be left behind through urban migration. This is the primary choice of the younger Quechua generation in de la Cadena's analysis ("Matrimonio"). The emotional turmoil that Rosita's death causes her family, lover, and the viewers calls on an ethos of mutual care and trust as the key to reuniting a divided community. A utopian ideal, perhaps, that nevertheless appeals to the social ethos underlying *ayllu* solidarity. Gender relations are a key problem that needs to be addressed in strengthening such values. The valorization of indigenous culture and knowledge goes hand in hand with an interrogation of how these relations themselves have morphed since the conquest and how they might be imagined more adequately for the present.

Loving Each Other in the Shadows follows melodramatic convention when the film restores male agency and integrates transgression into the law. Juancito ultimately has the power over Rosita's destiny and that of the community: to turn her into a walking ghost that will haunt the village (as happens in *Vest Made of Money*) or to set her free. If Quechua knowledge is criticized, it is also vindicated together with indigenous male authority. Rosita's freedom is only possible in death. Restoring male agency at the end of this video balances out the way the film foregrounds female agency directed against a patriarchal order, which, as the video emphasizes, is upheld with the key participation of women like Rosita's mother.[25] As Rosita claims the right to emotion, sexuality, and self-determination, *Loving Each Other in the Shadows* certainly resonates with the feelings of many of the young indigenous people in the highlands and beyond. Since the video is circulated through CAIB's network, perhaps it even calls upon the greater power and freedom of indigenous women in the Yungas and other lower elevation regions of indigenous migration from the highlands, like the Alto Beni (cf. Spedding, "Esa mujer"). Although *Loving Each Other in the Shadows* is about female self-determination and the critique of existing social orders, its classic melodramatic resolution appeals again, like the other videos by indigenous video makers in Bolivia, Ecuador, and Colombia, to gender complementarity.[26]

In 2004 the indigenous video maker Maria Morales proposed a script that overtly criticizes gender inequality. *Overcoming Fear* is set in the Yungas, the subtropical valleys north of La Paz that have been a prime destination for Aymara migrants since the Bolivian Revolution and partial land reform in the 1950s. The video tells the story of a family's move from the highlands to the valleys and the couple's arduous labor in clearing their plot. When the husband abandons his wife in the middle of their efforts to go live in the city, he hispanicizes his Aymara surname, changing Quispe into Quisbert. His wife, in contrast, remains on the land. She establishes close relations with the community there and becomes an outspoken leader—motivating her neighbors to resist their exploitation by middlemen and instead organize to sell their agricultural produce directly in the cities. She also argues for women's equal rights within the family and their right to land tenure. When her husband returns to claim the land and his children he is ousted. Against his insistence that he holds the title and she has no rights, the community asserts that, by consensus, the laws have changed. Even the overtly critical *Overcoming Fear*, however, couches the vindication of women's rights in the principle of complementarity—"women are as important as men and they need to have the same rights," says the protagonist in the film. The community's economic and social progress is based on their coming together—literally—in meetings where consensus or at least majorities are built.[27] Again the film is shot with the familiar stable frame, the scenes and shots edited with continuity, and the story told chronologically. The protagonist is a talented actress who, like Aidée Alvarez, is attractive, though not explicitly cast as an erotic object. Like *Loving Each Other in the Shadows*, *Overcoming Fear* ultimately advocates community solidarity, here taking complementarity at its word and explicitly stating that traditions need to be transformed.

The film takes place in newly founded community, characterized by the transformations and destabilizing effects that migration can entail. It is perhaps no surprise that the video makers can explore gender equality in this setting and not in one of the more traditional villages seen in *Qati qati* or even *Loving Each Other in the Shadows*. Yet one might ask, why is there not a more radical solution to addressing gender relations in indigenous communities? Why not experiment more with cinematic form? *Loving Each Other in the Shadows* and *Overcoming Fear* are certainly no more experimental than other indigenous video fictions. Why is there is no explicit undermining of the "conventional voyeurism and sadism of the male spectator's relation to the woman on the screen" (Penley 6)?

The answer may lie in part with the need to satisfy the audience's desire for narrative pleasure. Another possible reason is that since these videos are products of a collaborative process, decisions are made together with the other male members of the production group and the communities themselves. Such an answer implies, however, that if women could choose they would represent gender relations differently. Yet, as we have seen, most other films signed by women are even less overtly critical of indigenous patriarchy than *Loving Each Other in the Shadows* and *Overcoming Fear*. Rather, it may be necessary to understand the strategy of emphasizing complementarity as a response to the logic of coloniality. Films like *Loving Each Other in the Shadows* and *Overcoming Fear* frame the gender problem as part of a larger need to deal with divisions. Racism and class differences create structures of discrimination and privilege among women. Indigenous women face discrimination by a colonial society not as women but as indigenous women. The colonial gaze integrates patriarchal and colonial viewing habits and constructs indigenous women not only as objects of the male gaze but also as objects of an imperial patriarchal eye. Solving oppressive gender relations thus becomes a joint task, one that needs to be confronted by men and women together. Race and gender are inseparable, and women do not confront only sexism or only racism. Reforming gender relations requires cultural change, a collaborative project of women and men against patriarchy and colonialism and not a struggle against men. In this sense, gender relations are conceptualized principally as a cultural form and not primarily as the result of political structures that require a unified political subject voicing demands. Indigenous videos suggest that changes in gender relations cannot be solved according to an analysis that reduces feminism to the struggle against a universally defined patriarchy.

Relationships among women have been fractured by class interests, racial prejudices and privileges and, at times, the same theoretical arrogance that informs the geopolitics of knowledge at large (Mohanty).[28] These differences cannot be reduced to multicultural diversity. Especially when indigenous communities represent themselves to the outside—an outside that is constituted primarily of other indigenous and peasant communities but also of the wider audience these films encounter at festivals—the production crew chooses to emphasize the collaborative nature of transformation. The structure of coloniality compels an identification that cannot place either racism or sexism as the priority. The Zapatista uprising in Mexico includes the vindication of women's rights, and it claims the right to equality in difference. These demands "interpellate the indigenous communities, asserting the need to change customs and modify tradition in those cases where tradition and custom also mean domination, segregation, inequality, and abuse (Millán "Zapatistas" 4).[29] The bills drafted by the Ejército Zapatista de Liberación Nacional (EZLN) do not resolve gender issues but confirm the need to address them concurrently with the economic and political problems that the Mayan peoples face. Indigenous media activists in the Andean-Amazonian region similarly open up a space for addressing the question of knowledge and a range of social, economic, and, environmental issues, along with race and gender.

Representations of gender complementarity and women's participation in the process of video production create new opportunities for the reinvention of indigenous gender relations and knowledges as an alternative to Western modernity/coloniality. Just like women's participation in political organizations, indigenous video production requires reorganizing at least some of the gendered divisions of labor. Complementarity can become an open category that is severed from social roles and bodily functions, or it can reinscribe gender role prescriptions. In other words, the concept allows for a flexible interpretation of indigenous identity where traditions themselves are interrogated as to their desirability. Rooted in the principle of complementarity, the collaborative decision-making process, collective audience reception, and the enactments of gender relations and embodied knowledge on screen signal the rescue of indigenous culture as a process under negotiation. It requires transformation rather than a return to the past. Indigenous culture, knowledge, and tradition thus come into view as profoundly dynamic.

Beyond Complementarity

Social memory and subalternized knowledge is embodied and transmitted in gendered ways, but the enactment and representation of such links between knowledge and the female body has been a central point of debate for indigenous movements in Latin America and beyond. Partha Chatterjee asked whether decolonization must not "include within it a struggle against the false essentialism of home/world, spiritual/material, feminine/masculine propagated by nationalist ideology" (252). In part due to the philosophical importance of duality in the Andes, indigenous media in this region avoid interrogating the male/female binary itself. Certainly gender does not refer only to women. It is a construct that pertains to the ideas we hold about masculinity and femininity, about appropriate roles and about power relations. Gender is a historical and social category that is continuously enacted, albeit under the constraints of existing norms and imaginaries that differ across "geopolitical boundaries and cultural constraints on who is imagining whom, and for what purpose" (Butler 10).

Restricting gender identity to a binary option—male or female—is itself a product of history. Early European modernity, the era of conquest, for instance, was a time when Europe sought to fix a fourfold and more dynamic notion of gender and sexuality into the dichotomy of man and woman. George Mariscal argues that "virtually all forms of subjectivity in this period depended on different degrees and kinds of 'maleness' rather than on the historically more recent male/female binomial" (27). Not only gender—sociohistorically constructed and enacted ideas and roles—but biological sex itself was seen as dynamic and subject to change according to levels of body heat and humidity (Jones and Stallybrass 84). During the conquest, references to ambiguous gender roles and sexuality were abundant in colonial texts. Chronicles of Spanish and British expeditions (such as Gáspar de Carvajal's voyage down the Amazon or Sir Walter Raleigh's explorations of the Amazon delta) tell of encounters with indigenous peoples and betray the Renaissance anxiety about gender indeterminacy as the conquerors saw themselves battling monsters and virile women.[30] Before the influence of Christianity, Andean cultures similarly seem to have held the idea of a third gender, a central mediating force that was subalternized with the growing emphasis on gender duality during the colonial period. Based on a detailed analysis of different kinds of colonial texts (written, drawn, woven, and orally transmitted), Michael Horswell argues that Andean duality embraced the notion of a third space—that is, the ritual enactment of third gender ("Towards" 50–56; Decolonizing). The notion of Andean gender duality that informs the principle of complementarity in indigenous discourse is derived from the male/female dichotomy, but it may itself be a result of colonial discourse.

The question of gender, furthermore, is not limited to social roles. Even biological sex is more ambiguous and fluid than it seems. Today in the United States and elsewhere medical practices have changed the sexual morphology of newborns, at times without the consent of parents, in order to assure an anatomical correspondence between bodies and the sexual binary. The intersex movement in the United States has been drawing increasing attention to this practice.[31] Hormone treatments and therapies accompany surgical procedures that correct undesired ambiguity: "Until very recently, the specter of intersexuality has spurred us to police bodies of indeterminate sex. Rather than force us to admit the social nature of our ideas about sexual difference, our ever more sophisticated medical technology has allowed us, by its attempts to render such bodies male or female, to insist that people are either naturally male or female. Such insistence occurs even though intersexual births occur with remarkably high frequency and may be on the increase" (Fausto Sterling 54). Transgendered people take advantage of medical technology to overcome the painful disjuncture between their physical appearance and their gender identification. Sexual orientation itself is dynamic and can change over a lifetime, as Fausto Sterling's book argues.

The radical transgression of traditional gender roles and concepts (in both Western and indigenous systems of gender and sexuality) constitutes an important threshold that is yet to be considered by indigenous media in Bolivia, Ecuador, and Colombia. So far these discussions still shatter against a powerful taboo. CEFREC-CAIB's fiction videos frame men and women acting according to heterosexual gender stereotypes. In *Cursed Gold*, Juana makes up the bed, trades coca leafs on the village market, and sings in the *chichería* when encouraged to. The male protagonist Tito is an adventurer in quest of easy riches, and he stays out drinking all night. In *Vest Made of Money*, Satuco's wife spins wool and is in charge of the smaller animals while Satuco is a political authority, a post he is able to occupy because he is married, as he explains to his antagonist Cihualcollo. All videos enact a social system anchored in heterosexual couples. Only the lowland Moxos production *The Forest Spirit* destablizes, briefly and perhaps unintentionally, the notion of gender duality so prevalent in the highlands.

The story enacted on screen is based on a legend from Riberalta in the Bolivian lowlands. Two brothers who enter the forest in order to cut wood represent the central conflict. They confront the spiritual power of nature symbolized by a magical jaguar. The viewers only hear the growls of the animal off screen; when the spirit becomes embodied it appears to the young men as a woman, clothed, according to the classical codes of Hollywood cinema, in seductive, campy red. She is a tempting but dangerous force who sanctions the failure to believe in and respect the forest spirit with death. Again, it is not primarily the specifics of a particular forest legend that are at stake here but rather an indigenous ethical order. *The Forest Spirit* invokes respectful relations between humans and a feminized and powerful nature that provides for human life. While the older brother ridicules the "superstitious" beliefs of the younger, Julián (Henry Arredondo) warns his sibling not to disrespect the forests spirits. Julián thus embodies Moxeño culture and its regime of knowledge. His gender role is ambiguous. He assumes female-identified tasks (such as cooking), and the relation between the two men shifts between spousal, fraternal, and filial dynamics. This is the moment where the film opens up to the possibility of thinking third gender, a mediating presence (cf. Horswell, *Decolonizing*), but also a radical recuperation of gender roles that do not fall into the philosophy of duality. Ultimately, however, the video makers have Julian respond like his brother to female seduction, thus dispelling any further interrogation of male/female duality. Just as in *Qati qati*, the oedipal narrative underlying character distribution and plot line is splintered when both brothers die and the film fades out with shots of the jungle where female-identified nature prevails.

A similar destabilization of the gender binary, which is equally fixed at the very moment it appears, emerges in a bilingual book by the Quichua writer Luz María De la Torre Amaguaña from Ecuador. De la Torre Amaguaña highlights the value of female specific labor and the way Quichua cosmovision casts male and female as equally important. The myth of creation that de la Torre Amaguaña narrates attributes values to the sexes that partially correspond to Western Christian stereotypes, such as passivity and concrete thinking for women and the quest for what is beyond the mundane for men (13–19). But the author affirms the ideal of male-female complementarity rather than the male dominance inscribed by the Christian genesis. De la Torre Amaguaña supports her argument by citing a *yachac* (a Quichua elder). The *yachac* confirms the duality of gender as the two sides of the human spirit, where neither shall dominate the other: "both are like the sides of a leaf, a universe, that is created out of oppositional forces but that mutually hold each other in place" (13). Both men and women themselves embody duality (both have masculine and feminine parts), the *yachac* states, but "nobody can usually work on both sides of the page simultaneously" (13). De la Torre Amaguaña comes back to this doubling, arguing that "the inner part of the man is a man-woman and the inner part of the woman a woman-man. These parts make up a union leaving what is on the outside to act independently" (20). This doubling corresponds to the fourfold nature of duality that is based on the four cardinal points and that corresponds to the Inca Empire's spatial division.

What happens, then, if gender roles change? Although de la Torre Amaguaña opens up the possibility of thinking gender beyond the male-female dichotomy, she ultimately prescribes exclusive gender roles for men and women, essentializing woman as "the master of history. She is the master of presence, which has its roots in her body and which sprouts from within her, nourishing itself from the best and most sensitive part of her soul. Woman, mother, permanence and continuity, this is the great vital continuum of the *feminine cosmos in Andean understanding*" (36). Man in turn is the abstract thinker and seeker of truths and knowledge beyond the community. The roles correspond to those prescribed in the European Enlightenment, where woman was cast as the educator of the citizen and its emotional safe haven. Such an essentialized social inscription ties women and men firmly back into prescriptive and binary identities.

Gay, lesbian, and transgendered people do not enter the frame of indigenous discourse in the Andean-Amazonian region. Elsewhere some indigenous activists and artists openly identify as queer, such as the painter and video maker Kent Monkmoth in Ontario, Canada. The documentary *Blossoms of Fire*, made by the San Francisco resident Maureen Gosling, explores gender relations, including gay and transgender subjectivity among Zapotec Indians in Juchitán, Mexico. Yet even in these contexts queer subjectivity and indigenous activism is often fraught with difficulty, conflict, and denial. For the Andean region there are few studies dedicated to queer theory and subjectivity, whether in indigenous communities or urban centers.[32] The Andean-Amazonian audiovisual network continues to avoid the question of how and whether to incorporate women like Doña Marta Garay, who consciously reverted back to *chola* dress codes (she wears the *pollera* after having taken up Western dress for some time), drives a full-size truck (a traditionally male occupation for indigenous people, just like it continues to be in the West), and chooses to live as an urban migrant, not only because she is economically successful, but also because it allows her a life of independence from women's traditional responsibilities (Criales Burgos 62–65).

What might overstepping this threshold mean for the paradigm of gender complementarity? If videos such as *Loving Each Other in the Shadows* and *Overcoming Fear* question gender relations while maintaining the paradigm of complementarity, they also point to a dynamic understanding of indigenous culture, a sociocultural order in constant transformation and renovation. Considering what exceeds the idea of gender duality might only radicalize and democratize this process further and with it the transformations of the lettered city's patriarchal colonial gaze.

5

NATURE, INDIANS,
AND EPISTEMIC PRIVILEGE

*documentaries as key in the
construction of the colonial gaze*

As a film form, documentary is closely linked to the lettered city's production of knowledge. It can provide information about the sociohistorical world or become part of scientific research that is made public and directed at an audience of nonexperts. Ethnographic documentaries derive their power to define what is in front of the lens from this contextual inscription of the documentary form into the realm of news and pedagogy. Yet, like fiction films, the documentary has been instrumental to the construction of the colonial gaze. It tends to enthrall and convince its audience because it is armed with what Bill Nichols calls a "discourse of sobriety" (Nichols, *Representing Reality* 9), a scientific gaze that is assumed to be value-free.[1]

*discourse
of
sobriety*

Keith Beattie argues that Australian Aborigines have creatively adapted documentary and television's stylistic conventions as a means of talking back to the colonial gaze. Through parody, self-reflexivity, avant-gardist aesthetics that mix realism and antirealism, as well as poetic address, aboriginal filmmakers have at once made use of and undermined the documentary's truth claims.[2] Directed by the founder of Video in the Villages Vincent Carelli, the documentary *Video in the Villages Presents Itself* (*Video nas aldeias se apresenta*) reflexively and humorously addresses the relationship between indigenous video makers and the camera. In the Andean highlands, the Ukamau Group's docudramas from the 1960s and 1970s also reinvented documentary film form. Black-and-white film stock, handheld cameras, the casting of nonprofessional actors, and a focus on the sociopolitical issues within countries like Bolivia, Ecuador, and Peru exploited the truth value of documentary to convey urgency and realism in dramatic reenactments and fictionalized stories alike. In contrast with Aboriginal media, Video in the Villages, and even the Ukamau Group's solutions, however, most indigenous video makers and their collaborators in Bolivia, Ecuador, and Colombia have either abided by the established conventions of expository and interactive documentary form or opted for docudramas.[3] Yet, as I maintain in this chapter, these conventional indigenous documentaries use the documentary truth claim to undermine the idea of objective, disembodied truth. I trace the different ways in which a selection of shorts from Bolivia, Ecuador, and Colombia posit knowledge as inseparable from embodiment and interest and thus construct an epistemological privilege for pan-indigenous discourse that is, nevertheless, problematic.

Digital Film and the Trace of Light

In the Andean countries lowland and highland media activists have expressed that the essential criteria for the value of video are clarity, truthfulness, and representations that valorize indigenous culture. The position resembles what Eric Michaels noted for Australian Warlpiri video makers in the mid-1980s. He wrote that "when conformity to traditional values is encouraged in video training and production, Warlpiri video makers respond by inventing a version of direct cinema in order to subsume the text under the general requirements of sociability and veracity required by Aboriginal orality. People did not 'make things up' for the camera; rather, they were careful to perform everything in a true and proper manner" (Michaels 30). Yet, while video makers associated with Video in the Villages also opt for a direct cinema style—for example, in the 1999 production *The Initiation of a Young Xavante* (*Wapté mnhõnõ*)—CEFREC-CAIB prefers expository and interactive documentaries with alternating talking heads, even explicitly didactic and educational formats, because they permit straightforward address. Since the CRIC uses video as a pedagogical tool directed at children and adults, their documentaries similarly strive for clarity and simplicity. CONAIE's documentaries also offer clear-cut information about cultural practices and social-political issues rather than experimental subversion of existing codes. Direct cinema for the Warlpiri and the Xavante and more conventional approaches to documentary video in the Andean countries share an investment in the form's truth claim, which builds on an implied contract between viewers and filmmakers. This contract stipulates that what we see is indeed what is there and, in the case of expository formats, that what the commentators say is factual. The contract is bolstered by what Charles Peirce called the "indexical bond" between screen representation and referent: "The bond between representation and referent, that is, between the image and the real world, produces an impression of authenticity which documentary draws on as a warrant or guarantee of the accuracy and authority of its representation" (Beattie 13).

Like photography, film seems able not only to mimic reality but indeed to re-present it across time through a mechanical, apparently objective process, mediated solely by the camera lens. André Bazin thus likened photography to the making of a death mask, "a molding, the taking of an impression, by the manipulation of light" (Bazin 12n). He added that the impact photography caused resulted from a fundamental break with prior forms of representation. "For the first time," said Bazin, "an image of the world is formed automatically, without the creative intervention of man. . . . The objective nature of photography confers on it a quality of credibility absent from all other picture making" (13). Although some insist that the photographic image is not the same as its referent, photographic and cinematic media have had an uncanny ability to create the sense of a reality reproduced, the "punktum" or "the stubbornness of the referent in always being there," as Roland Barthes phrased it (6).

The illusion of realism, bolstered by film's ontological effect and the scientific discourse of sobriety, has been paradigmatic to the construction of the colonial gaze. Already early ethnography's perhaps most famous piece, *Nanook of the North*, staged a primordial scenario that no longer corresponded to Inuit life. Yet visual ethnography has understood film primarily as a means of *representing* rather than *constructing* reality (cf. Ruby, "Exposing"; Nichols, "Ethnographer's Tale"). Catherine Russel suggests that an ethnographic filmmaking that breaks with its colonial inscription hence entails a critique of representation as a relation between vision and knowledge. From this perspective, "the uncanniness of the Other in representation is the knowledge of its unknowability, the knowledge that to see is not, after all, to know. From that unknowability unfolds a resistance in and of representation." Russel concludes that the "failure of realism to present evidence of the real is the radical possibility of experimental ethnography" (25). If film's ontological quality constitutes one of the poles between which the experience of film is suspended, the other pole is the consciousness of film as artifice.

As spectators, we are, at least vaguely, always aware that what we see is not all that is there. Early on, filmmakers already drew attention to film as construct—think only of Djiga Vertov's radical experimentalism with form or

Sergei Eisenstein's use of montage as a means of involving the spectator emo-
tionally in his docudramatic re-creations.[4] These filmmakers demonstrated
that film is all but a mirror of reality: from the choice of the lens, to the composition of the image through lighting and camera angle, to the montage and
editing process film is a creative product.[5] For Russel and others, the solution to breaking with the capitalist/colonialist mode of film production lies
in revealing its fetishistic aspects through the composition of shots and the
duration of takes. Much indigenous video, however, does not strive to desta-
bilize the truth claims of documentary film. Rather, the video makers view
film as an evidentiary tool while at once putting forward an acute awareness
that it matters who makes a film. In other words, far from a naive approach
to film as a window upon reality, video makers use the camera to reflect a
different angle of perception of the world.

It is worth taking another look at the video memory *The Other Gaze.*
Directed by Iván Sanjinés, this expository documentary introduces viewers
in fifteen minutes to indigenous video making in Bolivia. Two narrators
provide general information on the scope of indigenous video training in
Bolivia, authorizing the way the images are supposed to be understood. The
short follows a realist framework that does not question the mimetic quality of its representations or delve into particularities or contradictions. The
voice-of-god narration ties together footage from video training workshops,
excerpts of the culture videos, interviews, as well as brief visual quotes from
CEFREC-CAIB's fiction pieces. *The Other Gaze* depicts video makers handling
camcorders but never frames the interaction between cameraperson and
those in front of the lens. The camera remains removed, objectively observ-
ing the speakers, actors, and participants in video training workshops. In
other words, viewers see video makers wielding camcorders, but we do not
hear or see them address the cameraperson filming them. Through the
voiceover and editing of *The Other Gaze*, however, the video makers strive to
adapt the format to a pan-indigenous social order. The documentary uses
documentary film conventions in order to privilege an indigenous point of
view. For example, in place of the deep male voice of scientific authority, the
commentary in this film alternates between a male and a female voice. These
commentators perform gender duality. Like the subjects on screen, they are
members of the multicultural organizations participating in the training
(CEFREC, CAIB, and CLACPI) many of whom identify as indigenous. *The Other
Gaze* thus decommissions the ethnographer's eye.

 the ethnographer's eye

The voice-of-god narration, nevertheless, reasserts an authoritarian structure. If structurally the existence of narrators seems to foreclose not the reinvention of social relations in themselves but perhaps more equitable ones, this may indeed be in accordance with traditional indigenous political and epistemic orders. Similarly, the repetitions within this documentary reflect a characteristic of oral communication. The video thus extends the reiterative nature of oral address beyond face-to-face interaction. At the same time, the repetition of community and video maker concerns across different cultures allows those on screen to enact what the ethnically diverse production group and their communities have in common with each other. In other words, videos such as *The Other Gaze* use the documentary form to reflect and produce structures of meaning that are pan-indigenous. The videos are meant to replicate sociocultural elements particular to the variety of indigenous cultures while also highlighting what is common to them. The participants' enactment of a pan-indigenous identity in diversity needs the truth-value of documentary film. At the same time, this appeal to a shared identity allows *The Other Gaze* to position indigenous peoples against a global order and reigning media representations.

In *Indigenous Peoples: This Is How We Think* (*Pueblos indígenas, así pensamos*), directorial responsibility is credited to the production collective CEFREC-CAIB. This more recent, even shorter self-representation of the National Indigenous Plan for the Audiovisual Communication of the Indigenous Peoples of Bolivia does not opt for more self-reflection or a longer, more complex rendering of the history and context of indigenous media production. Instead it further highlights the enactment of indigenous cultural diversity and strengthens the documentary's indexical effect: *Indigenous Peoples* shifts focus to a set of media activists and members of CAIB who are framed separately and set against diverse landscapes. They perform their ethnic identity and geographic belonging through clothing and language use. Marcelina Cárdenas, for instance, speaks in Quechua and is dressed in beautifully woven traditional dress. Cárdenas is university educated and also speaks fluent Spanish. Her dress and language choice highlight her identification with her village of origin, where most use Quechua for daily interaction. Marcelino Pinto, in contrast, speaks in Spanish and wears Western clothing, which is, like the language used in the Chapare, indicative of a society made up of largely Quechua- and Aymara-speaking migrants involved in coca production and trade and subject to the coca eradication programs of the nineties. Nicolas Ipamo is a Chiquitano Indian. His accented Spanish and brilliant white clothing again reflect a regional collective ethnic identity. When working on productions in the frigid highlands or when traveling to urban postproduction centers in Santa Cruz, video makers like Ipamo will of course dress differently. All the video makers included in this short comment briefly on the problems concerning their communities and on how the process of audiovisual communication helps address these issues. The footage is edited into a series of alternating talking bodies where the activists speak not only for themselves but also for the diversity of indigenous peoples involved in the National Indigenous Plan. Again, the film relies on the spectators taking the performance of those on screen at face value. Only inadvertently does this documentary reveal a trace of the camera's intervention when, in the alternating interviews, the video makers shift uneasily in front of the camera, exhibiting a slight nervousness—perhaps less in the face of this new technology, but because they are expected to speak publicly for their communities.[6] While constructing a common stance from which to speak, the visual quotations and alternating talking heads splinter the category of indigenous into multiple cultural entities. *Indigenous Peoples* thus subverts the discourse of colonialism that homogenizes native peoples into the racial and pejorative category *indio* but also refuses the in-depth information students and teachers in the North might desire.

The documentary's appeal to bodily presence and ethnic belonging are key in yet another way. Celina Ibazeta emphasizes the tone of camaraderie and familiarity that dominates indigenous documentaries such as *Let's Do Something about Plastic Garbage* (*Mana qhawakullaychu/hagamos algo contra la basura plástica*) and *Dusting Off Our History*. These videos reenact the moment of contact between filmmaker and community as deeply collaborative, where both agree to sit down and chat (Ibazeta 174). Documentary shorts such as *Lighting the Spirit* (*Kanchariy: Para encender la luz del espíritu*) and *Rebellions and Hopes* (*Rebeldías y esperanzas*) highlight the media activists' conviction that research dynamics and ends are changed when the video team and those seeking information are indigenous. In ethnographic film, white colonizers and scientists have objectified colonial others and bound viewers into their desires and anxieties. As Kaplan puts it, "the gaze of the colonialist thus refuses to acknowledge its own power and privilege: it unconsciously represses knowledge of power hierarchies and its need to dominate, to control. Like the male gaze, it's an objectifying gaze, one that refuses mutual gazing, mutual subject-to-subject recognition. It refuses what I am calling a 'looking relation' " (Kaplan, *Looking* 79).[7] Both *Lighting the Spirit* and *Rebellions and Hopes*, in contrast, show indigenous media activists who visit distant communities to interview them. In *Lighting the Spirit* the Aymara director, actor, and member of CEFREC Reynaldo Yujra explores medical practices among the Quechua-speaking Kallawaya. *Rebellions and Hopes*, directed by the Quechua member of CAIB, Marcelina Cárdenas, uses a fictional woman character who compares weaving practices in the high- and lowlands. In these documentaries, subjects, filmmakers, and spectators are bound into the same realm of reality. Although the encounter between filmmaker and members of the community are reenacted, both *Lighting the Spirit* and *Rebellions and Hopes* appeal to the ontological dimension of mutual recognition captured on screen.

The film's indexicality is the basis for intraracial-looking relations on screen and beyond. It is important to remember, in this sense, that unlike ethnographic film indigenous video does not usually seek to present an other to the West. Intercultural communication constructs sameness where indigenous peoples see each other and themselves on screen. They affirm the survival of indigenous cultures and address problems that often transcend the particular situation of individual communities. This response to the colonial encoding of vision operates on the same level of realism as conventional ethnographic documentary, but it does not subscribe to its claim for disinterested knowledge. Instead, the knowledge produced through these investigative documentaries is deeply interested and embodied. The knowledge about medicinal and weaving practices invites comparisons between different indigenous cultures rather than appropriating information.

The appeal to film as evidence is curious, even anachronistic, since indigenous videos are not filmed in analog format. "The analogical arts are fundamentally arts of intaglio, or worked matter—light literally sculpts microscopic hills and valleys in raw film, whose variable density produces a visible image" (1399), writes Rodowick eloquently. Digital recording radically challenges this relation between image and the real:

> Computer-generated imagery, alternatively, is wholly created from algorithmic functions. Whereas analog media record traces of events . . . digital media produce tokens of numbers: the constructive tools of Euclidian geometry are replaced by the computational tools of

Cartesian geometry. Analogy exists in digital technology as a function of spatial recognition, of course, but has loosed its anchors from substance and indexicality. . . . Because the digital arts are without substance and therefore not easily identified as objects, no medium-specific ontology can fix them in place. Digital production renders all expressions identical since they are all reducible to the same computational basis. The basis of all such "representation" is virtuality: mathematical abstractions that render all signs equivalent, regardless of their output medium. ("Dr. Strange" 1399)[8]

If the analog image has "spatial and temporal powers that reinforce photography's designative function with an existential claim" ("Dr. Strange" 1399), as spectators in indigenous communities and in the West alike we continue to view even digital films, especially when they are documentaries or broadcast as news programs, as reflections of reality captured by a camera lens. When indigenous communities today view ethnographic film and recognize their grandparents (as highlighted in the documentary *Video in the Villages Presents Itself*), the emotions stirred arise from film's ontological trace. The viewers hence subscribe to film's indexical effect. Indigenous videos, although now issued in digital form as mathematical codes, are expected to have similar effects in the future. As Alfredo Copa put it, "the community said, 'If our history becomes images, it, like memory, will help in remembering what our past was like'" (Flores 32). The video makers record continuity and change; they also transmit a sense of increased power and control over image production. Again, it matters who makes the film and who is seen/heard on screen. It is at this point that there emerges an acute awareness of image as construction.

Nevertheless, as viewers we might still expect that "another gaze" would present us with something different, not a film language that is all too familiar. Some suggest, for example, that "repetition, associative editing and non-narrative structures" are indigenous or at least opposed to the "centered and linear models of the West" (MacDougal, "Complicities" 97). Vincent Carelli noted that many of the Xavante and Waiãpi documentaries are indeed real time recordings: "They prize long, uninterrupted sequences and assemblage that closely follows events . . . the beauty of a ceremony is often measured, at least in part, by its completeness in detail and by repetition" (Aufderheide, "Making" 285). These real-time recordings of rituals do not seek to reveal the fetishism of continuity editing and narrative ellipses. Rather, like *The Other Gaze* and *Indigenous Peoples*, they again respond to the film's archival dimensions: the notion that film can render reality and hence conserve a document for future generations—in one case of indigenous peoples' access to the camera; in the other, of ritual practices as currently enacted or reenacted. Vincent Carelli notes that, indeed, one of video's effects has been to motivate the return to more traditional dress and body paint in rituals, since communities were unsatisfied with the way contemporary rituals had been performed, once they saw themselves on screen (quoted in Conklin 719). Conklin argues that these decisions, at least in Brazil, are related to the cultural politics of indigenous peoples when confronting the West. Exotic body paint and lip plates seem not only to guarantee authenticity but also to construct privilege vis-à-vis other tribes that are less spectacular to the Western eye (720).

CEFREC-CAIB's, CONAIE's, and the CRIC's use of realism indicates an understanding of video as a double-edged tool. This understanding takes advantage of the mimetic capabilities of the technology while simultaneously producing a particular perspective that denies the possibility of a universal and objective view of the world. Indigenous video makers represent knowledge as necessarily informed by perspectives (discursive regimes, ethical and political beliefs). Western knowledge is characterized here as one among several possible ways of understanding. It is denied its hegemonic status. Traditional ethnographic film's claim to objective truth gives way to a concept of knowledge as always already partial, especially when it pretends to the contrary. In other words, indigenous documentaries and docu-fictions deny the idea of Archimedean objectivity and with it any vindication of anthropology's mediating role.[9]

Tying the Body to the Land

Indigenous media are primarily directed at an audience that shares the temporal and spatial location of the producers. Despite geographical, climatic, or cultural differences, these spectators share certain characteristics. They live in rural villages and are exposed to the profit interests of regional and national industries, ranchers, loggers, and/or global corporations and non-governmental organizations. Land has always been at the center of indigenous anticolonial struggle. In the videos it acquires a new importance as a grounds from which to speak.

The Bolivian documentary *Mother Earth* and the Colombian *The Nasa Garden*, for instance, construct epistemic privilege in two, interrelated ways. The videos emphasize the tie between the body and the land. At the same time, both mix the discourse of sobriety with poetic address. *Mother Earth* is a largely conventional expository documentary where a female narrator (Nila Ruíz) articulates the ongoing struggle over land rights as a story of relative success, an oral narrative that the images corroborate. This video conveys information from a particular pan-indigenous point of view that calls attention to different modes of knowledge. Rationalism and photographic realism, like the voice-of-god narration, complement other forms of understanding. By arranging archival images, paintings of the colonial era, Eduardo Yañez's commentary on screen, and contemporary footage with the explanations of a female, apparently indigenous narrator, the film equates oral narrative, paintings, and photographic realism as corresponding to one and the same truth regime. The closing sequence shifts the mode of discourse from historical realism to poetic metaphors. In the poetic address, the narrator conceptualizes *la tierra* (land, earth, nature) as human responsibility. The narrator asserts that land is placed into human hands to be taken care of since it brings forth life. Footage of young mothers with their children by the riverside visually underlines the narrator's analogy. This final argument constructs a close association of indigenous women with the earth.

The symbolic images, however, offer a superficial rendering of the Andean notion of gendered relations with the lifeworld, where women are seen as closer to *Pachamama* and men as closer to the sun and sky. The equation is simplistic. The full gendering of the lifeworld in Quechua and Aymara cosmovisions includes agricultural space, where *Pachamama* is often but not exclusively associated with women. Quechuas and Aymaras gender mountains (rounded as female, peaks as male), valleys (female) and rivers (male), lakes and rain (female), and fields according to their locations, artifacts, potatoes, etc. Men and women themselves have both female and male parts.[10] In this sense, women are no closer to nature than men; both are like nature or nature like humans. This also means that my use of the terms "nature" and "humans" does not manage to conceptually grasp the relation between humans and the lifeworld. Spedding emphasizes that the correspondence between woman and *Pachamama* is fundamentally flawed, since it ignores that "*Pachamama* is not merely an image of the land in its totality, but rather she is related with other Earth spirits considered male or offering ambiguous aspects" ("Esa Mujer" 71). She "suspect[s] here rather a contamination [of Andean notions] with European and western concepts where woman is associated with 'nature' and even represented as 'naturally' peaceful (in the nineteen eighties) or 'ecological' (in the nineteen nineties), etc. and opposed to the violent and destructive male. . . . This is merely an extension of the marianist gender ideology . . . where woman is the guardian of honor, morality, and the values of the home, while man allows himself a double moral at the level of both sexuality and politics" (71). Despite this tendency toward gender essentialism that simplifies Andean understandings of the relation between humans and the lifeworld, *Mother Earth* challenges documentary realism by combining expository documentary and truth claims with a moral appeal articulated poetically that again plays on gender complementarity. These different orders of understanding—rational, sober documentary realism and poetic moralism are thus placed at the same level. Instead of a supposedly value-free investigation of historical documents and archival footage, the film issues a retrospective of indigenous struggle that carefully avoids taking the side of any political party. Instead, the video levels the grounds and projects indigenous unity in the present, based not only on a common struggle but also on a pan-indigenous, if simplified unity, between indigenous bodies and the land.[11]

Simplistically representing nature as female is not unique to CEFREC-CAIB's *Mother Earth* but quite common practice among Quechua and Aymara speakers. It forms part of an indianist discourse that works against colonial imaginaries made popular in national literature. As Josefa Salmón argues, Bolivian indigenista literature naturalized or essentialized the relation between indigenous people and the "natural" environment (Salmón, chap. 4). Naturalism, as a literary extension of ethology, showed the environmental determination of the subjects that inhabit particular spaces while simultaneously defining the characteristics of nature as primitive and crude (95). Biological racism, anchored in the environmental determinism of the psychology of the races was transformed, in time, into a cultural racism that maintained the conflation of subjectivity and territory. The idea of nature determining the psychology of the people (Andean melancholy) became a social determinism (based on an existential unity with nature in terms of mode of production) (99). Similar to the media activists, the Aymara Victor Ochoa counters that, "for us, the Aymara, the Pachamama is considered an Earth Mother that generates human life. . . . Often the *Pachamama* is identified as a 'Virgin,' a symbol that was adapted in ancient times as comparative to the Virgin Mary. We give the earth this name because she is like a mother that protects all human beings" (Ochoa, quoted in Mauricio Mamani 77).

The Colombian video *The Nasa Garden* very similarly appropriates the association of indigenous peoples with nature and femininity.[12] The personification of land is again key to creating a privileged position from which to speak. Complementing footage of earth, rivers, and rain, the voiceover commentator argues that *la tierra* is a person, a woman who has a vagina and breasts and who urinates. Landscape shots are cut to archival black-and-white footage of the destruction and rescue efforts after the great earthquake that struck the Cauca region in 1994. The narrator explains that this is why "sometimes, when we do not obey her, she gets mad." In *The Nasa Garden*, natural disasters like earthquakes constitute Nature's angry reactions. Nature at once demands human care, gives life, but also enacts terrible, uncontrollable violence and revenge. Devastating earthquakes perpetually threaten to sanction any lapses in human care. The relationship between humans and a personified nature have to be continuously renewed. Again, the Nasa representation of this link resonates across different languages and cultures. The Bolivian Aymara Mauricio Mamani summarizes in a language that parallels almost verbatim the words of the narrator in *The Nasa Garden*, "for mankind, the Earth Mother is a living being that needs to feed on certain organic elements: she needs light and air. In order to make use of her one must attend to her needs. In order to be protected one must protect her. If not, one runs the risk of being punished and abandoned" (Mamani 76).[13]

In *The Nasa Garden*, the relation between humans and nature is mediated by labor, but it is not an object relation where nature is transformed. Rather, it is a relation of reciprocity where the personhood of nature is integrated into the reciprocity among people.[14] The video thus collapses the difference between nature and human, object and subject. *The Nasa Garden* creates a likeness between gender complementarity and the indigenous relationship to the land. The conceptualization is not only based on an analogy between woman and nature (although it is also that). Neither is nature merely symbolized as woman. Rather, reciprocity between a humanized nature and actual humans is presented as an ethical mandate that nurtures an entire philosophy of life.

Vision, Knowledge, and Video Secrets

By uncoupling knowledge from the notion of objectivity, indigenous media articulate the body with particular viewpoints, places from where to look and understand. When this discourse enters into debates about development projects and the face of modernity, it resonates with environmental discourse and with a certain romanticized view of Indians in the West. The following videos implicitly appeal to these ideas while they carve out a space of epistemic privilege for an indigenous discourse enunciated from rural space. *Oil in Weenhayek Territory* is a *nota informativa*, an eight-minute news report shot in the territory of the Weenhayek peoples in the lowland region of Tarija (Bolivia) that borders on Argentina. *Oil in Weenhayek Territory* denounces the contamination caused by the Tesoro oil company, along with the lies of company representatives that the video makers caught on tape. *The Earth Is Bleeding* is a thirty-minute documentary produced by CONAIE in collaboration with Acción Ecológica.[15] Like *Oil in Weenhayek Territory*, *The Earth Is Bleeding* denounces the destruction of the environment, health, and living conditions by oil companies. It focuses on the devastating impact oil drilling has had on the fishing grounds of a lowland Huaorani community that seeks to maintain a traditional lifestyle. The third film, *Trinkets and Beads*, is directed by the North American filmmaker Christopher Walker. Unlike the indigenous videos *Oil in Weenhayek Territory* and *The Earth Is Bleeding*, this participatory documentary film of fifty-three minutes is directed primarily at a Western audience. *Trinkets and Beads* also treats the Huaorani struggle to recuperate their land from the international oil companies to whom they had granted drilling rights. It is not a film produced by indigenous organizations, although it is clearly sympathetic to the indigenous perspective.[16]

Trinkets and Beads denounces the destruction of the Ecuadorian rainforest brought on by Texaco/Chevron, Occidental Petroleum, Arco, and Maxus Energy Corporation, who have drilled on Huaorani land, and their collusion with North American missionaries.[17] Some of the most impressive scenes include footage from a 1950s U.S. television interview with the loquacious and still active missionary Rachel Saint. Two Huaroni women who never speak accompany her. Crosscut with this archival footage, Saint's present-day statements show no change in attitude as she continues to praise the civilizing force of her organization. For the spectators, this montage sequence successfully generates both outrage and ridicule of her ongoing colonial posturing. The intimate and longstanding connection between colonialism and capitalism is rendered through an offhand remark by one of Maxus Energy Corporations' officials visiting the Huaorani mission. The filmmakers capture him saying, "it's still trinkets and beads just like 500 hundred years ago," that are being offered for the land. The remark is so succinct that it becomes the title of the documentary.

Trinkets offers a scathing critique of North American evangelist missionaries and petrol companies, but it does not manage to fully break with the image of the tricked, infantilized Indian. The documentary calls attention to colonial relations and foregrounds the Huaorani's critique voiced by Moi, a community leader. The editing in this film, however, implies that his testimony is in need of corroboration by Western anthropologists and scientists—that is, by the discourse of knowledge and environmental protection located in the West. The documentary strives for objectivity, for a convincing representation of the complexities involved, including the seduction of the Huaorani by the missionaries and the fractures this has caused to the community. In this film, Indians are no longer equated with nature but represented as alienated from it. They remain in a space of limbo—not part of Western science and civilization but also no longer in harmonious relation with nature, due to the noxious influences of Christianity and capitalism. The land together with the indigenous peoples that inhabit it remains conceptualized as in need of protection by the West and against the West.[18]

At first sight, and although considerably shorter, *Oil in Weenhayek Territory* seems to echo the format of *Trinkets and Beads*. *Oil in Weenhayek Territory* also constructs indigenous peoples as the victims of a predatory Western civilization. However, this video transforms all three of the central strategies of representation in *Trinkets and Beads*: victimization, backing up the voice of the exemplary indigenous witness with scientific accounts, and the discourse of balanced representation. Instead of referring to the socioeconomic complexities affecting the Weenhayek community, *Oil in Weenhayek Territory* denounces the Tesoro representatives' environmental destruction and lies. We hear company officials arguing the collateral benefits of petrol drilling in the Tarija region, such as the building of roads and the provision of medicines to the Weenhayek community, while we see shots of oil spills, mud-choked roads contaminated by oil, empty medicine cabinets, petrol leaking into the natural water sources, and oil-covered birds. Interviews with the Weenhayek authorities additionally challenge the company officials' representation. Juxtaposing the footage of oil pollution and the testimonies of

Weenhayek authorities with those of Tesoro officials and national politicians, the video "proves" the declarations of the latter to be untrue. Despite being a digital video recording edited on a computer, *Oil in Weenhayek Territory* thus exploits film's lingering truth claims and assumed ontological warranty.

At the same time, this CEFREC-CAIB production, like *Mother Earth*, posits nature and rural space as a privileged place from which to speak. In contrast with the Huaorani leader Moi in *Trinkets and Beads*, Weenhayek community leaders and representatives are cast as subjects of knowledge in their own right. The "truth" of company officials is based on words alone, the "truth" of the Weenhayek community combines oral discourse and photographic images. *Oil in Weenhayek Territory* does not strive for a comprehensive representation of the complex social relations among company officials, anthropologists, missionaries, and indigenous peoples. One might argue that an effort at comprehensive objectivity would be overly ambitious given *Oil in Weenhayek*'s short duration of only eight minutes. In light of the total absence of an outside, nonindigenous expert's validation, however, it is more convincing to see this documentary short as a critique. It negates the possibility of disinterested or "objective" knowledge and at once affirms the need of indigenous peoples to speak for themselves.

CONAIE'S medium-length documentary *The Earth Is Bleeding* works with the same principle. *The Earth Is Bleeding*, in fact, includes some of the footage from *Trinkets and Beads* (particularly the fishbowl shots of the city and the wide angle shots of burning oil fields). Just as *Oil in Weenhayek Territory* and *Trinkets and Beads*, *The Earth Is Bleeding* denounces the practices of multinational oil corporations along with the profit principles guiding Western civilization. *The Earth Is Bleeding* also uses montage to enforce the argument and truth claim of the Huaorani, thus eliminating the recourse to Western experts. Indigenous testimonies are contrasted with those of Westerners and corroborated with visual proof for a particular perspective on reality. In other words, *The Earth Is Bleeding* and *Oil in Weenhayek Territory* construct representations that are consciously made to reflect a subjective, indigenous viewpoint. Where *Trinkets and Beads* highlights the complicities of indigenous leaders and parts of the communities in initially granting drilling rights, the indigenous videos insist on revealing a process of deception. Indigenous peoples emerge from *Oil in Weenhayek Territory* and *The Earth Is Bleeding* as actively resisting environmental destruction and as the transmitters of a seemingly uncontaminated and alternative ethics. That is, on the one hand, *The Earth Is Bleeding* and *Oil in Weenhayek Territory* both shun the representation of divisions within the indigenous community, especially those on the grounds of religion, in favor of projecting unity. On the other hand, in these shorts the indigenous peoples suffer the effects of Western capitalism, but they are not reduced to infantile dupes. In *Oil in Weenhayek Territory*, indigenous peoples are deceived by sophisticated promises. The video emphasizes that the Weenhayek themselves are capable of unmasking the false promises made, and, by using video, they are also able to present a different truth, not the whole truth but another view upon reality. Indigenous peoples are rendered then as innocent but not naive victims. The degree to which indigenous community authorities may at any point have been implicated in granting drilling rights—with or without the possible support of some but not other members of the community—is not addressed. The referent remains off screen, to emerge perhaps in the community discussions of the video and of the overarching issue of environmental destruction and sustainable development that CEFREC-CAIB and CONAIE foster.

At the same time, the montage sequences in these videos question hegemonic notions of modernity and national development. Oil fields and roads are not rendered the signs of economic progress. These documentaries oppose the business principles of transnational corporations and national governments that seek to exploit natural resources, whether in order to maximize profits, promote national development, or both. The communities' perspectives are offered, not as totally opposed to any kind of modernization, but rather as desires for a different kind of modernity guided by the ethical and environmental principals of the affected communities. This position includes the preservation of traditional lifestyles but cannot be reduced to premodern life.

Although *Trinkets* is clearly sympathetic to the Huaorani, *Oil in Weenhayek Territory* and *The Earth Is Bleeding* construct epistemic privilege for Huaorani and Weenhayek communities. These documentaries affirm indigenous points of view as emerging from an ethical relation with the life world, privileged vis-à-vis those points of view that result from an interest in the exploitation of natural resources. *Oil in Weenhayek Territory* directs attention to the contamination of foods, especially fish, which can no longer be successfully sold, thus depriving the Weenhayek community of income and its relation with the market. *The Earth Is Bleeding* argues the need to preserve nature not only as a food source and living environment but also as a habitat of the spirits. While indigenous lifestyles in *Oil in Weenhayek Territory* are defined by their relation with the market, both videos share the desire to mark a difference from Western capitalism that lies in the indigenous relation with and conceptualization of nature, a conceptualization that in the end these videos only hint at. *Oil in Weenhayek Territory* and *The Earth Is Bleeding* underscore that nature and humans are dependent on each other. Nature is part of the lifeworld, and the relation between humans and this lifeworld provides the space from where knowledge arises.

When *Trinkets and Beads* argues a clash in temporalities (the premodern and the postmodern/late capitalism) that causes the loss of authenticity, the North American production maintains a certain nostalgia for the past, a desire to reinstate the space of nature and its natural inhabitants. *Oil in Weenhayek Territory* and *The Earth Is Bleeding* in contrast propose the coevalness of temporalities where indigenous peoples are living in the same temporality as logging companies and petrol industries. Both documentaries construct an alternative relation to nature and production without renouncing technology—after all, the films are digital video recordings. They assert at once that indigenous lifestyles and ethics are incompatible with an ever expanding and intensifying capitalism and that a different modernity is possible. The alternative lies in strengthening social and cultural practices along with different experiences and ways of making sense of these experiences. Claiming the right or possibility of an indigenous ethics and relation with nature hence imposes a limit on capitalism and challenges its viability. This is not to say that the question of sustainable development, market relations, and monetary income are not debated (and controversially so) among indigenous peoples. Rather, indigenous videos intervene precisely in this pan-indigenous debate with a stance that is decidedly suspicious of neoliberal promises but at once claims the need for a different kind of modernization. *Oil in Weenhayek Territory* and *The Earth Is Bleeding* thus contradict the discourse of sobriety with an emphatically partial intervention that constitutes indigenous communities as ethically privileged subjects of environmental knowledge, without, however, renouncing film's indexical effects.

The distinction between nature (as object of study) and culture (as realm of intellectual production) has been key to the geopolitics of knowledge established with colonialism. It has also been a context where metaphors of femininity and masculinity have been attached to the realms of nature and civilization, private and public sphere, helping to keep both spaces conceptually separate. The lettered city and its visual economy have had considerable power in elaborating this spatial dichotomy. According to this logic, nature is to be studied, described, and integrated into the urban, civilized, modern—or postmodern—space where sustainable knowledge is created. From this perspective the idea that indigenous people in the countryside embark on a project of knowledge production enunciated through oral and audiovisual means is barely imaginable, especially if this knowledge claims to have equal if not privileged status vis-à-vis the scientific community. Yet these videos run the risk, at least in a Western context, of falling into a different colonial imagery: the romanticized idea of the bon savage. Certainly, insisting on Weenhayek market relations and on the use of video technology interrupts this pastoral. But since the camera remains outside the frame, even those films that forgo the pitfalls of invoking a simplistic gender-nature discourse (like the one offered in *Mother Earth* or *The Nasa Garden*) might be read as essentializing the equation of indigenous identity with nature. CEFREC-CAIB's Video Program No. 2 offers a counterpoint to this tendency.

Aymara Colonizers

Video Program No. 2 centers on the problem of environmental destruction. The package is titled "Gestión de recursos naturales y medio ambiente" (Managing Natural Resources and the Environment) and is accompanied by a bulletin for the facilitator's use.[19] The guide outlines instructions for the screening and gives some central arguments for guiding the discussion. As is the case for most of CEFREC-CAIB's video packages, this compilation of shorts mixes films that directly address the topic and others that function as news reports. Program No. 2 combines the five-minute piece *The Jungle* (*La jungla*), a video short representing a children's playground and park in one of Bolivia's coca growing regions that has turned into a popular ecotourist attraction (*Red Boletín* 3a); *Never Again* (*Nunca más*), a thirteen-minute documentary about a massacre of Indians in Chiapas accused of being members of the EZLN by the Mexican Army; *In the Amazon: San Ignacio de Moxos* (*En la Amazonía: San Ignacio de Moxos*), a nine-minute report on traditional dances in the Moxos lowlands; *Creating Life* (*Creando vida*), a nineteen-minute centerpiece on the search for alternatives to the environmental destruction caused by monoculture; and the fiction piece *Vest Made of Money* that argues against avarice. The package further contains a selection from the archive that includes two Bolivian animations on the environment for children, *The*

Earth Is Ill: How Can We Cure Her (*La tierra está enferma: Cómo podemos curarla*) and *The Forest Is Still Alive* (*El bosque aún vive*), and two documentaries on environmental destruction and indigenous/rural peoples in Mexico and Cuba, respectively *Woman, Production and the Environment* (*Mujeres, producción y medio ambiente*) and *You're Green* (*Sos verde*). The compilation of diverse documentary shorts on the environment prepares the grounds for an intercultural indigenous communication between highland Aymaras, Aymara migrants to the subtropical Andean valleys and those indigenous communities that have lived in the area since before the Aymara and Quechua "colonizers" arrived.[20]

Creating Life juxtaposes the problems with monoculture with ecologically sustainable methods of agriculture in the Alto Beni, a tropical valley region in the northeast of Bolivia. Unlike *Oil in Weenhayek Territory* and *The Earth Is Bleeding*, this educational video links environmental destruction to the disrespect for nature by indigenous peoples themselves. Environmental destruction is here not fixed to identity (the ecological Indian versus the destructive Westerner). Rather, it results from a particular history of development, severed ties to the land, and the prejudices of highland Aymara and Quechuas toward the indigenous peoples in the lowlands.[21] The land reforms of the Bolivian revolution in the early 1950s converted some of the holdings of the great estates into *minifundios*, small parcels allocated to individual owners rather than integrated back into the combination of individual and communal landholdings in the *ayllus*. The *minifundio* resulted from state policies adopted after 1952 and is criticized as one of the revolution's failings in *Mother Earth*. As a response to the unresolved problem of access to land, the state supported massive migration of Aymaras and Quechuas from the highlands to the tropical regions of the Alto Beni during the fifties and sixties.[22]

Creating Life, however, does not frame the problem of environmental destruction in the Alto Beni as an outcome of failed state policies in which Aymaras and Quechuas would pose as figures on a playing field manipulated by greater powers.[23] Instead, the film establishes a correlation between the practices of migrant indigenous peoples and Western profit-oriented companies in the area that complicates the construction of epistemic privilege in *Oil in Weenhayek Territory* and *The Earth Is Bleeding*. As the narrator explains, the indigenous peoples of the area were largely displaced by the *colonizadores* (as the highland migrants refer to themselves, following the terminology of the state issued during the 1950s and 1960s). The displacement was accompanied by a lack of communication between indigenous peoples that left the Quechua and Aymara migrants subject to the policies promoted by the state. The migrants adopted monocultural agricultural practices that depleted the soil, accelerated erosion, and have now become fully unsustainable since the crops are subject to massive insect and fungi pests.

The bulletin accompanying the video package details that the migrants had agricultural techniques that were well adjusted to highland ecology. When they moved to the tropical regions, they lacked the knowledge of how to create sustainable agricultural and living conditions. The effect has been devastating (cf. Red, *Boletín* 2, 1b). In the rational language of the social and environmental sciences, the bulletin affirms that "this exploitative mindset does not take into consideration the conservation of renewable resources or their sustainable productivity" (Red, *Boletín* 2, 2b). The farmers, who practice slash and burn agriculture and monoculture, share this lack of adequate knowledge with a number of companies who dedicate themselves to the overexploitation of the forests. Both large- and small-scale agricultural production and exploitation are declared responsible for environmental destruction and both seem only interested in short-term profits. This situation creates the urgency to which indigenous video responds. The documentary compares various sustainable agriculture initiatives and examines their alternative practices and farming experiments.

Stylistically, this video again follows an expository but indigenous-centered approach. The video makers represent each center through an interview with a male *agricultor* (farmer). (When *Creating Life* opts for the term *agricultor*, it avoids the common term *campesino*, with its highland ethnic and class connotations.) These talking heads are crosscut with footage of the fields and orchards. Like in *Oil in Weenhayek Territory* and *The Earth Is Bleeding*, and contrary to Western documentaries like *Trinkets and Beads*, there is no need for Western scientists, academics, or state officials to validate a discourse that can stand on its own, supported through the visual "proof" of images. The facilitator's bulletin, however, adds historical depth to the documentary. The predatory practices of the present are contrasted to how highland "indigenous communities' agricultural practices and behavior used to be" (Red, *Boletín* 2, 2b). The document affirms these farming methods as part of the past: Indigenous peoples had sustainable practices that allowed for gradual improvement of living conditions, although not for great economic profits. They also lived according to a mind-set that envisioned survival over generations and conceptualized "man as a mere part of nature. By damaging nature man is inflicting damage upon himself" (2b). These indigenous communal practices were abandoned because of *minifundio* and excessive parceling of the land. The bulletin collapses temporal difference more successfully than the film, by stating that both of these options are "realities," they coexist. The bulletin asks, "Faced with these two realities, what can we suggest?" (2b). The answer arises from a critique of state policies. The bulletin argues that these policies have not taken the actual causes of environmental destruction and low agricultural yields into consideration and instead have always tended to copy developmental models from other countries and other realities (2b). It is possible, the bulletin concludes, to suggest alternative solutions by thinking from the indigenous peoples, peasants, and their organizations themselves (2b).

The video's comparison of different ecologically sustainable projects is anchored in the present tense. It ends by documenting the efforts of Mosetén communities (an indigenous people originally from the Alto Beni). These communities reconceptualize agricultural practices through recovering Mosetén traditions, instead of getting inspiration from Western models put forth by international nongovernmental organizations and development agencies in the area. *Creating Life* thus concludes by focusing on an ethical component. This shift makes it possible for highland Indians to seek inspiration in lowland indigenous practices. The video affirms that the intellectual resources for sustainable relations between humans and nature are to be found in the recovery of indigenous knowledge and ethics. The solution is centered on the multilayered cultivation of crops that imitates the structure of natural forests instead of a renaturalization of cultivated lands (Red, *Boletín* 2, 2b). At stake is the protection of plants, animals, forests, and nature, as well as of indigenous peoples themselves.

Creating Life leaves the door open to reconfiguring the relationship with nongovernmental organizations on the basis of collaboration and complementarity. The indigenous approach, however, is not fully compatible with the Western environmental projects presented in the video. Although market relations and monetary income are desired, according to *Creating Life* the goal of indigenous cultural politics is to foster a long-term sustainable relation between humans and nature in a common life-world, and not short-term industrial growth and profit. *Creating Life*'s basic question to its viewers is whether development projects should be aimed at increasing profit or at recuperating nature (as a source of nutrition and spiritual well-being). Its argument is clear: there is a need to improve crop yields, along with a preservation of natural resources, for future generations. The solution is emphatically not industrial development in some areas, and nature preserves in others. The indigenous value system is rendered as a survival ethos serving past, present, and future generations and opposed to the immediacy of profit thinking that guides Western development initiatives.[24] Although the video allows for cooperation with Western development agencies, it does not endorse their tutelage. Similarly, by refraining from pigeonholing the state, indigenous communicators here construct themselves as potential interlocutors in the role of teachers, not pupils or enemies.

However much the video *Creating Life* may sideline the migrants desire for profit, it exemplifies a successful search for solutions. It extends the conversations that led to the documentary's making into other indigenous communities facing similar problems. As stated in the bulletin, this is a project in which all communities need to be involved on a continuous basis (Red, *Boletín* 2, 3b). According to the facilitators' manual, the discussion should incorporate a comparative analysis in the place where the video is shown, an analysis of nonsustainable practices, as well as the exchange and development of alternative ideas (3b). Market relations, development, integration, or alternatives to capitalism are not resolved here but brought to the table for discussion. The construction of epistemic privilege is in the end, then, quite straightforward. It is based on social practice that is linked to tradition, knowledge of the land, climate, and vegetation, accumulated over generations and to an ethics that guides the future, not to an essentialized bond between Indians and nature.

Produced in diverse contexts in Bolivia, Colombia, and Ecuador, videos such as *Oil in Weenhayek Territory*, *The Earth Is Bleeding*, *Creating Life*, and *The Nasa Garden* subtly undermine the discourse of pastoral fantasies put forth in conventional ethnographic film. Audiovisual communication creates a space for discussing indigenous communities' relation with (neo)liberal capitalism and for imagining alternative frameworks. Seen against a long colonial horizon, the struggle over land has always been a struggle for an alternative social and economic order. By insisting on the diversity of landscapes and indigenous cultures and by highlighting the figure of the migrant, the video *Creating Life* counters the homogenization of indigenous peoples. The figure of the Indian is complicated and diversified and so is the binary opposition between nature and culture. Seen together, these documentaries become educational tools for the debate over ecologically sustainable practices that transform the space of knowledge production. Rural peoples are at the center of this video politics of knowledge, not recipients or partners in a North-South transfer of knowledge and technology.

Most striking is perhaps the way video makers exploit documentary realism but forgo what the West would consider balanced accounts. The videos create a discourse that does not require Western scientific approval and at once creatively use editing strategies and narrative techniques to avoid the representation of a totalizing objectivity that is commonly associated with expository documentaries. Despite indigenous media's use of expository and interactive documentary form, both quintessential means of film as a pedagogical tool, the indigenous videos discussed in this chapter do not offer a well-rounded perspective. These documentaries hence challenge the expectations a Western audience brings to ethnographic film. This is by no means an exceptional strategy.

Consider again CEFREC-CAIB's video packages. They form a loose arrangement of news, documentaries, and video-short stories with a central topic. In the case of Video Program No. 3, for instance, the topic of the video debate is the relevance of indigenous medicine. Neither the cultural videos nor the video fiction, however, center on medical knowledge and practices. The video shorts compiled in this package are not primarily about the factual aspects of indigenous medicine at all. Similarly, CONAIE's *Between Spirits and Men* and *Woman, Wisdom and Power* address medical knowledge in different indigenous communities in Ecuador but offer no more than short sequences depicting healing practices set against a wider panorama of social relations. Indeed, no one could gain competence in shamanic medicine or midwifery by watching these films. Although the documentary shorts deal with multiple cultural and epistemic practices, viewers will not learn the intricacies of these practices by watching the tapes. Even more extreme in the case of CEFEC-CAIB's "culture videos," we are faced with snapshots that are devoid of explanation or analysis. Rather, these observational shorts serve as glimpses of traditions in practice, audiovisual postcards that address the international indigenous viewing community. They assert that indigenous traditions may be disregarded by some members of the communities but are still alive. These practices have survived, sometimes truncated, but are in any case recoverable. The elliptical quality of these films, their secrets, if you will, hence point to a transformed notion of knowledge and its relation to documentary representation. Indigenous media exploits an ambiguity: on one hand, there is film's ability to grasp the real; on the other, there is an awareness that there is more than one way of framing and seeing reality.

What may seem a shortcoming is actually a crucial element for the way video is contextualized within the dynamics of enactment, production, and reception. In Bolivia and elsewhere, the screenings of videos allow communities to negotiate their meaning and relevance, guided in their debates by indigenous facilitators. According to video makers like Alfredo Copa and Julia Mosúa, the videos give rise to discussions about whether or not the practices are represented accurately and what accuracy means (Mosúa, Copa, and Pinto, audiotape). At the same time, they put the general value of medicinal knowledge or ecologically sustainable agriculture up for debate. Because indigenous video is embedded in a collective production and reception process, it opens up a conversation rather than closing it off with an authoritative analysis of reality. To reiterate, these films put forth strong arguments; they are not based in value-free explorations of the complexities underlying the issues represented. Rather, they incite a debate that is at once philosophical and practical. They are always framed as conceived in the interest of the people represented and for the benefit of the communities making and watching the films.

In the process of constructing epistemic privilege, some videos like *The Nasa Garden* verge on the side of essentializing the relation between Indian and nature. In a Western viewing context, at least, they walk a thin line, often reminding viewers of colonial and environmental romanticized representations of Indians as guardians of nature, who for this very reason lack intellectual sophistication (cf. Schiwy, "Ecoturismo"). Others, like *Creating Life*, tend exaggeratedly toward the discourse of sobriety but vest agency from the scientist in favor of indigenous peoples who have always lived and cultivated in the forest. The videos discussed here parallel the multipronged strategies of indigenous movements who negotiate with local and international nongovernmental organizations, nation-states, and global institutions, making use of the cultural capital of international buzzwords while pushing a more profound decolonization of knowledge and subjectivity (Brysk 33–38).

6

SPECTERS AND BRAIDED STORIES

When Stanley Aronowitz spoke of cinema being the paradigmatic art form of late capitalism in the 1970s, he implied that the very technology itself, the succession of images in time, replicated and helped to constitute the rhythm of capitalist production. The moving image masked its production; it produced the memory of historical events as a montage sequence of images. Like other commodities, Aronowitz argued, film thus contributes to forgetting the actual agents of production (115–16). Aronowitz sets the stage for exploring how far films can break with their own fetishism. He asks, "Can the film be anything but the art form of late capitalism? Can the distortions of compressed and reversed time be themselves reversed so that politics may be expressed in and through film as the determining moment, rather than remaining subsumed under its technological reduction?" (121). James Weiner similarly argued that unless indigenous media explicitly undermine the fetishistic aspects of film production, the adoption of video technology by indigenous communities becomes a marker of their destruction, ultimately incorporating indigenous culture into the capitalist society of the spectacle. According to Weiner, since the audiovisual medium constitutes the society of the spectacle, its use by indigenous peoples can only convert societies that are based on ritual or "real" relations, not mediated ones, into cultures of the simulacrum. In contrast with Aronowitz, who looks for experimentation with cinematic time, Weiner suggests revealing fetishism by calling attention to the presence of the filmmaker in the diegetic space (Aronowitz 128; Weiner 208).

Third cinema's filmmaking practice anticipated much of Aronowitz' concerns. As Burton summarized her argument, "Latin American filmmakers' attempts to create a revolutionary cinema took as its point of departure not simply the introduction of a new content or the transformation of cinematic forms, but the transformation of the subjective conditions of film production and film viewing" (Burton, "Film" 180–81). The socialization of filmmaking was also to be achieved through film form. The Ukamau Group's experimental techniques—long shots and extremely long takes, for instance—were intended to allow for collective action and the distance filmmakers thought was required to facilitate critical thinking and understanding (Sanjinés and Grupo Ukamau 64). Third cinema also explicitly reversed the colonial gaze's entrapment of indigenous subjects, instead offering viewers identification with the colonized.

Most indigenous video, however, is not experimental in this way. Indigenous videos from Ecuador, Bolivia, and Colombia rarely meditate diegetically on the relation between filmmaker, film, and indigenous community. Indigenous media counter the prevailing images and plots in *indigenista* film and literature (which feature melancholic Indians, passive victims, and people equated with the mysterious and irrational forces of nature), but indigenous fiction and docudramas part with third cinema's politically committed aesthetics that had been inspired by Soviet realism and montage, the Grierson documentaries, and Italian neo-realism. Video makers instead opt for Hollywood genres such as the horror movie and the melodrama, computerized sound effects, and abundant close-ups. Both the kind of experimentalism that Aronowitz calls for and the self-reflexivity that Weiner demands are largely absent in indigenous media from the Andean countries and particularly in CEFREC-CAIB's award-winning fiction shorts.

Indigenous media's unabashed use of Hollywood's formulas hence raises a series of questions. What is the rationale for indigenous video's apparently commercial aesthetics? Do the formal strategies of indigenous fiction videos undermine the goal of strengthening local cultures and ways of knowing? Can indigenous societies indeed be characterized as premediatic?

Andean Mediascapes: *Telenovela*, MTV, and Jackie Chan

The Quechua fiction short *Cursed Gold* is a story about a young gold prospector who arrives in a small town seeking easy riches. Set in the coca-growing Chapare, the video is marked by takes of lush vegetation and village life that a light musical tune renders idyllic until the drama unfolds. An old man whom the protagonist meets at the town market tells him about an enchanted pond and incites the protagonist to offer a human sacrifice in return for gold. Tito (José Escalera) flirtatiously befriends a local girl and enlists her help as he seeks to respond to the old man's suggestion. As the drama unfolds, the viewers are led to believe that Tito sacrifices the girl until in the very last scene Tito himself becomes the victim. This twenty-five-minute fiction short combines elements of the horror movie with the melodrama. It abounds with extreme close-ups as the camera frames the devil's (Basilio Terraza) eyes watching over his victims from a distance. One of its most celebrated scenes, Juana's (Aidée Alvarez) flight from the jungle, uses an improvised traveling shot "to make the video more lively," as Marcelino Pinto, who wrote the script and directed this short, asserted in an interview with Salvadorian filmmaker Daniel Flores in New York City (Mosúa, Copa, and Pinto, audiotape). The soundtrack combines diegetic Andean pop music performed in a local chichería ("Black Eyes/*Ojitos negros*") with computer-generated Mickey Mousing that mimics footsteps and running sequences. All these are familiar techniques from Hollywood blockbusters. The focus on individual characters and the lack of depth that digital cameras achieve, on the other hand, remind viewers of *telenovelas*, as does the love story and day-to-day setting in the village in which the fiction short plays out.

These references are not surprising. Vincent Carelli, director of the Brazilian Video in the Villages argues that "Indians who have more familiarity with Brazilian and U.S. television adapt their visual styles to it" (Aufderheide, "Making" 285). Bolivian indigenous peoples similarly watch television soap operas, news shows, talk shows, and advertising spots. Television has become increasingly pervasive, even in the viewing habits of rural communities. Hollywood's dominant codes are familiar to many indigenous viewers and video makers from occasional visits to the cinema, from the proliferation of legal and pirated DVD and VHS copies, readily available at Andean markets and on buses, where VHS monitors have become steady travel companions for long trips. The *telenovela* melodrama is ubiquitous, screened on television sets in cities and ever-more remote villages.

Experimental film plays with and against film conventions and thus becomes subversive, challenging viewers into new associations and ideas. Yet third cinema's experimental and politically committed style often made for very difficult films to watch, even at a time when spectators were not yet used to the proliferation of close-ups and the rapid cuts between shots made familiar through television and MTV. The audiences that these films sought were often elusive. Filmmakers lacked national political support for the distribution of their cinema, but viewers also preferred the narratives of suspense, melodrama, and comic entertainment that commercially oriented national film industries and Hollywood—aided by its aggressive distribution policies—delivered to Latin American audiences. Today the solutions proposed by the Ukamau Group's revolutionary aesthetics are perhaps even less compelling for broad audiences. Extensive long-shot sequences, a slow editing rhythm, or the absence of close-ups—as in much of *Courage of the People*— run the risk of boring a younger audience used to the rapid cutting of MTV music videos or the ubiquitous Jackie Chan and Van Damme action movies.

In the 1960s, viewers also favored the locally produced B and C movies, exploitation films that replicated Hollywood genres and strategies for entertainment, shock, and other forms of emotional release, even if they did not achieve the same level of technical sophistication. As Gabriela Alemán writes for the case of Ecuador, the directors of these films

> are still well known in the alternative video or psychotronic circuits, although none of their movies has become part of the film canon in their own countries. . . . These movies can no longer be seen in Ecuador and can only be found through alternative film channels: pirated copies of late-night TV specials, copied and sold over the Internet; *bizarre* and paracinematic film websites such as bloodyplanet.com, specializing in gore and European horror flicks; or through El Santo's cult following and its specialized distribution circuits. These "exploitation" films successfully flooded the Latin American film market at the same time as the New Latin American Film Movement was gaining international acclaim and heralding political films as the only possible option for Latin American Cinema. (100–101)

The politically motivated Latin American films did not often achieve the goal of rousing the people into revolutionary action, in part, because their films could not live up to audience desires for schlock and escapism.[1]

If viewer expectations and associations are informed by the hegemonic language of cinema, indigenous media respond to these desires. Although the video makers, like the indigenous social movements they are associated with, criticize the power of U.S. media and their imitations in Latin America, the activists combine a desire to educate and incite discussion with the need to entertain and appeal to viewers. Despite its use of conventional genre formulas, fiction shorts such as the story of *Cursed Gold*, however, are not

merely about entertainment. *Cursed Gold* claims the importance of indigenous traditions and forms of knowing and condemns greed. Crucially, the
protagonist's demise is the result of his disregard for Juana's warning about
the dangerous and enchanted pond. Along with the girl's advice that she
takes from local tales, the protagonist also ignores his dreams of premonition. Guided by his desire for wealth, this Quechua speaker has lost the ties
to his community of origin and to the wider epistemic order that is transmitted through storytelling, dreams, specters, and bad omen in animal form. As
with the other indigenous fiction shorts discussed, *Cursed Gold* affirms these
elements as part of a Quechua order of knowledge. At the same time, with its
melodramatic personalization the video lends itself to an allegorical reading
where the protagonists represent the different social forces confronting each
other in the militarized coca-growing Chapare. In other words, if indigenous
videos generally aim for clarity (chronological narratives, explicitly moral-
izing summaries at the end), *Cursed Gold* allows for a reading that magnifies
the consequences of cultural abandonment.

The video vindicates the traditional use and marketing of coca leaves
while criticizing coca production for the global drug market. The protagonist,
Tito, who comes in search of gold, may be seen to represent outside drugs
traffickers who travel to the Chapare in search of large if not easy profits. The
local population is represented by Juanita, whose quotidian cultivation and
marketing of coca leaves has not lead to wealth but to a relatively dignified
survival. The devil, on the other hand, incarnates the violence committed
by the military troops, whose lower ranks are filled by indigenous peoples
themselves. Whether this allegory is intentional or not,[3] it is the form—the
borrowings from Hollywood cinema techniques and from melodrama—that
promote this interpretation. The video denounces the militarization of the
Chapare that has been defined by the low-intensity war between coca growers and the military, trained and supported by the United States. At the
same time, the film condemns those indigenous migrants in the area who
succumb to capitalist greed.

Video fictions like the Quechua *Cursed Gold* thus transpose the relation
between *rikuy* (seeing) and different levels of understanding (*yachay, unanchay,* and *hamuttay*), that Harrison (80) noted in her reading of Santacruz
Pachakuti Yamqui's text, once more back to the image and the act of looking.
In *Cursed Gold*, the lyrics to the popular folk song "Ojitos negros" (Black Eyes)
are rendered and repeated in Spanish and in Quechua, providing a direct

reference to the close-ups of two sets of eyes—those of Tito and those of the Devil (*rikuy*). On one level, these sets of eyes function as allegorical references to illegal coca production and the military eradication of coca crops (*unanchay*). On a more complex level they also invoke another two-eye metaphor (*hamuttay*), the need to struggle against both capitalism (seen by one eye) and racism (seen by the other), as Quechua and Aymaras have argued.[4]

The short thus intervenes in the national political debate over coca cultivation. At the same time, it references a Quechua epistemology based in storytelling, dreams, specters, snakes, and birds. These elements acquire significance because they allude to principles of a shared pan-indigenous cosmovision. In fiction shorts such as *Cursed Gold*, *Qati qati*, *Vest Made of Money*, or *Forest Spirit* the stories told and enacted for the camera are traditional tales, resituated into the present time. The adaptation of storytelling to the screen hence follows the conventions of so-called oral cultures, where ancient tales are continuously reinvented to reflect contemporary concerns.[5] *Cursed Gold*'s plot is based on a traditional Chipiriri story of an enchanted pond, and *Qati qati*'s compelling tale of flying heads is part of the oral literature of Carabuco. The tales of the living dead that might arise to punish those who transgress the social norms of reciprocity and community responsibility coexist with mythical accounts of indigenous survival and ongoing resistance to colonial rule. This living legacy forms a reservoir of understanding and transmitting knowledge that indigenous media draw on. Alfredo Copa, Julia Mosúa, and Marcelino Pinto have insisted that indigenous media in fact contribute to strengthening the tradition of oral storytelling rather than supplanting it (Flores 33–34).

Rendering storytelling in film has broad consequences. For Ginsburg, one of the key opportunities that indigenous media open up for native filmmakers in northern Canada are "narrative constructions of Inuit history on their own terms" ("Screen" 43). The implications are profound: "Their work not only provides a record of a heretofore undocumented legacy at a time when the generation still versed in traditional knowledge is rapidly passing; by also involving young people in the process, the production of these historical dramas requires that they learn Inuktitut and a range of other skills tied to their cultural legacies, thus helping to mitigate a crisis in the social and cultural reproduction of Inuit life" (42). Although CEFREC-CAIB's videos are situated in the present tense, their representations of traditional stories have similar consequences. The docudramas and fictions foreground the indigenous subject as protagonist and epistemic authority; they recover a marginalized history and strengthen the practice of storytelling by emphasizing its relevance. The films valorize indigenous language use and involve an entire community in the enactment of social values. Indianizing audiovisual media hence goes beyond the mimetic level.

K'anata, *Pampas*, and *Saltas*: Braiding and Weaving Video Narratives

The profound effects of indigenous media are partially due to the way storytelling itself cannot be fully separated from other forms of transmitting knowledge, such as music, song, dance, weaving, agricultural practice, even the construction of houses (Arnold and de Dios Yapita, *Hacia* 176). *Qati qati* replicates the structure of Andean storytelling as it blends the cinematographic horror genre with Andean tales of the walking dead. While the film criticizes the loss of belief in the traditional tales and divine manifestations that transmit a social ethos, the film braids together different story lines that shed light on each other. The complex plot intertwines two different main storylines as well as various renderings of the *qati qati* tale. Valentina performs storytelling on screen when she narrates the story of the flying head to her children. Tata Anselmo summarizes another version when trying to convince Fulo of the relevance of traditional beliefs. Valentina herself dies, turned into a flying head while her story is intertwined with an apparently unconnected story about a robbery. The community elders solve the robbery with the help of a *chullpa*, the buried remains of an *abuela* (literally a grandmother who is herself a microcosm of yet another story that is, however, not developed). This mummy reveals a young man and minor character in the film as the culprit. These story lines are connected through a dream scene: Fulo bathes in a cold mountain stream that turns to crimson, he laughs at a bloody dripping head that comes flying by, itself yet another version of the *qati qati* story. The color red then marks the lining in Valentina's bowler hat as Fulo watches her waving and departing on a truck. Water itself would have been enough of an indicator of impending doom, but the explicit bloody elements drive the point home. Both ritual lifting of footprints in the robbery case and the dream itself shed light on the principal *qati qati* story. Had Fulo heeded the dream's warning and performed a ritual like in the characters in the robbery tale, he may have been able to save his wife. This braiding of parallel plots incorporates the film into the format of storytelling and singing that Aymaras call *k'anata* (cf. *Hacia* 185).

K'anata or braiding is a common format for stories in the Andean high-lands and is mirrored in casual conversations and sentence structure. A speaker may begin a story or sentence, "then [the sentence] is interrupted by words that introduce a future idea, like seeds strewn casually across a text, they introduce an idea that will only come to fruition later, perhaps several sentences later. These strewn out words seem disparate to a person who doesn't speak Aymara well. Yet a native speaker is accustomed to this kind of style and usually expects for the apparently loose threads to eventually be completed" (*Hacia* 186). As Arnold and de Dios Yapita have pointed out, the early colonial chroniclers admired the mnemotechnical use of *khipus* (or *chinu* in Aymara) for remembering stories and legends. Arnold and De Dios Yapita ask if the order of recording knowledge by *khipu*—that is, by arranging knotted strings so that they lead from the most general down to the more specific—might not actually resemble the taxonomical order their Aymara co-author uses to arrange the stories he tells: "For Don Domingo there is a precise order to his stories. . . . 'Things are not all mixed, like in the museum in La Paz,' rather the sequence 'goes downward': *pir aynachar iraqtaña*" (*Hacia* 193; also 198–99). *K'anata* also refers to the braiding of *khipus* and perhaps even to certain structures in weaving. Weaving, on the other hand, is a form of representation that is intimately related to storytelling and the ritual invocation of forces beneficial to the communities and their agricultural means of subsistence (Heckman 97–105; Seibold 183).

These links between different modes and technologies of transmitting knowledge and social memory transcend the Andean context. It is no surprise that storytelling in the lowland video *Our Word* combines storytelling with performance, dance, and music in an interwoven fashion, alternating the telling and its reenactment. The structure of *Rebellions and Hopes*, Marcelina Cárdenas's documentary short about weaving that compares highland and lowland practices, is also arranged to resemble a braiding. The editing alternates and intertwines scenes from the high- and lowlands. Rather than neatly separate, weaving, braiding, storytelling, agriculture, and dance are intricately linked and together sustain indigenous epistemologies. In the Andes, weavers find inspiration in the landscape; they continue to symbolically represent social relations as well as call them into being. Weavings are sites where women manipulate miniature designs; transforming them, they "bring their larger counterparts into being in the *ayllu* macrocosm" (Arnold, "Making" 116).

Although the vast knowledge encoded in the Incan knotted strings called *khipus* may not be fully recoverable, *khipus* today still provide an important means of accounting and keeping track of local history (Salomon 21, 109–36, 209–36). Indigenous social memory and identity continue to be transmitted through the repertoire of embodied performance in rituals, celebrations, and parodies of colonial history enacted in Andean carnival but also in songs and through the daily embodiment of dress, hairstyle, and language use.[6] These material forms of signifying, along with bodily enactments and story-telling, are far from ephemeral. They have been transformed in the process of colonialism but have not disappeared (Taylor 43). In the Andes the prevalence of visual and other material forms of transmitting knowledge alongside storytelling remains overwhelming. The ties between what Taylor calls *repertoire* (performed and embodied forms of transmitting knowledge) and *archive* (material artifacts, such as weavings, *khipus*, and pottery design), as well as other means of transmitting knowledge, historical memory, and belonging—such as the meanings attributed to the ruins of buildings and roads or those ascribed to mountains, lakes, and *wak'as* (odd-shaped rocks and natural formations that in Quechua and Aymara worldview are the abodes of deities)—link material artifacts and the bodily transmission of knowledge.

Such interwoven modes and forms of knowledge characterize indigenous epistemological regimes in the entire region. Rappaport discusses the Nasa notion of sacred geography where tales told by local caciques "are linked to particular topographic sites that spatially locate the places at which the culture heroes were born, lived, and fought major battles, created resguardos and finally disappeared from human society. . . . Sacred geography is the medium in which history is experienced in everyday life: as a fleeting image, a brief mention, a vista, a resting-place, not a lengthy narrative" (*Politics* 161). While Rappaport argues that these inscriptions of meaning into the landscape foster "a moral continuity with the past, more than a detailed knowledge of it" (161), she also highlights the way these historical events often coincide with the abodes of mythical ancestors: high mountains that form borders between communities. Moreover, the Nasa both ritually and more casually remember by walking along marked sites in a precise temporal and spatial order. As Rappaport explains, "the riches of La Plata, destroyed by the colonial Nasa, are said to have been transported in single file via a mountain called la Muralla to Tumbichucue, a clear northwesterly movement. The story is preserved in the rock formation, which is said to be a line of petrified Indians. Juan Tama . . . also moved toward the northwest, battling the Guambiano in the Páramo de Moras and settling finally in the Juan Tama Lake. His unbaptized siblings were transformed into snakes whose fragments are also oriented upriver, toward the northwest" (166). Community members who walk from their villages to the market town and back "will pass numerous sites which encode Nasa history. The order in which they pass them causes them to relive the historical migration of the Nasa to the western slopes of the cordillera. Here again, through practice . . . temporal structure and history are experienced and enacted" (166–67). The video makers transpose this experience to the audiovisual medium, offering views of designated mountains readily recognizable to local Nasa viewers.

Film has been considered an archival form, opposed to the realm of performance. Diana Taylor (21), following Paul Connerton (41–71), has argued convincingly that performance is not ephemeral but acquires a staying power through the various ways it replicates itself. Taylor, however, also reiterates the notion that the *repertoire* demands presence in contrast with archival materials that are able to signify across time and space (20). Seeking to account for the difference between live performance and its recordings, she allocates video in the realm of the *archive* (see also Connerton 78). Even written documents, however, are unstable. The embodied reader and the context of reception construct and alter the meanings of what seem to be inalterable signs. The archive is in as much need of rethinking as the idea of ephemeral storytelling and ritual. The artifact is always involved in its reception—that is, in scenarios and embodied forms of understanding. In light of indigenous media, the line between what is *repertoire* and what is *archive* cannot be drawn neatly. Rather than neatly distinguish between archive and repertoire, indigenous media activists and communities link these semiotic systems on screen. In other words, representation and the communities' enactment of multiple forms of transmitting knowledge in front of the camera are fused in the audiovisual process. The videos allow tracing a continuity from traditional semiotic systems to the audiovisual medium. This continuity indicates a key strategy for turning video into a tool for indigenous movements. It constitutes a key component in the process of indianizing film.

Khipus are today used in a scaled-down form but used to be extremely complex. They not only conveyed statistical information about tribute and agricultural storage; they were also mnemonic devices for epic storytelling and had meanings encoded that are no longer fully understood (Salomon

11–20). Similarly, weavings offer multilayered means of signifying. Abstract designs and their location, visual metaphors—particularly those of animals located in the borders of weavings—can convey entire worldviews as well as particular stories (Seibold, 196–97; Heckman, 100–101). The plain central parts of a weaving, like the decorative borders, point to a relationship between human activity, natural forces, and agricultural or pastoral fields. Arnold and de Dios Yapita suggest that textiles function as archives that have been successfully used to complement written documents in struggles over territorial rights ("Caminos" 375), but their epistemic quality actually encodes all of the dimensions of the Andean lifeworld, including gender, cosmology, archeology, and the ideological and conceptual (376). Although men are traditionally responsible for knitting the metaphoric designs on their own and their sons' *ch'ullu* (hat), the intricate and complex fine yarn weaving and spinning of natural and synthetic fibers is women's responsibility (Heckman 102, 106; Arnold, "Making" 102–3). Arnold and Yapita emphasize that ignoring or even subalternizing textiles, as do not only historians but also members of the *ayllus* themselves (375), is deeply implicated with the association of this technology with femininity. Weaving remains a space where women encode their understanding of the world (Arnold, "Making" 130).

Either explicitly or through editing, or both, indigenous video revives technologies of knowledge grounded in storytelling, *khipus*, and weaving. The videos create a sense of logical extension, where these forms give way to audiovisual representation; a new form of weaving, one might say, that coexists with innovative and traditional weaving practice and designs. Again, this continuity transcends the Bolivian highland context. The Colombian *We Spin and Weave Giving Life to the Universe* and the Bolivian *Rebellions and Hopes* highlight weaving as a means of transmitting knowledge in related ways. *We Spin and Weave Giving Life to the Universe* follows the Nasa anthropologist Carmen Vitonás as she seeks to learn how to read the *chumbe* from her grandmother. The *chumbe* is a carrying belt rich in symbols and icons. The documentary crosscuts reenactments of the tales woven into the belt with footage of the two women's conversations. The video affirms a female genealogy of knowledge transmission across generations, which has gone into crisis but that the Nasa granddaughter-turned-visual-anthropologist recovers. Cárdenas's *Rebellions and Hopes*, on the other hand, follows the documentary filmmaker's voyage to the Bolivian lowland to show how textiles function similarly in the highlands and the Moxos. Her film enacts an instance of intercultural or inter-indigenous learning from and about the knowledge read and encoded in textiles. This documentary short braids the two primary sites of investigation, crosscutting between them, thus tying the visit of the fictionalized documentary filmmaker to the lowlands with one of her interlocutor's trips up to the highland. Significantly, both the Colombian and the Bolivian video again cast women as the bearers of indigenous knowledge who are responsible for its transmission, either from one generation to the next or as a reciprocal exchange across cultures.

Just as much information that used to be transmitted through *khipus* may have found its way into the abstract and metaphoric language of weaving, particularly the *tocapu* (Heckman, 48–51; Harrison 60–61), the resemblance between weavings and some of the videos indicates a correspondence between textiles and the audiovisual medium that is thematic, structural, and symbolic. *Vest Made of Money* perhaps illustrates this most clearly. The dramatic opening scenes include a fight between Satuco (Reynaldo Yujra) and his wife where she throws down her spinning in frustration. The sequence encapsulates a power struggle where Tomasa no longer makes economic decisions even though traditionally she is better poised to judge when livestock should be sold: "with their daily herding activity women are in a good position to make the vital decisions about the livestock of the household: which animals should be slaughtered, which shorn, which are good breeders, and which should be sold" (Harris quoted in Harrison 120). The scene also opposes a technology of knowledge transmission grounded in the visual and tactile qualities of wool, literally held by women, and a Western mind-set attuned to accumulation embodied by men. It is possible to read the entire structure of *Vest Made of Money* as a reference to weaving. The title itself names a textile (the vest), and its narrative and visual structure resembles a woven woman's shawl (*liclla*). The video deploys striking camerawork to reframe the Andean highlands that literature and film had coded as the site of melancholy, a place of suffering, oppression, and epic struggle. *Vest Made of Money* renders instead beautiful landscape and marketplace images, turning the highlands into a place of critical self-reflection. It deploys an almost touristic videography that introduces the setting slowly, through an ever-closer approximation that ends with close-ups of the protagonists' faces. The colorful sunset/sunrise sequence that opens and closes this short parallels the colorful border stripes on the two joined weavings of the *llicla*. While the *saltas* that border the plain weave can contain mimetic representations, often they are highly abstract. The postcard-like short takes of animals, church, ancient grain storage ruins, and small groups of people that structure the transition between the action scenes in *Vest Made of Money* resemble the use of such imagery in the iconic strips next to the plain weave borders. These shots succeed each other in relatively rapid rhythm, creating an almost photographic quality. The two major story lines—Satuco's greed and death and Cihuacollo's grave robbery and subsequent insanity—resemble the central plain weave parts of the *liclla* that reference community pastures.

Vest Made of Money's work with short montage sequences binds images of the village church, market scenes, the landscape, precolonial buildings, and the shots of animals to the framing of Aymara people themselves. These transitional sequences construct a visual iconography of the Aymara people that relies more heavily on images than on dialogue. In other words, *Vest Made of Money*, similarly to *Cursed Gold*, turns images into iconic metaphors, invoking systems of knowing while placing them into specific geographical locations and sociopolitical contexts. The images function as symbols that create particularity. Like visual shortcuts, they identify particular perspectives, meanings, and locations within the heterogeneous viewing community. These markers of place and ethnic specificity create viewing pleasure and affective identification for those who recognize themselves as the subjects of the film and as the objects of another spectator's gaze: the broader and divers pan-indigenous viewing community. Even if the details of the knowledge transmitted here might not be legible to all viewers, they will recognize a similar form of transmitting knowledge, a similar "script" as their own.[7] In other words, the symbols used in the videos signify across different cultural settings. The medium shot of a rooster that announces the break of a new day, the close-up of the moon in both *Vest Made of Money* and *Qati qati* signal the passing of time. Both are direct temporal references, but the former also refers to the power of transitional animals—those inhabiting both water and land, earth and sky—depicted in the weavings. Bad omens, like the subtropical snake in *Cursed Gold* parallel the highland snake Valentina calls a human intestine in *Qati qati*. Black birds in *Vest Made of Money* and in *Loving Each Other in the Shadows* similarly announce impending doom. The zigzag design on weavings, which may indicate water or a path, is reflected and reworked in the use of water on screen, along with other references to the landscape. In *Qati qati*, the *chullpa* that solves the robbery is never seen but is marked geographically. The lakes, mountains, and Mother Earth, whose power Fulo is accused of forgetting, are a visual presence in the video. The lake in *Loving Each Other in the Shadows* and the mountain stream in *Qati qati* are gendered differently (a lake is considered female and a stream male), but both refer to impending doom when seen in dreams. Water is also a transitional space between the living and the dead. In *Loving Each Other in the Shadows* the lake becomes the place of Juancito's rebirth and Rosita's freedom; in *Cursed Gold* the pond and waterfall are the devil's realm, a site of human sacrifice, bloody tragedy. In *The Forest Spirit* from the Moxos lowlands a river separates the reign of the jaguar spirit from the sphere of human society. Indigenous media activists frame the gods encoded in landscape and the meanings attributed to animals or water; they combine these shots with the visual representation of the ephemeral, such as the bird of bad tidings, ghosts, and devils.

Specters and the Space between the Living and the Dead

Several fiction shorts take the emphasis on the visual rather than on dialogue into yet another dimension. Not only are there references to the encoded, symbolic, even allegorical meanings rendered in weaving and landscape, but the films frequently visualize specters and dreams. In other words, these films make visible to all what is invisible or only visible to one. The videos thus enhance a regime of knowledge transmission that has, to a large degree, always relied on complex semiotic forms. The play between the visual and the invisible, the omnipresence of dreams, premonitions, and ghosts in all of CEFREC-CAIB's fiction videos are key references to subalternized systems of knowing.

We have already seen that the dreams in *Qati qati* and in *Cursed Gold* contain key premonitions that go unheeded and thus unravel the dramatic plot. *Cursed Gold* indeed operates with different levels of visuality. The devil in *Cursed Gold* is a syncretic figure rendered as a plain-clothed elderly man. He reflects the undead made visible in other films such as *Vest Made of Money* and *Loving Each Other.* In *Vest Made of Money* Satuco's ghost haunts the community, a visible warning not only to this community but others as well. In contrast to the theatrical makeup and staging of the devil in CEFREC-CAIB's *The Hunter* (*El cazador*), in *Cursed Gold* the devil maintains his trace of invisibility within the frame. His appearance shifts as he exchanges the polyester shirt of the village for the rags of a man living deep in the forest, but he is never explicitly made up as the devil. As he eats and drinks in town, he seems invisible to everyone except to Tito, the gold digger, and us, the audience. The allusion is subtle, as there are no crosscuts of missed looks. The figure symbolizes the devil in a manner not necessarily immediately obvious to an audience unaccustomed to the trope. The play between the visible and the invisible continues at the level of the spectator. The audience is both inside and outside the frame as the camera eye defines the devil's gaze as the audience's point of view. The devil thus symbolizes the spectators, a national indigenous audience, if we follow the allegorical reading of this video, where the figure can be seen to represent the indigenous military conscript. Only at the end of this short, when the corps that Tito offers to the waterfall emerges bloody and with a deep roar from the water is there no more doubt. The devil has killed Tito himself. Yet this is also the moment when the video distances us from the devil's gaze, finally identifying us with Juanita, the young Quechua woman who had warned Tito all along. Reading the devil as an allegory of military violence, as I suggested earlier, again frames the invisible and renders it visible as a trace. Reading Tito's loss of belief allegorically highlights the power such abandonment hands to military, narco-traffickers, and neo-imperialist forces.[8]

Video does not displace oral communication, however; rather, it indirectly stimulates oral forms of transmitting knowledge. The media activist Alfredo Copa emphasized in the interview with Daniel Flores that video entices especially younger audiences to ask elders about a story's details and variants. Oral, aural, and visual forms of transmitting knowledge are also fused on screen. In her study of Quichua songs and their relation to Andean ways of thinking that can be teased from colonial texts, Regina Harrison emphasizes that "in the contemporary lyrics I have collected in Ecuador, visual images dominate the poetic expression, and references to the verb of 'seeing' as 'experiencing' abound in the transcribed texts. 'Seeing' is a primary means by which information is stored and then later retrieved for expression in song" (79). While Harrison draws attention to the use of visual images in lyrics, I have argued that visual imagery structures video fictions like *Vest Made of Money*. On the other hand, the original soundtrack composed for *Vest Made of Money* creates sound bites, audio icons of a particular highland context in order to perform a contribution to the much wider inter-indigenous debate. Traditional instruments create a soundtrack that is not strictly folkloric but links the narrative through the repetition of musical motifs, a very particular "Andean sound" that alternates with computer-generated sound effects. The soundtrack thus becomes an audio-icon for a region. The Aymara dialogue in this video functions similarly. It becomes an affirmation of the continued existence of cultural practices and orders of knowledge transmitted through language.

The soundtrack and dialogue of the videos reinforce the sense of recognition while simultaneously taking advantage of the flexibility of the medium, which, unlike radio, allows one to project dialogue in one language and subtitles in another, while facilitators simultaneously interpret in yet another language during the screening. Reliance on oral communication in the fiction videos is minimal, nevertheless. The non-Spanish dialogue is transcribed (often not even completely) into Spanish subtitles (or English if the videos are screened at international festivals). Meaning is primarily generated through images, tone of voice, and soundtrack—that is, through aural and visual components. The audio-visuality of the medium thus takes advantage of the "human ability to 'grasp certain relationships visually at a glance but not to describe them in words with anything like equal precision" (Stillman Drake quoted in Boone, "Introduction" 9). Harrison equates the Quechua order of comprehension with findings in cognitive psychology. Quoting Michael I. Posner, she writes, "the capacity for storing information is enhanced by this facility for visual reproduction of complex hierarchical systems of knowledge. Human subjects, when questioned, often report that they can 'construct a visual representation which includes more information than they can verbalize'" (Harrison 81). Video thus re-creates and vitalizes the combination of oral-visual semiotics as a technology of knowledge, not at all an alien technology to indigenous contexts.

Indigenous media's use of visual and aural elements requires rethinking film as a representational medium. Indigenous material forms of signifying, along with bodily enactments and symbolism are strengthened through indigenous audiovisual communication. Certainly, social memory and identity continue to be transmitted through the repertoire of embodied performance in rituals, celebrations, the parodies of colonial history enacted in Andean carnival but also through the daily embodiment of dress, hairstyle, and language use. The processes of transmitting knowledge have been transformed by colonialism but have not disappeared (Taylor 43). Terence Turner writes that in Brazil, Kayapo video makers successfully integrate Kayapo notions of mimesis and representation into their documentaries of ceremonies ("Representation, Politics" 84).[9] Film is then no longer considered a foreign technology. Rather, following Turner, "representation, far from being an exclusively Western project foisted on the Kayapo through the influence of Western media, is as Kayapo as manioc meat pie" (84). Indigenous video in Bolivia similarly collapses the tenuous distinction between representation and ritual. Video making frequently involves the ritual reenactment or revitalization of rituals by the community for the camera. In this sense, representation/ritual is indeed as Kayapo as it is Aymara or Quechua. Unlike literary transculturation, where points of view sympathetic to indigenous figures were enhanced by the progressive incorporation of Quechua and Aymara words, poems, even grammatical changes to the Spanish language or to the narrative structures of novels, video making creates a space to not only represent/narrate indigenous worldviews but also enact them.

Ginsburg has found a similar logic at work in Aboriginal video from Australia. What Ginsburg terms "embedded aesthetics" is the tight interrelationship between what we see on screen and the process of evaluation and production that leads to enactment and filming ("Embedded" 368). Ginsburg argues that "the value or beauty of such videos for the Pitjantjatjara video makers is extratextual, created by the cultural and social processes they mediate, embody, create, and extend. The tapes underscore the cosmological power of ceremonies to invigorate sacred aspects of the landscape; they reinforce the social relations that are fundamental to ritual production; and they enhance the place of Pitjantjatjara among Aboriginal groups in the area" (370). Even camera movement and the length of takes are informed by aboriginal criteria. Ginsburg quotes Eric Michaels, who promoted indigenous video among the Warlpiri people in Australia, as saying "one is struck by the recurrent camera movement, [and] the subtle shifts in focus and attention during the otherwise even, long pans across the landscape" (371). As Frances Jupurrulrla Kelly, the Warlpiri producer and director of the film, explains, the movement corresponds to marking "important things in the landscape, like a tree where spirits live or a flower with symbolic value" (371). The camera not only represents but calls what it frames into being.

The screening and discussion of indigenous media create another site of performance, another level where social relations come into existence, where access to media technology and know-how are in reach of indigenous communities and communicators. Film technology—an oral, visual, and performative medium—expands and vitalizes the means of transmitting traditions. Although audiovisual technology seems to transcend the anchoring of performance (on screen) in the feeling of a shared time and space, it also affirms this joint experience. Seeing how other communities debate and enact contemporary issues on screen creates a common living experience with those in the audience. Furthermore, the screening itself enacts a shared moment in historical time where the technology becomes a part of indigenous culture, accessible, and now part of a self-determined modernity lived by indigenous peoples.

Beyond Literacy and Orality

In light of this process of adaptation, notions about indigenous cultures being premediatic fall short. So does the teleological assumption that locates orality as prior to literacy and audiovisual media.[10] As Michaels put it, "Aboriginal and other 'developing' people do not conform to this sequence [from orality to literacy, print, film and now electronics], and produce some very different media histories" (82). The process of audiovisual communication certainly bypasses literacy to a significant degree. Some of the indigenous video makers and their audiences are only partially literate, while others have gone through the state educational system and are reacting, like their intellectual counterparts in research institutions like Centro de Investigación y Promoción del Campesinado (CIPCA) and THOA, to the Eurocentric contents they encountered. Video makers take advantage of the communicative possibilities of the audiovisual medium in overcoming the limitations of alphabetic texts, usually monolingual and anchored in access to state education (literacy). Video is a technology that in both its production and reception relies only minimally on literacy. Even scripts for fiction films can be storyboarded or memorized, as Julia Mosúa insists (Mosúa, Copa, and Pinto, audiotape), especially if the dialogue is not scripted but improvised, as is the case in CEFREC-CAIB's docudramas and fictions. Film also more readily allows for multilingualism. Many indigenous films are spoken in Spanish, the lingua franca among the Latin American indigenous population (except in Brazil). Others are spoken in indigenous languages and subtitled in Spanish or English. To reiterate, in the context of the Bolivian communication network subtitles in Spanish may be read out loud by the facilitators showing the films. The facilitators may also translate the subtitles or dialogue into their native language, spoken in the community where the screening takes place. Literacy here is marginalized and integrated into a larger design of audiovisual communication; it does not become the primary vehicle of communication and thinking.

Considering that access to full literacy remains elusive for many—even undesirable in its present form and focus, as some communities continue to emphasize (Arnold and De Dios Yapita, *Rincón* 117)—the use of audiovisual technology by indigenous communities appears quite appropriate. Although it is also important to note that indigenous communities continue to demand better access to state education, the media activists are already creating alternative networks of knowledge production. These alternative networks provide the grounds to speak back at urban society "from the perspectives of our communities," as CEFREC puts it.[11] Yet audiovisual communication does not merely skip literacy. Indigenous media urge us to consider not only the way the lettered city's visual economy itself splinters the dichotomy of literacy and orality, but also press us to take note of the complex forms of signifying within so-called oral cultures. In other words, the binary of literacy and orality is insufficient on both terrains, that of Western "literate civilization" and that of supposedly "oral indigenous cultures."

The issue is crucial to indigenous knowledge politics. When Weiner asserts that indigenous cultures are based on orality and ritual instead of mediation, he constructs indigenous societies in terms of innocence—that is, as prior to mediation and opposed to the decadent superficiality of Western simulacra. At once he inscribes epistemic privilege. The idea of literacy arrived not only armed in the process of conquest but also harnessed to the notion of intellectual capacity: "All thought, including that in primarily oral cultures, is to some degree analytic: it breaks its materials into various components. But abstractly sequential, classificatory, explanatory examination of phenomena or of stated truths is impossible without writing and reading. Human beings in primarily oral cultures, those untouched by writing in any from, learn a great deal and possess and practice great wisdom, but they do not 'study.' . . . Study in the strict sense of extended sequential analysis becomes possible with the interiorization of writing" (Ong 8–9). This move from orality to literacy inscribes epistemic and intellectual hierarchies. As Alcida Ramos, put it, "to divide primitive mythic societies from historical societies is to add to the intellectual apparatus of domination, to build a sort of indigenist orientalism" (138). The teleological view on technologies of representation put forth the idea that alphabetic literacy allows for critical reflection, while oral modes of transmitting knowledge do not. When Weiner sets up the Western society of the spectacle as more complex than oral cultures, he reiterates what we might call a Western mythology of literacy and intellect. Like Ong, Weiner inscribes intellectual capacity as an outcome of mediation. In Weiner's case, the mythology of literacy and intellect serves, however, to construct epistemic privilege for the anthropologist, speaking from a place of critical and mediated distance. In this view members of indigenous communities would seem unable to critically reflect on their culture, let alone on the global economic dynamics rooted in colonialism.[12] The Western mythology of literacy and intellect merits a more detailed critique because it is quite pervasive.[13]

Weiner's assumptions are, indeed, fundamentally flawed. The myth of literacy is linked to entrenched beliefs about presence and mediation. These beliefs stipulate that oral expression is not mediated in the process of aural decoding or in the process of thinking and turning thoughts into words. Orality is thus seen to render a direct communication from subject to subject. The word is seen to represent the referent (thought ontologically). Alphabetic writing, in contrast, is mediated; it represents the word and is assumed capable of transmitting across space and time, which oral expression cannot. While orality promises immediacy, the written word seems to offer distance, critical distance to be sure. However, even in oral conversation or telecommunicative situations where all speakers are present in the same time (and space), communication never fully succeeds but always produces lacks and excesses of meaning. So does all semiotic exchange—including alphabetic writing, cinema, and video—especially, but not only, if it takes place cross-culturally (in space or time). On the other hand, phonocentrism attributes to alphabetic writing an omnipotence that fails to live up to closer scrutiny: A text is rarely read the same by different readers. With Derrida we might even insist that the word is no less of a representation than is the written sign, that thought is always already representation. The conceptual binary of orality and writing distinguishes what cannot be separated. Alphabetic literacy, like orality, is impure. Even Ong admits, "writing can never dispense with orality" (8). Orality, literacy, ritual, and visual forms of signifying do not exist in isolation from each other or from the complex embodied and performative dimensions of transmitting knowledge.

The telephone game that children are commonly taught in Western schools in order to prove the superiority and need for alphabetic writing fails to live up to the complex ways of signifying within so-called oral cultures. There are discourse types (think only of songs and poetry) and mnemonic devices (such as khipus and weavings) that impede arbitrary changes in oral messages over time and space (Street, *Literacy* 48). Most important, oral communication involves as much classificatory intellectual procedures as alphabetic writing and is in principal equally at work in all languages and cultural contexts (38). The binary construct of orality versus literacy is an abstraction from the mix of oral and semiotic practices present in all societies; there is no such thing as an unmediated society. All across Latin America indigenous communities in fact continue to practice multiple forms of representation and enactment (such as weaving, basketry, embodied storytelling, dance, and inscriptions of meaning into the landscape). These visual and performative ways of transmitting knowledge parallel the use of literacy by some community authorities and, increasingly, by larger parts of indigenous youth. From this viewpoint, indigenous cultures cannot be characterized as premediatic. Rather, indigenous media extend visual, tactile, oral, and performative traditions of transmitting knowledge.

Looking more carefully at the variety of semiotic systems through which so-called oral cultures communicate, it becomes evident that orality, visual, and embodied forms of transmitting knowledge and cultural memory go hand in hand. The argument can be extended to ritual as well. The notion of ritual as an unmediated form of calling into being falls short. Ritual is not opposed to mimetic representation where an imitative copy of reality is created. Rather the division between representation and life disintegrates if we accept that ritual involves enactment and representations frequently assume a presence of their own. How else can we explain the outrage over burning a national flag in the United States? Ritual just like other forms of representation transmits social memory over time (Taylor 14). In other words, ritual also functions semiotically across time. Denise Arnold, Domingo Jiménez, and Juan de Dios Yapita emphasize this interrelationship in the Andean context: "It is becoming ever clearer that each Andean story, as a text, cannot be understood in isolation. The spoken words of each story, at times sung, cannot be extracted from their contexts. The story is inseparable from the act of telling and the ritual that accompanies it. As anthropological research has described, there is a 'multilevel intertextuality' that connects the execution of supposedly separated activities such as story telling, music and dance, weaving, agricultural practice, the construction of houses, etc." (*Hacia* 176).

Indigenous media build on surviving and continuously re-created visual, performative, and tactile forms of signifying. Rather than being steeped in orality, the diverse indigenous cultures of the continent have combined oral modes of communication with visual and performative means of transmitting knowledge. Before the conquest and in a more subdued manner afterwards, such representations were realized through codices, glyphs, knotted *khipus* and weavings, inscriptions of meaning into the landscape, dance and rituals, etc. As Diana Taylor has argued, "the separation that Rama notes between written and spoken word, echoed in de Certeau, points to only one aspect of the repression of indigenous embodied practice as a form of knowing, as well as a system for storing and transmitting knowledge. Nonverbal practices—such as dance, ritual, and cooking, to name a few—that long served to preserve a sense of communal identity and memory were not considered valid forms of knowledge" (Taylor 18).[14] These material forms of signifying, technologies of knowledge if you will, along with bodily enactments and storytelling, have been crucial to the transmission of cultural memory. The adaptation and transformation of audiovisual media's profound effects relies on establishing a correspondence between indigenous mediatic traditions and the new technology. Indianizing film works through established codes of signifying, recombining codes that the film industry's global distribution practices have turned into formulas and connecting them with complex semiotic traditions. From this vantage point, indigenous peoples have always been mediatic.

7

**INDIGENOUS MEDIA
AND THE MARKET**

As if visualizing the Quechua/Aymara moral imperative—*ama sua, ama lulla, ama kella* (do not steal, do not lie, do not be lazy)—labor is an overwhelming presence in CEFREC-CAIB's videos.[1] Sowing, harvesting, herding, spinning, weaving, cooking, and childcare are regular chores. They form the backdrop to the narrative plots of *Vest Made of Money, Forest Spirit, Loving Each Other in the Shadows, Overcoming Fear,* and *Qati qati.* Many indigenous video documentaries and fictions explicitly criticize the desire to become part of a global, capitalist economy based on maximizing profits. *Qati qati* elaborately represents a self-sufficient Aymara household that relies on a complementary gendered division of labor and on barter. *Vest Made of Money,* like *Qati qati* filmed in the Aymara speaking highlands, brings monetary exchange to the forefront and criticizes its excesses. *Cursed Gold* invokes both the global drug trade and the traditional coca leaf market (that connects different regions, ethnicities, and ecological tiers) where the leaves are coveted for their role in ritual and medicine. The video vindicates traditional coca use and trade but allegorically condemns both the illegal profit-driven coca market and the eradication policies implemented under U.S. pressure in the Bolivian Chapare and Yungas valleys. Like *Vest Made of Money,* this video also criticizes the unchecked desire for wealth. The concern over economic order and development is paramount to indigenous communities in the lowlands as well. As discussed earlier, several of CEFREC-CAIB's educational documentaries and some of CONAIE's productions highlight alternative development projects and criticize the effects of logging and oil drilling on indigenous land. The Colombian CRIC's *The Nasa Garden* appeals to the communities in the Cauca region to reinstate traditional agricultural methods. These videos help prepare the communities to argue and struggle for human rights as a right to territory, including the management of natural resources above and below ground. The topic of environmental destruction and sustainable development is one of the most pressing for indigenous communities living in lowland subtropical and tropical agricultural regions and for those whose territories harbor subsoil mineral resources. The desire to achieve not only sustainable living conditions but also economic and technological improvements is an urgent matter for many indigenous communities regardless of their geographic location.

The activities preceding and accompanying the Bolivian Constituent Assembly (August 6, 2006–August 5, 2007) addressed these concerns through an indigenous media information campaign that worked through indigenous television, newspapers, radio, and multimedia packages distributed through CEFREC-CAIB's network. This media campaign extended and amplified a debate over economic, social, and human rights. As an intercultural process, it involved a variety of communities and indigenous and peasant organizations (cf. CEFREC, "Rumbo," n.p.). The ongoing focus on labor, economy, and territory responds to the pressure of indigenous and peasant communities in the low- and highlands who have been discussing how best to take advantage of modern technology and better their living standards while strengthening their cultures. Key concerns are how communities might redress poverty, limited healthcare, and lack of access to education without falling for the promises of neoliberal reforms that are proving illusory. In short, the videos represent indigenous peoples as self-reliant hard workers who are intensely engaged in trade across cultures and across ecological zones. They seek access to technology, electricity, health care, and so forth. At the same time, fiction and documentary shorts sharply criticize the unchecked desire for individual wealth. In other words, they challenge racist prejudices about "lazy Indians" but also criticize the profit principal guiding global capitalism. How do these concerns impact video production and distribution? How do media activists respond to the interests of a global market for multiculturalism?

On the one hand, video making includes the enactment of social and economic practices on screen, which resonate with audiences and can impact their cultural practices off screen. On the other hand, film and video are themselves products of labor relations and they circulate as commodities. Indeed, film is a particular kind of commodity. It is an intangible object of cultural consumption, a moving image projected in cinemas and broadcast on television and iPods. In its material quality film is rendered on DVDs or VHS tapes that circulate through official channels and pirate markets. It results from labor relations and it usually enters, often synergistically integrated with a wide range of ancillary products, into global marketing and distribution systems. The global film industry accommodates production and distribution practices to new profit opportunities. It has moved from imperialist policies to outsourcing, or to what Miller et al. describe as "runaway production" (111–72). Coproductions and a renewed interest in integrating successful directors and actors from Latin America directly into the Hollywood mode of production attest to the possibilities that seem to open up for multicultural content and so-called fresh perspectives. These opportunities lure young and not so young filmmakers and actors in Latin America into coproductions, realized on an ever-greater scale. Certainly, such participation comes at a price. If third cinema sought to promote social revolution in the sixties and seventies, international coproductions today are primarily expected to make a profit. Hollywood film and much of its aesthetics continue to constitute a global reference point. Despite highly productive media industries in India and Hong Kong, Hollywood still stands for compelling cinematic narratives and technological spectacle. Indeed, the prevalence of visual media and advertising, among them photographs, cinema, VHS, DVD, and television, have shaped the sense of being and perception globally, although certainly not homogeneously. Indigenous media activists in Bolivia, Colombia, and Ecuador face viewing habits, expectations, and a distribution practice that tends to keep national Andean productions out of mainstream cinemas unless they cater to a superficial taste for the local, presented within the genre frameworks that Hollywood hegemony in the twentieth century established in much of the world. Film and video hence need to be considered as socioeconomic practices, not only as a form of cinematic or digital representation. They realize an economic mode of production with profound cultural impact.

In the context of the cold war, leftist filmmakers in Latin America reconceived cinema as a revolutionary tool that would operate from a position external to the capitalist system. If socialism was understood as an alternative economic order that was opposed to capitalism, it was also seen as a necessary historical outcome brought about through a revolution incited from without. Following this logic, third cinema rejected Hollywood's formulas along with its modes of production and predatory distribution practices. The

Bolivian Ukamau Group, Solanas and Getino in Argentina, and the Instituto Cubano de Arte e Industria Cinematográficos (ICAIC) in Cuba socialized production and adjusted distribution practices so that workers and peasants could see the films.[2] Indigenous media, in contrast, operates at a political crossroads where the possibility of a militant socialist revolution has been displaced by the hopes set in electoral processes and where a global market economy seems all encompassing. In fact, cultural diversity itself has become a selling point. The collective process of video production and distribution confronts issues of image property rights and faces a world market defined by an increasing subsumption of the lifeworld to the logic of the market and the profit principal. Does this mean that capitalism has entailed the whole-sale integration or destruction of indigenous social and economic life? Does indigenous video constitute a commodity form that itself feeds the global market for multiculturalism, akin perhaps to literary *testimonio*'s fate in the North American academy?[3] Can indigenous media subvert established parameters by working within them or do they, like some of third cinema before them, reject commodification? The references and reenactment of a reciprocal economy in videos like *Qati qati* point to vestigial practices that stubbornly remain outside the logic of capital. We might then also ask if we should best understand global capitalism as creating a plane of immanence where change can no longer come from the outside or if indigenous media indicate a different dynamic.[4]

Capitalism and the Plane of Immanence

Indigenous media emerge in a context where overt racism and the desire for ethnically and culturally homogenous nation-states have largely given way to the dominance of multicultural markets where diversity sells. The global market has commodified postcolonial writers, Oscars are handed out for world cinema productions, and the national anchors of corporate capitalism have loosened. Capitalist centers are multiplying and increasingly creating a small but global middle class. Digital and satellite communication technolo-gies are helping to redraw the contours of a global map of economic power, but only slightly deviating from the lines engraved through colonialism.[5] Global capitalism thrives on access to knowledge and information. Accord-ing to Antonio Negri, these changes originate at least in part from the reform of the financial system under Nixon and Kissinger in 1971 and from changes in the dominant forms of production (Negri, "Toni" 32–33). Transnational corporate capitalism now generates much of its profit through speculation (stocks, land, and information) made possible by new digital communication technologies. Frederic Jameson maintains that abstraction (money) has been taken to a higher level: "Globalization is rather a kind of cyberspace in which money capital has reached its ultimate dematerialization as messages which pass instantaneously from one nodal point to another across the former globe, the former material world" (Jameson 154). Fornazzari explains that what he calls "casino capitalism" (17) relies in fact on a second-level abstraction: "Not only are goods substituted for shares, coins, vouchers, and papers, but these tokens are themselves abstracted and separated from whatever product they may have once represented. This process of abstraction renders the products immaterial, infinitely transferable to any part of the world (20–21). Robert Reich's book *Supercapitalism* includes a graph representing the increase in share values and trading volume at the global financial trading centers. It is a staggering visualization of the changes that are occurring in the financial sector as well as its exponentially increasing importance (96).

Hardt and Negri are not the only ones who see this transformation of emphasis from industrial production to the stock market as a sign of a new phase and form of capitalism, a paradigm shift with regard to modernity. As Fornazzari suggests, "what is at the heart of this regime of accumulation is a speculation on difference. The old stalwarts of stability and invariability do not produce profit; on the contrary, big fluctuations in prices do. Profit making takes place by gambling on wide margins of fluctuating differences. This kind of speculation takes place without the presence of goods or payments. Goods can be sold, purchased, and resold over and over again without the dealers ever physically exchanging them. It is only the difference that is being passed on, the merchandise is being rendered immaterial" (6–7). Others contend that the products of labor and our interaction with machines have also fundamentally changed. Mauricio Lazzarato (132–46) highlights that the industrial production process relies more and more on immaterial labor—thought, planning, and creativity—instead of on physical labor and machines.[6] Fornazzari finds a similar logic at work in financial trading and in the university. He suggests that those laboring at the stock market are no longer served by the old bourgeois values of frugality and rational planning. Rather, "it is all about gambling on novelty, surprise, and difference. It is the work of the creative artists" (17). Thus, the "neoliberal intellectual whose work consists of aestheticizing the visual culture of consumerism" complements the two new types of cultural producers identified by Bourdieu and Wacquant—"the expert" and the " 'communication consultant to the prince' who gives academic veneer to the political projects of neoliberal state and business nobility" (18). Intellectual and creative labor—including film-making—in this view, has become fully subsumed to capitalism.

Hardt and Negri (32) suggest, therefore, that the deployment and consumption of information, cultural performances, and intellectual debates are inherent to the capitalist system, constituting a plane of immanence. Immaterial labor indicates that capitalism has assimilated not only labor power but also emotions and intellectual production.[7] Critique and transformation hence no longer come from the outside. The alternatives to the global system arise precisely from within. In a manner resembling Foucault's totalizing and sometimes misunderstood notion of power, the capillary or rhizomatic distribution of power and sites of immaterial labor constitute both the moment of self-policing or "control" as well as the occasions for transforming the system. If Foucault's concept of power entailed resistance, immaterial labor's immanence to the system allows only for an inherent transformation: "the creative forces of the multitude that sustain Empire are also capable of autonomously constructing a counter-Empire, an alternative political organization of global flows and exchanges" (Hardt and Negri xv).

For Hardt and Negri the concept of immaterial labor achieves thus a double move. On the one hand, it extends the Marxist concept of the proletariat to a global level that is no longer anchored in industrial labor; on the other hand, it extends the Foucaultian idea of biopolitics to an all encompassing experience. As if trying to ground the virtuality of immaterial labor, Hardt and Negri reclaim the ontological dimension of life. They state that "in the biopolitical context of Empire . . . the production of capital converges ever more with the production and reproduction of social life itself; it thus becomes ever more difficult to maintain distinctions among productive, reproductive, and unproductive labor. Labor—material or immaterial, intellectual or corporeal—produces and reproduces social life, and in the process is exploited by capital" (402). Since social forces, or rather social life in its entirety, produce the responses of global capitalism, the ontological dimension of life grounds the possibilities for positive change, not only the exercise of power from above but also a productive biopower that transforms the world from below.[8] One of the consequences of this new form of capitalism, they argue, is that both imperialism and colonialism have reached their end and actually become counterproductive for capital accumulation (Hardt and Negri 200). Instead of an exploitation and repression of ethnic differences, global capital celebrates and incorporates cultural diversity (201).

There is a problem, however, in how Hardt and Negri conceive this ontological dimension of life. If we think of being in abstraction, uncoupled from the way subjectivity has been constituted through particular discourses and practices, all forms of creating links and social life become potentially transformative (Cf. Colectivo Situaciones 26).[9] Grounding the constitution of global capitalism historically and in connection with the production of subjectivity, however, creates a different outlook.[10] The consciousness of a global world and the establishment of global trade and exploitation in the sixteenth century rely on what we might also call immaterial labor—the colonial discourses on humanity and later race (indeed the cross-fertilization of gender and racial stereotypes) that served to justify geopolitical structures of economic exploitation. In short, the problem with globalization is not merely one of capital accumulation. Hardt and Negri would not disagree on that. As Santiago Castro-Gómez has pointed out, for Hardt and Negri "it is precisely in the enlightened project of normalization where colonialism fits so well. Constructing the profile of the 'normal' subject that capitalism needed (white, male, owner, worker, heterosexual, etc.) necessarily required the image of an 'other' located in the exteriority of European space. The identity of the bourgeois subject in the seventeenth century is constructed in opposition to the image of 'savages' who lived in America, Africa, and Asia that chroniclers and travelers had circulated throughout Europe" (Castro-Gómez, "Missing" 429–30). Today, according to Fernando Coronil, "as an 'economic' cultural dominant, discourses of neoliberal globalization coexist with celebratory discourses of cultural diversity, as well as with warnings concerning the coming 'clash of civilizations'; they subsume the world's multiple cultures and competing discourses about them as subordinate elements with an encompassing, planetary economic culture" ("Towards" 354).[11] If alterity can easily be read as a facet of the multicultural, the pretense of equality, nevertheless, masks ongoing processes of subalternization. For Hardt and Negri colonialism and postcolonialism remain derivative of modernity and postmodernity, not constitutive of them (Mignolo, "Colonialidad Global" 228). Yet colonialism and the control of the Atlantic are not byproducts of an industrial capitalism developed in European nation-states. Rather, they give rise to a global world system and a structure of power—the "coloniality of power"—that is constitutive of global capitalism as such (Mignolo, "Colonialidad Global" 227–34; Castro-Gómez, "Missing" 435). The majority of indigenous communities in South America have not only recently entered into contact with colonialism and capitalism. Without doubt, the conquest of Latin America's indigenous peoples and their colonial and post-independence exploitation have been foundational to the modern/colonial world system. As Quijano and Wallerstein put it, "the Americas were not incorporated into an already existing capitalist world-economy. There could not have been a capitalist world-economy without the Americas" (549).

Immaterial labor is crucial to capitalism whether as a direct source of value or as an indirect constitutive force of its imaginary. Immaterial labor and biopower, whether we conceive of it ontologically or in a poststructuralist sense as the metaphoric and material effects of discourse, are, in this sense, not novel elements of global capitalism, even if their importance for the creation of value has increased exponentially. Indeed, as Castro-Gómez argues, current bio-prospecting and international patent rights, together with an apparent interest in preserving biodiversity and the traditional knowledges of indigenous peoples reenacts forms of exploitation and epistemic hierarchies that colonialism established. According to Castro-Gómez, "95 percent of the biological patents are controlled by five big biotechnical companies, and the earnings produced by the issuing of patents was fifteen thousand million dollars [sic] in 1990. The patents are the juridical mechanism by which new forms of colonial expropriation of knowledge are legitimated ("Missing" 442). Donna Haraway made a similar argument in *Modest Witness*, where she showed how colonial racial-gender tropes are recycled in the advertisements of bio-prospecting companies (131–72).

Indigenous media signal a similar logic, but they also reshape capitalist forms of production. Film certainly constitutes a vital element of capitalism's immaterial labor. It produces intangible images, emotional experiences, and affective identification. It is also more than a form of representation. Performing forms of labor and economic exchange on screen at once entails a community's representation and enactment of socioeconomic practices. While representing them to other villages via video, the making of the documentary or fiction calls these practices into being, even if temporarily. *Qati qati*'s protagonists Fulo (Pedro Gutiérrez) and Valentina (Ofelia Condori) collaborate in the construction of a temporary shelter in their potato field, manufacturing all building materials from local plants. The couple engages in a labor-intensive process that is set to a light, Andean musical soundtrack and filmed against the backdrop of the high plains on the shores of Lake Titicaca. Valentina's tale of the *qati qati* is motivated by her belief to have heard a flying head to whom she offers salt and *ají*, a notion just as ridiculous to her husband as the story she tells. Yet the following day, in an uncanny but comical scene, Valentina receives a visit from a neighbor who asks her for these condiments. Valentina hands her the requested items, even as the woman denies having come around as a *qati qati* the night before. The figure of the *qati qati* thus refers to a spirit that reciprocity appeases. In a broader sense, the scene encapsulates the ethics of a socioeconomic system that finds its extension in wider ethnic relations implied in another sequence: When Valentina in *Qati qati* goes to the market and exchanges her highland produce for fruits from warmer, lower elevations, the sequence recalls an Andean vertical economy that was largely, but not completely destroyed by the process of colonialism and the capitalist market economy. In this vertical economy extended kinship networks traded agricultural produce through the diverse ecological zones of the Andes. Products gained from llama herds and vicuñas in the highlands above five thousand meters, potatoes in the high plains at about four thousand meters, and corn, tropical fruits, vegetables, and animals from lower elevations thus shaped a multilayered economy (Murra 83–142).

The market scene in *Qati qati* invokes the "adaptive vitality" (Larson, "Andean" 12) of indigenous communities where a monetary economy coexists with kinship-based relations of barter and exchange. Valentina's offering of salt and *ají* not only represent but also enact community solidarity, if only momentarily. The story she tells endorses this ethos, and disrespect for its wider significance gambles with the possibility of fatal sanctions. The actors thus perform on screen what Rivera Cusicanqui terms a "reciprocal economy" ("Trabajo de Mujeres"168).[12] Participating in the filming process entails a re-creation, a lived revitalization of such cultural elements, which can become influential for the communities' continuous self-fashioning. As Jorge Sanjinés wrote when speaking of making the *Principal Enemy* in 1972, "through the revealing, creative actions of the people the cinematic reenactment meshes with actual reality" (Sanjinés, "Problems" 64). Representation may thus be understood not only as a mimetic rendering of reality but as itself constitutive of this reality.

The enactment of socioeconomic relations in front of the camera indicates, moreover, that the effects of global capitalism are uneven. While indigenous communities have lived varying degrees of involvement with capitalism, other economic forms continue to survive alongside capitalist forms of production and market systems. The enactment of labor and reciprocal economy in *Qati qati* and the critique of profiteering in *Cursed Gold*, *The Hunter*, *Vest Made of Money*, and *Forest Spirit* point toward the existence of a border economy, rather than endorse late capitalism as a globally established logic of immanence. Indigenous videos' invocation of reciprocal economy attests to the existence of forms of production and market relations that are distinct from but coexist with global capitalism.

On screen and as a form of enactment, video recuperates and strengthens one of two "coexisting and fundamentally antagonistic economic orders: one governed by the ideals of communal self-sufficiency and reciprocity, the other by mercantile precepts and the norms of competitive individualism" (Larson, "Andean" 17). As Brooke Larson synthesizes, research on Andean economic systems has highlighted both dimensions. One approach, associated with John Murra and the discipline of anthropology, has focused on the adaptive capacity of communities to maintain socioeconomic relations outside of capitalist forms of production and exchange. The other, associated with Carlos Sempat Assadourian and the field of history and political economy, has highlighted the penetration of colonial and modern market economies and their destructive effects on Quechua/Aymara communities. These positions have been complicated in light of social agency. Karen Spalding, for example, shows how Indians actively shaped emerging commodity markets during the colonial period. Tristan Platt and Silvia Rivera Cusicanqui explain that indigenous forms of resistance and social mobilization seek to curb the effects of colonial and neo-imperial capitalism ("Andean" 18–19).

Although there was a profound shift toward the creation of more expansive regional and export economies in the twentieth century that demanded different modalities of negotiating their integration from peasant communities, anthropologists still find evidence "against broad teleological notions of progressive market penetration and dislocation in the southern highlands . . . Andean commerce complemented but never displaced, traditional trading alliances that moved crops, salt, and livestock between valley and puna" (Larson, "Andean" 33). Precolonial socioeconomic relations—particularly those built around the ethical ideal of reciprocity, or *ayni* as it is called in

Aymara, became subalternized, partially destroyed, and partially incorporated into the Spanish colonial exploitation of soil, subsoil, and human labor.
The intricate network of kinship-based relations of barter that connected the
diverse ecological zones of the Andean highlands and valleys were atomized
and realigned in function of transatlantic interests. Although deprived of
their reach and importance, vestiges of the reciprocal economy continue to
survive.

Evaluating the importance of this reciprocal economy is complicated
since indigenous peoples were long defined as peasants who lived outside of
the capitalist market economy. That is, those who engaged in travel to urban
markets or permanently migrated to the cities were seen—and understood
themselves—as changing their ethnic identity. As Harris argues, indigenous
identification (self and other) has corresponded to economic activity, changing from a racial classification, to fiscal and administrative categories, to
class criteria ("Ethnic" 367).

Gender further complicates the correlation between who or what economic activity counts as indigenous versus *mestizo*: "it is women who are the
bearers of Indian identity in areas of high migration, and also women—
the distinctive *cholas* with their marketing and trading activities—who
are the prototypical *mestizos*. In other words, women's ethnic identity is
more clear-cut because of their relatively stable relationships with consumer
markets. Peasant men, on the other hand, typically enter and leave markets
in a more fluid and mobile way and their ethnic identity is correspondingly
less clear-cut" ("Ethnic" 372). The instability of ethnic categories intersects
with the variety of economic forms that indigenous peoples have engaged
in. Anthropologists attest to the dual tactics at work here: "Andean peasants
redirected agriculture toward commercial ends; engaged in trade and commerce; pursued artisanry and wage labor; mortgaged, sold and purchased
lands; and sometimes even invested in the material and ideological trap-
pings of European prestige" while simultaneously engaging in "kinship based
and barter reciprocities" (Larson, "Andean" 19). Nevertheless, elements of
ayni, or reciprocal economy have found some continuation in urban settings,
and structure the relation between urban migrants and their rural family members, and even transcend national borders (Rivera Cusicanqui, "La
noción de 'nación' " 99; "Trabajo de Mujeres").

In view of the broader context of colonial economy in the Andes, Steve
Stern similarly argued that—instead of an incorporation of indigenous

economic forms into an expanding capitalist world system—colonial economies exhibited diverse modes of production and exchange that do not fit into
the categories of precapitalist, feudal, and capitalist economy. Thanks to the
diverse strategies of negotiating with colonial power, indigenous agents mod-
ified their integration and thereby influenced the responses by colonial mercantile capitalists. The interaction between indigenous economic strategies
and colonial forms of exploitation created thus a colonial mode of production
characterized by diversity. This diversity, writes Stern, "may speak not only
to material uncertainties, opportunities, and contradictions particular to
colonial life but also to distinctions in morality, ethos, and political culture
that differentiated colony from metropolis" (Stern 871).

In colonial and contemporary life, capitalism has thus not fully subsumed indigenous life. Rather, research on indigenous communities, like
indigenous media, point to liminal spaces where capitalist modes of production encounter a reciprocal economy. At the same time, the paradigm of
economic and epistemic power inaugurated with colonialism continues to
inform current material and immaterial labor exploitation. While finance
capitalism currently obtains its greatest gains from stock purchases and
money transfers where no actual money paper or coin materializes, con-
centrating on this aspect alone risks obscuring the way the coloniality of
power continues to drive global capitalism. Keeping this legacy in mind, in
contrast, helps to discern more specifically when and how the global system
is currently being challenged and reshaped.

What remains in question, then, are the implications for the product of
indigenous media at a time when global capitalism is indeed propelled by
immaterial labor. If we can now assert that the "new" global capitalism is still
shaped by colonial legacies, what happens to the forms and places of critical
transformation? Does the plane of immanence cover "the entire world market and global society" (Negri, "Toni" 45)? Is transformation achieved by the
social relations that would form an exodus from the state and from work, as
Paolo Virno has it (5)?

Who Owns the Image?

Indigenous media involve complex layers of performance and enactment—
on screen and off. Indigenous video makers engage the triple, interrelated
nature of performance in cinema: in front of the camera, in the production
process, and in video distribution. While in the sixties the socialist mode

of production constituted the guiding principal for an anticolonial cinema, indigenous video makers today shape audiovisual communication on and off screen in accordance with a socioeconomic, pan-indigenous order that is itself under construction. This transformation of the production process deepens the fissures in a supposedly smooth plane of immanence. As elaborated earlier, the production of indigenous video in Bolivia is a communal effort. Video makers and their collaborators see film as a medium that can avoid the fundamental heterogeneity at the heart of literature, where those represented in the narrative are of a different social and ethnic class than those writing, producing, and reading books (Cornejo Polar 23–24). If the practice of literature replicated a social structure that the narratives denounced, audiovisual media are seen as potentially able to incorporate the communities into the production process and to reach audiences regardless of their level of literacy. The Bolivian training workshops are aimed at providing all members of CAIB with the fundamental skills in each area of video making, from sound and lights to camera and editing. Yet the video makers are also moving toward individual specialization. Where Solanas and Getino emphasized the need for nonspecialized members in the film crew that could replace each other as revolutionaries ("Towards" 50), indigenous media indianize crucial roles in the filmmaking process, thus seeking to enact the same social ethos as we see vindicated on screen.

Consider for instance the artist/creator, a key immaterial laborer. While CAIB members eschew the term "director" because it invokes the individual artist in its bourgeois connotations, they nevertheless see a need to take individual responsibility for the final version of the film. Thus Marcelina Cárdenas is credited as responsible for *Loving Each Other in the Shadows*, Faustino Peña for *Forest Spirit*, Patricio Luna for *Vest Made of Money*, and so forth. CEFREC-CAIB prefers using the term *responsable* to that of "director" in order to mark the difference from both the Western director-star and the third cinema director-collective that maintained focus on the revolutionary vanguard and its leadership; in this case, the names of filmmakers that have become veritable icons of third cinema (e.g., Jorge Sanjinés, Glauber Rocha, Octavio Getino, Fernando Solanas, Fernando Birri, and Tomás Gutiérrez Alea).[13] The dynamics of producing indigenous media in an integral process resemble the collective process of Ukamau's filmmaking in the seventies, but the indigenous communicators emphasize a slightly different notion of collaboration.

Marcelino Pinto from the coca-leaf growing Chapare region of Bolivia, for example, wrote the script for *Cursed Gold* and directed the short. Some technical ideas are his, such as using an improvised traveling shot during the climax of the film in order to heighten suspense. Although in a mainstream media context Pinto might be considered the director or even the creative *auteur* of *Cursed Gold*, he insists on his film being a product of building consensus. Before his video was accepted for production, the collective (CEFREC and CAIB) had rejected Pinto's earlier scripts several times, arguing that they were either not promoting a positive self-image or were too risky in the national and international climate marked by the war on drugs. As Pinto puts it,

> The first script I wrote was based on the legend of the coca leaf, written by a Bolivian author. But that script didn't work because it implied that the coca leaf was evil, that it caused misfortune and led to death. So I threw that script aside. Then I did another, which was more like a denunciation, where the soldiers and the campesinos act out conflicts as they often happen there. But CAIB and CEFREC saw that it was premature to make that sort of video in what was and is a very tense time. Since the majority decides, they opted to make *Oro Maldito* [*Cursed Gold*], a traditional fairy tale that functions on the metaphorical level. It was selected by all of the indigenous peoples [involved in the National Indigenous Plan for Audiovisual Communication]. (Flores 35)

Because of this discussion process—among a crew of indigenous filmmakers from various ethnicities who represent their communities and technological advisers (some indigenous, some mestizos), Pinto insists that the film is the result of a collective decision, in Pinto's view, made by "all of the indigenous peoples." Since the video corresponds to the needs of Chipiriri, his community, and because the village participated in the filming the village is also part of the collaborative process that led to its production.

The process of collectively deciding on scripts and sometimes even postproduction submits itself to the structure of authority in the communities. It responds to the communities' needs—as articulated by the authorities—and to the cultural politics of indigenous organizations that underwrite the National Indigenous Plan for Audiovisual Communication.

In Bolivia video images are usually considered property of the community, but video makers report on diverging notions of ownership that correspond to local socioeconomic understandings. In an interview with Salvadorian filmmaker Daniel Flores y Ascencio, the Bolivian Moxeña media activist Julia Mosúa insisted that many members of the community who participated in the acting and oral history gathered for her docufiction *Our Word* considered these images a product of their gratuitous labor (Flores 31). Mosúa added that some in the community view her travels to film festivals with great suspicion (Flores 32). Some community members (but not all) insistently argue against her or CEFREC's right to sell the videos, raising the issue of financial reimbursement for their participation in the filming, or simply denying CEFREC the right to circulate the images beyond circuits approved by the community representatives (Mosúa, Copa, and Pinto, audiotape). In contrast, Alfredo Copa from the highland region of Potosí explained that his community considered the images obtained of them for the documentary *Dusting Off Our History* the property of CEFEC-CAIB—that is, of the producers and the multicultural organization of indigenous communicators (Mosúa, Copa, and Pinto; Schiwy, "Decolonizing" 122). Their images were obtained as part of a process of rescuing the oral narrative of the elders, but the community also participated in the production in terms of a reciprocal relation, or *ayni*.[14] When Pinto, Copa, and Mosúa refer to the collaborative process of indigenous media production and opt for the term *responsable*, they negotiate two different economic systems that encounter each other in the space of video production. Indigenous media operate in a borderland where capitalist forms of marketing film and inscribing authorship tensely coexist with ideals and surviving practices of collectivity, social responsibility, and redistribution of wealth.

Take another example, this time regarding Reynaldo Yujra, an Aymara member of CEFREC. Similar to Pinto, Reynaldo Yujra emphasized collective production during the international indigenous film festival in New York in 2000. He stressed that the idea for the script of *Qati qati* is based in oral tradition—that is, in legendary stories that do not assume an individual author but a long history of oral narrators. Yujra, however, also inscribes his responsibility for the film on screen. During the establishing shots in *Qati qati*, viewers briefly glimpse a close-up profile of Yujra's face, illuminated by the blue moonlight that introduces the mysterious ambience of this horror tale. Yujra thus becomes another narrator in the genealogy of storytellers while insisting on an expansive notion of collaboration that integrates all those involved in making the video. In *Lighting the Spirit*, Yujra performs his role as Aymara filmmaker on screen who travels to learn about medicinal practices among the Quechua-speaking Kallawaya. By placing himself into the center of the frame, Yujra invokes the documentary filmmaker as star—a role that Michael Moore has become famous for in the United States. At the same time, however, Yujra emphasizes his own ethnic identity. As a filmmaker figure he distinguishes himself from the anthropologist and ethnographic expert and instead places himself and the film crew on the same side of the colonial difference as the community that he visits.[15] The information obtained becomes part of the indigenous intercultural exchange instead of being integrated into the anthropological archive or the cineplex. Even as the video highlights the individual, it appeals to a collective identity that embraces the label of indigenous video. Yujra's enactment of the director figure points at once to individual creativity and talent and to the indigenous research imperative to benefit the community and make decisions based on debate and consensus. Straddling the line between Andean community responsibility and individual vocation, Yujra continues to lend his considerable talent as actor and director to the production collective as well as to the interests of his community of origin.

Individual and community are linked through *ayni* (reciprocity) and epistemic accountability. The labor of indigenous media activists includes mediating between their communities and urban centers, participating physically in communal construction efforts, as well as lending their communicative abilities and technological know-how to the needs of their villages. These collective needs are agreed upon through the process of consensus building in community assemblies, which the video makers have condensed, enacted, and idealized in *Overcoming Fear* and *In the Name of Our Coca*.[16] The procedures followed in such assemblies correspond to an ideal of equality that meshes social and economic considerations. Unlike contemporary Latin American filmmakers, such as Alejandro González Iñárritu, Pablo Trapero, or the late María Luisa Bemberg, indigenous communicators thus reject the romantic and marketable notion of the *auteur* and artist-creator who expresses his or her personality through the medium in favor of a conceptualization that is more adequate to the *proceso integral* that constitutes indigenous video making (Himpele, "Packaging" 358). Yet at the same time, the video makers embrace the collective label "indigenous video," emphasizing their access to the technology and responsibility for the films.[17]

Casting similarly traverses a borderland built of the tension between marketing, individual talent, and collective responsibility. In *Loving Each*

————————— 12. Aidée Alvarez being made up. Production still. —————————
http://videoindigena.bolnet.bo (CEFREC).

Other in the Shadows, Aidée Álvarez is again, as in *Cursed Gold*, cast as the young object of male desire. Her face and body are framed in close-ups and she appears on the production still announcing the film in 2001 on CEFREC's Web site (http://www.videoindigena.bolnet.bo) (fig. 12).

The advertisements on this site draw on the female image to attract potential viewers in the communities through a process of complex identification based at once on sexual desire and on ethnic recognition. Nevertheless, Alvarez does not form part of an elaborate, uncontroversial star system. Like Yujra, Alvarez is part the CEFREC-CAIB crew. Both have had lead roles in fiction shorts. Yujra in *Vest Made of Money* and in *Angels of the Earth*; Alvarez in *Cursed Gold* and *Loving Each Other in the Shadows*. They perform with less experienced members of CAIB and with the locals of the villages where the videos are filmed.

No one receives financial retribution for their part in these videos, and yet, in my conversations with the activists, Alvarez's and Yujra's talent provoked anxiety reminiscent of the concerns raised by revolutionary filmmakers in the sixties. Third cinema discarded the star system as part of the capitalist character of industrial cinema that stood in the way of a rational analysis of oppression, opting instead largely for the neorealist use of nonprofessionals. The process of creating stars through typecasting or by recognizing talented individuals is similarly under debate in indigenous media production. While some see the need to promote talented actors as actors, others want to maintain the collective and de-professionalized distribution of roles and tasks in the filming process. The debate over actors and directors forms part of the pan-indigenous self-reflection that seeks possibilities for incorporating Western elements of filmmaking into an indigenous order instead of being incorporated into that of the West, as Iván Sanjinés explained in 2003 during the New Latin American Film Festival in Providence, Rhode Island.

The dual strategy of embracing and resignifying existing staples of commercial filmmaking in light of the process of cultural reconstitution indicates a new approach to audience desire. Third cinema explicitly countered the escapism and complacency that film industries foster. The filmmakers from the sixties sought to raise consciousness among the people and willingness to engage in revolutionary struggle, thus transforming the act of passive consumption into social action (cf. Sanjinés, "Problems" 67). Indigenous media activists, though not promoting a socialist revolution, are similarly critical of pure entertainment. Like revolutionary third cinema, video makers also see an urgent need to reach their audiences. Building on acting and directing talent places the concern about quality and audience appeal in the foreground.

Carelli, director of Video in the Villages in Brazil, worries that indigenous video makers will orient themselves on the possibilities of making a career in film rather than on the project of cultural preservation. Carelli, therefore, "will not work with whose leadership is contested or [villages] whose political internal organization is not relatively stable" (Aufderheide, "Making" 286). CEFREC-CAIB's fiction production has followed a multipronged strategy, giving some space to their talented members but generally distributing the roles and integrating inexperienced actors, even if sometimes to the detriment of acting quality. Similarly, CAIB sends different media activists to present the films at international indigenous film and video festivals. (Iván Sanjinés, director of CEFREC, is always present, nevertheless.) CAIB thus subsumes the recognizable staples of Hollywood style to the pan-indigenous cultural and epistemic politics that is primarily focused on the intercultural process of debate and *concientización* among indigenous and peasant communities. This emphasis finds one of its most radical articulations in distribution.

Selling Diversity? Video Distribution, Reciprocity, and the Free Market

CEFREC-CAIB, CONAIE, and the CRIC have been reluctant to commercialize their films and do not strive to get their productions into mainstream theaters. Video in the Villages and the Chiapas Media Project/Promedios only make a small selection of their videos available to interested audiences in North America. The regional and international film and video festivals screen the videos free of charge. The Bolivian indigenous media network promotes the exchange of ideas and information among indigenous peoples without demanding pay. CAIB's rural distribution network is the key, nonprofit form of circulating indigenous films in Bolivia. In agreement with the National Indigenous Plan for Audiovisual Communication, CAIB's volunteer facilitators established distribution networks where the videos (compiled initially on VHS and now into multimedia packages) are circulated without monetary cost to the communities. They are, however, expected to provide room and board for the facilitators. Attending screenings also means making arrangements with respect to daily chores. In other words, the free distribution of indigenous video through autonomous networks among indigenous and peasant communities today is still an arduous process. It relies on reciprocal, nonmonetary forms of labor. It also requires that the communities designate and sponsor the facilitators who take VHS packages, and since 2005 DVD's and CD's, to the communities.

Indigenous media's distribution strategies resemble some of third cinema's efforts to bring cinema to the people. In Cuba, for instance, filmmakers carried electric generators and reels to rural villages in order to expose the peasants to audiovisual media even before the advent of television (Chanan, *Cuban* 25). Jorge Sanjinés and the Ukamau Group screened their films *Blood of the Condor*, *Courage of the People*, and *The Principal Enemy* in rural communities, factories, and universities in Ecuador, Peru, and Bolivia (Sanjinés, "Problems of Form" 69). Solanas and Getino showed *Hour of the Furnaces* at community and labor union centers in Argentina and beyond. All these films also circulate in Europe (Wood 26–78). Solanas and Getino proposed recuperating costs by entering their films into commercial viewing contexts (parallel to alternative screening sites) (Solanas and Getino 173). The Ukamau Group, in contrast, is only presently considering the commodification of their films. Filmmakers certainly have struggled with the high expenses of 16mm and 35mm film production that cannot always be recuperated through national distribution, while the international market has remained fairly closed to these films. At the same time, however, these filmmakers insisted on the importance of bringing their films to the intended audience: the poor and the working class and, in the case of Jorge Sanjinés, the indigenous and peasant peoples who lack basic needs and can often not afford cinema tickets, even if they live in urban centers. The video makers, in contrast, need to recuperate much less monetary investment than their revolutionary predecessors. Expenses are mainly those of updating and maintaining technological equipment and can be covered by the grants solicited from AECI, the Basque government, and nongovernmental organizations such as Mugarik Gabe (in the case of CEFREC-CAIB). Insertion into the global market economy is partial here.

The regional and international festivals contribute to the expanding indigenous communication network. Who gets to travel and participate in the workshops and screenings at the festivals is based on collective decisions and, in the case of CAIB, meant to give the opportunity to all on a rotating basis. As indigenous movements protest neoliberal policies, video makers make an effort to disconnect video from capitalist production systems, from individual ownership, and from commodification. Indigenous communities and media activists are generally aware of the colonial history of knowledge and exploitation. Experiences with having images and information taken from them without any further benefit or concern for those who provided them informs the limits placed on the distribution of audiovisual material. The question of distribution beyond the communities has been marked by worries over the sanctity of certain images and a general concern over image property rights.[18] The profit principal is not the guiding light for indigenous audiovisual communicators, but this does not mean that they completely eschew the market.

Well aware that video making constitutes a form of both immaterial and material labor and is subject to market exchange, the media activists prolong the enactment of socioeconomic ethics on screen and in the making of indigenous media to their mode of distribution. Indigenous media distribution follows the principle of reciprocity that can accommodate high- and lowland socioeconomic principles. When entering the monetary system, communicators experiment with adapting the principle of exchange.

As Iván Sanjinés emphasized, communities and video makers are mindful of avoiding the production of films for the international market simply because they sell well.[19] Until 2003, several of CEFREC-CAIB's videos were for sale but were not sold indiscriminately to everyone. The financing and distribution, just as the filming itself, have become part of relationships that include further obligations and responsibilities.[20] For example, when I first started researching indigenous video production in Bolivia in 1999, I was interviewed by members of CEFREC as to my intended use of their films. I was granted access once I explained that, to my mind, indigenous video offers an important counterpoint to the way indigenous culture is usually taught in the literary classroom. I believe that showing the films in universities in the United States and Europe can help to push decolonization forward at our end. Students may come to appreciate indigenous creativity and intellectual contributions to thinking about globalization. We also agreed on how I could reciprocate beyond the transfer of money, for instance, by occasionally lending my services as translator and interpreter.[21]

In 2003 the films by CEFREC-CAIB were placed on hold, despite lucrative offers such as Maori Television's in New Zealand, who offered $1,000 per film.[22] Community and regional assemblies throughout Bolivia as well as the production collective's special council discussed the question of how the money made from these videos may be used and redistributed over several years. The arguments differ according to indigenous cultural practices in the high- and lowlands and have been further complicated by anxieties over piracy. Concerns are exacerbated now that documentaries are selected and edited for broadcasting on the CEFREC-CAIB produced program *Among Cultures* (*Entre culturas*) aired on Bolivian National Television (Channel 7).

The interest from North and South American academics as well as Native Television stations is increasing, opening up possibilities for generating resources beyond the grants made available by Mugarik Gabe, AECI, and other institutions abroad. NGOs and the Spanish Agency for International Cultural Cooperation (AECI) have supported specific elements of CEFREC-CAIB's National Indigenous Plan on short-term or project-specific bases. For example, CEFREC's archive—which documents not only the experiences represented in the videos but also the process of video making and the implementation of the National Indigenous Plan for Audiovisual Communication itself—is made possible with funding from SEPHIS (South-South Exchange Programme for Research on the History of Development), a Dutch nongovernmental organization that has also supported academic publications. Indigenous media is not entirely delinked from the global neoliberal economy. Yet the organizations involved in the audiovisual communication process in Bolivia have for now decided to refrain from selling their videos in the free market. Indigenous videos from Bolivia can be seen at international festivals and some university libraries hold small collections (Duke University; University of Connecticut, Storrs; University of California, Riverside).[23] The National Museum of the American Indian continues to maintain its international video collection, which includes selections of CEFREC-CAIB's, CONAIE's, and CRIC's productions.

The Bolivian solution of largely bypassing the potential monetary value for indigenous media is the most radical. Like in the representations of labor and market relations, media activists engage the global indigenous video market in differentiated ways. In contrast with CEFREC-CAIB, CONAIE in Ecuador has assumed a flexible pricing policy for their films. Just like in Bolivia, CONAIE's primary distribution of indigenous media is directed at indigenous communities where recordings are made available free of charge. CONAIE has not made their films accessible through international distribution outlets or Web sites, but their communication department holds videos that are available for purchase. While indigenous communities use the archives in Ecuador and Bolivia for free, the sale prices and availability of the videos depend on the origin of the person purchasing. The CRIC's consulate in Bogotá similarly carries a selection of their indigenous videos for sale upon request. The Chiapas Media Project/Promedios in Mexico focuses on the nonprofit exchange of videos among diverse communities (Halkin, "Outside" 1). Parallel to the use of video as a means of communication among rural communities in Chiapas and Guerrero, they have more readily taken advantage of the marketability of their films in order to promote a thinking process that challenges the place of indigenous communities within the global economy. They see video as a means of drawing international attention and support to the political and cultural struggle of organizations such as the Zapatista National Liberation Army (EZLN). According to Halkin, "Video sales last year [2006] exceeded $17,000, with university sales making up the majority of the income. It has really only been in the last couple of years that the communities can see a direct financial benefit from video sales. Currently, video sales cover the monthly satellite internet connection fees in all four of the Regional Media Centers" (11). Chiapas Media Project videos approved for international circulation are easily available from their Web site in DVD format. CMP/Promedios had chosen not to pursue corporate support but changed its policy in 2004 when Halkin "nominated one of our staff for a high-profile human rights award sponsored by a U.S. corporation, and we received the award. The award recognition goes to an individual, but the money goes to their organization" (12). As Halkin highlights, one of the drawbacks of accepting corporate funding is that "the spectacle and individualization of it runs counter to indigenous philosophy" (12). The Brazilian Video in the Villages has also released a series of videos for international distribution. Their production has been financed by the North American Guggenheim, MacArthur, Rockefeller, and Ford foundations—that is, through grants obtained from corporate institutions in the United States and from the Cooperation of Norway, which became interested in Carelli's work in 1995, "enabling us to begin to design a long-term strategy." Video in the Villages became a nongovernmental organization in 2000 (Carelli, n.p.).

Indigenous media hence operate in a borderland where the capitalist market encounters reciprocal economy. The media circulate in limited ways, and video makers take advantage of the multicultural market to different degrees, but they all largely bypass mainstream media outlets and commercial film festivals, sponsorship by Hollywood producers, and other companies interested in making a profit. Usually their films enter the market for multicultural diversity by way of the university or other educational institutions and sometimes the media activists receive funding from corporate foundations associated with education and the arts.

The Logic of the Border Economy

Whether capitalism has entailed the wholesale integration and thus destruction of indigenous social and economic life, or whether, on the contrary, marginalized indigenous communities have been able to maintain much of their aboriginal forms of production and exchange has been a subject of debate. Indigenous media suggest that capitalism has incompletely permeated the Andean economy and that alternatives need to be conceived from the ties between reciprocal economy and a community ethos anchored in stories about ghosts, flying heads, and enchanted waterfalls, which many in the communities have begun to consider superstitions. The remains of such market economies, having survived on the border to global capitalism, are currently strengthened—along with traditional forms of governance and ethics—as indigenous media activists, intellectuals, and historians work with their rural communities of origin (cf. Choque Quispe and Mamani Condori; Stephenson, "Forging").

Indigenous media are a form of immaterial labor that rely minimally on outside funding and distribution and favor instead a regional exchange through pan-indigenous networks operating beyond the profit principle. The activists sidestep the way media corporations have refashioned themselves in the era of the neoliberal commodification of diversity. Video makers experiment with possibilities for transforming the rules of the market and maintaining a liminal space from which to think and act otherwise. Indigenous communicators and their collaborators either actively seek out an international audience and its solidarity politics (as in the case of the Chiapas Media Project) or reluctantly agree to form an alliance with the interests of researchers and teachers elsewhere (the case of CEFREC-CAIB). In all cases, the producers have decided to make a small selection of their films available to outsiders. Instead of indicating a wish to integrate into the existing global economic order, the multiple strategies making up the practice of indianizing film point to a transformation of this order. Again, these are not uncontroversial positions, but rather, as the video fictions attest to, issues of passionate debate in the communities themselves.

Indigenous socioeconomic forms, in any case, have not been fully integrated into a neo-colonial economy and neither is their material and immaterial labor fully subsumed to the "new" capitalism. Indigenous media strengthen these alternative economic, ethic, and epistemic traditions for cultural survival. The discourse on multiculturalism shapes this context as much as the nation-state that outsources its functions in an ever more expansive manner to private enterprises. Indigenous video proposes the need to reinterpret knowledge, genealogies, and perspectives that have themselves become subalternized and cast as unsustainable by the dominant national and global discourses of modernization and development. It draws attention to the way multiculturalism merely masks the continuing legacies of colonial subalternization. Whatever runs counter to the global capitalist market with its growth principal and ethics of profit maximization is at once a risk and a potentially new market to be colonized. Yet it is also a site for transforming the system. This view on transformation, however, is cast not from within but from the colonial fissures in the system. Indigenous movements insist that the global system continues to feed on colonial legacies. From this perspective the global capitalist system is not characterized by immanence but is structured by socioeconomic borders, akin to those existing at an epistemological level. Decolonization in the age of multiculturalism draws attention to the legacies of colonialism underlying global capitalism and its commodification of intellectual and cultural production.

If we understand capitalism to create borders and to integrate other economies in an uneven manner, we can see the representations of labor and exchange in indigenous media as mobilizing the resources for alternatives to modern development and capitalism from these borders. Indigenous media production and distribution thus join two different socioeconomic practices, one reciprocal and subalternized and the other profit oriented and dominant. Their interaction resembles what Mignolo calls "border thinking," where epistemological traditions that have been poised against each other in unequal ways through the colonial experience are brought to bear on each other in order to produce a thinking that transcends Eurocentrism (Mignolo, *Local* 49–90). The horizon for indigenous media's economic transformation indicates, in an analog manner, a challenge to the hegemony of capitalist development. Indigenous media in Latin America look beyond the idea of film as a commodity, a means of generating income for impoverished communities, for example. The principal of indianizing film—of appropriating an industrial, capitalist, and colonial art form to a cultural politics of decolonization that is critical of capitalism—is hence opposed to the ideas of development designed by Western agencies (private or otherwise) who promote a greater share in wealth for indigenous peoples without also challenging the colonial epistemic and economic structures that originated contemporary global power relations. At the same time, even if the ethics of reciprocity resemble a communist ideal of shared wealth, the affirmation of market relations and the existence of differences in wealth and power within indigenous communities as well as a long history of hybrid economic practices exceed the Andean Marxist perspective on indigenous life that Mariátegui had so influentially proposed.

As indigenous video producers increasingly make their gaze part of national and international vision-scapes, they certainly take advantage of the marketability of their videos (among indigenous communities worldwide, social activists, and some academics). However, this partial commodification of some videos cannot be reduced to an easy coexistence with the global capitalist market. The logic of profit maximization is held in check, countered and partially disrupted through the rural distribution networks, and through production practices anchored in local indigenous social relations. If the so-called New Latin American Cinema of the sixties had aimed to transform cinema from an art form of late capitalism into a socialist and revolutionary practice, indigenous activists and their collaborators today are transforming the medium into an epistemic tool grounded in (and reproducing) socioeconomic relations on the border to capitalism. These relations are constructed as alternatives to capitalism as we know it.

The process of indianizing audiovisual communication challenges the notion of capitalism as an all-encompassing order that can only be transformed from within. Video is not simply a Western technology that is appropriated; it is one that is indianized. Indianizing film can be understood as a conscious strategy of incorporating a technology that is apparently other. Video becomes a technology that mirrors and produces indigenous social and economic relations instead of, like the movement associated with cultural and literary transculturation, incorporating them into a national projected whose horizon is set on the West.[24] In other words, indigenous discourse, articulated in audiovisual form, indicates ways of understanding cultural and economic change in terms of creating autonomous networks that bypass established centers reshaping whatever these new flows sweep into their stream. If these national projects are now invested with the idea of multiculturalism, video makers push the meaning of multiculturalism so that the contours of colonial legacies become visible beneath the colorful marketing of diversity.

If one feels convinced by arguments about the total capitalist permeation of life, or the subsumption of life to its regime, change appears immanent to its logic. However, biopower here also becomes amorphous. Upon closer examination the creative adaptations of indigenous rural communities have produced alternative spaces that are neither inside nor completely outside of the logic of capitalism but rather constitutive of an economic and epistemological border.

When in the mid-1980s Kayapo video makers performed what still appears as a clash between body paint and camcorders, they drew international attention to their struggles against the incursion of cattle ranchers, gold miners, and transnational development projects (such as the building of hydroelectric dams in the Brazilian Amazon). News agencies and the rock star Sting broadcasted Kayapo resistance into international media, capturing an audience keen on saving the rain forest. Instead of directly countering the appeal of cultural diversity, the Kayapo used, exposed, and subverted the colonial legacies at work in the discourse of multiculturalism. The Kayapo— like the coca-growing communities in Bolivia allegorized in *Cursed Cold* and *In the Name of Our Coca* or the reciprocal Andean economy featured in indigenous videos like *Qati qati*—bring sharply into view the limits of what can be integrated into the existing global order. Decolonization requires transforming the global economic order as much as the epistemological discourse that has justified and naturalized ideas about indigenous peoples. The process conceives of culture not simply as a folkloric product for the market or the classroom, but rather as an epistemic intervention that addresses questions of ethics, knowledge, and economic systems of exchange. Documentaries about territorial struggle, about the use of indigenous languages, medicinal practices, dances, oral history, and myths thus acquire meanings that go beyond documenting what may be lost. Culture here becomes a resource, a potential for rethinking, or, more precisely, decolonizing knowledge and the market.

AFTERWORD

With Ecuador's indigenous organizations deposing two presidents in the last decade, and with Aymara Indian Evo Morales's election to the Bolivian presidency in 2006, much scholarly discussion has centered on the relation between indigenous movements and the state. The state and the Colombian constitution of 1991, which acknowledges the pluricultural makeup of the nation, are also the major referents in the study of Colombian indigenous movements, together with their negotiation of the violent civil war between guerrillas, paramilitary and government troops, and the U.S. war on drugs.[1] Bridging social sciences and political theory with cultural studies, one might also look at indigenous movements as part of a newly configured multitude shaped by *piqueteros* and factory takeovers in Argentina, by the Movimento Sim Terra (Landless Movement) in Brazil, the Zapatistas efforts to create another campaign in Mexico, and by organizations in the urban *barrios* of Caracas that support Chávez. Indigenous movements here would appear as one among several social groups constituting a New Left.[2]

In this book I have argued, in contrast, that the cultural politics of indigenous movements in the Andean countries are effecting long-lasting and profound changes that transcend election policies and the state. I have sought to illuminate the use of video as part of a politics of knowledge designed by indigenous organizations. These indigenous cultural politics share affinities with native and aboriginal efforts to decolonize knowledge in North America, Australia, and New Zealand. Working with Creole/white and *mestizo* collaborators, indigenous media activists have constructed audiovisual communication networks that reframe the way indigenous subjectivity, culture, and systems of knowledge have been represented in mainstream literature and media. My study suggests that in the Andean-Amazonian region this audiovisual knowledge production becomes sustainable for the villages and peoples linked through video networks. In other words, indigenous media invest the philosophical and religious knowledge that was hidden or deemed as superstition with new value.

The video fiction *Angels of the Earth*, a 2001 CEFREC-CAIB production, and *Secret Nation*, made in 1989 by the Ukamau Group, differ markedly in their visual aesthetics, yet both highlight the loss of family ties and community solidarity as the painful cost caused and suffered by urban migrants who desire to become recognized as *mestizos* and integrated into Western society. Indigenous media activists across the region speak of a trend toward assimilation brought on by exposure to state education that is no longer affecting only those living in the city. As Alfredo Copa puts it, "Many old people say to me, 'Interview me, tape-record me with music. I want to leave something that my children never asked me, that my grandchildren never asked me.' I worry about what they are not being asked. Education in my country does not concern itself with this. They teach us the history of ancient Greece and Rome, but not our own history. So more and more memories are being lost. Video demonstrates that you have to remember. . . . Video is a motivation; people who are losing their culture can strengthen themselves in this way" (Flores 33). Copa insists that indigenous media counters the prevailing tendency toward assimilation. It fosters pride in indigenous identity and traditions. The video makers thus contribute to a process of decolonization that begins with indigenous and peasant self-perceptions. Many people living in indigenous and peasant communities today have interiorized the dominant national cultures' inscription of Indians as poor, backward, and destined to integrate into Western society. Indigenous cultural politics, in contrast, highlight histories of survival, ongoing resistance to colonialism, even emerging alternative modernities.

Here I have argued that indigenous movements are indeed enacting a revolution of a new kind and that indigenous media partake in this struggle. It is a revolution of knowledge politics. Media activists foster pride in local traditions, agricultural systems, and medicinal knowledge. They vindicate religious beliefs that have survived since precolonial times as part of a greater ethos that sustains indigenous alternative visions of modernity across very diverse cultures. As Copa argued, indigenous media strengthen local technologies of transmitting these forms of memory, knowledge, and social relations. Storytelling, song, dance, weaving, bodily performance, and rituals are all represented on screen, but they are also enacted for the camera, and, most important, they become part of community reflection and discussion. In other words, the media activists strengthen indigenous philosophical and religious systems and vindicate the practical know-how relating to agriculture and medicine, systems of law and community rule, and the technologies of transmitting such knowledge that were increasingly being considered backward or irrelevant by a younger generation of indigenous peoples exposed to state education. Indeed, what we might tend to analytically separate into philosophical and practical knowledge is intimately linked.

Local, regional, and national organizations have rearticulated the long history of indigenous peoples' struggle for more political power, for territorial rights, and against racism in their countries. They make use of global institutions, such as the United Nations, nongovernmental organizations that operate internationally, and individual activists and collaborators. They reframe their demands in the readily recognizable keywords of global activism: human rights, women's rights, multiculturalism, ecological sustainability, and so forth (cf. Brysk). These terms are appropriated and adapted in a process of global communication in order to find allies and international support for indigenous movement struggle. Older and newer forms of struggle are used to express indigenous demands: protest marches, road blockades, radio shows, oral history, testimonial writing, written publications by university graduates and researchers, film, and video. Like the buzzwords of global activism, the media are at once reinterpreted and given new meaning in a grassroots discussion process. The process of indigenous audiovisual communication transforms the technology's dominant use and significance. While corporate media and the profit principal today dominate what is seen on small and big screens, indigenous media activists employ the technology not only to grassroots activism. They shape the visual and aural aesthetics to reproduce the cultural particularities of indigenous traditions of transmitting knowledge.

I have suggested that the tireless efforts of individual media activists in rural communities, along with low-cost digital video production and screening technology, have enabled intercultural communication networks and the creation of audiovisual archives. In addition to regional, hemispheric, and global indigenous film and video festivals, these networks contribute to making indigenous knowledge sustainable. By this I mean that the values attributed to local peasant and indigenous communities' forms of knowing, working, and living that went into crisis within the communities themselves are being reversed in what seems like a snowballing and lasting manner. To reiterate, indigenous media is not alone in this process; it is part of a wider sociocultural indigenous politics. The founding of intercultural universities in Bolivia and Ecuador, the hopes invested in Evo Morales's government, and the Aymara movement to reconstitute the *ayllu*, in which the THOA has played a key role, are indicative of a widespread cultural transformation grounded in decolonizing knowledge. According to Catherine Walsh, "as a political and epistemic project of the indigenous movement, the UINPI [Universidad Intercultural de las Nacionalidades y Pueblos Indígenas] challenges academic-institutional enclosures and epistemological borders that are always crossed by power relations and that limit study to the confines of occidental-universal-liberal knowledge. By recognizing epistemic diversity, by working with it and at the same time recognizing and confronting epistemic-colonial violence, the UINPI creates a strategic model of struggle and education" (87). The impact is not locally restricted but entails putting forth sociocultural frameworks that can serve to reshape defunct national societies.

Marcia Stephenson explains that the movement to reconstitute the *ayllu* began in the early 1980s as a response to the austerity measures that neo-liberal reform brought to bear on highland communities already suffering the consequences of ongoing drought (111). The THOA, which was founded around the same time by young Aymara university graduates, "recognized the reconstitution of the *ayllu* as a political act of decolonization" (111) that entailed "turning away from the organizational arrangement set forth by syndicalism" (112). In response to requests by part of the *ayllu* communities, the THOA subsequently became involved in the movement. Its members took on advisory roles and the *Estructura orgánica* that Jesús de Machaqa, a highland Aymara community, adopted was published as a booklet that the THOA distributed widely. Stephenson emphasizes that "this booklet has served as a useful guide for other communities wanting to strengthen their traditions and reconstitute customary forms of governance" (113).

Carlos Mamani and Maria Eugenia Choque Quispe, who both served as directors of the THOA at different times, have offered a similar description of the THOA's role in the movement to reconstitute the *ayllu*. They describe the *ayllu* as a kinship-based community that commonly ties different, not necessarily adjacent territories into a tight relationship of economic exchange and reciprocity. Within the *ayllu* the relations are structured by duality, usually comprising two complementary units. *Ayllus* extend relations with each other following the same model. The communities are governed by authorities who are called to serve. Criteria for appointment are based on a couple's economic abilities to redistribute wealth, prior political experience (in minor posts), and at times their talent (Choque Quispe and Mamani Condori 157–59). Political representation is thought within a strictly hetero-normative mold that extends the Andean paradigm of duality. The authorities are commonly required to be married; the wives are seen as sharing in the political responsibilities of their husbands. The reconstituted *ayllu* recognizes collective property; it "traces its origin to the most remote pre-colonial past" and unites colonial and pre-Hispanic traditions in its social and political organization where family relations are fundamental (Mamani y Choque Quispe 152).[3] The movement to reconstruct the *ayllu* and its forms of governance, in which the work of the THOA in the 1980s and 1990s was instrumental, has had tremendous impact in revitalizing indigenous traditions of governance, laws, and relations among a growing number of highland communities. Indeed, the impact has been social and epistemological. The THOA has offered a critique of Western epistemology and has instead elaborated an understanding of historical and social transformation from its collaborative process of oral history research in highland communities. One of the key contentions here has been a challenge to the vision of Andean indigenous uprisings as disarticulated events that ultimately testify to a history of increasing assimilation of indigenous peoples. The THOA instead argued that indigenous uprisings attest to a historical awareness in the communities of the different strategies deployed in a history of survival and anticolonial struggle. Members of the group worked with both men and women elders and have thus also been able to draw out and highlight to the communities and beyond the influential contributions of women in this struggle (Rivera Cusicanqui and THOA, "Potencial"; Stephenson 103). The THOA's findings have been published in inexpensive mimeographs and as radio shows, always with the goal of making its research findings available to the communities they have worked with and beyond (Stephenson 104–7). It has thus contributed to constituting what Stephenson calls an "indigenous counterpublic sphere" (103) where alternatives to the dominant Bolivian historiography and political and social theory are elaborated. Indigenous media activists extend this sphere even more widely as they circulate hundreds of video shorts transnationally and among diverse indigenous peoples.

The United Nations Declaration of the Rights of Indigenous Peoples in part reflects the global scope of this knowledge politics. The general assembly finally passed the declaration after more than twenty years of debate and negotiations involving states and indigenous organizations and representatives on September 13, 2007. The United Nations Web site offers PDF files of the document in its official languages as well as in Miskito, Maori, Portuguese, and Guarani. Its historical overview is worth quoting at length. It summarizes the process and gives a sense of the contentious issues:

> The efforts to draft a specific instrument dealing with the protection of indigenous peoples worldwide date back over two decades. In 1982 the Economic and Social Council (ECOSOC) established the Working Group on Indigenous Populations (WGIP) with the mandate to develop a set of minimum standards that would protect indigenous peoples. WGIP was established as result of a study by José R. Martínez Cobo on the problem of discrimination faced by indigenous peoples throughout the world. The study outlined the oppression, marginalization and exploitation suffered by indigenous peoples. WGIP submitted a first draft declaration on the rights of indigenous peoples to the Sub-Commission on the Prevention of Discrimination and Protection of Minorities, which was later approved in 1994. The Draft was sent for consideration to the then U.N. Commission on Human Rights for further discussion and if it was deemed to be appropriate, to approve the proposed declaration before its submission to ECOSOC and the U.N. General Assembly.[4]

The historical narrative offered on the United Nations Web page casts indigenous peoples in the familiar light of poverty and marginalization—the declaration was envisioned as a response to the "oppression, marginalization, and exploitation suffered by indigenous peoples"—and highlights the key role of researchers (Martínez Cobo) and official United Nations committees. However, it also indicates a change in perception: "The process moved very slowly because of concerns expressed by states with regard to some of the core provisions of the draft declaration, namely the right to self-determination of indigenous peoples and the control over natural resources existing on indigenous peoples' traditional lands." In other words, the major points of contention have been indigenous sovereignty (and the implications this may have for the coherence of nation-states) and, perhaps most important, the control over natural resources on indigenous lands. Although the document does not spell them out, at stake are particularly oil, precious and other metals, as well as plant and human genetic information. Those opposing the declaration were not surprisingly the so-called CANZUS states: Canada, Australia, New Zealand, and the United States.[5]

These issues of contention hence configure indigenous peoples as landowners with tremendous assets in biotechnology and fossil fuels, which, nevertheless, they often have little interest in fully exploiting. This is not a contradiction. The UN narrative highlights that the declaration "is a comprehensive statement addressing issues such as collective rights, cultural rights and identity in addition to rights to education, health, employment and language among others. The Declaration emphasizes the right of indigenous peoples to maintain and strengthen their own institutions, cultures and traditions and to pursue their development in accordance withe [sic] their aspirations and needs. The Declaration will undoubtedly assist indigenous peoples in their efforts to combat discrimination and racism." Embedded in the declaration is hence a veiled reference to the decade-long process of formulating indigenous designs for "development" as an indigenous politics of knowledge based on strengthening "their own institutions, cultures and traditions."

The declaration is not legally binding, even for the United Nations' member states, but it points to a complex interrelationship between the geopolitics of knowledge, cultural and spiritual frameworks, place, and socioeconomic visions for development. Unlike the Web page summary, the declaration itself spells out the "urgent need to respect and promote the inherent rights of indigenous peoples which derive from their political, economic and social structures and from their cultures, spiritual traditions, histories, and philosophies, especially their rights to their lands, territories, and resources." At the same time, it acknowledges indigenous agency: "the fact that indigenous peoples are organizing themselves" (*DRIPS* 2). The Declaration of Indigenous Rights was indeed drafted with the key participation of indigenous organizations and representatives; it symbolizes a concern with reconfiguring the European tradition of science and research, which has separated disciplines and cast sustainable knowledge as rational, objective, and secular (cf. Wallerstein et al.).

Articles 11, 12, 13, 14, 15, 23, 25, and 31 specifically address indigenous peoples' rights to strengthen their own knowledge systems. Article 16 directly addresses media access: (1) "Indigenous peoples have the right to establish their own media in their own languages and to have access to all forms of non-indigenous media without discrimination. (2) States shall take effective measures to ensure that State-owned media duly reflect indigenous cultural diversity. States, without prejudice to ensuring full freedom of expression, should encourage privately owned media to adequately reflect indigenous cultural diversity." The articles regularly emphasize two correlations. One is the link between culture, spirituality, society, and economy. The other ties particular rights linked to sovereignty on the part of indigenous peoples to their right to access all services provided by the state. The articles also reiterate the need to conduct all laws, regulations, and policies with due respect to customs and traditions and *in conjunction* with the indigenous peoples concerned.

Oldham and Frank point out that the declaration merits consideration for anthropologists with respect to its implications for the field's professional codes of ethics regarding issues of prior informed consent and intellectual property, and with respect to thematic areas of anthropological research (e.g., children, gender, health, and development). They suggest that "additional consideration could be given to the development of specific guidance to inform anthropological training and practice in research with indigenous peoples. The emphasis here would be placed on the promotion of constructive research relationships with indigenous peoples and demonstrating anthropology's ongoing commitment to ethical research relationships grounded in an understanding of international human rights norms" (9).

Indigenous scholars, however, have long been calling for an even more extensive decolonization of research methodologies and goals. Linda Tuhiwai Smith, Andrea Smith, Michelle Raheja, and Melanie Fitzgerald, for example, emphasize that linking community needs, critical understanding, and scholarly production is essential. Like the THOA and indigenous media activists, they demand privileging knowledge production in the interest of indigenous and native communities.

What happens when the knowledge politics of indigenous media enter the cultural studies classroom? Doesn't video become merely another commodity with multicultural content that sells best when most exotic? When the subalternized voices featured in literary *testimonio* entered the space of literary institutions, they added new perspectives and changed parts of the content of literary studies. *Testimonio*'s force seemed to lie in its ability to

incite the political solidarity of a university-educated readership in the so-
called First World with the oppressed of the so-called Third World. The films
of the Chiapas Media Project/Promedios that circulate readily at U.S. universities similarly point to an acute solidarity politics. Like *testimonio* they are
synchronic with the activity of the critic and their viewers. Beverley's words,
written in regard to *testimonio* may also be relevant for video: "*testimonio* was
intimately linked to international solidarity networks in support of revolutionary movements . . . detached from these contexts . . . [it] runs the risk
of becoming a new form of *costumbrismo*, the Spanish term for 'local-color'
writing" (*Testimonio* 281). Once integrated into the literary or cultural studies canon, *testimonio* lost its subversive force in a double way: it became a
multicultural commodity and an object of study that no longer encounters a
contemporary referent or constituent (Beverley, "Real"; Sanjinés C., "Beyond").
Testimonio no longer subverts (if it ever really did) the notion of the canon or
the power of the literary institution (Moreiras, "Aura" 202–4).[6]

Like the *testimonios* collected by the THOA, indigenous video—whether
in the Andes, Chiapas, or Brazilian Amazon—is not primarily in search of
academic solidarity elsewhere. Its interlocutors are not consumers but indigenous communities involved in a process of cultural revolution. Indigenous
media largely bypass the requirements of literacy and create an epistemic
process where solidarity politics are ultimately not the key. Obtaining the
funds to purchase, maintain, and replace digital media equipment is certainly a concern. At the moment, video makers rely on the interest and
support of nongovernmental organizations and other institutions, yet their
actions and relations with funding agencies are constantly under revision.
Like the earlier dependency on the state in Mexico, indigenous media activists are likely to creatively shift their attention elsewhere if they feel pres-
sured by these institutions or if their resources dry up. Yet critically engaging
and teaching indigenous video in North American universities—whether in
cultural studies or film studies programs—proposes a similar dilemma. Like
testimonio, indigenous video risks becoming another object of multicultural
consumption, a subject of the critical apparatus of cultural and cinema
studies.

We might limit ourselves to comparing indigenous media to other cinematic forms, or use them as complementary illustrations of indigenous
life that accompany textual representations offered in academic writing. I
suggest that indigenous media also offer themselves to a different reading:

Indigenous media contribute ideas and positions on our common preoccupations. While chapters 1 and 2 outlined the knowledge politics and dynamics of collaboration that characterize indigenous media in the Andean-Amazonian countries, in the following chapters I tried to think about several key concepts in Latin American cultural theory from the perspectives offered by indigenous video. In Chapter 3 I showed that, in light of indigenous media, concepts such as the lettered city and orality appear flawed and demand reconceptualization. Chapter 4 engaged with the media activists' privileging of gendered bodies in order to rethink the way the "coloniality of power" has been theorized. Chapters 5 and 6 further elaborate the way indigenous media activists adapt film form, documentary, and fiction respectively to carve out epistemic privilege for indigenous positions. Chapter 7, finally, points toward the way indigenous media may help to reconsider how we conceptualize social change under conditions of speculative capitalism's apparently all-encompassing force. In other words, I have tried to show in this book that indigenous videos offer a way of critical engagement that contributes to rethinking where thinking takes place.

NOTES

INTRODUCTION

1 http://videoindigena.bolnet.bo. Accessed March 1, 2006.

2 Conklin discusses some of the implications that the Kayapo politics of the exotic has had for other Amazonian Indians who do not use lip plates and have assumed Western clothing.

3 http://videoindigena.bolnet.bo/caib.htm. Accessed July 1, 2008.

4 Raheja states that native filmmaking in North America began in the silent period with directors Edwin Carewe and James Young Deer ("Reading" 1182 n. 7).

5 For Bolivia, see especially Rivera Cusicanqui, *Oprimidos*; Rivera Cusicanqui "Pachakuti"; Hurtado; and Mamani and Choque Quispe. For Colombia, particularly, Gros (*Colombia* and "*Indigenismo*"), Rappaport (*Politics* and *Cumbe*), and Dagua Hurtado et al. Walsh ("[Re]Articulation"), and Macas Ambuludi and Lozano Castro make the case for Ecuador, among others. From the perspective of a Quichua media activist, Lema outlines the role of new communication technologies, including video, for indigenous cultural politics in the Ecuadorian highlands.

6 Confederación Sindical Única de Trabajadores Campesinos de Bolivia (CSUTCB), the dominant peasant union in the Bolivian highlands; (Confederación Sindical de Colonizadores de Bolivia (CSCB), the main union organizing highland migrants now working in the Andean valleys; and Confederación de los Pueblos Indígenas de Bolivia (CIDOB), the regional umbrella organization of the indigenous peoples living in the eastern Bolivian lowlands.

7 Bolivia's peasant and indigenous movement history is long and very complex. Published in English, Gustavson provides an overview of indigenous politics that strives to give equal weight to the high- and lowlands. Rivera Cusicanqui's *Oprimidos pero no vencidos* remains the classic history of highland Indian organizing written in Spanish. See also Hurtado's study of Katarismo as well as publications by Xavier Albó.

8 Personal communication with Iván Sanjinés, September 2006, La Paz, Bolivia. CEFREC-CAIB declined the offer. I explain the politics of indigenous media distribution and sales in detail in chapter 7.

9 Theodore Macdonald (176–87) offers a concise history of Ecuador's indigenous movements in English. Walsh ("[Re]Articulation") situates Indigenous and Afro-Ecuadorian movements into the context of decolonizing knowledge.

10 http://conaie.org/es/di_comunicaciones/index.html. Accessed November 28, 2007.

11 ECUARUNARI (RUNACUNAPAC RICCHARIMUI/Confederación de los Pueblos de Nacionalidad Kichua del Ecuador), the Confederation of the Peoples of Kichua [Quichua] Nationality, is one of Ecuador's regional organizations that CONAIE represents. Quechuas live in Peru and Bolivia; Quichuas, in Ecuador.

12 http://conaie.org/clacpi/convocatoria.html. Accessed November 28, 2007. My translation.

13 ONIC is the National Organization of the Indigenous Peoples of Colombia (Organización Nacional Indígena de Colombia).

14 Christian Gros's *Colombia Indígena* is a classic comparative study of the rise of indigenous movements in Colombia since the early 1970s. Joanne Rappaport's *Politics* and *Cumbe Reborn* offer in-depth looks at how the Nasa (Paéz) Indians construct their regional organization as a historical continuity with past struggles for territorial rights. See also Gros, "*Indigenismo*" 39–52; Findji; and Jackson. Lame Chantre, Avirama and Márquez, and Dagua Hurtado, Aranda, and Vasco articulate perspectives from within the Nasa and Guambiano movements in the Cauca region.

15 For indigenous evaluations of the goals and accomplishments of indigenous movements in Latin America see, for instance, the volume edited by Raquel Gutiérrez and Fabiola Escárzaga.

16 Unless otherwise noted, all translations are mine.

17 In a controversial essay published in 1997, James Weiner asserts that video is not a valid tool for strengthening indigenous cultures, which he sees as based on ritual and oral tradition (208). According to Weiner, indigenous video falls into the trap of realist ethnographic documentary, and it constitutes a fundamental break with indigenous social relations. Indigenous cultures, in Weiner's view, are premediatic in the sense that they are based on ritual. He understands ritual as a form of "calling into being" and "hiding" that is closer to European medieval practices than to representation in a "specularized as well as spectacularized society" in which vision is the privileged sense. In his opinion, unless their use consciously undermines the idea of mimesis, audiovisual media can only lead to reproducing the Western society of the spectacle (199). Those working on indigenous media have insisted that Weiner's arguments are not only grossly misinformed with respect to indigenous media but also indicative of his limited understanding of indigenous peoples' history of colonial contact and current exposure to mainstream audiovisual media (cf. the comments by Ginsburg, Hamilton, Piccini, Pinney, Strathern, and Turner published in the same volume of *Current Anthropology*). Indigenous peoples in Latin America are certainly not isolated from Western capitalism. Rather, with Aníbal Quijano and Immanuel Wallerstein, I maintain that capitalism itself has been constituted through the colonial experience and the conquest of the Americas. Indigenous media, on the other hand, often includes the kind of self-reflexivity Weiner calls for, particularly productions by Video in the Villages. Yet Weiner's doubts have lead me to interrogate more profoundly how indigenous media activists deal with the colonial gaze of mainstream film and media as well as with the way they have negotiated the dominance of a global media industry.

18 Many of the key documents and critical studies can be found in Chanan, *Twenty-five*; Julianne Burton, *Social*; Martin's two-volume *New Latin American Cinema*; Pick; King; and in Spanish the indispensable *Hojas de cine*. Wood's thesis

offers a thorough exploration of the similarities and differences between Bolivian and Colombian third cinema.

19 In 1981 Bonfil Batalla used the term in a similar way in his introduction to a compilation of essays by writers of the emerging indigenous movements of the sixties and seventies ("Utopia" 44).

20 Cf. Quijano, "Coloniality"; Mignolo, *Local* 52–54; Mignolo, *Idea* 32.

21 This approach has been considered crucial for scholarship on third cinema (Burton, "Film"). Understanding cultural production as both a socioeconomic practice and as a text is not particular to film and video. Antonio Cornejo Polar's groundbreaking essay "*Indigenismo*" theorized Latin American literature as the product of textual and material dynamics. Like literature, audiovisual cultural production entails forms of representation as well as conditions of possibility and material effects.

22 The Cuban anthropologist Fernando Ortiz coined the term in 1940 as a new approach to understanding the complex ways of cultural transformation resulting from colonialism. If acculturation implied a total cultural loss on the part of the colonized, transculturation pointed to the transformation of both parts (colonizer and colonized), and thus the creation of one or more new cultures (*Contrapunteo* 96–97). Transculturation, in Ortiz's sense, always carries the trace of colonial violence as well as the affirmation of life (cf. Coronil, "Introduction"). Angel Rama later took up the concept again to theorize the literary boom's transformation and fusion of European and North American modernist elements of style with indigenous and other local symbolic traditions in his book *Transculturación narrativa*. Transculturated texts have offered literary and cultural studies a fruitful matrix for reading the subaltern voice against the grain. That is, transculturation indicates a move toward imagining, in Benedict Anderson's sense, a modern nation that requires a homogenous community. Indigenous elements of culture are incorporated into a project whose horizon is the modern, Western state.

23 John Beverley suggests that there is a difference between transculturation as a project designed by the state in contrast with reverse transculturation or "transculturación al revés" (271) designed by indigenous social movements in the brief essay "Siete aproximaciones al problema indígena," a comparative study of the drama Ollantay, the Sandinistas, and Rigoberta Menchús *testimonio*.

24 See the achievements and goals of indigenous media outlined in Lema and in the Spanish language description of the National Indigenous Plan on CEFREC's home page http://videoindigena.bolnet.bo/. Last accessed July 19, 2008.

25 Beverley has discussed the hopes invested in testimonio and its pitfalls in detail in his articles "On Testimonio" and "The Real." See also the other articles in the collection of essays edited by Gugelberger for a broader view.

26 This does not mean that indigenous media can't be seen in the North. The films and videos are shown regularly at festivals, and some university libraries as well as the National Museum of the American Indian hold collections that can be viewed upon request. See also Domínguez for an detailed report prepared for SALALM (Seminar on the Acquisition of Latin American Library Materials).

27 Walter Mignolo and I have elaborated on this process: the movement of Marxist-Leninist thinking into an indigenous context, its profound transformation through this contact, which then allows an also transformed indigenous

perspective to speak back to national society (Mignolo and Schiwy, "Translation/Transculturation" 264–65.)

28 Pinhanta's article "You See the World of the Other and You Look at Your Own" is published on Video in the Villages' Web page, at http://www.videonasaldeias. org.br/home_ingles.htm (accessed July 4, 2008).

29 Scholars associated with the group have published a number of edited volumes, special editions of journals, and monographs in Spanish and English. See, for example, Lander; Castro-Gomez, *Reestructuración*; Mignolo, *Local*; Mignolo and Schiwy; Walsh, Schiwy, and Castro-Gomez; Schiwy and Ennis; Walsh, *Pensamiento crítico*; Mignolo, *Idea*; Escobar, *Hybrid Nature*; *Cultural Studies* 21.2–3 (2007); and Nelson Maldonado-Torres.

30 For example, Carelli; Pinhanta; Aufderheide, "Making"; Turner, "Representing," "Visual," and "Representation, Politics"; Conklin; and Moore.

31 Jeff Himpele's conclusion to *Circuits of Culture*, published after the completion of my manuscript, briefly discusses the history of the Indigenous Peoples' National Plan in light of a progressive history of the indigenization of popular culture in Bolivia. I regret not being able to fully integrate his findings on Bolivian media and popular culture into my book.

32 Gabriela Zamorano is currently finishing a thesis on the production and distribution practices of CEFREC-CAIB and indigenous media's conceptions of the state.

CHAPTER ONE

1 Video in the Villages maintains a trilingual Web site that lists some of their video productions as well as related essays (http://www.videonasaldeias.org.br/ abertura/index.html). See also Aufderheide and the documentary *Video in the Villages Presents Itself* (*Video nas Aldeias se apresenta*).

2 On indigenous media in Mexico, see also Cusi-Wortham, "Narratives" and Brígido-Corachán.

3 For a review of the festival, see Wortham, "Building."

4 Peru, apart from the Peruvian Amazon, has played a minor role in indigenous media. There are some isolated projects, such as the testimonial videos by Chirapaq, as well as an emerging digital video production of feature length B-movies. These low-budget B-videos are made by young Andean filmmakers who resist the labels of indigenous or even Andean video. They are not connected to the strong indigenous social movement organizations, as is the case with the productions from Bolivia, Ecuador, and Colombia. Since some of these films are available on pirated DVDs in Andean urban markets and travel with their consumers, they do become part of the audiovisual diet of urban migrants and rural communities within and outside of Peru. I am indebted to Mildred López for information on the young filmmakers from the Peruvian Andes.

5 At the time of writing, CEFREC-CAIB's media productions have additionally been endorsed by Consejo Nacional de Ayllus y Markas del Qollasuyo (CONAMAQ) and the Federación Nacional de Mujeres Campesinas Indígenas Originarias de Bolivia Bartolina Sisa (FNMCIOB-BS).

6 SEPHIS has funded mostly academic work, such as the translation of several essays by the Indian Subaltern Studies group into Spanish (cf. *Debates postcoloniales*, edited by Silvia Rivera Cusicanqui and Rossana Barragán).

7 CEFREC-CAIB is not the only producer of indigenous video in Bolivia. The Andean Oral History Workshop (THOA), for instance, has also supported a series of videos. The Women's Center Gregoria Apaza made short documentaries together with Aymara women living in El Alto for television during the early nineties. The series was also directed by Iván Sanjinés. Sanjinés also mentions AVE (Audiovisuales Educativos) in Cochabamba who have promoted Quechua women's and young people's access to video and the Centro de Educación Popular "Qhana" (Luz) in La Paz ("Panorama" 36).

8 My use of the term "coloniality of power" follows Quijano ("Colonialidad") and Mignolo, (*Local* 12) but includes both racial and gender constructs, as I explain in detail in chapter 4.

9 For a discussion of the dynamic conceptions of racial identity in the Andes, see also Harris, "Ethnic Identity"; De la Cadena, *Indigenous*; and Sanjinés, *Mestizaje*.

10 James Siekmeier provides a useful discussion of research to date on the issue and a contextualization of the debate about the role of the Peace Corps in Bolivia. According to an interview conducted with Jorge Sanjinés in 1971, a radio station in Huatajata reported that North American gynecologists had sterilized a woman from the village. According to Siekmeier, "Sanjinés also stated that he was not interested in sterilization, per se. For him, as an artist, the issue served as a metaphor to make a broader point. The scene on sterilization was used to dramatize how U.S. influence, through the Peace Corps as well as the Alliance for Progress, reached the most remote places in Latin America. Metaphorically, Sanjinés held, North American hegemonic power had sterilized the *mestizo* culture, cutting it off from its Indian roots" (82–83).

11 Thanks to Keith Richards for reminding me of this article. *Blood of the Condor* achieved an indigenous gaze through point-of-view shots with a hand-held camera, and by estranging Western-modern contexts with a surrealist soundtrack. Sanjinés, however, ultimately became very critical of his film. Its aesthetics—not only the nonchronological narrative but also the soundtrack, and the use of close-ups that would promote affective identification and the star system did not correspond to Quechua representational strategies and could not achieve an indigenous point of view. For the Ukamau group, nonlinear narratives and chronology, such as the complex flashback structure in *Blood of the Condor*, failed to re-create both the Andean concepts of time and space and the need for clarity (Lopez, "Limits" 422–23; Sanjinés and Grupo Ukamau 57–66; Jorge Sanjinés "Problems" 62–66). *To Receive the Bird Songs* (*Para recibir el canto de los pájaros*) revisits the problems of sociocultural interaction, particularly the failure of the Ukamau Group to achieve a true collaboration with the Quechua community where *Blood of the Condor* was filmed. Deploying aesthetic solutions akin to magical realism, *To Receive the Bird Songs* frames the arrogance of the white urban filmmakers in the countryside and their failure to consult the proper authority figures in the Quechua community. In the film, with the help of a foreign anthropologist (acted by Geraldine Chaplin), the members of the production crew become aware of their own prolongation of internal colonialism. After filming *Blood of the Condor* at the end of the 1960s, Ukamau significantly changed both their social and aesthetic cinematic practice. *To Receive the Bird Songs* has been criticized because it again constitutes a fundamental aesthetic change and because it includes a famous North American actress in a leading role.

12 Cf. Albó, "From MNRistas to Kataristas"; Rivera Cusicanqui and THOA, *Pachakuti*; Sanjinés, *Mestizaje* 14–15; 160–63; Hurtado.

13 The example is from Stam and Spence 16.

14 In Bolivia, hopes that the Constituent Assembly will change the constitution have created an increased sense of urgency for this process. CEFREC-CAIB fosters an ongoing process of critical reflection on the goals and strategies for alternative development, on indigenous and human rights, and indigenous culture and ethics. Indigenous media helped prepare indigenous communities to participate effectively at the local and regional levels of debate and to voice demands to the Constituent Assembly (cf. CEFREC, "Communication Strategies" 1).

15 See Fernández Osco on Aymara law. The video fiction *The Justice of Our Peoples* (*Markanakasan Jucha T'aqawipa/La justicia de nuestros pueblos*) stresses how these laws are being increasingly reinstated in response to a corrupt and inefficient national judicial system.

16 CEFREC, CLACPI, and the national organization of indigenous people of Colombia (ONIC, or Organización Nacional Indígena de Colombia) have reestablished contact and are working toward expanding the use of video to communicate indigenous people cross-culturally. (Personal conversation with Iván Sanjinés, director of CEFREC and former director of CLACPI in Providence, Rhode Island, March 2003).

17 Personal conversation with Graciela Bolaños, director of the Consulate of the CRIC in Bogota, February 2000.

18 For an account of Quintin Lame's role in the Nasa struggle, see also Rappaport, *Politics* (117–74), as well as Lame Chantre.

19 For a brilliant reading of *Atanarjuat, the Fast Runner* that shows how this film nevertheless creates relevance for the present and includes a colonial critique, see Raheja, "Nanook's Smile."

20 This may be a fundamental distinction to films such as *Woman of Courage* (*Qamasan warmi*) and *The Soul* that are made with the participation of indigenous actors and based on indigenous legends but are not part of the indigenous movement's appropriation of media.

21 Raheja's reading of *Atanarjuat* suggest that the Quechua order of knowledge shares affinities with other indigenous cultures. In addition, complex metaphorical meaning and colonial critique is not necessarily sidelined in fiction films set in the mythical past. Raheja argues that without study of the paratextual materials—the companion book and *Inuit Studies Reader*—the non-Inuit audience does not fully understand the film; "the audience is also, unwittingly perhaps, engaged in a game with the filmmakers, one in which the filmmakers obviously have the upper hand" (1175). Specifically, the battle or *illuriik* between the two shamans Tuurngarjuaq and Kumaglak in the spirit world, she argues, are "an expression of a tribally specific episteme; *illuriik* in the film is a form of visual sovereignty that both places this practice within a local context in the services of linguistic and cultural revitalization and simultaneously makes a broader argument for self-representation and self-determination by involving the spectator in the process of decolonization" (1176). Indeed, as Raheja explains, the *illuriik* functions metaphorically for the Inuit viewers. On an extranarrative level, "read metaphorically as a seductive, foreign presence, the visiting shaman [Tuurngarjuaq] can be seen to represent both an individualized

destructive power and the destructive power of Euro-Canadian colonialism. The community struggles over the course of the next two and a half hours to purge itself of the damage caused by the introduction of malevolent forces and begins to heal again. This is instructive for the contemporary community at Igloolik and its environs who can take these lessons about negotiating the potentially dangerous terrain of the 'other' to apply to the present colonial and environmental context in their homeland" (1177).

22 Personal conversations in La Paz (July 1999); Quetzaltenango (August 1999); La Paz (March 2000).

23 The catalog on CEFREC's home page includes a selection of their films. Cf. http://videoindigena.bolnet.bo.

24 On the colonial subalternization of languages, see Mignolo, *Local* 217–311; also Ngugi. On the use of indigenous languages in film, see also Castells i Talens.

25 Employees of the film and video section of the National Museum of the American Indian (part of the Smithsonian Institution) and others write the English subtitles for CEFREC-CAIB's videos. These versions are screened at indigenous film and video festivals in the United States and Canada. I was asked to write the subtitles for *Overcoming Fear* and *In the Name of Our Coca* in 2006 while visiting CEFREC's office in La Paz.

26 For the Bolivian context, see the analysis of literary representations, gender, and spatial metaphors in Josefa Salmón, *Espejo*. Also Stephenson, *Gender*. In the Peruvian case, this geographic mapping is further complicated because of the competing bids for hegemony articulated from the coast and the mountains. The Andean highland capital Cuzco's claim to privilege similarly builds on geographic gender imaginaries, however in this case, the Cuzco elite mobilizes a Quechua association of mountains with virility and the sea with the effeminate (cf. Valcarcel, *Tempestad*; De la Cadena, *Indigenous* 145–47).

27 See http://videoindigena.bolnet.bo.

28 The electronic version of the journal *Entre culturas* issued by CEFREC and linked on their home page used to provide updates on current activities for several years but is now no longer available online. Instead, *Entre culturas* now is a news show that CEFREC-CAIB broadcast on Bolivian National Television.

29 I elaborate on the distribution and financing of indigenous media in chapter 7.

30 At the time of writing, CLACPI is planning the creation of a central Latin American indigenous video collection outside of Bolivia. Iván Sanjinés (director of CEFREC) was replaced as director of CLACPI in June 2004 by Juan José García (personal conversation with Alex Halkin, LASA Conference Las Vegas, October 8, 2004). Consejo Nacional Indígena de Ecuador (CONAIE) in Quito has a similar archive, although of smaller scope. The newly founded Latin American Indigenous Video Initiative (LAIVI) or Red de Iniciativas por el Video Indígena Latinoamericano (RIVIL), currently headed by Alexandra Halkin of the Chiapas Media project and Amalia Cordova of the National Museum of the American Indian, is preparing a comprehensive digital archive that will include not only indigenous videos but also recordings of interviews with indigenous filmmakers. The preparation for this archive is partially funded through a grant from the John Simon Guggenheim Memorial Foundation (cf. Halkin and Cordoba).

31 Indigenous audiovisual communication in this sense parallels the general strategy of indigenous movements that take advantage of global institutions and networks in their struggles (cf. Brysk). These processes raise important questions regarding the role and relevance of the nation-state for the transformations initiated by indigenous social movements. Thoroughly engaging with this problematic, however, exceeds the scope of this study.

32 http://videoindigena.bolnet.bo/. Accessed July 19, 2008. My translation.

33 Mignolo introduced the term "colonial difference" to indicate thinking that takes the foundational experience of colonialism in the Americas as a key starting point for understanding the global world today (*Local* 50–56). He clarifies the term in *The Idea of Latin America* as indicating an epistemic power differential set up with the colonization of the Americas (10). I borrow the concept for reference to the colonial subalternization of knowledge systems but also follow indigenous communicators and intellectuals who distinguish between those colonized and those located on the side of the colonizers, structurally benefiting from colonization even if unconsciously so.

CHAPTER TWO

1 The volume *The Real Thing*, edited by Gugelberger offers a good selection of key texts on the *testimonio* debate.

2 The idea of authorship is certainly also questionable in light of the study of reception and the theory of discourse, where the subject or author is seen as the outcome of constitutive discourses and practices. This perspective is as valid for film and video as it is for written texts.

3 Cf. Bermúdez Rothe, credits, n.p.

4 Amalia Córdova and Melanie Schnell write that CLACPI has also organized workshops and meetings in Cuba and Paraguay. They state that "funding for CLACPI programs has come from the Agencia Española de Cooperación Internacional, Mugarik Gabe (an NGO in the Basque country of Spain), and the World Association for Christian Communication, with additional support from the United Nations Educational Scientific and Cultural Organization's cultural office in Havana, Cuba, and the International Film School of San Antonio de los Baños, Cuba." http://www.cs.org/publications/Csq/csq-article.cfm?id=1829. Accessed July 7, 2008.

5 Ginsburg sustains a similar argument for aboriginal video makers in Australia ("Screen" 51).

6 At the time of writing, the members of CLACPI include Vincent Carelli (Video in the Villages, Brazil), Guillermo Monteforte (Ojo de Agua Comunicaciones, Mexico), Alberto Muenala (CONAIE, Ecuador), Iván Sanjinés (CEFREC, Bolivia), Juan José García (Ojo de Agua Comunicaciones, Mexico), and Alexandra Halkin (Chiapas Media Project).

7 Although CEFREC-CAIB have profoundly altered the scope of Ukamau's "cinema with the people," in the Andes the link between indigenous video and third cinema is personal. Iván Sanjinés, director of CEFREC and of CLACPI until June 2004, is the son of the Bolivian filmmaker Jorge Sanjinés, who worked not only in Bolivia but also in Peru and Ecuador. Reinaldo Yujra, responsible for *Qati qati*, once remarked with slight irony that he was discovered by Jorge Sanjinés, who cast him as the protagonist of *The Secret Nation*. (Personal conversation with Yujra, La Paz, November 2001.) The Peruvian César Pérez, in turn, is credited as cameraperson and photographic advisor to fiction shorts like *Vest Made of Money*.

Pérez worked in Cuzco at the Cine Club de Cuzco (CCC) with Luis Figueroa, who, together with the Bolivian Jorge Ruíz was one of the most important *indigenista* filmmakers in the Andean Region. (Personal communication with Luís Figueroa, Tulane University, March 26, 2001.) Luís Figueroa's best-known film is *Kukuli.*

8 See also CEFREC's Web page at http://videoindigena.bolnet.bo for a similar view. In an early article, Iván Sanjinés also points out the importance of Aymara radio in La Paz and El Alto, particularly the Centro de Comunicadores Aymara "Saphi Aru" and of the historical Cadena Minera (Sanjinés "Panorama" 37–38).

9 Scripts are not necessarily written, as I explain below.

10 See also Luis Macas Ambuludi and Alfredo Lozano Castro, "Reflexiones" 13–15; Luis Macas Ambuludi, "Como se forjó" 23–24; and Walsh "(Re)articulation" 85–87 on the Quichua-dominated multiethnic efforts to create an intercultural university in Ecuador. Recently, the online publication *bolpress* printed a short article on the first indigenous university to open in the Bolivian provincial capital Oruro. As the article states, "this is not a traditional university but a research center that seeks to recuperate the local customs and traditions." The article includes the comments by Carlos Quenaya, the jilacata of the *ayllu* Sullca Salli de Turco who expressed his satisfaction by stating that "I find the methodology that they propose interesting in the sense of learning by doing. As a result of that we—everyone in the community who has knowledge about the *ayllu*, the raising of cameloids or colateral knowledge (*ch'alla* o festivities in honor of the animals)—need to contribute with something to the knowledge of the university." http://www.bolpress.com/art.php?Cod=2007031509. Accessed June, 23, 2008.

11 In personal conversations, as well as during discussions of their videos at international film and video festivals, for instance in Guatemala (1999) and New York (2000), Alfredo Copa (Quechua), Julia Mosúa (Moxeña), Marcelino Pinto (Quechua), Faustino Peña (Moxeño), and Patricio Luna (Aymara), among others, have emphasized that decisions about the selection of scripts, framing strategies, and soundtrack are made collectively. See also Flores and more detailed Mosúa, Copa, and Pinto, audiotape.

12 Outside advisors include, besides Ivan Sanjinés, independent filmmakers such as Alberto Muenala (Quichua filmmaker from Ecuador), Francisco Cajías (Bolivia), Francisco Ormachea (Bolivia), and César Pérez (Peru).

13 I further discuss the production process in chapter 7.

14 While there are numerous studies of indigenous movements at the national level, Brysk and Van Cott offer regional overviews that emphasize the multipronged strategies of indigenous organizations in securing global support while pushing forward local and national changes. See also Yashar 89–90.

15 The critical essays and manifestos by filmmakers collected by Michael Martin offer a good survey of these strategies. See also Michael Chanan's *Twenty-five Years*; *Hojas de cine*; and for the socialization of the cinematic process in Cuba Chanan, *Cuban* 88–89, 355–72.

16 The metaphorical association between cinema and the gun dates back to the beginnings of cinema and its involvement in the colonial enterprise. As Shohat puts it, "it is perhaps not surprising that from the early days the camera was referred to as a gun, precisely because the camera has been used as a gun by colonial powers. (Etienne-Jules Marez, a French physiologist interested in animal locomotion and in wildlife photography called his 1882 camera a 'fusil cinématographique' because of its gunlike apparatus, which made twelve rapid exposures on a circular glass plate that revolved like a bullet cylinder)" (Shohat, "Imaging" 68).

17 Solanas and Getino kept their perspectives closely in tune with Peronist designs. Their film *Hour of the Furnaces* (*La hora de los hornos*) is a tour de force, considered a masterful piece of propaganda. *Hour of the Furnaces* portrays colonization as an outside force that prolongs itself through the national elites. The film's target audience is the people, a class-based category, that calls for revolutionary leadership by those imbued with consciousness, a relation that the film itself performs.

18 For an explanation of how *Courage of the People* overcomes the problems that Sanjinés saw in *Blood of the Condor* and achieves an adequate collaboration and vision of the Bolivian miners, see Sanjinés and Grupo Ukamau 57–66; Sanjinés, "Problems."

19 Jorge Sanjinés, quoted in Iván Sanjinés, "Panorama" 32.

20 Mariátegui 13, 28; see also Quijano, "Prólogo."

21 Sanjinés and the Ukamau group build explicitly on the Peruvian *indigenista* thinker Mariátegui (cf. Sanjinés and Grupo Ukamau). García Pabón argues that Ukamau's films have evolved in a way similar to that of *indigenista* literature from *Raza de bronze* to *Huasipungo* and the novels of José María Arguedas, moving from an outsider perspective to a more and more interior point of view (García Pabón 253).

22 The cost of making the thirty-five-minute fiction short *Qati qati*, in contrast, was approximately only $5,000, as Iván Sanjinés once commented in response to a question at the Latin American Film Festival in Providence, Rhode Island, in 2002.

CHAPTER THREE

1 Cf. Mamani Condori. On the appropriation of alphabetic writing by indigenous authors and administrators trained in the missionary and colonizing apparatus during the colonial period, see, for example, Mignolo (*Darker*, chapters 3 and 4) and Lienhard (chapters 1 and 2).

2 Stephenson, "Forging" offers an instructive view of how the THOA collaborated with other organizations in the creation of a "counterpublic sphere" that has significantly contributed to the highland movement to reconstitute the *ayllu*. See Rappaport, *Politics*, for an in-depth look at Nasa historians and political leaders Don Juan Tama, Manuel Quintín Lame Chantre, and Julio Niquinás. Particularly Lame Chantre and Niquinás conveyed their thoughts through oral history and in written documents. Rappaport also emphasizes that "the contemporary Nasa express their historical tradition through political rhetoric, myth, ritual, and visual images, conveyed both in Spanish and Nasa Yuve" (21).

3 Jesús Martín-Barbero made the case most optimistically in *De los medios*, and Nestor García Canclini similarly attributes great power to mass media and consumer choice in *Consumers*. I return to the relation between indigenous media and the market in the last chapter of this book.

4 Indigenous cosmovision and language have served as a literary platform for imagining *mestizaje*: the assimilation of indigenous traditions to a newly crafted Western society. Although indigenous perspectives shape the notion of *mestizaje*,

they are subordinated to the paradigm of Western civilization. Undoubtedly the so-called *indigenista* novels and short stories—a fundamental pillar of the national literary canon in Bolivia, Peru, and Ecuador—have shaped the idea of indigenous subjectivity in the present. Although Colombia is regarded as not having developed a literary tradition of *indigenismo* or an institutionalized state policy targeting its diverse indigenous peoples because of their relatively small number (Gros, "Guerrillas"; Raymond L. Williams), writers like Antonio García betrayed racial anxiety and reproduced *indigenista* views (*Pasado*). José Antonio Figueroa argues that nineteenth-century literary works emptied the landscape of its inhabitants or, as in the case of the Santa Marta Indians in Colombia, represented indigenous peoples as incapable of self-representation, lacking in political rationality and wedded to rituals and magic that kept them far from the practical world ("Excluidos"). Across the Andes the prevailing image of Quechuas and Aymaras is that of the tragic victim, divested of education and thus incapable of rational thought. This victim longs for the urban intellectual's solidarity. The destiny of indigenous communities is to assimilate or perish. Literature thus developed its own colonial gaze, realized in visual metaphors and plot lines. On the other hand, as a hegemonic framework and technology of representation, literacy/literature did not fully obliterate subalternized voices. Glimpses of strategic adaptations on the part of the subaltern might be caught, as in the use of graffiti (cf. *Lettered* 37–39). Indigenous perspectives and understanding of the world have permeated literary writing that deals with ethnic diversity and the legacy of colonial exploitation. They have shaped the language and narrative structure of novels and have been read as a subversive mode that infiltrates the texts of Creole writers and reveal the trace of a colonized presence that has never quite assimilated. See, for example, Lienhard's detailed discussion in *La voz y su huella*.

5 Although Adorno's argument is based, in part, on a reading of Guaman Poma, in this article there is no reference to the illustrations in Guaman's text. See in contrast López-Baralt's detailed analysis of how Guaman Poma's use of symbolism in *Nueva coronica* subverts the lettered text. According to López-Baralt, Guaman Poma articulates a subalternized perspective through the use of mimetic iconography, which is modeled on existing Christian and colonial painting, but also through the symbolic structure of his images, which let an Andean worldview emerge (*Icono y conquista* 209). Harrison (55–84) offers a similarly insightful reading of Santacruz Pachakuti Yamqui Salcamaygua's *Relación de las antigüedades deste reyno del Pirú*. Román de la Campa ("El desafío") and Gustavo Verdesio ("Revisando un modelo") begin to consider both literacy and visual practice. See also Horswell (*Decolonizing*), who bases his analysis of third gender in part on the structure of Guaman Poma's and Santacruz Pachakuti Yamqui's drawings.

6 Julio Ramos, in his translated and revised study *Divergent Modernities*, complicates Rama's argument by detailing how the nineteenth century brought about a significant split among the lettered classes that was related to the aesthetics of representation. Ramos shows that in the nineteenth century state thinkers such as Domingo Sarmiento, who was influential beyond his native Argentina, sought to discipline and control populations steeped in oral traditions by converting orality into literary representation and thereby symbolically enacting the subjection of rural social groups to the educated urban elites. Ramos, however, also indicates that the professionalization of the writer and modernist poetry

allowed not only for a resistance to positivism in the figure of the *literato*, but also for a lettered practice that resisted the state. Similar to Julio Ramos, Carlos Alonso ("Rama y sus retoños") argues that Rama demonizes writing and produces an immanent vision of the *literato*. According to Alonso, Rama therefore runs the risk of losing sight of historical contexts of cultural production and doesn't see the specifics played out in the discourse of literature

7 According to Gruzinsky, sculpture among the Aztecs was not re-presentation but a ritual practice where spirits or gods were made visually present. Catholic statues of saints were held to be representations, not incarnations. Gruzinsky argues that the church struggled as it tried to substitute the veneration and representation of saints for "idols" (30–60). Although the church may have promoted this view, the veneration of saints, like those of national flags one might add, imbues these items with a sacred value. In any case, whether we understand the notion of ritual as presentation or enactment, it is certainly an ethnocentric fallacy to reduce societies where rituals are practiced to a presignifying state.

8 Rony argues that by turning one's attention to the way the participants of ethnographic film have experienced the process, it is possible to discern performance—that is, a means of seeing with a "third eye" rather than reifying "empirically represented Primitives in timeless picturesques" (13). Wood references an account by Marta Rodríguez who showed *Nanook of the North* at an indigenous video workshop in 1992. He writes, "Rodríguez found that the indigenous delegates at the workshop saw in Nanook not Flaherty's self-aggrandizing discourse, but a picture of the 'communal labour that sets us apart as ethnic groups'" (21). See also Raheja's discussion of *Nanook of the North* in "Reading."

9 The realist illusion created by cinema has coexisted, of course, with experimental montage and self-reflective filmmaking. Jay Ruby distinguishes the conventional kind of ethnographic film from the experimental and more self-conscious practice of ethnographic filmmakers such as Jean Rouch (cf. *Picturing*).

10 I have been using the terms imperial gaze and colonial gaze interchangeably. The idea of the imperial gaze, as elaborated by Kaplan, is primarily based on the analysis of colonial-looking relations in the context of British and French Imperialism. Shohat's analysis of the "disciplinary gaze of empire" takes the colonial context of the Americas into consideration. She links the imaginaries developed during early colonialism with the cinematic representations of Africa and India during the twentieth century (cf. "Imaging"). Similarly, Stam and Spence connect both phases of colonialism.

11 Although beyond the scope of this study, it may be additionally revealing to critically study the enactment of indigenous savagery by *mestizos* in the carnival parades in Oruro and La Paz.

12 See also Himpele's study of the history of Bolivian media in *Circuits of Culture*.

13 For an analysis of Ecuadorian cinema, see Gabriela Alemán. The Ministry of Education in Colombia has supported the production of documentaries such as *The Voyage: Sons and Daughters of the Mountain* (*El viaje: Hijos de la montaña*) that represent indigenous peoples there to television audiences. See also David Wood's dissertation.

14 See also Carelli (n.p.) and Pinhanta (n.p.).

15 See Wood for an insightful comparative analysis of third cinema in Bolivia and Colombia.

16 Pedro Susz lists seventy-five documentary shorts and feature films directed by Ruiz between 1948 and 1960, as well as twenty-six news shorts between 1968 and 1971. Ruiz also co-directed and collaborated in a large number of other documentary shorts (114–16). The key reference work on Jorge Ruiz is Jose Antonio Valdivia's *Testigo de la realidad*. See also Himpele's discussion of Jorge Ruiz in *Circuits*.

17 For a more generous reading, see Gumucio Dagrón 175–79. Gumucio reminds his readers, according to Oscar Sorias (a member of the much more radical Ukamau Group), that in 1954 the Bolivian authorities resisted entering *Come Back, Sebastiana*, as the national contribution to the Montevideo Film festival because "a film about Indians cannot represent the country" (179; my translation).

18 Besides Javier Sanjinés's Mestizaje *Upside Down*, see also Josefa Salmón for a critical treatment and survey of *indigenismo* in Bolivia.

19 Mel Gibson's *Apocalypto* combines both portrayals in the same film as endearing rural Mayans battle the cruel decadence of their urban counterparts.

20 Later the unity between low- and highland indigenous organizations was broken precisely because the high lands claimed that the lowland Indians let themselves be tricked by promises of the state. See Albo, "And from Kataristas."

21 *Mother Earth* is very different from *Achacachi*, an independent film that was produced with the collaboration of CEFREC. *Achacachi* denounces ongoing racism and economic oppression while constructing Aymara protagonism and leadership during the recent uprisings. The title, *Achacachi*, refers to an Aymara community in the highlands that has acquired a reputation for its tenacious anticolonial struggle. It is also the home of the politician Felipe Quispe, *El Mallku*, who voiced the need to indianize the white man rather than become integrated into the national project of *mestizaje* and Western modernity.

22 One could object that armed struggle in Colombia's context of long-standing civil and paramilitary war is of little promise, especially since the whole of indigenous peoples in Colombia constitutes only a small minority. Indeed, indigenous and Afro-Colombian social movement organizations in Colombia have been deliberately and increasingly promoting nonviolent ways of social change, thus countering the dominant discourse of violence underwritten by the U.S. war on drugs (Libia Grueso in Chapel Hill, North Carolina, in June, 2004). See Gros's *Colombia* for a historical account of indigenous movement organizing in Colombia, including its violent aspects.

23 A key intellectual of the Aymara movement, Fausto Reinaga was among the first writers to claim indigenous identity and articulate Andean utopian thinking in the book form. Reinaga self-published essays and books in the late sixties. He framed the *indio* as intellectual and protagonist of anticolonial struggle, including its epistemic dimension. In contrast to the rhetoric of *indigenismo* and *mestizaje*, Reinaga's arguments resonate with the anticolonial struggle and proposals of Frantz Fanon and the Black Panthers (Marcia Stephenson, personal communication). He insisted on the binary of colonizer and colonized but inverted the values attached to each. Reinaga spoke of the total oppression of the *pueblos originarios* (aboriginal peoples) over centuries and resignified the negative image of the *indio* by exalting Aymara culture and highlighting the evils that had come of white, enlightened civilization: nuclear war, ecological devastation, the Holocaust, etc. ("Mi palabra" 61). Reinaga's ideas are still very influential, yet indigenous media relativize many of his radical stands. On the emergence of Aymara indianism, or *Katarismo*, and the influential role of Fausto Reinaga, see Rivera Cusicanqui, *Oprimidos* 124–49. See also Hurtado's study of *Katarismo* as well as Mignolo, *Local* 180.

24 For a more nuanced vision of precolonial ethnic relations, though also from a political position partial to highland anticolonial struggle, see Rivera Cusicanqui and THOA, *Pachakuti* 4.

25 In Quechua language past and present tense are identical, signified by the same temporal suffix. In Aymara the past and present are considered to be before the future but both are not radically separate. Past and present can be seen, while the future has not yet manifested itself (Layme Pairumani 139). In addition, both languages distinguish through suffixes what has been seen by the speaker from that which has only been told to him or her. Harrison discusses the relation between vision and knowledge and the use of different suffixes to indicate Quechua speakers' relations to experience, reported events, and myths or dreams in detail (71–82.)

26 See Escobar (*Hybrid*) for a discussion of the difference between alternative modernities and alternatives to modernity. I use the former expression since indigenous media indicate that the debate in the Andes involves both notions.

27 Archondo as well as Himpele (*Circuits* 140–85) analyze Palenque's radio and televisual campaign and political career cut short by an inexplicable heart attack in 1997.

28 Just before CEFREC and CAIB launched the Indigenous National Plan for Audiovisual Communication in 1996, Javier Sanjinés argued that the use of mass media by political figures, such as Carlos Palenque, who performed Aymara reciprocity and gender complementarity in a popular television talk show in the late eighties, attests to the way audiovisual technology lends a hand to the neoliberal commodification of diversity devoid of a socially transformative impact ("Beyond" 261–62).

29 Wood and García Pabón have each offered a different reading of this film (Wood 176–89; García Pabón 249–62). Ukamau's film poster also emphasizes that "only those men and peoples who assume their identity can again be themselves."

30 I discuss the gender dynamics in this video in more detail in the next chapter.

31 See also Chakrabarty's discussion of subaltern history and Guha's notion of peasant consciousness in his introduction to *Provincializing Europe*. Chakrabarty, however, is more concerned than I am with national liberation and democratic citizenship, which are not necessarily at the center of indigenous decolonization in Latin America.

32 Mignolo argues that ultimately subaltern studies has been unable to escape what he calls "Chakrabarty's dilemma": the desire to hold on to a history of liberation informed by the parameters of Western enlightenment and to let go of Europe as the central referent, even of Indian historiography (Mignolo, *Local* 203–5).

CHAPTER FOUR

1 In the Latin American context gender has usually entered into reflections on the coloniality of power and processes of decolonization as an afterthought; for instance, when Mignolo draws attention to the blindness of "white" feminism

to the coloniality of power (Mignolo, *Local* 124–26; 314–15). More recently, gender has been taken as shorthand for "woman," leading some to ask about the participation of women in decolonization efforts (e.g., Escobar, *Hybrid*, chap. 5). How gender imaginaries have entered colonial constructs and continued to mesh with the idea of race has not received the same attention. Instead, the invention of race—through discourses and practices—has been privileged as a marker of the coloniality of power and as the defining characteristic of what distinguishes this globalization (1492 to the present) from other forms of imperial rule and expansion. I maintain, however, that ideas about gender have not disappeared but continue to shape colonial attitudes and power relations. The way gender is interrogated marks the depth of thinking in indigenous movements' efforts to sustain decolonizing processes.

2 As I argued earlier, ethnic identification among indigenous peoples has fluctuated. It has increased with the proliferation of indigenous social movements and constitutional reforms acknowledging the multicultural makeup of Latin American nation-states. Land rights granted to indigenous communities have similarly prompted many to acknowledge or assume an indigenous identity where formerly racial discrimination was a strong deterrent that instead exerted pressure to embrace other ethnic categories such as *mestizo/a* (cf. Harris, "Ethnic").

3 Although spectator identification is complex, there is a tendency for feminine viewers to identify with the male heroes in a kind of oedipal nostalgia that lives out a fantasy of not succumbing to the law of femininity. According to this logic, there is no space for the woman-spectator in this regime, because it is always already a male gaze constructed by the narrative and the look of the camera (8). The question of identification has been complicated significantly since Mulvey's first article, not only by de Lauretis but also by other feminist film critics such as Elizabeth Cowie, Janet Bergstrom, or Mary Ann Doane, as well as by Mulvey herself in her exploration of female spectatorship in "Afterthoughts" (Penley, "Introduction"). Fatimah Tobing Rony, in turn, insists that Hollywood cinema never quite manages to interpellate its colonial and postcolonial spectators. Neither actors nor spectators can smoothly integrate themselves into the disparaging portrayals of themselves, returning the gaze through a "third eye" that "acknowledges performance rather than empirically represented Primitives in timeless picturesque" (Rony 13). bell hooks's discussion of African American viewers is particularly suggestive with regard to subversive and self-empowering ways of looking ("Oppositional").

4 *Qati qati* was filmed in digital format and produced by CEFREC-CAIB in Bolivia. The dialogues are in Aymara with Spanish subtitles.

5 Certainly, robbery exists and existed in indigenous communities. See Fernández Osco for the traditional judicial structures in Aymara communities that focus on sanctioning robberies. The 2006 CEFREC-CAIB fiction short *The Justice of Our Peoples* depicts an intact local system of crime investigation and punishment that the protagonists call upon when confronted with the corruption and inefficacy of the state's judicial system. Here two young llama thieves are found with the help of a traditional coca reading and sacrificial *mesa*.

6 Thanks to Reynaldo Yujra for clarifying this point in a personal conversation in Xela (Quetzaltenango), August 8, 1999.

7 Gender roles are idealized constructs. Those shaped in the West since the Renaissance, hardened during the European Enlightenment, and opened

up somewhat since then, do not exactly correspond to gender role ideals in Quechua and Aymara communities. On gender ideals and concepts in the Andes, see for example, Silverblatt; Arnold ed., *Más allá*; Harrison 114–43; and Weismantel.

8 A strict psychoanalytic approach to the gaze in the context of Andean film (and culture) carries significant limitations. In a context where Greek mythology is largely absent and Christian mythology (and its relation to the Greek) has been integrated into Quechua and Aymara mythologies, subject identification and formation do not render the patriarchal tales of later Greek mythology but rather an ideology of gender complementarity.

9 See, for example, Harris, "Complementarity"; "Power" 72–87; Isbell 275–85; Rössing 81–84.

10 For Ramiro Reynaga, the " 'progressive' mestizo prefers as his wife a repulsive white whore instead of a pure beautiful Indian" (Wankar 296). His father sees "the greasy prostitute miniskirt" as a symbol of Western civilization (Fausto Reinaga, *América India* 129).

11 However, see Calani Gonzales, who eliminates references to women from his history of indigenous thought while using complementarity in reference to the idea of "diversity with unity" (Calani Gonzales 93).

12 See also the anthropological studies collected in Perrin and Perruchon.

13 Though not part of indigenous social movement politics, Estermann's effort to bring Western and Quechua philosophy in dialogue argues along similar lines. See, particularly, his discussion of Andean complementarity in relation to Western Logic and Dialectics (Estermann 126–35). Raheja notes that in her dissertation, Karla Jessen Williamson, an Inuit scholar from Greenland, "asserts that traditional conceptions of gender equality and complementarity among the Inuit inform contemporary structures of gender equality and, among other things, attitudes toward sexual orientation in Artic communities" (Raheja, "Reading" 1185 n. 53.)

14 See also Stephenson, *Gender*. Rossana Barragán argues that nineteenth-century urban migration supplanted vertical gender relations with more horizontal ones in the rural highlands of Bolivia.

15 See Cervone et al.; Brito Sandoval; Mosúa, Copa, and Pinto; Barrios de Chungara; as well as Condo Riveros. See De la Torre Amaguaña and De la Cadena, "Matrimonio," for details on Andean gender ideals among speakers of Quichua (in Ecuador) and Quechua (in Peru). See Olivia Harris's work as well as the studies by Denise Arnold and Juan de Dios Yapita for Aymara gender ideals. Rivera Cusicanqui's edited volume *Ser mujer* includes three detailed studies on the transformations of gender roles in different rural contexts (low- and highlands). The studies draw attention to changes occurring with the increased migrations of men and the developmental interventions by nongovernmental organizations. Rivera Cusicanqui's essay in this volume is a sophisticated study of urban Aymara women vendors and their gender roles and relations.

16 See Rivera, "Noción" as well as Criales Burgos for the Aymara context; de la Cadena "Mujeres" and "Matrimonio" for Quechua communities in Peru; Lehm and Ciddebeni on the Moxos. Jesús Avirama of the Columbian CRIC dismissed indigenous feminism when he stated that "the emergence of foundations subject to the rhythm and whims of international fashion—focusing on the

environment, women's issues, or development, for example, is troubling" (Avirama and Márquez 99).

17 *Our Word* won the Premio Especial of the International Film and Television School (Escuela Internacional de Cine y TV) in San Antonio de los Baños, Cuba, and the Special Prize at the VI Festival Americano de Cine y Vídeo de los Pueblos Indígenas in Guatemala 1999.

18 See de la Cadena, "Mujeres" and "Matrimonio," for the devaluation of women's labor in Chitapampa, Peru. Starn (166) offers a similar self-evaluation by women with regard to their roles in the *rondas* in northern Peru. Starn's narrative, however, also opens up a possibility of reading the rhetoric of "auxiliary" as *indispensable* help. See also Domitila Barrios de Chungara's testimonio *Si me permiten hablar*. As such it would enter into the representation of complementarity without hierarchy, a discourse where women can emphasize their roles as equally important to those of men.

19 Personal communication with Ivan Sanjinés, Duke University, March 27, 2002.

20 Religious affiliation is indicated by the family's consumption of alcohol. In the case of the Catholic suitor, the parents want to integrate the gift and consumption of alcohol into the Quechua ritual of prenuptial negotiations. As protestants, Rosita's family, however, abstains.

21 Brooks, *The Melodramatic Imagination* (New Haven: Yale University Press, 1976), 14–15. Quoted in López, "Tears" 152.

22 One of the first fiction pieces produced by CEFREC-CAIB, *Jichi Woman* explores the cave as a female coded place of ancestry in more depth.

23 On the water as the borderland between the living and the dead, see also the 35mm fiction short *Soul*.

24 According to Iván Sanjinés, personal conversation at Duke University, March 27, 2002.

25 Cf. again Starn (155–91) on how Quechua women provoked men to assume their roles as protectors of family and community during the war of the Shining Path.

26 My reading of *Loving Each Other in the Shadows* has benefited from discussion with undergraduate students in a class on indigenous media that I taught at the University of California, Riverside, in the winter of 2008.

27 In *Overcoming Fear* the women actively participate in the community debate and are even responsible for setting the agenda. See, in contrast, the characterization of *ayllu* meetings in Ticona Alejo 125–34.

28 Feminist critique by women of color has been outspoken about this issue and has been offering extremely suggestive venues for understanding. As Linda Tuhiwai Smith put it, "the work being carried out by western feminists has been countered by the work of black women and other 'women with labels.' In fact, the very labeling of women demonstrates the pluralism within the feminist world, and the multiple directions from which feminist theory has emerged and to which it may be heading" (167). In order to understand violence against women, Andrea Smith suggests that "by putting Native Women at the center of analysis . . . we can develop more comprehensive strategies for ending gender violence that benefit not only indigenous women and women of color, but all people affected by gender violence" (5). These quotes are just a few examples of scholarship currently under way that changes the paradigms of inquiry. Instead of looking at the lives and thinking of subalternized and colonized peoples as particular cases from a universal framework developed in the North and with white women at the center, women of color scholarship explores what happens when these peoples are privileged in the practice of theorizing.

29 Millán's article includes a reprint of the Law of Indigenous Women that appears for the first time in the EZLN's publishing organ, *El Despertador Mexicano*, on January 1, 1994. See also the EZLN Web site.

30 See Mott 43; Montrose 17; Schiwy "Discovery" 12–13.

31 Fausto-Sterling 45–77; Butler 7–16. See also the award-winning Argentine film *XXY* whose protagonist is an adolescent hermaphrodite struggling with his/her emerging sexual identity. Thanks to Susan Antebi for calling my attention to this film and letting me borrow it.

32 For a theorization of *chola* market women as transgressing Andean and Western notions of gender, see Weismantel. Monasterios offers a collection of essays on Mujeres Creando, an urban group of lesbian performance activists that includes Aymara migrants in La Paz.

CHAPTER FIVE

1 Documentary film, as Nichols notes, has not been accepted as an equal to scientific discourse, but rather a form of subordinate illustration and accompaniment. Nevertheless, such a stand "neglects the extent to which image, ideology, and utopia are fundamentally joined. Images help constitute the ideologies that determine our own subjectivity" (*Representing* 9–10).

2 Cf. Beattie 69–79. Ten years prior to Beattie's account, Faye Ginsburg ("Embedded" 368) noted that for most Australian Aboriginal video makers, form and innovative solutions do not seem relevant. The aesthetic criteria used by aboriginal people privilege instead the strengthening of community ties. See also Eric Michaels's collection of essays in *Bad Aboriginal Art*. Beattie states that Aboriginal filmmakers have grown tired of documentary form and are moving into fiction where there seems to be greater space for creative reframing (cf. Beattie 66). See also Jennifer Deger's book on the late Aboriginal media activist Bangana Wunungmurra. Perhaps indigenous video in Latin America will follow a similar trajectory, already visible in the increasingly experimental and parodic fictions of Video in the Villages, such as the four Waiãpi tales of the cannibal monster compiled on *Jungle Secrets* (*Segredos de mata*).

3 I follow Bill Nichols's distinction of documentary genres. Nichols defines five general types of documentary modes: Expository, observational, interactive, reflexive, and performative (*Representing* 32–75). Keith Beattie has added two types, derived in large degree from television studies: reconstructive and observational-entertainment (24–25).

4 Eisenstein sought to consciously influence the audience in a desired direction through "a series of calculated pressures on its psyche," effected through montage, a procedure he called "agit" (39).

5 Seen from the interstice of these two tendencies, one true desire that film technology expresses is not the creation of art made possible through technology. Rather it is the longing for total realism, "a total cinema that is to provide that complete illusion of life" (Bazin 20). Bazin argues that despite and beyond montage, the search for this realism in film continues. Early experiments with montage lead to the in-depth shot, deep focus panning shots, that restore to

reality its ambiguity; at the same time, however, these operations reveal even more the constructed nature of this realism effect: "The image—its plastic composition and the way it is set in time, because it is founded on a much higher degree of realism—has at its disposal more means of manipulating reality and of modifying it from within. The film-maker is no longer the competitor of the painter and the playwright, he is, at last, the equal of the novelist" (39–40).

6 Julia Mosúa explicitly expressed her discomfort with the need to speak publicly in an interview with Daniel Flores (Copa, Mosúa, and Pinto, audiotape). Cf. Ibazeta, chapter 3, for an elaboration of the staging of indigenous self in front of the camera in CEFREC-CAIB's documentaries.

7 See also Shohat and Stam, especially chapter 3. On the return of the gaze, see also Rony.

8 As I argue, making this relation explicit may be a goal of digital video art, but it only functions as an artistic interruption, because the truth claims of documentary film continue despite digital technology. I further explore the relationship between digital media, speculative capitalism, and analogue readings in a forthcoming article in the journal *Social Identities*.

9 Weiner insists on the need for and possibility of creating objective knowledge, generated from the outside and based on a critical distance (210). He argues that anthropological research is a privileged mode of attaining knowledge about indigenous cultures since indigenous video conceals more than it reveals (205–6). Faye Ginsburg anticipated such a position, suggesting that knowledge production might better be seen as a collaborative undertaking where anthropologists and video makers contribute different perspectives, ultimately leading to a more comprehensive understanding ("Parallax"). Ginsburg has also been very clear that audiovisual media, no matter what anthropologists may think, primarily serve the purposes of indigenous communities. Clearly, indigenous communities and social movements may have a different conception than academics about what is useful in indigenous media. Representing to the West or to the academy is not the primary issue on their agenda. In this sense, indigenous media resemble the indigenous testimonials and oral histories gathered for internal use rather than the international *testimonio* in search of political solidarity.

10 See Estermann 206–12; Spedding "Investigaciones"; Rössing; and De la Torre Amaguaña.

11 The trope becomes central in *The Nasa Garden* and in *Jichi womanu*, where nature is personified by a woman, and in *The Forest Spirit*, where nature is cast as a seductive but dangerous young woman. It is striking that videos made in diverse indigenous cultures from the South of Bolivia to the Cauca region in Columbia share this trope. *Pachamama* has become a pan-indigenous referent that is not, at first sight, complicated by the notion of a thoroughly gendered life world that remains hegemonic in the Andean highlands from Bolivia to Ecuador.

12 Gros's *Colombia* and Rappaport's *Politics* and *Cumbe* thoroughly discuss the complex history of indigenous struggle for territory in light of the Colombian state's historical legislation concerning reservations (*resguardos*).

13 See also Estermann for the same conceptualizations of nature among Quichua speakers in Ecuador. Estermann says that according to the Quichua the

Pachamama lives; "it is an organic being that gets thirsty, angry, untouchable, that can be dead or sterile and that gives reciprocally" (176).

14 The video elaborates on this conflation of nature and culture. The narrator explains how everything is connected and personified and useful, how everything exists with the goal of harmony, abundance, and happiness. It all depends on reciprocity. The footage illustrates the narrator's explanation's of the complexity of relations between plants, humans, when to sow, etc.

15 The camera work is done by Paco Chuji, a member of CONAIE, and Rainer Stöckelmann, an independent documentary filmmaker from former East Germany. The translations from Quichua are by Paco Chuji and Lucila Lema, both Quichua members of CONAIE's communication department.

16 *Trinkets and Beads* is a documentary directed by Christopher Walker, produced by Tony Avirgan in collaboration with Phantom/Sunny Side Faction Films and TVE (Television Trust for the Environment) and distributed by First Run/Icarus Films. It is in English and Spanish with English subtitles.

17 For a brief history and update on the Huaorani struggle, see for example Amnesty International's Web site at http://www.amnestyusa.org/chevron-corp/chevron-in-ecuador/page.do?id=1101670&n1=3&n2=26&n3=1242. Accessed July 4, 2008.

18 See Schiwy's "Ecoturismo" on the perpetuation of Western epistemic privilege in ecotourism through the deployment of gender and colonial imaginaries.

19 The accompanying manual for the members of CAIB's Red Nacional is called *Boletin guía de acompañamiento* 2.

20 State policies after the Revolution of 1952 encouraged migration to solve land issues in the highlands. The indigenous migrants are called *colonizadores* ("colonizers") in official terminology. The union representing these migrants is Confederación Sindical de Colonizadores de Bolivia (CSCB), one of the underwriters of the Indigenous National Plan for Audiovisual Communication.

21 This is not the only video with such an approach. The fiction piece *The Hunter* and CRIC's *The Nasa Garden* frame indigenous peoples as participants in the exploitation and destruction of nature.

22 For a vivid account of these experiences, see Luciano Tapia, *Ukhamawa*, part 5.

23 These migrant peoples became part of the modernization and development discourses that Jorge Ruíz synthesized in his film *The Mountains Don't Change*, which endorses the state discourse promoting monoculture and modern agrobusinesses. Ruíz's feature fiction film *The Slope* (*La vertiente*) celebrates the modernization undertaken in the Alto Beni during the fifties, starring a white male hero. *Overcoming Fear* is set in the same geographical context but brings none of the interethnic or environmental issues to the forefront.

24 The film's economic critique is magnified when *Creating Life* is viewed as part of the video package, followed by the fiction piece *Vest Made of Money*, which critiques avarice and greed.

CHAPTER SIX

1 Cuban cinema is a notable exception since many of ICAIC's films early on opted for the comedy as a way of combining audience entertainment, constructive criticism of the revolutionary process of building a new society, and the innovative possibilities of mixing documentary with fiction film footage, and found clips. Cf. Chanan, *Cuban Cinema* for a detailed account of the diversity of Cuban film produced by ICAIC.

2 They are also radically different from B-videos, such as *The Little Orphan* (*El huerfanito*) or *Incest in the Andes* (*Incesto en los Andes: La maldición de los jarjachas*), produced in the Peruvian Andes in recent years. See "Páginas del cine andino" for an overview at http://www.ayllumedia.org/cineandino.htm. Thanks to Mildred López for calling my attention to this Andean video production.

3 In the interview with Daniel Flores, Pinto insists that—despite the suggestive title—*Cursed Gold* is simply a legend where coca marketing and consumption frames a cultural backdrop and that a denunciation of human rights violations in the region is impossible in the present political climate (Mosúa, Copa, and Pinto). Franco Gamboa, however, suggests that the allegorical reading of *Cursed Gold* clearly imposes itself for a Bolivian audience that has witnessed the struggles and protests of the coca growers in newspapers and on the streets since the beginning of the U.S.-backed national policy of coca eradication by military troops in 1998 (personal conversation, February 2001, Duke University).

4 Cf. Rivera Cusicanqui *Oprimidos*, 154–55; Albó, "From MNRistas" 402; Javier Sanjinés, *Mestizaje* 14. This understanding also underlies the Movimiento al Socialismo (MAS) that Evo Morales represents.

5 The story of the *kharisiri*, *ñakaj*, or *pishtaco* is a famous example that has morphed from the fat-sucking priest of colonial times to the postmodern medical doctor who harvests the organs of innocent indigenous victims. In each case the tale attest to the acute sensitivity of Andean communities to forms of colonial and neocolonial/neoliberal exploitation. Although the specific circumstances and characteristics of the culprits may change, the stories maintain a continuity in setting (the dark of night), unawareness of exploitation (the victims don't remember being assaulted) due to the magical procedures of the assailants (blowing magical dust into their victims' eyes). The consequences, delayed but inevitable death, have also remained the same. See also Weismantel 3–16; Gareth Williams 214–72; and Portocarrero et al. for suggestive discussions of the *pishtaco* tales. See also the short Peruvian film *Ñakaj*.

6 For a classic study of colonial continuities and change in Quechua songs, see Harrison. There is much literature on embodied forms of transmitting social memory and indigenous identity. E.g., Dover, Seibold and McDowell; Abercrombie; Harrison; Taylor.

7 "William J. Conklin has contributed significantly to the understanding of visual representation in Andean textiles through the concept of 'structure as a carrier of meaning.' He suggests that researchers' preconception that there must have been a written language with some resemblance, such as an alphabet, to our own may have created an obstacle to understanding 'other modes that involve formal visual constructions that were used across the culture and conveyed complex meanings' " (Heckman 38–39, quoting from Elizabeth Hill Boone). See also Harrison 55–71.

8 For an explicit treatment of the subject see CEFREC-CAIB's video *In the Name of Our Coca*.

9 Turner seems to imply that ritual equals mimetic representation and can hence be shown on screen. It may, however, be helpful to understand ritual as a form that collapses the distinction between mimesis and making present. The binary

opposition begins to disintegrate if we accept that both representation and ritual involve enactment.

10 Adolfo Colombres, for instance, has suggested that indigenous video is an apt form of mediation that allows indigenous cultures to skip over the developmental step of alphabetic literacy, extending orality into the audiovisual realm. He considers audiovisual media to be "less mutilating for it [indigenous culture] than writing . . . it is easier for an oral culture to jump towards this new orality (a mediated orality) than to submit itself to the laws of writing" (103).

11 The quote is from the booklet accompanying CEFREC-CAIB's multimedia package Estrategia Nacional de Comunicación Derechos Indígenas y Originarios Hacia la Asamblea Constituyente, n.p., 2006.

12 Weiner insists that it is possible to generate objective knowledge through critical distance and from outside indigenous communities (210). He argues that anthropological research is a privileged mode of attaining knowledge about indigenous cultures since indigenous video conceals more than it reveals (205–6). The argument is confusing since its logic does not seem to apply to Western societies. See also the critical debate following Weiner's article in the same issue of *Current Anthropology*.

13 The visual and performative dimensions of transmitting knowledge and social memory have rarely found their way into the critical discussion of the lettered city. Despite its ethnocentrism and limited definition of what constitutes "writing," the myth of literacy has proven quite tenacious. See, for instance, Lienhard's important study on literature and subalternity that traces the persistence of indigenous voices in hegemonic literary forms. Seeking an explanation for why indigenous peoples accepted the hegemony of alphabetic literacy, Lienhard argues that Amerindians become subject to the fetish of writing not primarily because it is a colonial imposition (as in Rama's lettered city), but precisely because they believe in its transcendental power. Lienhard suggests that indigenous peoples acknowledged a technological-civilizational superiority of the West. Similarly to Jack Goody and Walter Ong, Lienhard suggests that alphabetic writing, in contrast with orality and Amerindian semiotic systems, is capable of communicating speech over space and time and is therefore producing a different kind of knowledge than the oral, one that creates the foundation for empire (22–23). Lienhard himself here becomes a victim of the magic of writing. His narrative reflects an ethnographic pastoral imaginary that seeks to rescue indigenous peoples from imperial guilt. The imperial expansion of the Inca Empire indicates that the capacity to re-present the state across time and space is not limited to alphabetic writing. The Andean *khipus* and the *ceques* system sustained the telecommunication of the Inca state; the paintings of maps and visual histories in Mesoamerica were fundamental to the Mayan Empire (cf. Boone and Mignolo; Mignolo, *Darker*). Santiago Castro-Gómez, similarly, reiterates the teleological narrative of technologies of representation in his efforts to show the lettered city as an ideologically fractured space. Castro-Gómez asserts that alphabetic writing is inherently reflexive, which is what distinguishes it from orality ("Los vecindarios" 129). For Castro-Gómez this capacity for critical thought constitutes the lettered city as a form of power that can serve oppression as well as liberation. It is for this very reason that literacy has frequently been seen as the master's tool capable of dismantling the master's house. For a similar position, see also Hugo Niño as well as Guillermo Mariaca. I developed

my critique of such arguments further in the article "Indigenous Media and the End of the Lettered City."

14 Rama does not elaborate on how the power of alphabetic writing entailed the creation of orality as an idea that abstracted from the plethora of complex visual, oral, and performative forms of representation across different indigenous cultures. Rather, his attention remains focused on how power articulates itself. Roman de la Campa argues that Rama is thus following the first tendency in the study of power, an archeology of power that does not focus on its subversion but, similar to the early Foucault and Said, attests to its articulation (cf. "El desafío" 34–35).

CHAPTER SEVEN

1 I would like to thank Thomas Reese, Tulane University, for calling my attention to the pervasive representation of labor in CEFREC-CAIB's fiction videos.

2 Cf. Chanan, *Cuban* 357–72; Solanas and Getino, *Cine, cultura* 60; Burton, "Film."

3 Some consider that culture and economy, even the performance of indigenous politics, have become reciprocally permeated: "Not just as a commodity—which would be the equivalent of instrumentality—but as a mode of cognition, social organization, and even attempts at social emancipation, seem to feed back into the system they resist or oppose" (Yudice 28).

4 Antonio Negri, Michael Hardt, Paolo Virno, and others associated with the autonomous radical philosophers in Italy have proposed thinking the global capitalist system in terms of an all-encompassing empire that no longer allows for an external critique. Rather, it has created a global plane of immanence. Negri's writing, in particular, has been widely discussed in Argentina but has had less impact in the Andean countries.

5 See any global Internet map, such as the one advertised by TeleGeography at http://www.telegeography.com/products/map_internet/index.php. Accessed June 2, 2008. Bandwidth and major communication lines connect and expand the power of European and U.S. American corporations with increasing contact to the Asian economies. Miller et al. discuss the complex strategies of diversification deployed by the Hollywood media industry. The authors maintain that "Hollywood's hegemony is built upon and sustained by the internal suppression of worker rights, the exploitation of a global division of labour and the impact of colonialism on language" (Miller et al. 131). See also John Sinclair's succinct discussion of television and the concentration of ownership in Sinclair and Turner.

6 Lazzarato argues that immaterial labor is of key importance to late capitalism. Immaterial labor is equally or perhaps even more productive or essential to the process of creating surplus value, as is the traditional production of goods (cf. Lazzarato 132–46).

7 The new global order, marked by networks, immaterial labor, and biopower is seen as coming into being as a response to the actions of labor movements, the emphasis on labor being stronger in Negri than in Hardt (Hardt and Negri xii–xv, 8–9, 19; cf. also Negri, *Time for Revolution*).

8 A collection of essays forthcoming in the journal *Social Identities* discusses the relation between immaterial labor, global capitalism, and digital technologies. See especially the articles by Fornazzari and Rogers.

9 For a detailed and eloquent discussion of the revolutionary potential of the multitude, see Beasley-Murray. Beasley-Murray similarly finds multitudinous eruptions throughout history regardless of the nature of these revolts or their relation to anticolonial struggle. His, however, is a less utopian vision. As he summarizes his critique, "absolute immanence would not only end history; it would also end the play of encounter, the series of events that give rise to either pleasure or pain. All contingency and accident would be abolished in favor of absolute necessity, for Spinoza coterminous with absolute freedom. There would be no encounter because everything would already be in its place. What would endure would be pure intensity, outside of time or, better, of time rather than in time. Should the multitude come into its own, and the state and transcendence disappear, there would be no objectivity, only the pure subjectivity of the divine presence and power. Heaven is a place where nothing ever happens. Future Perfect or *perfectum est*: It would be perfect, but it would be dead" (67).

10 Maldonado Torres's discussion in "Topología" (97–107) is suggestive, although like Mignolo and Quijano he does not see gender constructs as constitutive of the coloniality of power.

11 Coronil proposes—in the face of the declining power of Eurocentrism and the deterritorialization of capitalism—that we might more appropriately speak of globalcentrism rather than of coloniality of power: "what I call the globalcentrism of dominant globalization discourses *expresses the ongoing dominance of the West* by a number of representational operations that include: the dissolution of the 'West' into the market and its crystallization in less visible transnational nodules of concentrated financial and political power; the attenuation of cultural antagonisms through the integration of distant cultures into a common global space; and a shift from alterity to subalternity as a dominant modality for constituting cultural difference ("Towards" 354).

12 See Rivera Cusicanqui, "Desafío" 32 and "Trabajo" for accounts of how some women maintain these characteristics of peasant economy and transport them into the urban environment in different regions in Bolivia.

13 Wood suggests that these filmmakers themselves rejected or only strategically embraced the label of *auteur*. Rather, their status as "talented intellectual revolutionaries" and "film-artists" were attributed to them by the intellectual circles in Latin America and Europe where their films were seen (19).

14 Alfredo Copa continuously affirms his ties with his community of origin. He is required to provide manual labor (to participate in the construction of houses, for instance) as well as his intellectual capacity in return for his communities' participation in video production. He may be called upon to mediate administrative issues with the state, to help voice demands of community needs to the outside, and to continue to make video production available (Mosúa, Copa, and Pinto, audiotape; Flores 33–34).

15 See also Ibazeta, chapter 3.

16 Ticona Alejo paints a more hierarchical picture of political decision-making in the *ayllus* (125–44).

17 Discussions in film studies concerning the idea of the auteur in Europe and his or her importance within Hollywood's industrial cinema have resurfaced again since the initial debates in *Cahiers du cinema*. Catherine Grant argues that in the context of affirming those traditionally excluded from outstanding positions in

film production, the emphasis on the identity of the director can be politically useful even as this emphasis shrouds the collective nature of all film production, the determining role of producers in industrial cinema, and the fact that meaning is ultimately not determined by authors and filmmakers but by the audience (Grant 124).

18 The indigenous struggle for intellectual property rights finds itself forced onto the hegemonic ground of copy right and private property laws that are themselves not global laws but extensions of European and U.S. legislative traditions (cf. Rosemary Coombe).

19 Personal conversation with Iván Sanjinés, La Paz, August 2005.

20 When indigenous videos were sold during the 2002 *Eye of the Condor Bolivian Video Tour* these requirements were softened. The activists took advantage of the one-time opportunity to sell a limited amount of films to interested audiences at the screenings. If the question of image property rights is revisited, the international sales-dimension may open up further.

21 I have since then interpreted for members of CEFREC and CAIB during film festivals in New York and Rhode Island, translated written documents, and most recently I wrote the English subtitles for two CEFREC-CAIB fiction shorts, *Overcoming Fear* (*Venciendo el miedo*) and *In the Name of Our Coca* (*Cocanchej sutimpy*).

22 Personal conversation with Iván Sanjinés, La Paz, Bolivia, August 2005. For a schedule and overview of Maori Television programming, see their Web page at http://www.maoritelevision.com/. Accessed July 4, 2008.

23 I facilitated these library acquisitions. As part of my reciprocal relationship with CEFREC-CAIB I am still allowed to trade my services for videos, though in a limited way. I use them for teaching and research and have committed to not creating unauthorized copies of them.

24 See Ortíz's classic study of transculturation; Rama (*Narrative*); and Beverley, "Siete."

AFTERWORD

1 This is of course particularly true for the social sciences. See, for example, the collected volumes edited by Van Cott; Maybury-Lewis; Clark and Becker; and Yashar's "Indigenous Politics."

2 The collected volume *Left Turns*, edited by Eric Hershberg, Maxwell Cameron, and Jon Beasley-Murray, currently in preparation, is informed by this perception. The volume joins social sciences and cultural studies approaches to understanding the New Left.

3 Ticona Alejo describes the ideal and reality of governance in Quechua and Aymara communities and at regional levels (137–44).

4 http://www.un.org/esa/socdev/unpfii/en/declaration.html. Accessed June 30, 2008.

5 Brazil, Bolivia, Ecuador, Peru, Venezuela, and Mexico—the Latin American states with large fossil fuel reserves and indigenous territories—are not included in the CANZUS group. Of the Latin American countries, the only one to abstain was Colombia, citing contradictions with its national constitution. http://www.un.org/News/Press/docs/2007/ga10612.doc.htm. Accessed July 12, 2008.)

6 Raheja's notion of sovereignty indicates that Native American cinematic and literary testimonios continue to carry important epistemic potential. Raheja

suggests "a reading practice for thinking about the space between resistance and compliance wherein indigenous filmmakers and actors revisit, contribute to, borrow from, critique, and reconfigure ethnographic film conventions, at the same time operating within and stretching the boundaries created by these conventions. Terming this approach 'visual sovereignty,' I demonstrate how this strategy offers up not only the possibility of engaging and deconstructing white-generated representations of indigenous people, but more broadly and importantly how it intervenes in larger discussions of Native American sovereignty by locating and advocating for indigenous cultural and political power both within and outside of Western legal jurisprudence" ("Reading" 1161). In their introduction to a special issue on American Indian autobiography, Raheja and Fitzgerald further explain that much previous scholarly discussion of Native American autobiographies and testimonials "often obscured the Indian voice of the text and shifted the focus on the scholarship away from indigenous lived experience to that of the non-Indian editor" (Raheja and Fitzgerald 1). Their collection, in contrast, builds on the insight that native life stories contribute "in meaningful ways to tribal communities' processes of nation building and the reconfiguration of tribal intellectual and cultural sovereignty through the recovery of Native voice and agency in mediated texts" (1). Though nonprescriptive this approach signals that *testimonios* can also acquire a new meaning for literary and cultural studies scholarship.

BIBLIOGRAPHY

Abercrombie, Thomas A. *Pathways of Memory and Power. Ethnography and History among an Andean People*. Madison: U of Wisconsin P, 1998.

Adorno, "La *ciudad letrada* y los discursos coloniales." *Hispamérica* 16.48 (1987): 3–24.

Albó, Xavier. "From MNRistas to Kataristas to Katari." *Resistance, Rebellion, and Consciousness in the Andean Peasant World, 18th to 20th Centuries*. Ed. Steve J. Stern. Madison: U of Wisconsin P, 1987. 379–419.

———. *¿ . . . Y de Kataristas a MNRistas? La sorprendente y audaz alianza entre aymaras y neoliberales en Bolivia*. La Paz: CEDOIN; UNITAS, 1993. Translated as "And from Kataristas to MNRistas? The Surprising and Bold Alliance between Aymaras and Neoliberals in Bolivia." Trans. Charles Roberts. *Indigenous Peoples and Democracy in Latin America*. Ed. Donna Lee Van Cott. New York: St. Martin's Press and Inter-American Dialogue, 1995. 55–81.

Alemán, Gabriela. "An International Conspiracy. Ecuadorian Cinema in the 1960s and 1970s." *Journal of Latin American Cultural Studies* 13.1 (2004): 97–113.

Alonso, Carlos J. "Rama y sus retoños: Figuring the Nineteenth Century in Spanish America." *Revista de Estudios Hispánicos* 28 (1994): 283–92.

Archondo, Rafael. *Compadres al micrófono: La resurrección metropolitana del ayllu*. La Paz: Hisbol, 1991.

Arguedas, Alcides. *Pueblo enfermo*. La Paz: Gisbert & Cia, 1979.

Arnold, Denise. "Hacer al hombre a imagen de ella: aspectos de género en los textiles de Qaqachaka." *Revista chungará* 26:1 (1994): 79–115.

———. "Making Men in Her Own Image: Gender, Text, and Textile in Qaqachaka." *Creating Context in Andean Cultures*. Ed. Rosaleen Howard-Malverde. Oxford Studies in Anthropological Linguistics. New York: Oxford UP, 1997. 99–134.

———, ed. *Más allá del silencio. Las fronteras de género en los Andes*. La Paz: CIASE/ILCA, 1997.

Arnold, Denise, and Juan de Dios Yapita. "Los caminos de Qaqachaka." *Ser mujer indígena, chola o birlocha en la Bolivia postcolonial de los 90*. Ed. Silvia Rivera Cusicanqui. La Paz: Ministerio de Desarrollo Humano, Secretaría de Asuntos Etnicos, de Género y Generacionales, Subsecretaría de Asuntos de Género, 1996. 303–91.

———. *El Rincón de las cabezas. Luchas textuales, educación y tierras en los Andes*. Colección Académica 9. La Paz: Facultad de Humanidades y Ciencias de la Educación, UMSA and ILCA, 2000.

———, eds. *Madre Melliza y sus crías/Ispall mama wawampi: Antología de la papa*. La Paz: Hisbol/Ediciones ILCA, 1996.

Arnold, Denise, Jiménez A. Domingo, and Juan de Dios Yapita. *Hacia un Orden Andino de las Cosas. Tres pistas de los Andes meridionales.* Serie Biblioteca Andina. Dir. Javier Medina and David Tuchschneider. 2nd ed. La Paz: Hisbol/ILCA, 1998.

Aronowitz, Stanley. "Film—The Art Form of Late Capitalism." *Social Text* 1 (1979): 110–29.

Asamblea Nacional de Organizaciones Indígenas, Originarias, Campesinas y de colonizadores de Bolivia (CSUTCB, CONAMAQ, CIDOB, CSCB, FMCBBS, CPESC, CPEMB, MST, A.P.G.). *Propuesta para la Nueva Constitución Política del Estado.* Sucre, 2006.

Aufderheide, Patricia. "Grassroots Video in Latin America." *Visible Nations. Latin American Cinema and Video,* ed. Chon A. Noriega. Minneapolis: U of Minnesota P, 2000. 219–38.

———. "Making Video with Brazilian Indians." *The Daily Planet: A Critic on the Capitalist Culture Beat.* Minneapolis: U of Minnesota P, 2000. 274–88.

Avirama, Jesús, and Rayda Márquez. "The Indigenous Movement in Colombia." *Indigenous Peoples and Democracy in Latin America.* Ed. and Trans. Donna Lee Van Cott. New York: St. Martin's Press and Inter-American Dialogue, 1995. 83–106.

Barrios de Chungara, Domitila with Moema Viezzer [1978]. 'Si me permiten hablar . . .' *Testimonio de Domitila, una mujer de las minas de Bolivia.* Mexico: Siglo XXI, 13th ed., 1991.

Barthes, Roland. *Camera Lucida: Reflections on Photography.* Trans. Richard Howard. New York: Hill and Wang, 1981.

Batchen, Geoffrey. *Burning with Desire: The Conception of Photography.* Cambridge and London: MIT Press, 1997.

Baumann, Thereza, and B. Baumann. "Imagens do 'outro mundo': O problema da alteridade na iconografia cristã occidental." *América em tempo de conquista.* Org. Ronaldo V. Vainfas. Rio de Janeiro: Jorge Zahar, 1992. 58–76.

Bazin, André. *What Is Cinema?* Comp. and Trans. Hugh Gray. Berkeley, Los Angeles, and London: U of California P, 1974.

Beasley-Murray, Jon. "Conclusion: Negri and Multitude." June 18, 2008 <http://posthegemony.blogspot.com>

Beattie, Keith. *Documentary Screens: Nonfiction Film and Television.* New York: Palgrave MacMillan, 2004.

Bermúdez Rothe, Beatriz, ed. *Pueblos indígenas de América Latina y el Caribe: Catálogo de cine y video.* Caracas: Biblioteca Nacional and CLACPI, 1995.

Beverley, John. *Against Literature.* Minneapolis: U of Minnesota P, 1993.

———. "The Real Thing." *The Real Thing: Testimonial Discourse and Latin America.* Ed. George M. Gugelberger. Durham: Duke UP, 1996. 266–86.

———. "Siete aproximaciones al problema indígena." *Indigenismo hacia el fin del milenio: Homenaje a Antonio Conejo-Polar.* Ed. Mabel Moraña. Pittsburgh, PA: Instituto Internacional de Literatura Iberoamericana, 1998. 269–83.

———. *Subalternity and Representation. Arguments in Cultural Theory.* Durham: Duke UP, 1999.

———. *Testimonio: On the Politics of Truth.* Minneapolis: U of Minnesota P, 2004.

Bonfil Batalla, Guillermo, ed. *Utopía y Revolución: El pensamiento político contemporáneo de los indios en América Latina.* México: Nueva Imagen, 1981.

Boone, Elizabeth Hill. "Introduction: Writing and Recording Knowledge." *Writing without Words: Alternative Literacies in Mesoamerica and the Andes.* Ed. Elizabeth Hill Boone and Walter Mignolo. Durham: Duke UP, 1994. 3–26.

Brígido-Corachán, Anna. "An Interview with Juan José García, President of Ojo de Agua Comunicación." *American Anthropologist* 106.2 (2004): 368–73.

Brito Sandoval, Sonia. *Mujeres indígenas protagonistas de la historia.* La Paz: Tijaraipa, 1998.

Brysk, Alison. "Acting Globally: Indian Rights and International Politics in Latin America. *Indigenous Peoples and Democracy in Latin America,* ed. Donna Lee Van Cott. New York: St. Martin's Press, 1995. 29–51.

Burton, Julianne. "Film Artisans and Film Industries in Latin America, 1956–1980: Theoretical and Critical Implications of Variations in Modes of Filmic Production and Consumption." 1981. *New Latin American Cinema,* vol.1. Ed. Michael T. Martin. Detroit: Wayne State UP, 1997. 157–84.

———, ed. *The Social Documentary in Latin America.* Pittsburg: U of Pittsburg P, 1990.

Butler, Judith. *Undoing Gender.* New York: Routledge, 2004.

Calani Gonzales, Esteban. *Pensamiento político ideológico campesino.* La Paz: PAZ, 1996.

Canessa, Andrew. "Género, lenguaje y variación en Pocobaya, Bolivia." *Más allá del silencio: Las fronteras de género en los Andes.* Ed. Denise Arnold. La Paz: CIASE/ILCA, 1997. 233–50.

Carelli, Vincent. "Moi, un Indien." July 4, 2008. http://www.videonasaldeias.org.br/texts_ok/moi_un_indien_ok.htm.

Carnero Hoke, Guillermo. "Teoría y práctica de la indianidad." *Utopía y revolución: El pensamiento político contemporáneo de los indios en América Latina.* Ed. Guillermo Bonfil Batalla. México: Nueva Imagen, 1981. 111–26.

Castells i Talens, Antoni. "Cine indígena y resistencia cultural." *Chasqui* 84 (December 2003): 50–57.

Castro-Gómez, Santiago. "Los vecindarios de la ciudad letrada: Variaciones filosóficas sobre un tema de Angel Rama." *Angel Rama y los estudios latinoamericanos.* Ed. Mabel Moraña. Pittsburgh: Instituto Internacional de Literatura Iberoamericana, 1997. 123–33.

———. "The Missing Chapter of Empire: Postmodern Reorganization of Coloniality and Post-Fordist Capitalism." *Cultural Studies* 21.2–3 (2007): 428–48.

———, ed. *La Reestructuración de las ciencias sociales en América Latina.* Colección Pensar. Bogotá: CEJA, 2000.

CEFREC, CAIB, CIDOB, CSCB, CSUTCB. *La otra mirada: Memoria del Plan Nacional Indígena Originario de Comunicación Audiovisual.* La Paz: CEFREC, 2000.

CEFREC. "Communication Strategies and Indigenous Rights: Report on the Indigenous Aboriginal National Plan for Audiovisual Communication, 2000–2004." Unpublished report. Trans. Freya Schiwy. La Paz, 2005.

———. *Comunicar Desde Adentro: Investigación sobre la comunicación Indígena en las Tierras Bajas de Bolivia.* Plan Nacional Indígena Originario de Comunicación Audiovisual. Santa Cruz, Bolivia: CEFREC, 2006.

———. Homepage. March 1, 2006 <http://videoindigena.bolnet.bo>

———. "Plan Nacional." September 15, 2001 <http://videoindigena.bolnet.bo/plan1.htm>

————. "Presencia del Plan Nacional." September 15, 2001 <http://videoindigena. bolnet.bo/camino/pag2/pag2.htm>

————. "Rumbo a la Asamblea Constituyente. Conociendo Nuestros Derechos Impulsamos Nuestras Propuestas." Multimedia package, La Paz 2005.

Cervone, Emma, Alicia Garcés, Sissy Larrea, Abelina Morocho, Mercedes Prieto, Nely Shiguango, Berta Tapuy, Dolores Yangol. *Mujeres Contracorriente: Voces de Líderes Indígenas.* Quito: CEPLAES, 1998.

Chakrabarty, Dipesh. *Provincializing Europe: Postcolonial Thought and Historical Difference.* Princeton Studies in Culture/Power/History. Princeton: Princeton UP, 2000.

Chanan, Michael. *Cuban Cinema.* Vol. 14, *Cultural Studies of the Americas.* Minneapolis: U of Minnesota P, 2004.

————, ed. *Twenty-five Years of the New Latin American Cinema.* London: British Film Institute and Channel Four Television, 1983.

Chatterjee, Partha. "The Nationalist Resolution of the Women's Question." *Recasting Women: Essays in Indian Colonial History.* Eds. Kumkum Sangari and Sudesh Vaid. New Brunswick: Rutgers UP, 1990. 233–53.

Choque Huanca, Germán. "El Proyecto de Reconstitución del Kollasuyo." *Asamblea constituyente: Hacia un Nuevo Estado Boliviano Nacional, Multinacional, Federal, de Autonomías o Comunitario.* Ed. Jorge Kafka Z. La Paz: Colegio de Politólogos; Universidad Católica Boliviana, comisión Episcopal Pastoral Social–Caritas, 2005. 85–94.

Choque Quispe, María Eugenia. "Colonial Domination and the Subordination of the Indigenous Woman in Bolivia. Trans. Christine Taff with Marcia Stephenson. *Modern Fiction Studies* 44.1 (1998): 10–23.

Choque Quispe, María Eugenia, and Carlos Mamani Condori. "Reconstitución del Aylluy de derechos de los pueblos indígenas: El movimiento indígena en los Andes de Bolivia. *Los Andes desde los Andes: Aymaranakana, Qhichwanakana, Yatxatawipa, Lup'iwipa,* ed. Esteban Ticona Alejo. La Paz: Yachaywasi, 2003. 147–170.

CLACPI. "Festival." June 18, 2004 <http://www.puebloaymara.cll/festivaldecine/cefrec-clacpi.htm>

Colectivo Situaciones. *Apuntes para el nuevo protagonismo social* (19 and 20). Buenos Aires: Ediciones de Mano en Mano, 2002.

Colombres, Adolfo. "El cine y los medios audiovisuales como sustrato de una nueva oralidad de los pueblos indígenas." *Casa de las Américas* 35.199 (1995): 97–103.

Condo Riveros, Freddy. *Las Bartolinas: Sus orígenes, su historia y futuro. FNMCB "BS."* La Paz: CESA, 1996.

Conklin, Beth A. "Body Paint, Feathers and VCRs." *American Ethnologist* 24.4 (1997): 711–37.

Connerton, Paul. *How Societies Remember.* Cambridge: Cambridge UP, 1998.

Coombe, Rosemary J. *The Cultural Life of Intellectual Properties: Authorship, Appropriation and the Law.* Durham, Duke UP, 1998.

Córdova, Amalia, and Melanie Schnell. "Resources for Indigenous Film and Video Makers." *Cultural Survival Quarterly* 29.2 (2005). July 7, 2008 <http://www.cs.org/publications/Csq/csq-article.cfm?id=1829>

Cornejo Polar, Antonio. "Indigenismo and Heterogeneous Literatures: Their Dual Socio-Cultural Logic." Introduction and trans. by John Kraniauskas. *Journal of Latin American Cultural Studies* 7.1 (1998): 13–27.

Coronil, Fernando. "Transculturation and the Politics of Theory: Countering the Center, Cuban Counterpoint." In *Cuban Counterpoint*, ed. Fernando Ortiz. Durham: Duke UP, 1995. ix-lvi.

———. "Towards a Critique of Globalcentrism: Speculations on Capitalism's Nature." *Public Culture* 12.2 (2000): 351–74.

Criales, Lucila. *Mujer y conflictos socio-culturales : El caso de las migrantes de Caquiaviri en la ciudad de La Paz*. La Paz: Aruwiyiri; Taller de Historia Oral Andina, 1994.

Dagua Hurtado, Abelino, Misael Aranda, and Luis Guillermo Vasco. *Guambianos: Hijos del aroiris y del agua*. Bogota: Los cuatro elementos, Fondo Promoción de la Cultura, Fundación Alejandro Angel Escobar, CEREC, 1998.

De la Cadena, Marisol. *Indigenous Mestizos: The Politics of Race and Culture in Cuzco, Peru, 1919–1991*. Durham: Duke UP, 2000.

———. "Las mujeres son más indias: Etnicidad y género en una comunidad del Cuzco." *Revista Isis Internacional*. Ediciones de las mujeres 16 (Santiago de Chile), 1992.

———. "Matrimonio y etnicidad en comunidades andinas (Chitapampa, Cusco)." *Más allá del Silencio: Las fronteras de género en los Andes*. Vol. 1. Ed. Denise Y. Arnold. La Paz: CIASE; ILCA, 1997. 123–49.

De la Torre Amaguaña, Luz María (Achiq pacha Inti-Pucarapaxi). *Un universo femenino en el mundo andino: Runapaqpacha kawsaypi warmimanta yuyay, yachaykunapash*. Bilingual publication. Quito: INDESIC and Hans Seidel Stiftung, 1999.

Deger, Jennifer. *Shimmering Screens: Making Media in an Aboriginal Community*. Minneapolis: U of Minnesota P, 2006.

De Lauretis, Teresa. *Alice Doesn't: Feminism, Semiotics, Cinema*. Bloomington: Indiana UP, 1981.

Dominguez, Daisy. "Indigenous Film and Video in Latin America: Starting Points for Collection Development." June 2004. Typescript.

Dover, R.V.H., K. E. Seibold, and J.H.C. McDowell, eds. *Andean Cosmologies through Time: Persistence and Emergence*. Bloomington: Indiana UP, 1992.

Dubey, Madhu. "The 'True Lie' of the Nation: Fanon and Feminism." *Differences: A Journal of Feminist Cultural Studies* 10.2 (1998): 1–29.

Eisenstein, S. M. "The Montage of Film Attractions." *Selected Works. Vol 1. Writings, 1922–34*. Ed. and Trans. Richard Taylor. London and Bloomington: BFI Publishing and Indiana UP, 1988. 39–58.

Escobar, Arturo. *Hybrid Nature: Cultural and Biological Diversity at the Dawn of the Twenty-First Century*. Durham: Duke UP, forthcoming.

Estermann, Josef. *La filosofía andina*. Quito: Abya-Yala, 1998.

Fals Borda, Orlando. *Ciencia propia y colonialismo intelectual: Los nuevos rumbos*. Bogotá: C. Valencia Editores, 1971.

Fanon, Frantz. *Black Skin, White Masks*. Trans. Charles Lam Markmann. New York: Grove P, 1967.

———. *Studies in a Dying Colonialism*. Trans. Haaken Chevalier. Intro. Adolfo Gilly. New York: Monthly Review Press, 1965.

Fausto-Sterling, Anne. *Sexing the Body: Gender politics and the construction of sexuality*. New York: Basic Books, 2000.

Fernández Osco, Marcelo. *La Ley del Ayllu: Práctica de jach'a justicia y jisk'a justicia (Justicia Mayor y Justicia Menor) en comunidades aymaras*. La Paz: PIEB, 2000.

Figueroa, José Antonio. "Excluidos y exiliados: Indígenas e intelectuales modernistas en la Sierra Nevada de Santa Marta." *Modernidad, Identidad y Desarrollo: Construcción de sociedad y recreación cultural en contextos de modernización*. Ed. María Lucía de Sotomayor. Bogota: Instituto Colombiano de Antropología, Ministerio de Cultura, Colciencias, 1998. 361–78.

Findji, María Teresa. "From Resistance to Social Movement: The Indigenous Authorities Movement in Colombia." *The Making of Social Movements in Latin America. Identity, Strategy, and Democracy*. Eds. Arturo Escobar and Sonia E. Alvarez. Series in Political Economy and Economic Development in Latin America. Boulder: Westview Press, 1992. 112–33.

Flores, Daniel. "Bolivian Links: Indigenous Media. Interview with Julia Mosúa, Alfredo Copa and Marcelino Pinto." Transcription Freya Schiwy and trans. Susan Briante. *Bomb* 78 (2001/2): 30–35.

Fornazzari, Alessandro. "A Stock Market Theory of Culture: A View from the Latin American Neoliberal Transition." *Social Identities* 15.3 (2009).

Franco, Jean. *The Decline and Fall of the Lettered City. Latin America in the Cold War*. Cambridge: Harvard UP, 2002.

García Canclini, Néstor. *Consumers and Citizens: Globalization and Multicultural Conflicts*. Trans. and intro. George Yúdice. Minneapolis: U of Minnesota P, 2001.

García Espinosa, Julio. "For an Imperfect Cinema." *New Latin American Cinema*. Vol. 1. Ed. Michael T. Martin. Detroit: Wayne State UP, 1997. 71–82.

García Pabón, Leonardo. 1998. *La Patria Intima: Alegorías nacionales en la literatura y el cine de Bolivia*. La Paz: CESU/Plural Editores-CID.

Getino, Octavio. *Cine y televisión en América Latina. Producción y mercados*. Colección Imágen y Sonido. Santiago de Chile: LOM, 1998.

Ginsburg, Faye D. "Comment." *Current Anthropology* 38.2 (1997): 213–16.

———. "Embedded Aesthetics: Creating a Discursive Space for Indigenous Media." *Cultural Anthropology* 9.3 (1994): 365–82.

———. "Indigenous Media: Faustian Contract or Global Village?" *Cultural Anthropology* 6.1 (1991): 92–112.

———. "Screen Memories: Resignifying the Traditional in Indigenous Media." *Media Worlds: Anthropology on New Terrain*. Eds. Faye Ginsburg, Lila Abu-Lughod, and Brian Larkin. Berkeley: U of California P, 2002. 39–57.

———. "The Parallax Effect: The Impact of Aboriginal Media on Ethnographic Film." *Visual Anthropology Review* 11.2 (1995): 64–76.

Ginsburg, Faye D., Lila Abu-Lughod, and Brian Larkin. "Introduction." *Media Worlds: Anthropology on New Terrain*. Berkeley: U of California P, 2002. 1–36.

———, eds. *Media Worlds: Anthropology on New Terrain*. Berkeley: U of California P, 2002.

Gramsci, Antonio. *Selections from the Prison Notebooks*. Ed. and Trans. Quintin Hoare y Geoffrey Nowell Smith. 11th ed. New York: International Publishers, 1992.

Grant, Catherine. "Secret Agents: Feminist Theories of Women's Film Authorship." *Feminist Theory* 2.1 (2001): 113–30.

Gros, Christian. *Colombia indígena: Identidad cultural y cambio social*. Trans. Jesús Alberto Valencia. Serie Amerindia No. 2. Bogota: Editorial CEREC, 1991.

———. "Indigenismo y etnicidad: El desafío neoliberal." *Antropología en la modernidad*.

Eds. María Victoria Uribe and Eduardo Restrepo. Bogota: Instituto Colombia no de Antropología and Colcultura, 1997. 15–59.

Gruzinsky, Serge. *Images at War: Mexico from Columbus to Blade Runner (1492–2019)*. Trans. Heather Maclean. Durham: Duke UP, 2001.

Gugelberger, Georg M. *The Real Thing: Testimonial Discourse and Latin America*. Durham: Duke UP, 1996.

Guha, Ranajit. "The Prose of Counter-Insurgency." *Selected Subaltern Studies Reader*. Eds. Ranajit Guha and Gayatri Chakravorty Spivak. New York: Oxford UP, 1988. 45–86.

Gumucio Dagrón, Alfonso. *Historia del cine en Bolivia*. Enciclopedia Boliviana. La Paz: Editorial Los Amigos del Libro, 1982.

Gustavson, Bret. "Paradoxes of Liberal Indigenism: Indigenous Movements, State Processes, and Intercultural Reform in Bolivia." *The Politics of Ethnicity: Indigenous Peoples in Latin American States*. Ed. David Maybury-Lewis. Cambridge: Harvard University David Rockefeller Center for Latin American Studies, 2002. 267–306.

Gutiérrez Alea, Tomás. "The Viewer's Dialectic." *New Latin American Cinema*. Vol.1. Ed. Michael T. Martin. Detroit: Wayne State UP, 1997. 108–31.

Gutiérrez, Raquel, and Fabiola Escárzaga, eds. *Movimiento indígena en América Latina: resistencia y proyecto alternativo*. Vol. 2. Mexico: Casa Juan Pablos; Centro de Estudios Andinos y Mesoamericanos; Benemérita Universidad Autónoma de Puebla, 2006.

Halkin, Alexandra. "Outside the Indigenous Lens. Zapatistas and Autonomous Videomaking." May 15, 2008 <http://www.antropologiavisual.cl/halkin_imprimir.htm>

Halkin, Alexandra, and Amalia Córdova. "Red de Iniciativas Por el Video Indígena Latinoamericano (RIVIL)/Latin American Indigenous Video Initiative (LAIVI)." Typescript, n.p.

Hardt, Michael, and Antonio Negri. *Empire*. Cambridge: Harvard UP, 2000.

Harris, Olivia. "Complementarity and Conflict: An Andean view of women and men." *Sex and Age as Principles of Social Differentiation*, ed. J. La Fontaine, ASA 17. London: Academic Press, 1978. 21–40.

———. "Ethnic Identity and Market Relations: Indians and Mestizos in the Andes." *Ethnicity, Markets, and Migration in the Andes*. Eds. Brooke Larson and Olivia Harris with Enrique Tandeter. Durham: Duke UP, 1995. 351–90.

———. "The Power of Signs: Gender, Culture and the Wild in the Bolivian Andes." *Nature, Culture, and Gender*. Eds. Carol P. MacCormack and Marilyn Strathern. Cambridge, Cambridge UP, 1980. 70–94.

Harrison, Regina. *Signs, Songs, and Memory in the Andes: Translating Quechua Language and Culture*. Austin: U of Texas P, 1989.

Heckman, Andrea M. *Woven Stories: Andean Textiles and Rituals*. Albuquerque: U of New Mexico P, 2003.

Heidegger, Martin. "The Question Concerning Technology." *The Question Concerning Technology and Other Essays*. Trans. William Lovitt. New York: Harper and Row, 1977. 3–35.

Hess, John. "Neo-Realism and New Latin American Cinema: *Bicycle Thieves* and *Blood of the Condor*." *Mediating Two Worlds*. Eds. John King, Ana M. López, and Manuel Alvarado. London: BFI, 1993. 104–18.

Himpele, Jeff. *Circuits of Culture: Media, Politics, and Indigenous Identity in the Andes.* Minneapolis: U of Minnesota P, 2007.

———. "Packaging Indigenous Media: An Interview with Iván Sanjinés and Jesús Tapia." *American Anthropologist* 106.2 (2004): 354–63.

Hojas de Cine: Testimonios y documentos del Nuevo Cine Latinoamericano. 3 vols. Series: Colección Cultura Universitaria. Mexico: SEP, UAM, Fundación Méxicana de Cineastas, 1988.

hooks, bell. "The Oppositional Gaze: Black Female Spectators." *Feminist Film Theory: A Reader.* Ed. Sue Thornham. New York: New York UP, 1999. 308–20.

Horswell, Michael J. *Decolonizing the Sodomite: Queer Tropes of Sexuality in Colonial Andean Culture.* Austin: U of Texas P, 2005.

———. "Toward an Andean Theory of Ritual Same-Sex Sexuality and Third-Gender Subjectivity." *Infamous Desire: Male Homosexuality in Colonial Latin America.* Ed. Pete Sigal. Chicago: U of Chicago P, 2003. 25–69.

Hurtado, Javier. *El Katarismo.* La Paz: Instituto de Historia Social Boliviana, 1986.

Ibazeta, María Celina. "Desafíos y límites del género documental: Cine etnográfico, cine político y video indígena." Ph. D. diss., U of New York, Stony Brook, 2006.

Isbell, Billie-Jean. "De inmaduro a duro: Lo simbólico femenino y los esquemas andinos de género." *Más allá del Silencio.* Ed. Denise Arnold. La Paz: CIASE, ILCA, 1997.

Jackson, Jean. "Caught in the Crossfire: Colombia's Indigenous Peoples during the 1990s." *The Politics of Ethnicity: Indigenous Peoples in Latin American States.* Ed. David Maybury-Lewis. Cambridge: David Rockefeller Center Series on Latin American Studies. Cambridge: Harvard U, 2002.

Jameson, F. *The Cultural Turn: Selected Writings on the Postmodern, 1983–1998.* New York: Verso, 2000.

Jones, Ann Rosalind, and Peter Stallybrass. "Fetishizing Gender: Constructing the Hermaphrodite in Renaissance Europe." *Body Guards: The Cultural Politics of Gender Ambiguity.* Eds. Julia Epstein and Kristina Straub. New York: Routledge, 1991. 1–28.

Kaplan, E. Ann. *Looking for the Other: Feminism, Film, and the Imperial Gaze.* New York: Routledge, 1997.

King, John. *Magical Reels: A History of Cinema in Latin America.* New York: Verso 1990.

Lame Chantre, Manuel Quintin. *Los pensamientos del indio que se educó dentro de las selvas colombianas.* Bogotá: Organización Nacional Indígena de Colombia, 1987.

Lander, Edgardo, ed. *La colonialidad del saber: Eurocentrismo y ciencias sociales. Perspectivias latinoamericanas.* Caracas: Clacso, Unesco, 2000.

Larson, Brook. "Andean Communities, Political Cultures, and Markets: The Changing Contours of a Field." *Ethnicities and Markets in the Andes.* Eds. Brooke Larson and Olivia Harris with Enrique Tandeter. Durham: Duke UP, 1995. 5–53.

Larson, Brooke, and Olivia Harris with Enrique Tandeter, eds. *Ethnicities and Markets in the Andes.* Durham: Duke UP, 1995.

Layme Pairumani, Félix. "El idioma aymara." *La cosmovisión aymara.* Comp. Hans van den Berg and Norbert Schiffers. La Paz: UCB, Hisbol, 1992.

Lazzarato, Maurizio. "Immaterial Labor." Trans. Paul Colilli and Ed Emory. *Radical Thought in Italy: A Potential Politics.* Eds. Paolo Virno and Michael Hardt. Theory Out of Bounds 7. Minneapolis: U of Minnesota P, 1996. 132–46.

Lehm, Zulema, and Centro de Investigación y Documentación para el Desarrollo del Beni (CIDDEBENI). "El saber y el poder en la sociedad mojeña: Aproximación desde una perspectiva de género." *Ser mujer indígena, chola o birlocha en la Bolivia postcolonial de los años 90*. Ed. Silvia Rivera C. La Paz: Subsecretaría de Asuntos de Género, 1996. 393–453.

Lema, Lucila. "Digamos lo que somes, antes que nos den diciendo lo que no somos." Boletín ICCI "RIMAY" 3.22 (2001). <http://icci.nativeweborg./boletin/22/lema. html>

Lienhard, Martin. *La voz y su huella: Escritura y conflicto étnico-social en América Latina, 1492–1988*. Hanover, NH: Ediciones del Norte, 1991.

López, Ana M. "At the Limits of Documentary: Hypertextual Transformation and the New Latin American Cinema." *The Social Documentary in Latin America*. Ed. Julianne Burton. Pittsburg: U of Pittsburg P, 1990. 403–32.

———. "Early Cinema and Modernity in Latin America." *Cinema Journal* 40.1 (2000): 48–78.

———. "Tears and Desire." *Mediating Two Worlds: Cinematic Encounters in the Americas*. Ed., John King, Ana M. López, and Manuel Alvarado. London: BFI Publishing, 1993. 147–63.

López-Baralt, Mercedes. *Icono y conquista: Guamán Poma de Ayala*. Madrid: Hiperión, 1988.

Lozano, Alfredo. "Síntesis de la propuesta técnica académica de la U.I.N.P.I." *Boletín ICCI-RIMAI* 2.19 (2000): 26–61.

Macas Ambuludi, Luis. "¿Cómo se forjó la Universidad Intercultural?" *Boletin ICCI-RIMAI* 2.19 (2000): 20–25.

Macas Ambuludi, Luis, and Alfredo Lozano Castro. "Reflexiones en torno al proceso colonizador y las características de la educación universitaria en el Ecuador." *Boletin ICCI-RIMAI* 2.19 (2000): 10–19.

MacDougall, David. "Complicities of style." *Film as Ethnography*. Ed. Peter Ian Crawford and David Turton. Manchester and New York: Manchester UP, 1992. 90–98.

MacKenzie, Scott. "Mimetic Nationhood. Ethnography and the National." *Cinema and Nation*. Eds. Mette Hjort and Scott MacKenzie. New York: Routledge, 2000. 241–59.

Mader, Elke. "Waimiaku: Las visiones y relaciones de género en la cultura shuar." *Complementariedad entre hombre y mujer: Relaciones de género desde la perspectiva amerindia*. Coords. Michel Perrin and Marie Perruchon. Biblioteca Abya-Yala 43. Quito: Abya-Yala, 1997. 23–46.

Mamani Condori, Carlos. "El intelectual indígena hacia un pensamiento propio." Conference paper. Latin American Studies Association Convention, Miami. March 2000.

Mamani P., Mauricio. "Agricultura a los 4000 metros." *Raíces de América: El mundo Aymara*. Comp. Xavier Albó. Madrid: Unesco, Sociedad Quinto Centenario, and Alianza Editorial, 1988. 75–131.

Marcos, Subcomandante, Major Moisés, Comandante Tacho, Yvon Lebot, and Maurice Najman. *El sueño zapatista: Entrevistas con el subcomandante Marcos, el mayor Moisés y el comandante Tacho, del Ejército Zapatista de Liberación Nacional*. Barcelona: Plaza y Janes, 1997.

Mariaca Iturri, Guillermo. "Los refugios de la utopía: Apuntes sobre estudios culturales desde América Latina" *Escarmenar: Revista boliviana de estudios culturales* I (1995): 5–9.

Mariátegui, José Carlos. *7 ensayos de interpretación de la realidad peruana.* Mexico: Ediciones Solidaridad, 1969.

Mariscal, George. *Contradictory Subjects: Quevedo, Cervantes, and Seventeenth Century Spanish Culture.* Ithaca: Cornell UP, 1991.

Martí, José. *Nuestra América.* Prólogo Josep Fontana. Barcelona: Editorial Ariel, 1973.

Martin, Michael T., ed. *New Latin American Cinema.* 2 Vols. Detroit: Wayne State UP, 1997.

Martin-Barbero, Jesús. *De los medios a las mediaciones: Comunicación, cultura y hegemonía.* 5th ed. Santafé de Bogotá: Convenio Andrés Bello, 1998.

McClintock, Anne. *Imperial Leather: Race, Gender and Sexuality in the Colonial Contest.* New York: Routledge, 1995.

Menchú, Rigoberta. "Rigoberta Menchú: Hemos sido protagonístas de la historia." Interview with Alice A. Brittin and Kenya C. Dworkin. *Nuevo texto crítico* 6.11 (1993): 207–22.

Michaels, Eric. *Bad Aboriginal Art: Tradition, Media, and Technological Horizon.* Foreword by Dick Hebdige. Introduction by Marcia Langton. Theory Out of Bounds 3. Minneapolis: U of Minnesota P, 1994.

Mignolo, Walter D. *Local Histories/Global Designs: Coloniality, Subaltern Knowledges and Border Thinking.* Princeton Studies in Culture/Power/History. Princeton: Princeton UP, 2000.

———. *The Darker Side of the Renaissance: Literacy, Territorialiy and Colonization.* Ann Arbor: Michigan UP, 1995.

———. *The Idea of Latin America.* Blackwell Manifestos. Victoria: Blackwell, 2005.

———. "Descolonización epistémica y ética: La contribución de Xavier Albó y Silvia Rivera Cusicanqui a la reestructuración de las ciencias sociales desde los Andes. *Revista Venezolana de Economía y Ciencias sociales* 7.3 (2001): 175–95.

———. "Colonialidad Global, Capitalismo y Hegemonía Epistémica." *Indisciplinar las Ciencias Sociales: Geopolíticas del conocimiento y colonialidad del poder: Perspectivas desde lo andino.* Eds. Catherine Walsh, Freya Schiwy, and Santiago Castro-Gómez. Quito: UASB; Ediciones Abya-Yala, 2002.

Mignolo, Walter, and Freya Schiwy. "Translation/Transculturation and the Colonial Difference." *Beyond Dichotomies.* Ed. Elizabeth Boyi. Syracuse: Syracuse UP, 2002.

Millán, Márgara. "Los zapatistas de fin de milenio: Hacia políticas de autorepresentación de las mujeres indígenas." *Chiapas* 3 (2001): I–II. January 29, 2001 <http://www.ezln.org/revistachiapas/ch3millan.html>

Miller, Toby, Nitin Govil, John McMurria, Richard Maxwell, and Ting Wang. *Global Hollywood 2.* London: British Film Institute, 2005.

Mohanty, Chandra Talpade. "Under Western Eyes: Feminist Scholarship and Colonial Discourse. *Feminist Review* 30 (1988): 61–88.

Monasterios, Elizabeth, ed. *Tecnocracia de género y feminismo autónomo: Mujeres Creando.* La Paz: Plural, 2006.

Montrose, Louis. "The Work of Gender in the Discourse of Discovery." *Representations* 33 (1991): I–42.

Moore, Rachel. "Marketing Alterity." *Visualizing Theory: Selected Essays from V.A.R. 1990–1994*. Ed. Lucian Taylor. New York: Routledge, 1994. 126–39.

Moreiras, Alberto. "The Aura of Testimonio." *The Real Thing: Testimonial Discourse and Latin America*. Ed. Georg M. Gugelberger. Durham: Duke UP, 1996. 192–224.

Mosúa, Julia, Alfredo Copa, and Marcelino Pinto. "Entrevista." Interview with Daniel Flores. Audiorecording. International Indigenous Film and Video Festival, New York, November, 2000.

Mott, Luiz. "As amazonas: Um mito e algumas hipótesis." *América em tempo de conquista*. Org. Ronaldo V. Vainfas. Rio de Janeiro: Jorge Zahar, 1992. 33–57.

Mujeres Indígenas de la CONAIE. *Memorias de las Jornadas del Foro de la Mujer Indígena del Ecuador*. Quito: CONAIE and UNFPA, 1994.

Mulvey, Laura. "Afterthoughts on 'Visual Pleasure and Narrative Cinema' inspired by *Duel in the Sun*." *Feminism and Film Theory*. Ed. Constance Penley. New York: Routledge; London: BFI Publishing, 1988. 69–79.

———. "Visual Pleasure and Narrative Cinema." 1975. *Feminism and Film Theory*. Ed. Constance Penley. New York: Routledge; London: BFI Publishing, 1988. 57–68.

Murra, John V. *El Mundo Andino: Población, medio ambiente y economía*. Lima: Pontificia Universidad Católica del Perú, Fondo Editorial, IEP, 2002.

Nachtigall, Horst. *Tierradentro: Archäologie und Ethnographie einer kolumbianischen Landschaft*. Zürich: Origo Verlag, 1955.

Negri, Antonio. *Time for Revolution*. Trans. Matteo Mandarini. New York: Continuum, 2003.

———. "Toni Negri en Buenos Aires." In *Diálogo sobre la globalización, la multitud y la experiencia Argentina*, eds. A. Negri, G. Cocco, C. Altamira, and A. Horowicz. *Espacios del Saber*. Vol. 35. Buenos Aires: Paidós, 2003.

Ngugi wa Thiong'o. *Decolonizing the Mind: The Politics of Language in African Literature*. London: J. Currey; Portsmouth: Heinemann, 1986.

Nichols, Bill. "The Ethnographer's Tale." *Visual Anthropology Review* 7.2 (1991): 31–47.

———. *Representing Reality: Issues and Concepts in Documentary*. Indianapolis: Indiana UP, 1991.

Nicholson, Heather Norris, ed. *Screening Culture: Constructing Image and Identity*. Oxford: Lexington Books, 2003.

Niño, Hugo. "El Etnotexto: Voz y actuación en la oralidad." *Revista de Crítica Literaria Latinoamericana* 26.47 (1998): 109–21.

Ong, Walter. *Orality and Literacy: The Technologizing of the Word*. London: Methuen, 1982.

Ortíz, Fernando. *Contrapunteo Cubano del Tabaco y el Azúcar: Pról. y cronología Julio Le Reverend*. Caracas: Biblioteca Ayacucho, 1987.

———. *Cuban Counterpoint: Tobacco and Sugar*. Trans. Harriet Ortíz and introduction by Fernando Coronil. Durham: Duke UP, 1995.

Penley, Constance. "Introduction—The Lady Doesn't Vanish: Feminism and Film Theory." *Feminism and Film Theory*. Ed. Constance Penley. New York: Routledge; London: BFI Publishing, 1988. 1–24.

Perrin, Michel, and Marie Perruchon, coord. *Complementariedad entre hombre y mujer: Relaciones de género desde la perspectiva amerindia*. Biblioteca Abya-Yala 43. Quito: Abya-Yala, 1997.

Pick, Zuzana M. *The New Latin American Cinema: A Continental Project.* Austin: U of Texas P, 1993.

Pinhanta, Isaac. "You See the World of the Other and You Look at Your Own." July 4, 2008 <http://www.videonasaldeias.org.br/home_ingles.htm>

Poole, Deborah. *Vision, Race, and Modernity: A Visual Economy of the Andean Image World.* Princeton Studies in Culture/Power/History. Princeton: Princeton UP, 1997.

Portocarrero Maisch, Gonzalo, Isidro Valentín, and Soraya Irigoyen. *Sacaojos: Crisis social y fantasmas coloniales.* Lima: Tarea, 1991.

Pratt, Mary Louise. *Imperial Eyes: Travel Writing and Transculturation.* New York: Routledge, 1992.

Quijano, Aníbal. "Colonialidad del Poder, cultura y conocimiento en América Latina." *Anuario Mariateguiano* 9.9 (1997): 113–21.

———. "Coloniality of Power, Eurocentrism, and Latin America." *Nepantla: Views from South* 1.3 (2000): 533–80.

———. "Prólogo: José Carlos Mariátegui: Renencuentro y debate." In *7 ensayos de Interpretación de la realidad peruana,* by José Carlos Mariátegui. Caracas: Biblioteca Ayacucho, 1995.

Quijano, Aníbal, and Immanuel Wallerstein. "Americanity as a Concept, or the Americas in the Modern World-System." *ISSI* 134 (1992): 549–57.

Quispe Huanca, Felipe. *El indio en escena.* Chukiyawu-Qullasuyu: Ed. Pachakuti, 1999.

Rabasa, José. *Inventing America: Spanish Historiography and the Formation of Eurocentrism.* Norman: U of Oklahoma P, 1993.

Raheja, Michelle. " 'I Leave It with the People of the United States to Say": Autobiographical Disruption in the Personal Narratives of Black Hawk and Ely S. Parker." *American Indian Culture and Research Journal* 30.1 (2006): 87–108.

———. "Reading Nanook's Smile: Visual Sovereignty, Indigenous Revisions of Ethnography, and *Atanarjuat (The Fast Runner)."* *American Quarterly* 59.4 (2007): 1159–85.

———. *Redfacing and Visual Sovereignty.* U of Nebraska P, forthcoming.

Raheja, Michelle, and Stephanie Fitzgerald. "Literary Sovereignties: New Directions in American Indian Autobiography. *American Indian Culture and Research Journal* 3.1 (2006): 1–3.

Rama, Angel. *La Ciudad Letrada.* Hanover: Ediciones del Norte, 1984.

———. *La transculturación narrativa en América Latina.* Mexico: Siglo XXI, 1982.

———. *The Lettered City.* Ed. and Trans. John Charles Chasteen. Durham: Duke UP, 1996.

Ramos, Alcida R. *Indigenism: Ethnic Politics in Brazil.* Madison: U of Wisconsin P, 1998.

Ramos, Julio. *Divergent Modernities: Culture and Politics in Nineteenth-Century Latin America.* Trans. John D. Blanco. Durham: Duke UP, 2001.

Rappaport, Joanne. *Cumbe Reborn: An Andean Ethnography of History.* Chicago: U of Chicago P, 1994.

———. *The Politics of Memory: Native Historical Interpretation in the Colombian Andes.* Latin America Otherwise: Languages, Empires, Nations. Durham: Duke UP, 1998.

Red Nacional Indígena de Comunicación Audiovisual (CEFREC-CAIB, CIDOB, CSUTCB, CSCB). *Boletín Guía de Acompañamiento* 2 (n.d.).

Reinaga, Fausto. *América India y Occidente.* La Paz: Partido Indio de Bolivia, 1974.

———. "Mi Palabra." *Utopía y Revolución: El pensamiento contemporáneo de los indios en América Latina.* Ed. Guillermo Bonfil Batalla. Mexico: Editorial Nueva Imagen, 1981. 60–68.

Reynaga, Ramiro. "Ideología y Raza en América Latina." *Utopía y Revolución: El pensamiento político contemporáneo de los indios en América Latina.* Ed. Guillermo Bonfil Batalla. Mexico: Nueva Imagen, 1981. 87–110.

Richards, Keith. "Popular theatre: Lo'il Maxil and Sna Jtz'ibajom." *Pop Culture Latin America.* Eds. Stephanie Dennison and Lisa Shaw. Santa Barbara, CA: ABC-Clio, 2005. 134–35.

Rivera Cusicanqui, Silvia. *Birlochas. Trabajo de mujeres: Explotación capitalista y opresión colonial entre las migrantes aymaras de La Paz y El Alto.* Prólogo Alison Spedding. 2nd rev. ed. La Paz: Mama Huaco, 2004.

———. "La noción de 'derecho' o las paradojas de la modernidad postcolonial: Indígenas y mujeres en Bolivia." *Temas sociales* (Revista de Sociologia UMSA) 19 (1997): 27–52.

———. "La noción de 'natión' como camisa de fuerza de los movimentos indígenas." *Movimento indígena en América Latina: resistencia y proyecto alternativo.* Vol. 2. Eds. Raquel Gutiérrez and Fabiola Escárzaga. Mexico: Textos Rebeldes; Centro de Estudios Andinos y Mesoamericanos; Gobierno del Distrito Federal; Universidad Autónoma Metropolitana, Benemérita Universidad Autónoma de Puebla; Diakonia, Centro de Investigación n Desarrollo; UMSA, Universidad Pública de El Alto, UNAM, 2006. 98–102.

———. *Oprimidos pero no Vencidos: Luchas del campesinado aymara y qhechwa, 1900–1980.* Prologue by Luis H. Antezana. Preface by Silvia Rivera C. La Paz: Aruwiyiri and Ediciones Yachaywasi, 2003.

———. "Presentación de la edición japonesa" [de *Oprimidos pero no Vencidos*]. Typescript.

———. "Prólogo: Los desafíos para una democracia étnica y genérica en los albores del tercer milenio." *Ser mujer indígena, chola o birlocha en la Bolivia postcolonial de los años 90.* La Paz: Ministerio de Desarrollo Humano, Secretaría de Asuntos Etnicos, de Género y Generacionales, Subsecretaría de Asuntos de Género, 1996. 17–83.

———. "Trabajo de Mujeres: Explotación capitalista y opresión colonial entre las migrantes aymaras de La Paz y El Alto, Bolivia." *Ser mujer indígena, chola o birlocha en la Bolivia postcolonial de los años 90*, ed. Silvia Rivera Cusicanqui. La Paz: Ministerio de Desarrollo Humano, Secretaría de Asuntos Etnicos, de Género y Generacionales, Subsecretaría de Asuntos de Género, 1996. 163–300.

———, ed. *Ser mujer indígena, chola o birlocha en la Bolivia postcolonial de los años 90.* La Paz: Subsecretaría de Asuntos de Género, 1996.

Rivera Cusicanqui, Silvia, and Rossana Barragán, eds. *Debates postcoloniales: Una introducción a los estudios de la subalternidad.* La Paz: Historias/Sephis/Aruwiyiri, 1997.

Rivera Cusicanqui, Silvia, and THOA. "El potencial epistemológico y teórico de la historia oral: De la lógica instrumental a la descolonización de la historia." *Temas Sociales* 11 (1991): 49–75.

———. *Pachakuti: Los aymara de Bolivia frente a medio milenio de colonialismo.* La Paz: THOA, 1991.

Rivera Cusicanqui, Silvia, Filomena Nina Huarcacho, Franklin Maquera Cespedes, Ruth Flores Pinaya. *La mujer andina en la historia*. La Paz: THOA, 1990.

Rocha, Glauber. "An Esthetic of Hunger." *New Latin American Cinema*. Vol. 1. Ed. Michael T. Martin. Detroit: Wayne State UP, 1997. 59–61.

Rodowick, D. N. "Dr. Strange Media; or, How I Learned to Stop Worrying and Love Film Theory." *PMLA* 116.5 (2001): 1396–1404.

Roel Pineda, Virgilio. "Raíz y vigencia de la indianidad." *Utopía y Revolución: El pensamiento político contemporáneo de los indios en América Latina*. Ed. Guillermo Bonfil Batalla. Mexico: Nueva Imagen, 1981. 127–36.

Rogers, Ken. "Capital Implications: The Function of Labor in the Video Art of Juan Devis and Yoshua Okón." *Social Identities* 15.3 (2009).

Rony, Fatimah Tobing. *The Third Eye: Race, Cinema, and Ethnographic Spectacle*. Durham: Duke UP, 1996.

Rössing, Ina. "Los diez géneros de Amarete, Bolivia." *Más allá del Silencio: Las fronteras de género en los Andes*. Comp. Denise Arnold. La Paz: CIASE; ILCA, 1997.

Ruby, Jay. "Exposing Yourself: Reflexivity, Anthropology, and Film." *Semiotica* 30.1/2 (1980): 153–79.

———. *Picturing Culture: Explorations of Film and Anthropology*. Chicago: U of Chicago P, 2000.

Russel, Catherine. *Experimental Ethnography*. Durham: Duke UP, 1999.

Ruétalo, Victoria, ed. *Latsploitation, Latin America, ad Exploitation Cinema*. Routledge Advances in Film Studies. New York: Routledge, forthcoming.

Saldaña Portillo, María Josefina. *The Revolutionary Imagination in the Americas and the Age of Development*. Durham: Duke UP, 2003.

Salmón, Josefa. *El espejo indígena: El discurso indigenista en Bolivia, 1900–1956*. Facultad de Humanidades y Ciencias de la Educación, UMSA. Colección Academia 5. La Paz: Plural Editores/CID, 1997.

Salomon, Frank. *The Cord Keepers: Khipus and Cultural Life in a Peruvian Village*. Durham: Duke UP, 2004.

Sanjinés C., Javier. "Beyond Testimonial Discourse: New Popular Trends in Bolivia." 1995. *The Real Thing*. Ed. Georg M. Gugelberger. Durham: Duke UP, 1996. 254–65.

———. *Mestizaje Upside-Down. Aesthetic Politics in Modern Bolivia*. Illuminations: Cultural Formations of the Americas Series, ed. John Beverley and Sara Castro-Klarén. Pittsburgh: U of Pittsburgh P, 2004.

Sanjinés, Iván. "Panorama del cine y video en Bolivia. Reflejos de un país indio mestizo." *Pueblos Indígenas de América latina y el Caribe. Catálogo de Cine y Video*. Comp. Beatriz Bermúdez Rothe. Caracas: Biblioteca Nacional y Comité latinoamericano de Cine de Pueblos Indígenas, 1995. 31–43

Sanjinés, Jorge. "Problems of Form and Content in Revolutionary Cinema." Trans. Richard Schaaf. *New Latin American Cinema*. Vol. 1, *Theory, Practices, and Transcontinental Articulations*. Ed. Michael T. Martin. Detroit: Wayne State UP, 1997. 62–70.

Sanjinés, Jorge, and Grupo Ukamau. *Teoría y práctica de un cine junto al pueblo*. México: Siglo XXI, 1979.

Sarmiento, Domingo Faustino. *Facundo: Civilización y Barbarie*. Buenos Aires: Losada, 1963.

Schiwy, Freya. "Decolonizing the Frame: Indigenous Video in the Andes." *Framework* 44.1 (2003): 116–32.

———. "Digital Ghosts, Global Capitalism, and Social Change." *Social Identities: The Journal for the Study of Race, Nation and Culture* 15.3 (2009).

———. "Discovery and the Construction of Gender in the Amazon." *Inroads: Women and Gender across the Academic Landscape.* Seventh Annual Women's Studies Graduate Research Conference. Duke University, January 31–February 1, 1997. 11–16.

———. "Ecoturismo, mujeres indígenas y globalización: Rearticulaciones de la naturaleza en este fin de siglo." *La naturaleza en disputa: Retóricas del cuerpo y el paisaje en América Latina.* Ed. Gabriela Nouzeilles. Buenos Aires: Paidós, 2002. 203–34.

———. "Entre multiculturalidad e interculturalidad: Video indígena y la descolonización del pensar." *Construcción y poética del imaginario boliviano.* Ed. Josefa Salmón. La Paz: Plural, 2005. 127–47.

———. "Reframing Knowledge: Indigenous Video, Gender Imaginaries, and Colonial Legacies." Ph.D. diss., Duke University, 2002.

———. "We Are all Presidents: Bolivia and the Question of the State." Forthcoming.

Schiwy, Freya, and Michael Ennis. "Knowledges and the Known. Andean Perspectives on Capitalism and Epistemology: Introduction." *Nepantla: Views from South* 3.1 (2002): 1–14.

Seibold, Katherine E. "Textile and Cosmology in Choquecancha, Cuzco." *Andean Cosmologies through Time: Persistence and Emergence.* Eds. R.V.H. Dover, K. E. Seibold, and J. H. McDowell. Indiana UP, 1992. 166–201.

Shohat, Ella. "Gender and the Culture of Empire: Toward a Feminist Ethnography of the Cinema." *Quarterley Review of Film and Video* 13.1–3 (1991): 45–84.

———. "Imaging Terra Incognita: The Disciplinary Gaze of Empire." *Public Culture* 3.2 (1991): 41–70.

Shohat, Ella, and Robert Stam. *Unthinking Eurocentrism: Multiculturalism and the Media.* New York: Routledge, 1994.

Siekmeier, James F. "A Sacrificial Llama? The Expulsion of the Peace Corps from Bolivia in 1971." *Pacific Historical Review* 69.1 (2000): 65–87.

Silverblatt, Irene. *Moon, Sun, and Witches: Gender Ideologies and Class in Inca and Colonial Peru.* Princeton: Princeton UP, 1987.

Sinclair, John, and Graeme Turner. *Contemporary World Television.* London: British Film Institute, 2004.

Singer, Beverly R. *Wiping the War Paint Off the Lens: Native American Film and Video.* Foreword by Robert Warrior. Minneapolis: U of Minnesota P, 2001.

Smith, Andrea. *Conquest: Sexual Violence and American Indian Genocide.* Foreword by Winona Duke. Cambridge: South End Press, 2005.

Smith, Claire, Heather Burke, and Graeme K. Ward. "Globalisation and Indigenous Peoples: Threat or Empowerment?" *Indigenous Cultures in an Interconnected World.* Eds. Claire Smith and Graeme K. Ward. Vancouver and Toronto: UBC Press, 2000. 1–24.

Smith, Linda Tuhiwai. *Decolonizing Methodologies: Research and Indigenous Peoples.* London: Zed Books, 1999.

Solanas, Fernando, and Octavio Getino. "Towards a Third Cinema: Notes and Experiences for the Development of a Cinema of Liberation in the Third World." *New*

Latin American Cinema. Vol. I. Ed. Michael T. Martin. Detroit: Wayne State UP, 1997. 33–61.

Solanas, Fernando E., and Octavio Getino. *Cine, Cultura y Descolonización.* Buenos Aires: Siglo XXI, 1973.

Spedding, Allison. " 'Esa mujer no necesita hombre': En contra de la 'dualidad andina'—imágenes de género en los Yungas de La Paz." *Más allá del silencio: Las fronteras de género en los Andes.* Ed. Denise Y. Arnold. La Paz: CIASE/ILCA, 1997. 325–44.

———. "Investigaciones sobre género en Bolivia: Un comentario crítico." *Más allá del silencio: Las fronteras de género en los Andes.* Ed. Denise Y. Arnold. La Paz: CIASE/ILCA, 1997. 53–74.

Spivak, Gayatry Chakravorty. "Can the Subaltern Speak?" *Colonial Discourse and Post-Colonial Theory: A Reader.* Eds. Patrick Williams and Laura Chrisman. New York: Colombia UP, 1994. 66–III.

———. "Subaltern Studies: Deconstructing Historiography." *Selected Subaltern Studies.* Eds. Ranajit Guha and Gayatri Chakravorty Spivak. Foreword Edward W. Said. New York and Oxford: Oxford UP, 1988. 3–32.

Stam, Robert. *Tropical Multiculturalism: A Comparative History of Race in Brazilian Cinema and Culture.* Durham: Duke UP, 1997.

Stam, Robert, and Louise Spence. "Colonialism, Racism, and Representation—An Introduction." *Screen* 24.2 (1983): 2–20.

Starn, Orin. *Nightwatch: The Politics of Protest in the Andes.* Durham: Duke UP, 1999.

Stephan, Nancy Leys, and Sander L. Gilman. "Appropriating the Idioms of Science: The Rejection of Scientific Racism." *The 'Racial' Economy of Science: Toward a Democratic Future.* Ed. Sandra Harding. Bloomington and Indianapolis: Indiana UP, 1993. 170–94.

Stephenson, Marcia. "El uso de dualismos y género sexual en la formulación del discurso indianista de Fausto Reinaga." *Identidad, ciudadanía y participación popular desde la colonia al siglo XX.* Eds. Josefa Salmón y Guillermo Delgado. *Estudios Bolivianos* I. La Paz: Plural, 2003. 153–62.

———. "Forging an Indigenous Counterpublic Sphere: The Taller de Historia Oral Andina in Bolivia." *Latin American Research Review* 37.2 (2002): 99–118.

———. *Gender and Modernity in Andean Bolivia.* Austin: U of Texas P, 1999.

Stern, Steve J. "Feudalism, Capitalism, and the World-System in the Perspective of Latin America and the Caribbean." *American Historical Review* 93.4 (1988): 829–72.

Street, Brian V. "Introduction." *Literacy and Development: Ethnographic Perspectives.* Ed. Brian V. Street. London: Routledge, 2001. 1–17.

———. *Literacy in Theory and Practice.* Cambridge: Cambridge UP, 1984.

Susk, K. Pedro. *Cronología del cine boliviano (1897–1997).* Serie Cinemateca Boliviana Notas Críticas 61. La Paz: Cinemateca Boliviana, 1997.

Tapia, Luciano (Lusiku Qhispi Mamani). *Ukhamawa Jakawisaxa: Así es nuestra vida. Autobiografía de un aymara.* La Paz: Hisbol, 1995.

Taylor, Diana. *The Archive and the Repertoire: Performing Cultural Memory in the Americas.* Durham: Duke UP, 2003.

THOA (Taller de Historia Oral Andina). *Mujer resistencia comunaria: Historia y Memoria.* La Paz: Hisbol, 1986.

Ticona Alejo, Esteban. "El Thakhi entre los Aimara y los Quechua o la Democracia en los Gobiernos Comunales." *Los Andes desde los Andes: Aymaranakana, Quichwanakana Ytaxatawipa, Lup'iwipa.* Ed. Esteban Ticona Alejo. La Paz: Ediciones Yachaywasi, 2003.

Turner, Terence. "Representation, Politics, and Cultural Imagination in Indigenous Video: General Points and Kayapo Examples." *Media Worlds: Anthropology on New Terrain.* Eds. Faye Ginsburg, Lila Abu-Lughod, and Brian Larkin. Berkeley: U of California P, 2002. 75–89.

———. "Representing, Resisting, Rethinking: Historical Transformations of Kayapo Culture and Anthropological Consciousness." *Colonial Situations: Essays on the Contextualization of Ethnographic Knowledge.* Ed. George W. Stocking Jr. Madison: U of Wisconsin P, 1991. 285–313.

———. "The Social Dynamics of Video Media in an Indigenous Society: The Cultural Meaning and the Personal Politics of Video-making in Kayapo Communities." *Visual Anthropology Review* 17.2 (1991): 68–76.

———. "Visual Media, Cultural Politics, and Anthropological Practice." *Independent* (New York) (January–February 1991): 34–40.

Valcarcel, Luis Eduardo. *Tempestad en los Andes.* Lima: Editorial Minerva, 1927.

Valdivia, José Antonio. *Testigo de la Realidad. Jorge Ruíz: Memorias del cine documental boliviano.* La Paz: Conacine and Cinemateca Boliviana, 1998.

Van Cott, Donna Lee, ed. *Indigenous Peoples and Democracy in Latin America.* New York: St. Martin's Press, 1994.

Virno, Paolo. "Virtuosity and Revolution: The Political Theory of Exodus." October 17, 2005 <http://www.generaton-online.org/c/fcmultitude2.html>

Wade, Peter. *Race and Ethnicity in Latin America.* London: Pluto Press, 1997.

Wallerstein et al. *Open the Social Sciences: Report of the Gulbenkian Commission on the Restructuring of the Social Sciences.* Stanford: Stanford UP, 1996.

Walsh, Catherine. "The (Re)Articulation of Political Subjectivities and Colonial Difference in Ecuador: Reflections on Capitalism and the Geopolitics of Knowledge." *Nepantla: Views from South* 3.1 (2002): 61–97.

———, ed. *Geopolíticas del conocimiento.* Special issue of *Comentario Internacional: Revista del Centro Andino de Estudios Internacionales* 2.2 (2001).

Walsh, Catherine, Freya Schiwy, and Santiago Castro-Gómez, eds. *Indisciplinar las ciencias sociales: Geopolíticas del conocimiento y colonialidad del poder: Perspectivas Andinas.* Quito: Duke (Global Studies and the Humanities), UASB, Abya-Yala, 2002.

Wankar (Reynaga, R.). *Tawantinsuyu: Cinco siglos de guerra qheshwaymara contra España.* La Paz: Mink'a, 1978.

Weiner, James F. "Televisualist Anthropology: Representation, Aesthetics, Politics." *Current Anthropology* 38.2 (1997): 197–235.

Weismantel, Mary. *Cholas and Pishtacos: Stories of Race and Sex in the Andes.* Chicago: U of Chicago P, 2001.

Willemen, Paul. "The Third Cinema Question: Notes and Reflections." Ed. Michael T. Martin. *New Latin American Cinema.* Vol. 1. Detroit: Wayne State UP, 1997. 221–51.

Williams, Gareth. *The Other Side of the Popular: Neoliberalism and Subalternity in Latin America.* Durham: Duke UP, 2002.

Williams, Raymond. *Keywords: A Vocabulary of Culture and Society*. New York: Oxford UP, 1976.

Wood, David. "Revolution and *Pachakuti*: Political and Indigenous Cinema in Bolivia and Colombia." Ph.D. diss., King's College, U of London, 2005.

Worth, Sol, and John Adair. *Through Navajo Eyes: An Exploration in Film Communication and Anthropology*. New foreword, afterword, and illustrations by Richard Chalfen. Albuquerque: U of New Mexico P, 1997.

Wortham, Erica Cusi. "Between the State and Indigenous Autonomy: Unpacking Video Indígena in Mexico." *American Anthropologist* 106.2 (2004): 363–68.

———. "Building Indigenous Video in Guatemala." *Jump Cut* 43 (2000): 116–19.

———. "Narratives of Location: Televisual Media and the Production of Indigenous Identities in Mexico." Ph.D. diss., Department of Anthropology, New York University, 2002.

Yampara Huarachi, Simón. " 'Economía' comunitaria aymara." *La cosmovisión aymara*. Comp. Hans van den Berg and Norbert Schiffers. La Paz: UCB, Hisbol, 1992. 143–86.

Yudice, George. *The Expediency of Culture: Uses of Culture in the Global Era*. Durham: Duke UP, 2003.

FILMOGRAPHY

Achacachi: The Aymara Uprising (*Achacachi: La insurgencia aymara*). Dir. Magdalena Cajías de la Vega, Jhony Canedo, Zenón Quispe, Pablo Quisbert and Raúl Reyes. Documentary, 33 min. Betacam. Spanish. Bolivia, 2002.

Among Cultures (*Entre culturas*). Dir. Collective. Prod. CEFREC-CAIB. Television news show, 30 min. Airing weekly on the Bolivian CANAL 7 since 2005.

Among Spirits and Men (*Entre los espíritus y los hombres*). Dir. CONAIE. Prod. ECUARUNARI. Prod. Ejecutiva Mario Bustos. Script: Lucila Lema, Edicíon: Lucila Lema and Rebeca Llasag. Documentary, 32 min. Spanish. Quito, 1998.

Angels of the Earth (*Angeles de la tierra*). Resp. Patricio Luna. Prod. CEFREC-CAIB. Fiction. 25 min. Quechua with Spanish subtitles and Spanish. CEFREC, Bolivia, 1997.

Angels of the Earth (*Angeles de la tierra*). Resp. Patricio Luna. Prod. CEFREC-CAIB. Fiction. 50 min. Quechua with Spanish subtitles and Spanish. CEFREC, Bolivia, 2001.

Apocalypto. Dir. Mel Gibson. Yucatec Maya with English subtitles. Fiction. 139 min. Touchstone Pictures, USA, 2006.

Atanarjuat, The Fast Runner. Dir. Zacharias Kunuk. Prod. Igloolik Isuma Productions. Fiction. 172 min. Canada, 2001.

Blood of the Condor (*Yawar mallku*). Dir. Jorge Sanjinés. Prod. Ukamau. 35 mm, Fiction. Black and white. Ukamau, Bolivia, 1969.

Blossoms of Fire (*Ramo de fuego*). Dir. Maureen Gosling. Documentary. 74 min. USA, 2000.

The Civilizers (*Die Zivilisationsbringer*). Dirs. Uli Stelzer and Thomas Walther. 130 min. Spanish and German with English subtitles. Bayrischer Rundfunk and ISKA e.V. Germany, 1997.

Come Back, Sebastiana (*Vuelve Sebastiana*). Dir. Jorge Ruiz. 16mm, Documentary. Prod. Boliviana, 1953.

Courage of the People (*El coraje del pueblo*). Dir. Jorge Sanjinés. Prod. Boliviano-Italiana, Ukamau. 16mm, documentary. 90 min. Ukamau, Bolivia, 1971.

Creating Life: Agro-Forest Systems in the Alto Beni (*Creando vida: Sistemas agraoforestales en Alto Beni*). Prod. CEFREC-CAIB. Documentary. 25 min. Spanish. CEFREC, Bolivia 1998.

Cursed Gold (*Oro maldito, el*). Resp. Marcelino Pinto. Prod. CEFREC-CAIB (Santa Cruz). Digital video recording. Fiction. 35 min. Quechua with Spanish subtitles and Spanish. CEFREC, Bolivia, 1999.

Dead Birds. Dir. Robert Gardener. 80 min. USA, 1964.

Dusting Off Our History (*Desempolvando nuestra historia*). Resp. Alfredo Copa. Prod. CEFREC-CAIB. Docufiction. 27 min. Quechua and Spanish. CEFREC, Bolivia, 1999.

The Earth Is Ill, How Can We Cure Her (*La tierra está enferma, como podremos curarla*). Dir. Jesús Pérez. Prod. Luciérnaga. Animation. 18 min. CEFREC, Bolivia, 1992.

The Earth Is Bleeding (*Sangra la tierra*). Prod. Acción Ecológica y CONAIE (Departamento de Comunicación). CONAIE, Ecuador, 1998.

The Forest Is Still Alive (*El bosque aún vive*). Dir. Jesús Pérez. Prod. Luciérnaga. Animation. 14 min. CEFREC, Bolivia, 1995.

The Forest Spirit (*El Espíritu de la Selva*). Resp. Faustino Peña. Prod. CEFREC-CAIB. Digital video recording. Fiction. 25 min. Spanish. CEFREC, Bolivia, 1999.

Gender and Ethnicity in the Moxos Plains (*Etnicidad y género en los llanos de Moxos*). Resp. Julia Mósua. Prod. CEFREC-CAIB. Documentary, 25 min. Spanish. CEFREC, Bolivia, 2000.

The Hour of the Furnaces (*Hora de los hornos*). Grupo Cine Liberación. Dir. Fernando Solanas and Octavio Getino. 260 min. Argentina, 1966–68.

How Tasty Was My Little Frenchman (*Como era gostoso o meu Francês*). Dir. Nelson Pereira Dos Santos. Fiction. 80 min. Condor Films, Brazil, 1971.

The Hunter (*El cazador*). Resp. Nicolás Ipamo. Prod. CEFREC-CAIB. Fiction. 17 min. Spanish. CEFREC, Bolivia, 1998.

In Search of the Warrior (*En busca del guerrero*). Resp. Regina Monasterios. Prod. CEFREC-CAIB. Fiction. 25 min. Spanish. CEFREC, Bolivia, 1999.

Incest in the Andes (*Incesto en los Andes: La maldición de los jarjachas*). Dir. Palito Ortega Matute. Fiction, digital recording, 120 min. Quechua with Spanish subtitles. Peru, 2003.

Indigenous Peoples, This Is How We Think (*Los pueblos indígenas así pensamos*). Dir. Collective. Prod. CEFREC-CAIB. Report, 8 min. Various languages with Spanish or English subtitles. CEFREC, Bolivia, 2000.

The Initiation of a Young Xavante (*Wapté Mnhõnõ*). Dir. Video in the Villages. Photography by Bartolomeu Patira, Caimi Waiassé, Divino Tserewahuy, Jorge Protodi and Whinti Suyá. Coordination Estevão Nunes Tutú and Vincent Carelli. Centro de Trabalho Indigenista, Brazil, 1999.

In the Amazon: San Igancio de Moxos (*En la Amazonía: San Ignacio de Moxos*). Resp. Faustino Peña. Prod. CAIB. Report. 9 min. CEFREC, Bolivia, 1998.

In the Name of Our Coca (*Cocanchej sutimpy*). Resp. Humberto Paz. Prod. CEFREC-CAIB. Fiction. 50 min. Quechua and Spanish. Subtitles in Spanish or English. CEFREC, Bolivia, 2005.

The Jichi Woman (*La Mujer Jichi*). Resp. Humberto Paz. Prod. CEFREC-CAIB. Fiction. 17 min. Spanish. CEFREC, Bolivia, 1998.

The Jungle: A Recreational Park in the Chapare (*La Jungla: Parque de Recreación en el Chapare*). Resp. Marcelino Pinto. Prod. CEFREC-CAIB. Documentary. 5 min. CEFREC, Bolivia, 1998.

Jungle Secrets (*Segredos de mata*). Dirs. Dominique Gallois and Vincent Carelli. Prod. Video in the Villages. Collection of four fiction shorts. 37 min. Waiãpi with Portuguese and English subtitles. Centre de Trabalho Indigenista, Brazil, 1998.

The Justice of Our Peoples (*Markanakasan Jucha T'aqawipa/La justicia de nuestros pueblos*). Resp. Sonia Chiri. CEFREC-CAIB, Bolivia, 2006.

Kayapo: Out of the Forest. Dir. Michael Beckham, Granada Television. Author: Terry Turner. Series: Disappearing World. Documentary, 52 min. English, Portuguese with subtitles. Chicago: Films Incorporated Video, 1991.

King Kong. Dir. Peter Jackson. Fiction. 187 min. New Zealand and USA, 2005.

King Kong. Dir. Merian C. Cooper and Ernest B. Schoedsack. Fiction. 100 min. USA, 1933.

Kukuli. Dir. Eulogio Nishiyama, Luís Figueroa, and César Villanueva. Prod. Kero Films. Fiction. 35 mm, 80 min. Quechua with Spanish subtitles. CCC, Peru, 1961.

Let's Do Something about Plastic Garbage (Mana qhawakullaychu). Resp. Jacinto Rodríguez. Documentary, 17 min. Quechua with Spanish subtitles. CEFREC-CAIB, Bolivia, 2000.

Let's Save the Forest and the Peoples' Lives (Salvemos el bosque y la vida de los pueblos). Prod. Acción Ecológica and CONAIE. Ecuador 1998.

Lighting the Spirit (Kanchari). Resp. Reynaldo Yujra. Documentary, 37 min. CEFREC-CAIB, Bolivia 2003.

The Little Orphan (El Huerfanito). Dir. Flaviano Quispe Chaiña. Fiction, 105 min. Quechua with Spanish subtitles. Peru, 2004.

Loving Each Other in the Shadows (Llanthupi munakuy). Resp. Marcelina Cárdenas. Prod. CEFREC-CAIB. Fiction. 50 min. Quechua with English subtitles. CEFREC-CAIB, Bolivia, 2001.

Les Maîtres Fous. Dir. Jean Rouch. 29 min. France, 1955.

Mother Earth: For the Right to Land and Territory (Tierra madre: Por el derecho a la tierra y el territorio). Prod. CEFREC-CAIB. Documentary. 19 min. Spanish. CEFREC, Bolivia, 1999.

The Mountains Don't Change (Las montañas no cambian). Dir. Jorge Ruiz. Prod. Instituto Cinematográfico Boliviano, Documentary. 35 min. 35mm, black and white. Spanish. Cinemateca Boliviana, 1962.

Ñakaj: Fabula andeium. Dir. Daniel Aizenstat. 20 min. Peru, Taruka Films, 1987.

Nanook of the North. Dir. Robert Flaherty. Silent docudrama, 70 min. USA, 1922.

The Nasa Garden (Nasa tul: La huerta de los nasa). Dir. Jesús Bosque and Inocencio Ramos. Prod. CRIC (Unidad tierra y cultura). Documentary. 24 min. Nasa with Spanish subtitles and Spanish. CRIC, Columbia, 1996.

Never More (Nunca más). Prod. Independiente. No credits. Documentary. 13 min. CEFREC. Mexico, 1998.

A New Country, A New Way (Un nuevo país, Un nuevo camino). Prod. CEFREC-CAIB. Docu-fiction. 18 min. Bolivia, 2005.

Oil in Weenhayek Territory (Petroleo en territorio weenhayek). Resp. Abel Ticona and Humberto Paz. Prod. CEFREC/CIAB. Documentary ("Nota informativa"). 5 min. Spanish. CEFREC, Bolivia (Tarija), 1999.

Opening a Way (Yi pyandena). Dir. Jesús Bosque. Prod. CRIC. Documentary. 17 min. Spanish. Colombia, 1996.

The Other Gaze (La Otra Mirada). Dir. Iván Sanjinés. Prod. CEFREC-CAIB. Documentary. 15 min. Spanish. Bolivia, CEFREC, 1999.

Our Language Is Important (Nasa yuwe' walasa': Nuestra lengua es importante). Dir. Jesús Bosque. Prod. CRIC. Documentary. 23 min. Nasa and Spanish. Colombia 1994.

Our Word: The History of San Francisco de Moxos (*Nuestra palabra: La historia de San Francisco de Moxos*). Resp. Julia Mosúa. Prod. CEFREC-CAIB. Docufiction. 22 min. Moxeño with Spanish voiceover and Spanish. Bolivia, CEFREC, 1999.

Out of Here (*Fuera de aquí*). Dir. Jorge Sanjinés. Prod. Ukamau (Ecuador). 35mm, Fiction. UKAMAU, Bolivia 1977.

Overcoming Fear (*Venciendo el miedo*). Resp. María Morales. Prod. CEFREC-CAIB. Fiction. 50 min. Aymara with Spanish or English subtitles. CEFREC, Bolivia, 2005.

The Principal Enemy (*El Enemigo Principal*). Jorge Sanjinés. Prod. Ukamau. Fiction, black and white. Prod. in Peru, 1973.

Qati Qati: Whispers of Death (*Qati qati: Susurros de muerte*). Resp. Reynaldo Yujra. Prod. CEFREC-CAIB (La Paz). Fiction. 35 min. Aymara with Spanish subtitles. CEFREC, Bolivia, 1999.

Rebellions and Hopes (*Rebeldías y esperanzas*). Resp. Marcelina Cárdenas. Documentary, 35 min. CEFREC-CAIB, Bolivia 2005.

Secret Nation (*Nación clandestina, la*). Dir. Jorge Sanjinés. Prod. Ukamau. Fiction. Boliviana, 1989.

Seed and Memory: The Nasa Chumbe (*Semilla y memoria: Chumbe nasa*). Dir. Jorge Mario Alvarez. Prod. Tiempos Modernos; Ministro de Cultura. With Carmen Vitonás. Documentary. 30 min. Nasa and Spanish. CINEP, Colombia, 1997.

The Slope (*La vertiente*). Dir. Jorge Ruiz. Prod. ICB. Docufiction, 90 min. Spanish. Bolivia, 1958.

The Soul (*Ajayu*). Dir. Francisco Ormachea. Fiction. 29 min. Aymara with English subtitles. Bolivia, 1995.

The Spirit of TV (*O Espíritu da TV*). Dir. Vincent Carelli. Prod. Video in the Villages. Documentary, 18 min. Brazil, 1990.

Taking Aim. Dir. Mónica Frota. Rio de Janeiro, Brazil. 41 min. Prod. Institute for Anthropology, University of California, Los Angeles. Documentary with footage by Kayapó video makers. Portuguese and Kayapo with English voiceover and subtitles and English. 1993.

This Is How We Organized (*Nawëthaw püt': Así nos organizamos*). Dir. Jsús Bosque. Prod. CRIC. Documentary. 28 min., Spanish. CRIC. Colombia, 1996.

To Receive the Bird Song (*Para recibir el canto de los pajaros*). Jorge Sanjinés. Prod. Ukamau. Fiction. Bolivia, 1995.

Traditional Medicine: Health in Our Communities (*Medicina tradicional La salud en nuestras comunidades*). Prod. CEFREC-CAIB. Documentary, 5 min. Spanish. CEFREC, Bolivia, 1998.

Trinkets and Beads. Dir. Christopher Walker. Prod. Sony Avigan. Phantom/Sunnyside/Faction Films and Television Trust for the Environment. Documentary. 53 min. First Run/Icarus Films, USA, 1996.

Vest Made of Money (*Qullqi chalika*). Resp. Patricio Luna. Prod. CEFREC-CAIB (La Paz). Fiction. 25 min. Aymara with Spanish subtitles and Spanish. CEFREC, Bolivia, 1998.

Video in the Villages Presents Itself (*Video nas Aldeias se apresenta*). Dir. Vicent Carelli and Mari Correa. Documentary. 33 min. English subtitles. Brazil 2002.

The Voyage: Sons and Daughters of the Mountain (*El viaje: Hijos de la montaña*). Prod. Luna López. CINEP; Ministerio de Educación Nacional; Viceministerio de la Juventud. Documentary. 25 min. Spanish. CINEP, Columbia, 1997.

The Way Things Are (Ukamau). Dir. Jorge Sanjinés. Prod. ICB. Black and white. Fiction, 90 min. Spanish and Aymara with Spanish subtitles. Ukamau, Bolivia, 1966.

We Spin and Weave Giving Life to the Universe (Hilamos y tejemos para darle vida al universo). Dir. Jorge Mario Alvarez. Prod. Tiempos Modernos, Ministerio de Cultura. With Carmen Vitonás. Documentary. 30 min. Nasa and Spanish. CINEP, Colombia, 1997.

Whose Truth Is It? (¿Ahora de quién es la verdad?) Prod. CEFREC-CAIB. Docufiction. 35 min. Spanish. Bolivia, 2004.

Woman of Courage (Qamasan warmi). Dir. José Miranda. Docudrama, 42 min. Prod. Centro de la Mujer Gregoria Apaza. Spanish with English subtitles. Bolivia, 1993.

Woman, Production and the Environment (Mujeres, producción y medio ambiente). Prod. Centro de Desarrollo Comunitario. Documentary, 15 min. Mexico, 1996.

Woman, Wisdom, and Power (Mujer, sabiduría y poder). Prod. CONAIE. Script and editing Lucila Lema. Digital video recording. Documentary. 33 min. Spanish. CONAIE, Ecuador, 1998.

XXY. Dir. Lucía Puenzo. Fiction. 90 min. Prod. Historias Cinematográficas, Wandavisión, and Pyrámide Producciones. Argentina and Spain, 2007.

You're Green (Sos verde). Dir. Daniel Diez. TV documentary (TV Serrana). 16 min. CEFREC, BOLIVIA. Cuba, 1996.

INDEX

Page numbers in *italics* refer to figures.

ABOUT THE AUTHOR

FREYA SCHIWY is assistant professor of Latin American Media and Cultural Studies at the University of California, Riverside. She is coeditor of *(In)disciplinar las ciencias sociales* (Quito, 2002).